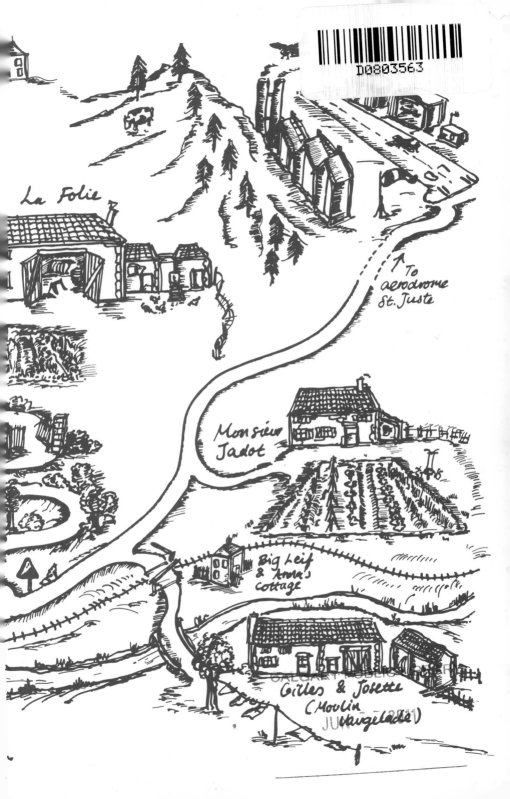

La Folie

To
aerodrome
St. Juste

Monsieur
Jadot

Big Leif
& Anna's
cottage

Gilles & Josette
(Moulin
Jumangelade)

# JE T'AIME À LA FOLIE

*Also by Michael Wright*

C'est La Folie

For more information on Michael Wright and his books,
see his website at www.lafolie.co.uk

## AUTHOR'S NOTE

### I

This is a true story. And if any of the people upon whom my characters are based should wish to thump their fist on a table and declare: 'But it was not like that at all,' then that is their right. A questionable authority on anyone's life but my own, I shall happily hold up my hands and agree.

### II

Jolibois is the name I have given to the nearest town to La Folie. Though you will not see it on any map, it is not hard to find. And perhaps you will not feel the urge to try. For there are many other incarnations of Jolibois, waiting to be explored and appreciated, all over France.

For Amélie and Mirabelle,
so that they will know

TRANSWORLD PUBLISHERS
61–63 Uxbridge Road, London W5 5SA
A Random House Group Company
www.rbooks.co.uk

First published in Great Britain
in 2010 by Bantam Press
an imprint of Transworld Publishers

Copyright © Michael Wright 2010

Endpapers map © Nicholas Peall 2010

Michael Wright has asserted his right under the Copyright, Designs
and Patents Act 1988 to be identified as the author of this work.

This book is a fictional account based on the life, experiences and recollections of the
author. In some cases names of people, places, dates, sequences or the detail of events
have been changed to protect the privacy of others. The author has stated to the
publishers that, except in such minor respects, the contents of this book are true.

A CIP catalogue record for this book
is available from the British Library.

ISBN 9780593059951

Addresses for Random House Group Ltd companies outside the UK
can be found at: www.randomhouse.co.uk
The Random House Group Ltd Reg. No. 954009

The Random House Group Limited supports the Forest Stewardship
Council (FSC), the leading international forest-certification organization. All our titles that
are printed on Greenpeace-approved FSC-certified paper carry the FSC logo.
Our paper procurement policy can be found at:
www.rbooks.co.uk/environment

Typeset in 11/14pt Sabon by
Falcon Oast Graphic Art Ltd.
Printed and bound in Great Britain by
CPI Mackays, Chatham, ME5 8TD

4 6 8 10 9 7 5

# Michael Wright

# Je t'aime à La Folie

One man's quest to fulfil
a life-long dream

## BANTAM PRESS

LONDON · TORONTO · SYDNEY · AUCKLAND · JOHANNESBURG

'Flying is done largely with one's imagination.'

*Stick and Rudder: An Explanation of the
Art of Flying*,
Wolfgang Langewiesche

the Mallard, which is my favourite steam train, and Queen Victoria, who is my favourite ruler, apart from Mary, Queen of Scots and Princess Anne. The year is 1972.

One day, the headmaster comes into our classroom and whispers something to Miss Dembinska, who is in the middle of drawing a jet aircraft on the blackboard. She says that an aircraft is the fastest way of travelling to a place called Abroad. But when I have a Spitfire, I think I shall just fly it over the white cliffs of Dover.

The headmaster's bald head is shiny. I can see the strip-lights glinting off it as he leans forward to talk to her, resting one hand on her shoulder like an eagle clutching an egg. Then he points at me, and everything changes.

'You're being moved up,' Miss Dembinska whispers, after the headmaster has left. 'You'll have a new teacher now.'

'But I want to stay with you,' I reply. One of the boys sitting behind me blows his nose, and the others laugh. Beside me, my friend Davenport nudges me in the ribs.

In my new class, the other boys are much older than me, and we have to learn a new subject called French, which is a foreign language from Abroad. In French, everything is either masculine or feminine. Bread is a him, whereas jam is a her. Even Mr Thompson, who has been to France three times and has a hedgehog moustache, does not know why this should be.

At breaktime, Miss Dembinska says it's best if we don't hold hands any more, because I'm too grown up for all that now. But I'm still six years old. And I feel hollow inside.

Three years later, my parents climb into a jet aircraft and move to Bogotá, which is Abroad, and very far away.

A boarding school is my home now. Windlesham is good, because there are girls as well as boys in my class. This reminds me of when my dad brought home the colour television to replace our old black-and-white one. The programmes are the same, but everything suddenly looks

# THE MAGIC ALLIGATOR

I am six years old, snow is falling on Surrey and my girl-friend is called Miss Dembinska. Miss Dembinska wears black leather gloves, like Alvin Stardust, and I think she is quite old. I wear itchy grey shorts and a maroon blazer, with the motto of my first prep school, Greywalls, embroidered on the breast pocket: *Quaerite et invenietis*.

At breaktime, when she is on duty, Miss Dembinska and I hold hands and stroll through the icy playground together. This is my favourite time of day, apart from watching *Blue Peter* and *Captain Pugwash*. Hand in hand, we crunch a path through the frozen leaves, while the other boys play football with an empty Coke can, or practise walking-the-dog with their Butterfly yo-yos. Compared with them, I know that I am different in some way. My legs tingle with the cold, but I do not mind, because Miss Dembinska's hand feels like warmed velvet in mine.

My heart is full of sky. When I grow up, I am going to be a train-driver or a Spitfire pilot and we will get married. For Spitfires are my favourite thing in the world. In fact, I love Spitfires almost as much as I love Miss Dembinska. But I have not told her about any of this yet. Mostly we talk about

# Part One

lives in Malaysia, where his dad has been posted from Islington, like an airmail letter. This explains why he has a stuffed tarantula and a snake pickled in a jar of formalin in his tuck-box, whereas all I have is a Corgi Spitfire and Stuka, a Butterfly yo-yo, a pot of Slime and a pile of free stickers from Goodyear, Ferodo and Billy Graham. Toby has useful gadgets, too. One day, he produces two army pouches from the tuck-box, and over the next few weeks we both assemble survival kits, in case the Russians drop a bomb on Storrington.

Each survival kit contains an army tin-opener; a bundle of matches waterproofed with nail varnish and wrapped in wire for fishing or making snares; a small brown bottle of potassium permanganate crystals for disinfecting wounds and purifying water; and a shiny gold space blanket which I bought at the Kennedy Space Center in Florida, on the way back from Bogotá. We also have salt tablets and some beef Oxo cubes, although my Oxo supply is dwindling, because I often feel obliged to check that they haven't gone off.

Having a survival kit will be useful if we have to sleep in the woods. I shall light a fire for Clara Delaville, and then she will love me.

One day, during the summer holidays, I spot a stuffed baby alligator in a shop run by a wizened old Inca lady in Bogotá, and immediately want it for Toby. Standing a foot tall on its hind legs, the reptile carries an umbrella in one claw and a miniature briefcase in the other. Wearing a big smile, with all its razor teeth on show, it somehow speaks to me. My mother isn't so sure. She says it's cruel to treat an animal like that. Whereas I just think it is the coolest thing I have ever seen.

'What did the shopkeeper say?' I ask my mother as we are leaving the shop with my precious alligator wrapped up in brown paper. All I know in Spanish is *sandwich combinado por favor* and *muchas gracias*.

more glorious, especially on cold, dark winter evenings, when we all sit together – boys next to girls, masculine beside feminine – in our brightly lit classroom, doing our Latin prep with the light spilling out into the black Sussex countryside.

French is now my favourite subject, because in French I sit next to Clara Delaville, who is the prettiest girl I have ever seen. She has shiny auburn hair, cut almost as short as a boy's, and laughing brown eyes that seem to sparkle when she talks to you. I never manage to reply. Clara is ten, and I am nine. Yet the beautiful, athletic Clara shines so far above me that she might as well be a princess and I a peasant.

In dorm, after the speakers playing us Greek myths and Chopin ballades have been switched off, I go to sleep thinking about Spitfires or Clara Delaville; I wake up thinking about her, too, wondering if I will be on the same table as her at breakfast. I yearn for our next French lesson, when we will pore over our shared copy of *Tricolore* and the elbows of our knitted sweaters may perhaps, fleetingly, touch.

I would never dare venture across the glass corridor to the forbidden territory of the Girls' Wing, where Clara sleeps. But one of the senior boys went there once, for a dare. He says the girls have carpets, and thick mattresses, and dressing-tables with flowers painted on them. In our boys' dorm, we have splintered wooden floorboards, and bunk beds with saggy mattresses, and a boy who lights his own farts with a box of Swan Vestas. We tell jokes, too.

'Knock knock.'

'Who's there?'

'Corn Flakes.'

'Corn Flakes who?'

'Wait till next week, it's a cereal.'

My best friend in dorm is called Toby Melbury. Like me, Toby lives Abroad. Lots of children at our school do: Miles in Brunei, Lilibet in the Virgin Islands, Joanna in Peru. Toby waiting is going to last. But this is rural France, so the only things aloft are a pair of buzzards, wheeling over the distant hills. And the only plane-spotters are a handful of sheep, gazing at me across the perimeter fence. Everyone else is still having lunch, and will be for the foreseeable future.

The hangar doors rumble like coal trucks on rails as I heave them apart. It is cool in here, and I stand for a moment amid the aircraft packed inside, allowing my sun-dazzled eyes to adjust to the darkness.

There she is.

I still find it hard to believe that I have now lived in France for two whole years, striving to toughen myself up with heroic adventures, doing my best to learn about things that matter, and failing to plant any spuds. As I haul the yellow Luscombe Silvaire out of the shadows, I find it even harder to believe that this jaunty cocksparrow of a two-seater air-craft, with its leather-lined cockpit and curves in all the right places, is *mine*. I first dreamed of learning to fly a Spitfire when I was six years old. And now here I am, aged thirty-eight, readying a vintage plane for flight. The Luscombe is no Spitfire. But it was built in the 1940s, and that is about as close as I am likely to get.

The air is beginning to cool, but the tarmac still feels warm to the touch as I lean down to chock the wheels and inspect the brakes. Above me, the sky burns deep blue, and a hint of a breeze flirts with the uninterested windsock. Perfect flying weather. No wonder the place is deserted. And no matter: after my two years as a trainee peasant in darkest France, I have grown used to being alone.

Seconds later, footsteps crunch upon asphalt, and my heart sinks as I recognize the hunched silhouette of Marcel, the aeroclub grouch, coming to bait me. As usual, the butt of an unlit cigarillo is glued to his sneering lips, like a comma in the middle of a death-threat. I think he has been sucking upon this same grey cheroot ever since I first visited St Juste,

# I

## SEPTEMBER

I am thirty-eight years old, alone in France, and I seem to think about women all the time. As I drive down a sunlit road towards an aerodrome in the heart of nowhere, there are three things I want to achieve while I am still young enough to appreciate them. I want to cook and eat a potato grown by myself. I want to fly a Spitfire. And I want to meet someone wonderful with whom to share the rest of my life. Unfortunately, on a September afternoon in darkest France, as the poplars flash past me like years on a calendar, all three of these ambitions feel about as unlikely as each other. Even the potatoes.

It is four o'clock, and the slate-grey runway at St Juste shimmers in the sun as I park my battered Espace, with its whiff of dead dog, behind one of the hangars. Today is Sunday, so the clubhouse is shuttered, and the chimneys of the paper factory opposite are like a pair of snuffed candles, waiting to be relit. There is a hint of garlic, rather than sulphur, in the air.

If this were England, the aerodrome would be buzzing with Cessnas and microlights; with anoraks with binoculars, and windswept wives wondering how much longer the

'She said it's a magic alligator.'

'It does tricks?' This is getting better and better.

'No,' replies my mother, eyeing the parcel in my hands. 'She said it would help you to find something you have lost.' She is silent for moment, vanished in her own thoughts. And then she laughs. 'Silly, really, isn't it?'

But I don't think it's silly at all.

On the first day of term, I give the alligator to Toby.

'That is so cool,' he says, examining it closely. I never see the alligator again. Probably Toby has managed to swap it for something more desirable, like a pot of Slime or some Bennett Pro trucks for his skateboard.

'Knock knock,' says Toby, when we are washing our faces at the long line of basins outside the dormitory that night.

'Who's there?' I reply.

'Cabbage.' Toby is already laughing, so I can tell this is going to be a really funny one. I like 'knock-knock' jokes.

'Cabbage who?'

'Cabbage Jones.' Toby falls on the floor and bangs his head on a pipe, he is laughing so much. I am laughing, too. I just don't seem to be able to stop myself.

'Why is that funny?' I ask.

'It isn't.' Toby rubs his head. His shoulders are still shaking with the giggles, his cheeks wet with tears. 'My little sister made it up. It's her first joke. But everything she says is hilarious.'

Lying in bed, I consider this for a while. Toby has invited me to join him on a day out to Brighton at the weekend, because his mother is over from Malaysia with his sister, who is coming to Windlesham next term. I feel intrigued to meet this little girl who is already making up her own jokes. And so I doze off, my head filled with thoughts of Clara Delaville and Cabbage Jones. I am twelve years old, and – when I am not thinking about aeroplanes – I seem to think about girls all the time.

breath, and swing the prop through eight blades. Two shots of prime. Another six blades. 'Throttle set, CONTACT!' I give the propeller a hefty swing, and the engine splutters into life first time – an occasional miracle – huffing and puffing and straining and clattering before gradually settling into a familiar *pocketa-pocketa-pocketa* rhythm, like a quartet of cyclists cresting a hill.

The niggle of fear I often feel just before I go flying almost melts away in the prop-blast as I drag away the chocks and climb up into the cockpit, where the needles of the instruments are vibrating in the din. Almost, but not quite. Perhaps seeing Marcel has unsettled me. With the stick held back between my knees, I grab my headset from the empty seat beside me, release the brakes, and taxi out to the holding-point on the runway threshold, testing the brakes as we go.

And then we're off and up, the fields and trees falling away like forgotten troubles as the Luscombe climbs inexorably towards the one wispy cloud in the sky. Up here, I can forget about sick chickens, about encroaching brambles and my ongoing failure to master the subjunctive in French. If only Miss Dembinska could see me now. Flying my own little aircraft, and over France, of all places. Abroad. Alone.

Flying is not brave. Yet I do find it bracing to think, each time I take off, that the ancient 65-horsepower engine clattering in front of me could stop at any time. As the pilots' cliché has it: it's much better to be down there, wishing you were up here, than up here, wishing you were down there. And though I fancy my chances in a fair fight with an open field, I also know that a forced landing in inhospitable terrain could coffin my French adventure sooner than planned. Behind my seat, in my flight bag, I have tucked one of the shiny gold space blankets I bought at the Kennedy Space Center all those years ago, for me and Toby Melbury. I don't know what happened to my nail-varnished matches and the rest of my survival kit.

almost three years ago. It looks far too damp and shrivelled still to be combustible.

'Big car for one person,' growls Marcel, in French. He must have seen my bashed-up Espace, parked behind the clubhouse.

'Sometimes I carry a few sheep in the back of it,' I reply.

'So you still haven't found *une copine* to warm your bed on these cold nights?' he chuckles. Marcel is never happy unless he's being downright miserable.

I shake my head, and unclip the engine cowling to check the oil.

'*Froid*,' he repeats, with an emphatic shiver.

'Who needs a girlfriend,' I reply, wondering if we can have been experiencing the same weather, 'when they have a cat and an aeroplane for company?'

Marcel snorts. 'I do,' he snarls, with a scowl, beginning to slope away. 'Life is wretched when you get to my age and you're all alone.'

'You should get yourself a dog.'

'I can't stand dogs.'

'Nor can I,' I reply. And we both stand for a moment, in awe of the fact that we appear to have something in common after all.

'You'll find someone, Marcel,' I add, at last. 'It's never too late.'

'Ah, but it is,' he says, over his shoulder. 'You'll see for yourself, if you haven't crashed this thing before then.'

'Thanks for the encouragement,' I call, as he slopes away. Cussed as he is, I like Marcel. The old boy has walked away from more plane crashes than anyone else I know. His footsteps stop in the shadows, and I hear the *click-click-click* as he tries to light his wet cigarillo – until a muttered expletive tells me that he has given up in disgust, yet again.

Wheels chocked, brakes on, stick tied back. Fuel on, switches off. 'Sucking in,' I mutter to myself under my

Today's flight is a celebration of sorts, since it marks the second anniversary of my solitary life in darkest France. In that time, I have struggled to learn how to turn myself from a soft townie into a rugged peasant, to learn about sheep and chickens and manly power-tools and, with rather more success, how *not* to weed my *potager* or woo a wonderful *copine*. So it feels appropriate that the Luscombe and I should have this big French sky all to ourselves, yet again.

With the needle of the oil-pressure gauge holding steady, and the sixty-year-old Continental engine clattering along like an angry sewing machine in front of me, I am as happy as any six-year-old in a thirty-eight-year-old's body can be. Above the racetrack, I set course for Jolibois, my local town, which lies just beyond that tree-lined ridge of low hills. The sky is as clear as vodka. Clearing the ridge, I can already see what look like three white golf-tees – the water towers of Jolibois – glowing in the evening sun, and the glinting slate roof of the church at the top of the hill. A drab medieval sprawl that was once one of the hubs of the French tanning industry, Jolibois is now most famous for its summer traffic jams. People get stuck here for hours or, in my case, several years.

'Why Jolibois,' the locals still ask me, 'when you could have chosen anywhere else in France?'

'Because it has a pipe-organ and a tennis club and a landing-strip,' I always used to reply. Yet the reasons change, with hindsight, the longer I am here. Now I simply admit that I like the place. Its rugged simplicity, and the feeling of living in the past, suits me. Especially after London, where I always seemed to be living with one eye on the future. It is living in the present that is so difficult to achieve.

'I only chose this place because I hadn't amassed enough points to choose anywhere better,' is what Jacques the flying schoolteacher once told me, over lunch at the house of Raphaël the priest. 'If you have maximum points, you can choose a good school in the centre of Paris, or a cushy billet in Provence. If you have zero points, they send you to Jolibois.'

'But surely, Jacques,' I replied, 'by now you must have enough points to be able to move on?'

And, even now, I can picture the shy smile with which he conceded, 'Somehow, once I was here, I could never quite bring myself to leave.'

On the side of a scrubby hill, seven black dots stop chewing and gaze up into the sky, at the little yellow aeroplane flying low overhead. Strange to think that those sheep are *mine*; I, who used to go to the theatre four nights a week in London, and who lived in a terraced house in East Dulwich with a garden made of concrete and a talent for murdering shrubs.

Mine, too, that khaki hillside, with the ramshackle farmhouse that I began to renovate two years ago. And that tiny smudge of grey-and-white on the front step, which must be Cat, brought kicking and screaming from South London to share the adventure. One day, I hope she will forgive me.

On the ground, La Folie is an isolated wilderness, miles from civilization. '*Ah, c'est le bout du monde ici,*' say French visitors when they arrive. It is the house at the end of the world. But from up here, at two thousand feet, I can see that the place is not really isolated at all. The world is like one of those pictures made up of splodges or dots: it makes sense, and all connects up, only when you stand far enough away from it. There are other terracotta roofs dotted across the valley; other settlements whose inhabitants imagine that they are at the end of the world, because they have never flown high overhead and seen how connected they are. Even Jolibois itself is only a mile or two away.

Dipping the Luscombe's nose towards the church where I play the organ for Mass on Saturday nights, I bank in a slow arc over the peach clay courts of the tennis club where I never win any matches, and over the Gothic stone bridge on which I have so often stood, gazing into the dark waters, wondering if I shall always be alone. And if not alone, then with whom?

When I was in my teens, I imagined I would get married in my twenties. By my late twenties, I assumed I would get married in my thirties. By the time I reached my mid-thirties, I really didn't think I would marry at all. Leaving aside the minor detail that nobody ever showed much sign of wanting to marry me, I suppose I had begun to feel that marriage was an ending rather than a beginning; something that other people did, after they stopped having fun.

Levelling the wings, I swoop low over Gilles's farm – where the same blue-grey laundry is hanging on the washing-line as has been hanging there ever since I first visited the house of my heroic neighbour and chief peasant mentor – and fly along the single-track railway line that runs past the bottom of the drive to La Folie. Four trains a day rattle along this line, clattering out a rhythm of *today-today-today* as they pass the level-crossing beside old Monsieur Giblin's cottage. A single steam train passes once a year, too, its pistons puffing *yesterday-yesterday-yesterday* as it hammers through the valley in a cloud of smoke and dreams. At last, I set course back to St Juste, climbing to clear the tree-lined ridge for a second time.

And then I swallow, hard. Because Houston, we have a problem. Really quite a big problem.

We are not going to clear the ridge.

I yank out the carburettor heat knob, bite my lip and stare at the rev counter. The drumming of the engine in my headset has roughened, as if the little 65-horsepower engine were straining even more than usual and, scanning the instruments, I notice that the needle of the oil-temperature gauge is reading hotter than normal. It's nothing. Yet my skin prickles, even so.

Why won't she climb?

I stare again at the needle, and the blurred pointer creeps another millimetre to the right.

These nerves jangling in my spine are just plain silly. I can't be about to crash and burn, can I? Not on this bright day, when I only came flying for the hell of it. Calm, calm. The aerodrome at St Juste is only twelve minutes' flying time away, on the far side of those tree-lined hills. If I need to turn back, the grass landing-strip at Jolibois is only five minutes behind me.

Squeezing the stick to the right, I start a gentle turn to give the labouring Luscombe a little more time to clear the ridge. There's nothing to worry about, I tell myself, as I listen to the engine grinding away, picturing push-rods splintering, cylinders disintegrating and the cam-shaft exploding in a shower of sparks. But when I scan the steep forests beneath me for a friendly field, I feel a silent surge of alarm well up inside me. Inside my little yellow tin box, I am sitting very, very still.

Two minutes later, I skim the top of the ridge, low enough to see a cow blink as I roar overhead, a few metres above her horns. Sorry, love.

Jolibois is a long way behind me and I still can't spot St Juste. I count my lucky stars that I am alone and have not put anyone else's life at risk. Mind you, I wouldn't mind having a fellow pilot with me right now; preferably an expert one, with several emergency landings under his belt. Not Marcel, then. No, my friend Jethro in England, who can fly anything with his eyes shut. Or Peter Viola, another pilot at St Juste, who is so confident of his own airmanship that sometimes he cuts the engine of his Thruster at a thousand feet, just so that he can feel the buzz of an emergency landing for real.

The vibrating needle of the oil-temperature gauge has already risen higher than I have ever seen it before: two hundred degrees and climbing. Now I'm no mechanic, but even I can tell that this is not promising. My feet are getting hot, my heart is racing and I feel slightly sick. And then a thought strikes me, with the force of a sledgehammer thwacking the head of a fence-post: nobody knows I'm here, except perhaps that cow on top of the ridge.

I have spoken to no one on the radio. If the engine shakes itself to pieces and I fail to make a decent emergency landing in one of the non-existent fields beneath me, there will be no search party. With Marcel the only unreliable witness of my folly, it may be weeks before anyone even notices that I am missing. The post will build up outside the front door. Cat will grow thinner. My mother will leave a series of agitated messages on the answerphone. The organ will be silent during the Saturday-evening Mass. And, eventually, some grizzled *randonneur* will come upon a heap of twisted yellow wreckage on a tree-lined hillside, and there will be a small funeral for the cheerful English writer who lived alone, played tennis very badly, and never found love, poor fellow.

As gingerly as if I were defusing a bomb, I ease back the throttle-knob with my right hand and peer out across the lengthening shadows of the countryside, searching for a big, flat field. Just in case. But there's nothing, and nowhere: only trees and powerlines and fields almost too steep for sheep.

Nobody is expecting me home. Nobody will telephone tonight. I shiver in the cold air of the cockpit; twist shut one of the perspex air-vents that is blasting a hundred-mile-an-hour breeze up my sleeve.

Longing to hear a human voice, I flick on the radio and listen for other traffic. Silence. It seems nobody else is flying today: there isn't even the occasional rasp of static to let me know of other pilots transmitting in the far distance. I switch to the frequency for Limoges Approach, announce my call-sign into the silence, and feel a whoosh of relief when the controller finally responds.

'Go ahead, Golf-Zulu-Alpha,' crackles his voice in my headset, in English. 'Pass your message.'

So I tell him who I am, and where I am heading, hoping that he cannot hear the fear in my voice. This man cannot see me on his radar. I am too far away for his binoculars. He cannot help me in any practical way. Even so, it is good to know that he is there; that I am connected to the earth by the radio waves passing between us, carrying our voices through the darkening sky.

In the distance, St Juste appears at last. Still too far to glide. But I can see the dash-dot-dash smudge of hangar three with its doors still open, and the grey splodge of Carrefour just to the rear, where the beautiful lady behind the fish counter – a haughty Botticelli in white wellies, whom I secretly admire – will by now be packing away her monk-fish tails and, unaware of my plight, scraping what is left of her crushed ice down the plug-hole. In another minute I will be close enough for a glide approach, even if the engine – whose laboured clattering now sounds to me like an angry armadillo trying to escape from a washing machine – packs up.

Second by second, the minute passes. After signing off from Limoges – *Field in sight, merci bien, monsieur, Golf-Zulu-Alpha,* I click the radio frequency-selector to St Juste and inform the uninhabited sky that I will be joining down-wind for runway zero-seven. And then, as I turn on to base leg with a surge of relief, knowing that I have the runway made, I do something I have often considered, but have never in my life done before. If Peter Viola can do it, why shouldn't I? With steady fingers, I reach for the ignition key, hesitate for a second, and switch off the magnetos. I'd rather stop the engine now, when I am expecting it, than have it quit on me on the short final, when I am not.

It takes only a few seconds for the propeller to stop, and I feel a lurch of self-induced fear in the pit of my stomach; a zing of adrenaline coursing through my shoulders and back. As I push the stick forward to maintain seventy mph on the airspeed indicator, the sudden silence of an aircraft that has been converted into a makeshift glider takes me by surprise. All I can hear through my headset is a distant hiss of wind, and my view is partially obscured by the black stripe of the propeller, stuck at ten to six. I would guess that my heart rate is now up around 150 beats per minute. Watch your speed and don't get low. Now you're too high. Pushing the stick to the left, and dabbing at the rudder pedal with my right foot, I side-slip to lose the extra altitude and then, fifty feet off the ground, straighten the nose.

My silent glider rapidly sinks in a down-draught, and then the white runway numbers – 07 – are flashing beneath me. I ease the stick back as gently as my tense left arm will allow, to catch the last whispers of lift before the Luscombe settles on to the earth in the sort of perfect three-point landing that I only ever manage once a year when nobody is watching. Behind me, I hear a sound I have never heard before: the roar of the tailwheel as it booms down the aluminium megaphone of the plane's hollow fuselage.

Creaking, clunking and rattling, the Luscombe slows as if it were coasting through treacle, and with the last of its ebbing momentum I manage to steer it off the runway and on to the grass.

I am home safe.

As I glance across at the hangars, instinctively looking out for the cheering crowds of well-wishers celebrating my safe return, I can see that the aerodrome is still deserted. Even old Marcel must have gone off to sulk at home. I am a space-man, safely back on planet earth. Unbuckling my straps, I sit for a moment, listening to the hot motor still ticking as it cools in the silence. Another uneventful local flight. I am alive. Not just alive, but somehow more alive than I was before I took off. And I wish there were someone I could tell;

someone waiting at home with a glass of wine and something hearty bubbling on the hob.

My legs feel like blancmange as I stride across the apron to fetch my little two-wheeler trailer. This I hitch under the Luscombe's tailwheel and heave the aircraft backwards into the hangar. Later, I drive back to La Folie and sit with Cat on the terrace, sipping a glass of Pastis as we gaze out at the view across the valley and at the orange glow from Jolibois that lights up the brown sky, as we do every night.

My mum phones, and I tell her how happy I am in my unfinished, ramshackle farmhouse.

'All's well,' I say. 'I went flying today, and the Luscombe is going fine.'

'Oh, that's nice,' she replies. 'Is it really safe to go flying on your own?'

'Actually, I prefer it,' I lie. 'There's a kind of freedom in being alone.'

'Which you don't have enough of at La Folie?'

'That's different.' I pause, hearing the familiar cogs ticking and whirring in my mother's brain, the same cogs fitted into the brain of every mother with an unmarried son who shows no sign of settling down with a Nice Girl. 'And I've learned to enjoy being on my own.'

This is what I always tell myself these days. Yet today's flight has given me second thoughts. It is one thing to live by myself, in the house at the end of the world. It is quite another to come face to face with the fact that nobody would have noticed if I had killed myself in a crash tonight.

On top of this, the more time I spend alone, close to nature, the more beautiful the world somehow becomes. And the more beautiful the world becomes, the sadder it seems to have no one with whom to contemplate it. I cannot help but dream of finding someone with whom to share this beautiful landscape, instead of keeping these stars and this moon, the whirr of these crickets, all to myself.

Yet I am almost forty years old. If I were going to meet someone perfect for me, would I not already have met her by now, when our young lives were still ahead of us, and when I was still surrounded by all those charming, available young women who had not already been snapped up by young men far more eligible – or at least more willing to commit – than me?

The night is drawing in, and the air is cooling fast. Finishing up my drink, I head back inside, while Cat slinks into the undergrowth for another bout of hair-raising shrieks and hell-raising with the shrews.

# 2

## OCTOBER

Come with me, and let me show you La Folie.

A few furlongs outside the town of Jolibois, deep in darkest France, an unmarked lane curves up into the trees. As steep and sharp as a sheep-track, it looks almost too much for a car. But up we roar, you and I, while birds flit and dart across our path, and sunlight strobes through the oaks and sweet chestnuts that curtain either side.

We slow as we pass a stooped old man with a stick and a carrier bag. He waves at us, gives us a sad shrug. No mushrooms yet, then, *monsieur*.

Before you ask, these are not my woods. This is not my land. No one is quite sure who owns this place.

Another sharp bend, and now we are driving beneath a fan-vaulting of oaks and chestnuts, dappling the road ahead as if it were painted by Corot or Pissarro. A blue arrow daubed on one of the trunks points out the direction of the old pilgrims' route. But we head straight on, through a pair of rusting gates, and there – up ahead – you can just see the crumbling façade of a primitive farmhouse fronting the valley. This is La Folie. I always think the place looks its best from down here, where you can see the render peeling off the ancient stone, and not the zinc peeling off the doors of the barn; the lavender shutters, and not the blank stares of the windows at the far end.

The Egg Squad have come dashing down the hill to greet us, so we'd better slow down. Chickens do play chicken, and really will cross the road without a reason, given half a chance. I love the way they run. Look at them now: seven fat madams in feather boas, racing to catch a bus with their hands tied behind their backs. That vast cockerel, who reminds me of Holbein's Henry VIII, is Titus, king of the roost. And there, just behind him, is Hotspur, the young pretender to his throne. Keeping two cockerels is, frankly, a recipe for disaster. It's also a recipe for *coq au vin*, although I don't like to think in those terms. My chickens are for company, not casserole.

Bump, bump, bump. Sorry about that. I still haven't called the *Travaux Publics* to ask them to repair the rutted drive in front of the house. And please don't look too carefully at the scene of vegetative carnage that is looming, even now, to our right. That fenced jungle of weeds haunts my every waking moment, and the bounteous *potager* into which I hope to transform it is the single most important project on my mind, if we discount the small matter of finding a soul-mate. Or any sort of mate, come to think of it.

Over there, just behind the once-and-future *potager*, is the makeshift kennel where old Zumbach, my predecessor, or some peasant long since departed, used to chain up his guard dog. Once upon a time, I would have loved a dog myself. And then, on one of my long walks on the ancient cart-tracks that seem to radiate from La Folie, I was pursued for almost half a mile of pure terror by a great grey, limp-lolloping fang-slavering blood-eyed mongrel hellhound, straining at every stride to sink its jaws into my flailing limbs. And I changed my mind. I fear dogs now, at least the French ones. I will cross the road to avoid the evil beasts.

Reassuringly, Cat is a hundred per cent behind me on this one. Not to mention grouchy old Marcel at the aeroclub.

On the left, where the ground rises steeply, you may be able to see my seven tiny Ouessant sheep, Rastafarians in dreadlocks, as wild and ragged as if they had galloped straight out of the Bronze Age.

In all, I must have about five acres of rough hillside, skirting a house that clings to its craggy outcrop of rock like a solitary barnacle on the side of an old boat. This is where I have lived, with a cat and a grand piano, as I strive to become the kind of man I always wanted to be, as opposed to the dusty jumble of doubts and fears that I somehow became in my London life. A townie all at sea in the countryside, I am doing my best to learn from the earth. I am practising being brave.

I am still not quite sure how this has happened. How a life that was heading on rails in one direction – as a newspaper arts critic, butterfly-sociable and in love with the bright lights of the metropolis – has branched off the gleaming main line into an unkempt siding lined with wild flowers. In darkest France, of all places.

I know that I came here to have an adventure, because the buzzing sleepwalk I called a career had become uncomfortably comfortable, and because I had achieved nothing in my life of which I could feel proud. I wanted to learn about nature, not art. I wanted to see if I could survive abroad, alone, amid the leafy stillness of a place so remote that it felt like the end of the world. I wanted to start training myself to be a hero.

So here I am in my late thirties, alone in France with a cat, a piano and an aeroplane. I feel as if I am almost-slightly-just-beginning-vaguely-to-become integrated in this strange old world, still so new to me. I have a handful of French good friends. I am happy with my cat and my chickens. I take comfort in my piano, and delight in my aeroplane. The sheep may safely graze.

I have everything for which I could possibly wish.

Yet even as I register this thought, I know that it is a lie.

On 3 October at three o'clock in the afternoon, I fall in love at first sight. A car comes labouring up the drive, and I stand on the front steps to watch my unexpected visitor approach.

Cleopatra does not arrive on a burnished throne. From head-on, her vehicle looks and sounds like one of those white vans that all the farmers drive around here. I am half expecting it to be old Boulesteix, who they say hates *les Anglais*, in search of a lost sheep.

I blink and gape. It is like the moment when you are expecting to feel a smooth egg underneath a chicken, and instead touch a fluffed-up, bright-eyed chick. If this were a cartoon, I would rub my eyes. But it is not a cartoon. And a lovely young woman really has just turned up on my doorstep, all pale, chiselled features and glossy black hair. This is not supposed to happen in Jolibois, where a mystery virus appears to have wiped out almost every female human being between the ages of eighteen and fifty-five. It is certainly not supposed to happen to me.

As she winds down the window, I take a step backwards. I am a smocked peasant in front of the carriage of a princess. Oh, blimey. This must be how Titus the cockerel feels every time he catches sight of Melissa, his chicken pin-up. I feel a similar urge to unfurl one wing rakishly to the ground, and do a sideways matador dance, while squawking falsetto at my visitor. For the glowing directness of that smile blows every paper off the untidy desk of my heart; makes me want to bask in it for very much longer than it takes her to say:

'*Bonjour, monsieur. Madame Crillon, elle est là?*'

I have a strong urge to tell her that Madame Crillon has just popped out to buy chewing-tobacco, but will be back any minute.

'I don't know Madame Crillon,' I confess. '*Vous avez son adresse, madame?*'

She glances down at a crumpled piece of paper on her lap. '*Elle habite à St Sulpice.*'

St Sulpice is the village just across the valley. The princess is charmingly off-track, but the road will be easy to find. This doesn't stop me from crouching beside her door and explaining the route several times. I can't take my eyes off her, and I don't want her to leave.

'Do you know where you're going once you get to St Sulpice?' I ask.

'I understand there's a chapel,' she says, examining my face with a hint of a smile. 'I can find it from there.'

'*Ah, oui, la chapelle.* You can't miss it. You'll be fine.'

'*Merci, monsieur,*' she beams.

And then she is bumping back down the drive, and I have a three-second conversation with myself about courage and regret.

'I'm just popping over to St Sulpice,' I tell myself, as innocently as possible. 'I'll be back shortly.'

In St Sulpice, there are more houses than I remembered, and more white cars, too. The road forks at the chapel, so the princess could have gone in either direction. I drive both ways around the village, twice, waving at all the old boys on the first circuit, ducking their questioning gazes on the second. Then I sit on the chapel steps, and wait.

Twenty minutes later, a bulldozer passes.

'Taking the air, *monsieur*?' yells the driver cheerily, reminding me how rarely people loiter in Jolibois.

'Just waiting for someone,' I reply.

After forty-five minutes or so, my undying love for a complete stranger begins to falter. Even if I find her, she's going to think I'm her stalker. I haven't a clue what I plan to say to her, nor any idea, for that matter, why I am pursuing her at all. Has it come to this? Am I really so emotionally desperate that I must go hurtling around the countryside pursuing mystery women, simply because they happen to be extremely pretty and make me feel as if I am eighteen again?

Fortunately, she doesn't come. I drive twice more around the little village, picturing worried matrons phoning the gendarmes to tell them about the strange man casing the joint in a bashed-up green Espace. She is nowhere to be found. Perhaps she was never even there at all.

Blinding sunlight and the grinding rumble of yet another diesel engine jolt me awake at 8 am. Blast it. It is much too early for it to be Marie-Claude, my terrifying cleaning lady. Don't tell me it is that beautiful lost damsel again, still seeking Madame Crillon. Cat must still be out mousing, or she'd have woken me an hour ago, rasping clean her fishy tongue on my unshaven chin. By the time I have galloped down to the winter sitting-room, taking the stairs two at a time, Gilles is already standing at the front door, making binoculars of his bare hands as he attempts to peer through the glass. With any luck, that glass is too dirty for him to see all the washing-up piled up beside the sink.

Gilles is my heroic neighbour and peasant mentor, who lives with his silent wife Josette, on the other side of the railway line at the bottom of the valley. He serves as my conscience, too, always turning up unannounced with that same wry smile to make me feel I should have leapt out of bed an hour earlier; always with that none-too-surreptitious glance at the un-vegetable patch, silently upbraiding me for my idleness.

'*Salut, Gilles,*' I croak, attempting to sound as if I have been up for hours.

'*Salut, Michael,*' he replies, shaking my hand with his vice-like Masonic grip, and glaring at my stripy pyjama trousers, which I have done my best to cover up with an oilskin coat. Rumbled.

A grizzled *paysan* who has been farming since he left school at thirteen, Gilles's face is carved with almost six decades of wind and sun and life experience. Most of the lines deepen when he smiles or laughs. But there are some darker marks that do not match his smile, too, which have appeared in the time since we met. Either sheep-farming in France is becoming tougher with each passing season, or else the pressures of helping a hopeless English townie learn about animals and nature are beginning to take their toll.

'Is there something you . . . ?' I begin, and then stop myself. I am still learning the ways of the French country-side; still learning that when Gilles drops by to say hello, he doesn't like to have to announce why he has come without some gentle chit-chat first, to work up to it. So we stand in silence for a second or two, gazing up at the old box tree outside the front door. That tree must have stood here, rustling in this breeze, for nigh-on two hundred years.

'*Ça va, avec le beau temps?*' he asks, at last.

'*Oui, ça va, ça va,*' I reply. There's no way I'm inviting him in, to see my kitchen shambles. '*Mais le potager . . .*' I point at the jungle of my un-vegetable patch, knowing that he is already gazing at my all-too-public disgrace.

'Oh, don't worry about that now,' he says, waving his hand. 'But since you mention it . . .' He steps from foot to foot; looks uncomfortable. I have hurried him on to his chosen subject before he has finished his warm-up. 'Are you serious about doing the work this year?'

'Absolutely I am.' I hang my head at the way he says 'this year' – meaning the coming one – for we both know how badly I failed earlier this summer, with my bumper crop of weeds, and two dirty great sacks of unplanted seed potatoes turning to spaghetti in the barn. 'Next year is going to be *l'année de la patate* at La Folie.'

'*Ah, c'est bien,*' says Gilles, unconvinced. 'I thought you

would be too busy terrorizing my sheep with that noisy
yellow aeroplane of yours.'

'Um, *je* . . .'

'I saw you flying overhead the other day. Engine sounded
a bit rough; I wondered if you'd crash.'

'Actually, I think I nearly did,' I reply. He appears to find
this hilarious.

'In the meantime, if you're interested,' he continues, rubbing
the side of his nose with his finger. 'I've found someone to help
you with your garden. Claude Jadot, a former *cantonnier*.'

I don't know what a *cantonnier* is, and I don't recall asking Gilles if he knew anyone who might give me a hand with
taming what remains of the La Folie jungle, let alone
with training me in the art of potato-charming. If I did, I
think I was rather hoping he might put himself forward for
the job. He obviously has even less confidence in me than I
feared.

'But won't you be . . . ?'

'I'm rather busy with the sheep,' he says. 'And besides, it's
not so long until I retire.'

I never take Gilles's references to his retirement very
seriously. Partly this is because he seems, at fifty-nine, far too
young to be swapping his sheep farm for an armchair. And
partly because he is, for me, the quintessential *paysan*: a
vision of the French countryside in his faded check shirt and
wellington boots, as inseparable from his sheepdog and his
mud-spattered white van as red wine from bread and
Camembert. He is part of eternity.

'You'll never retire, Gilles. I can't believe it.'

'It's the law,' he shrugs, kicking at a stone. And then he
asks if the gendarmes have been to see me yet today.

'You mean to ask me whether you're serious about
retiring?'

Gilles chuckles, stroking his beard at the thought. 'A pair
of them came to see us. Apparently they're looking for an

attractive young woman in a white Clio who has burgled several houses around here in broad daylight.' Gilles hesitates; leans a little closer to me. 'Are you all right?'

'Yes,' I say, with a high-pitched laugh that takes us both by surprise. 'I'm fine.'

'You can't be too careful, these days.'

'No, Gilles,' I reply, gazing wistfully out across the valley towards the little chapel at St Sulpice. 'You certainly can't.'

And before I can ask him how he feels about saying good-bye to the only way of life he has ever known, let alone apologize for buzzing his sheep, he begins to climb back into his van. 'Anyway,' he says, 'I've asked Jadot to come and see you. He's a bit special. You'll see.'

As I watch Gilles disappear down the drive in a cloud of dust and smoke, Cat comes and strokes herself insistently against my legs almost as if she were attempting to smooth the creases out of my pyjama trousers. I shiver. It's cold out here on the steps, even in my oilskin coat. Much to Cat's chagrin, I head off in the direction of the chicken house to release the Egg Squad from their confinement and rattle some grain into their tin. Their water is almost finished, so I bring the upturned drum of their drinker inside, feed Cat – now clawing at my calves – and then return the replenished drinker to the chicken house.

'*Puck puck puck puck*,' declares Martha, my black-and-gold favourite, bending her head to drink before tipping it back, beak to the sky, and letting the water glug down her throat as if it were a particularly succulent earthworm. Titus leaps up on to the gate and begins to belt out his trumpeted *cocorico*, while the rest of the girls queue up to drink. Hotspur, the outsider, waits in the shadows. I think I know how he feels.

'*Puck puck puck puck*,' I reply to Martha. And from the way she blinks at me – much like the locals, when I first began to try out my spoken French in Jolibois – I think it is safe to say that I do not yet speak fluent Hen.

After trudging round the side of the house to count the sheep quietly ruminating on the hillside, I trudge back inside to have a shower in the subterranean bathroom, enjoying the gushing zing of the water as it massages my shoulders and scalp, feeling myself slowly reinhabiting the crumpled corners of my body, and thinking how grateful I am not to have been burgled, not to have caught up with the young lady in the white Clio and – perhaps more than anything – not to have been born before hot showers were invented. Back in those days, it would have been unthinkable for an English bachelor in his late thirties to inhabit a tumbledown farmhouse in darkest France and to presume to integrate himself into local life.

'You do know that the French look with suspicion upon single men living alone, don't you?' my friend Jérôme once told me, with a wink. 'I should know.'

Jérôme is a retired banker from Paris, who lives a few miles from La Folie with nine horses, nine donkeys and nine bicycles stabled on his 81-hectare estate. These are all awaiting the visits of his nine grandchildren, who, more and more, are discovering the pleasure of exchanging the heated chaos of the city for the cool simplicity of the countryside. Kindly as his words are meant, I wish he hadn't actually told me.

I need to be speedy in the shower today for, in less than half an hour's time, I have a date with a fearsome lady of approximately my age, statuesque as the Arc de Triomphe, who would, I suspect, be beautiful if she were not so scary. Her name is Marie-Claude, and she arrives in her little red car to give me a weekly lecture on a subject of her choice, namely *les Anglais*, and what is wrong with us. By the by, she also cleans the house until it feels as polished and disinfected as an old-fashioned hospital. But I like to persuade myself that it is her lectures for which I am paying, because this makes me feel better about the exorbitant social-security bill I must foot for the pleasure of seeing her. I also like to persuade myself that there is a secret frisson between us; a silent awareness that we are alone together at La Folie.

Today, when the red car pulls up outside the front door, I am caught in a familiar position: with my hands in the sink, attempting to finish a week's worth of washing-up.

'*Bonjour*,' says Marie-Claude, in her nasal whisper. I lean forward to give her a peck on each cheek, but she firmly sticks out her hand, almost pushing me backwards as she shakes mine. Then she begins to remove the several thick layers of woollen outer garments that she has donned for the short drive from her house.

'*Bonjour, Marie-Claude*,' I reply, cheerily. '*Ça va?*'

Tall and admonitory as a stack of overdue library books, fearsome as a rolled-up bundle of electrified stock fencing, Marie-Claude betrays no lack of self-esteem. She examines me through narrowed eyes to see if I am teasing her. '*Oui, ça va, merci*,' she replies, raising her eyebrows as if to suggest that it is a miracle that she has survived another week. And then she smiles, and adopts a warmer tone to add, 'I think I may have run over one of your chickens.'

Glancing at her sphinx-like smile to see if she is serious, I race out of the front door and peer down the drive in search of a dark pile of flattened feathers. But there is no road-kill to clear, no departed friend to grieve, and a quick head-count of my familiars – Titus and the girls pecking in the long grass around the *fosse septique*, with Hotspur lurking lower down, closer to the un-vegetable patch – reveals that all are present and correct after all. I could swear that Marie-Claude looks almost disappointed when I tell her the news. Her lips purse, and another unreadable smile flickers across her eyes. Standing in front of her reminds me of attempting to attract the attention of one of the perfumed shop assistants in a Jermyn Street shirt-maker's, most of whom look far too grand even to shop there, let alone work there themselves.

'There was a programme about *les Anglais* on television the other night,' she says, launching straight into her lecture even as she is still tying the straps of her apron behind her back. 'Did you see it?'

I shake my head. '*Je n'ai pas de télévision.*' Marie-Claude must know this already, but she still looks at me as if I had just told her that I had my tonsils removed last week.

'It was about how many of them – of you – are moving to the Limousin, the Dordogne, the Lot and the Charente,' she continues. 'Buying up small farms because they want to be *paysans*. Even with *la Crise*, they said the property prices in England are four times as expensive as here in France.'

Is it really as bad as that? I love France; feel as if I have begun a personal relationship with my adopted country. I hadn't realized I was just another lemming, leaping off the white cliffs at Dover. But the credit crunch must have begun to stem the émigré rodent tide.

'So does it bother you, all these English people coming here?' I ask, hoping to smile her into softening.

'*Non*,' she declares, after a pause. 'But they say it's an invasion.'

'Well, yes, I suppose it is. But this region was English once before, in the fourteenth century, so it's nothing new.' A wise old Frenchman in a neighbouring village told me this, but I haven't had the chance to try it out on anybody until now.

'Exactly. And the English captured Poitiers.' She fixes me with a cast-iron stare. For a moment I wonder if she is expecting an apology on behalf of Richard the Lionheart, until it dawns on me that Marie-Claude is not playing a game of cat-and-mouse semi-flirtation with her employer. No, she is genuinely worried about her country being toppled by the Brits.

'So do you think the English queen will ever be the queen

of France?' I ask. In those rare moments when Marie-Claude shows a chink of vulnerability, she becomes strangely attractive. There is a fragile femininity behind all that electrified barbed-wire fencing, like a petite ballet dancer surrounded by a burly entourage, that makes me want to play along with her English-baiting. Once I even asked her if we might call each other *tu*, instead of the more formal *vous*. But she wasn't having any of it. 'People can take advantage of each other like that,' she told me. And she is not about to humour my humour now.

There is a long, frosty silence.

'It's true that the English humour is very different to the French humour,' she says, at last, changing the subject as she fetches the basket of cleaning products from under the sink, each aerosol and spray-gun of lethal carcinogens bought according to her express instructions, as laid out in a numbered list.

Much as I enjoy the cut-and-thrust of my chats with Marie-Claude, it feels wrong to be standing here idle, watching her hard at work. So I make my excuses and slip into the summer sitting-room to play the piano. I am about to launch into one of the Schubert sonatas I have been attempting to perfect since my teens, and then stop myself, in case she should see through so bald an attempt to worm my way into her affections. She will think I am showing off. So I stick studiously to scales: the harmonic and melodic minors in all keys, four octaves, legato, instead. I cannot help thinking that, if I am ever to win myself the woman of my dreams, then music will somehow play a part.

# 3

## NOVEMBER

The days are shortening, Cat rolls herself into a tighter ball with each week that passes, and my bedroom feels a little danker with each dusk. To pay the firewood bill at La Folie, I write a weekly newspaper column about my attempts to turn myself from a soft townie into a rugged French peasant. Here, my occasional references to my single status, and my abject failure to find myself a dishy French *copine*, have begun to bear strange fruit.

Today, when Didier the postman roars up the drive in his muddy yellow Clio, there arrives a pink envelope from which, when I open it, fall three photographs of a young woman in a bikini, in a cocktail dress and on horseback. I do not recognize the woman, and feel a familiar shyness – as if I am overhearing a conversation I am not supposed to be hearing, and wish I could cough or whistle to make it stop – as I begin to read the accompanying letter.

'I hope you don't mind me sending you these pictures of my niece,' it begins. 'And for goodness' sake don't tell Rosie that I've done so. But she is just such a lovely girl, of about your age, and she deserves to find love. So I thought of you . . .'

I gaze at the pictures of a young woman, gazing shyly into the camera lens, and – unwittingly – into the eyes of a stranger in France. Yes, I think to myself, she does deserve to find love. But me?

This is not the first such touching letter I have received, from kindly women doing their very best to find a man who is not a drunk or an axe-murderer for their single daughters, nieces, goddaughters and unmarried best friends. Flattered as I am, I feel embarrassed, too. But mostly I feel bemused. Is there really such a shortage of men who are not beasts?

'You're probably going to think I'm completely bonkers,' writes another lady, 'but here goes. Having read your column since you first started writing it, I have a feeling that my daughter, Rachel, could possibly be your *copine*. Rachel is thirty and single. She's caring and thoughtful, potty about animals, gardening and music, a bit fey and not at all materialistic. I would love her to find "the one", but kind men who love the countryside and want to settle down are thin on the ground in London. I'm attaching a picture of Rachel with her cat, Flaubert, otherwise known as Fifi . . .'

Yes, I do love the countryside, and a cat called Flaubert appeals, in the absence of a parrot. But my own cat is unlikely to concur, and I am sure I have never suggested anything about wanting to settle down. No, settling down is what children are told to do in dormitories when they are showing too much spirit, rather than the ambition of fledgling *paysans* bent on heroic adventures with their manly power-tools. This unacknowledged urge must have slipped out, between the lines; a secret so secret that I wasn't even aware of it myself.

All I want, all I have ever wanted, is someone to share the adventure; a co-pilot to occupy the right-hand seat of my plane. Does this woman, Rachel's *maman*, have no idea how many manly power-tools I possess? Not for me a wedding list at John Lewis and every motorist in Jolibois tooting his horn at my nuptial cortège: I have no yearning for children and a labrador to make my life complete. On the contrary, there are enough children in the world already, without my adding my DNA to the mix. And they say that labradors are the bitiest dogs in the world.

For now, more than anything, I want to live my life. I want a relationship that is a beginning, not an end; a life whose trajectory is upwards and skywards, not down into the well-sprung depths of a sofa built for two.

'My challenge should you choose to accept it is to be a Knight on a white charger for a remarkable damsel in your neck of the woods,' writes a woman who claims to work for the Home Office, and whose tone at first seems a little more encouragingly upbeat than some of the other well-meaning mums desperate to save their daughters from what they must perceive as the death-in-life of spinsterhood.

'My daughter Maria is not French as I know your dream woman should be,' continues Home Office lady, 'but she speaks the lingo fluently and lives not far from you. She fled these shores in June this year after her heart was broken at the end of a relationship which promised much but delivered little (he was an estate agent . . . say no more). So I think you could call her a damsel in distress, though she would probably not agree (see enclosed photos).'

I peer at the photos, of a young woman who looks as tall as a supermodel and far too chic for me. 'Anyway, from what I've read I think you would suit each other perfectly. In Italy, Versace tried to talk her into modelling (which if you've now looked at the pics, you can see she is well qualified for) but she refused. She used to be a champion fell-walker, and is now a ferocious climber, deep-sea diver and tennis player. I think you would suit each other perfectly.'

This woman obviously hasn't seen my backhand, I think to myself, before reading on: 'I am only sorry I never taught her plastering or plumbing which would, I guess, have made her irresistible. Maria would be absolutely furious if she knew anything about this and so a felicitous/fortuitous contact would have to be engineered. Intrigued? I hope so.'

Without even the excuse of one glass of wine too many, I reply, although I feel almost ashamed of myself as I do, like a hunter pursuing a wild boar on a day set aside for the hare.

Fortunately, Home Office lady comes back with a series of suggested deceptions so fantastical as a means of hoodwinking her own daughter into meeting me that I am able to duck out of her scheme without any backward glance of regret. A wise man once told me that all women turn into their mothers in the end.

I know my heart should leap at these and other advances-by-proxy, but I am too busy feeling uneasy to feel like leaping. I appear to have become the kind of man a woman wants her daughter to marry, which is not at all the same thing as becoming the kind of man a woman wants to marry herself. How is it that these women can have no idea who I really am, yet are nevertheless willing to woo me on behalf of others who have no inkling that they are being set up?

All the letter-writers know of me is that version of myself that I carefully construct on a weekly basis; a cut-and-pasted single-malt snapshot of my life distilled into 750 words. I do strive to tell the truth, as best I can, and isolation has certainly brought me face to face with my emotions in rather the same way that my Rastafarian sheep, conditioned to scarper if anyone else is with me, will gallop towards me if I approach them alone. But all I can write is one of many possible versions of the truth: a passport photo, not a Leonardo likeness. And lovely women are now writing to me, offering me their daughters, all wrapped in shiny paper and tied up with satin bows.

It is always mothers and aunts, not fathers and uncles, who write, seeking to make the universe match up. I try to imagine who they are; attempt to picture them sitting in their comfortable houses, night after night, wringing their hands, wanting nothing more than the happiness of others. Inordinately touching as I find their advances, they make me want to hide, too. After I have glanced at the pictures, of course.

These pictures make me feel more separate than ever, as I sit and gaze at the strangers who smile back at me from them. For these women whom the universe is intent upon offering me on a silver salver do not merely not fit the gap in the jigsaw puzzle with which I am toying. No, they seem to belong to a different puzzle entirely, like some of the houses the more obtuse French estate agents would take me to see when I was searching for La Folie.

'Why have you brought me here?' I would ask, even before we had climbed out of their company car to look at the next unsuitable property on the list. I knew I was shallow, for first impressions mattered to me; if the house didn't look right from the outside, I was uninterested in taking the time to look inside. Even names mattered more than they ought: houses in Bellac or Lussac called out to me far more strongly than those in Nieul or Niort.

And then with Émilie, an estate agent who reminded me of one of the lovelier woodland characters in a Disney cartoon, I drove up the drive to the last house on my list. And all my questions were so thoroughly answered that I felt quite daunted at the suddenness with which my life was about to be transformed.

For there was nothing about La Folie that I could have wanted to change. As Émilie and I wandered from room to room, gazing up at oak beams held together with spiders' webs, everything about this ancient *fermette* was precisely as I would have ordained it were I lying on a couch, describing my dusty, unfinished fantasy to a shrink who specialized in ramshackle French farmhouses. A section of my life's puzzle was finally complete. And the slap-in-the-face certainty I felt has left me with an inkling of the kind of lurch in my heart I will one day need to feel, if I am to know that I have finally met the woman who is the missing jigsaw-puzzle piece of my dreams – and not some glamorous house-thief, come to steal the last cold sausage in the fridge.

I shiver. Though the sky is still bright and clear enough to make me want to leap into the Luscombe and take to the air, each day the temperature seems to drop by another degree. Titus crows as lustily as ever, yet there is an unmistakable frostiness to his rousing cock-a-doodle-doo. This morning, the thermometer in the winter sitting-room says it is twelve degrees indoors. So I give in to my shivering, and prepare to light the wood-burning stove at last. This is my only source of heat, although Ralph the artist, an overgrown bumblebee of a man, and one of my few English friends in Jolibois, did lend me a portable gas heater a while ago, largely out of pity for Cat. But using it makes the house feel as damp as Glencoe, without markedly changing the temperature: it smells and feels a bit like trying to melt an iceberg with a Zippo lighter. So heavier ordnance is required.

This pains me, not just because it is an admission that winter is beginning to envelop La Folie in its iron grasp, but also because having a vast, untouched wood-store stashed away for a rainy day or twenty gives a fellow a warm feeling. It is like taking off in a small plane from a runway that is much longer than you need, or cooking enough oven chips for two when you are alone.

Each year, Jean-Louis – the genial sheep-farmer whose beard is so thick that it feels as if I am talking to him through a hole in the hedge – asks me if I will be wanting another *dix stères* of seasoned oak this year. And each year, I say yes, please, Jean-Louis. I just can't help myself. Never mind that, even without these extra ten cubic metres, my wood-pile already stretches the entire length of the barn, and is too high for me to reach the logs on the top layer. Like a miser with his gold hidden under his mattress, the knowledge that it is there lulls me to sleep at night.

One of the reasons I fell for La Folie was its wood-burning stove. Never mind that the big black Godin *cuisinière* I inherited from my predecessor, old Zumbach, sucked all the light from the winter sitting-room. The beast felt reassuringly familiar, for I once started a chimney-fire with something similar, years earlier, on holiday in France. I can still recall the sight of the fire's red-black flames licking at the ceiling from the flue. These did little damage. I remember, too, the bitter stink of the blue-grey powder that came rasping from my extinguisher. And this did a lot.

The La Folie stove is a squat black lump, roughly the size of a Texel ram, with a fire-box on one side, an oven on the other, and a crooked chimney that puts one in mind of an early steam locomotive by Trevithick. Oiled and polished, its vast cooking plate looks big enough to simmer a cauldron of soup for a platoon. Yet I have never really used it for cooking, apart from (a) a few attempts at Nigel Slater's rabbit with grainy mustard to impress early female visitors to La Folie; (b) one pan of eggs shamelessly scrambled for the benefit of a photographer who came to take pictures of my hermitic existence; and (c) one favourite pair of socks, tragically incinerated.

Hence the fact that I have asked Monsieur Duruflé the tiler to replace the inky leviathan with a smaller and more efficient stove. Best of all, this new stove will have a glass door. So I will shortly be able to spend hours gazing at the combustion of the logs I have sawn on the fire I have lit: Promethean television.

Leaping into the Espace, I drive down to Jolibois to return Ralph the artist's portable gas heater.

'Oh, but you should have *kept* it, my boy,' he booms from the doorstep of his townhouse, making me wish I had a pair of dark glasses and a false moustache in my pocket. Marie-Claude is always warning me that *les Anglais* are far too loud. 'I feel closer to my poor dear Rembrandt when I work in the cold,' continues Ralph, glancing theatrically over his shoulder at the small postcard of Rembrandt that he has taped to the side of his easel. He wants me to join him and Olga for a mid-morning snorter, but I explain that I am off to buy firelighters from the *droguerie* on the rue du Coq and cannot stop.

'Ah, yes, the Nicest Man in the Universe,' nods Ralph. 'Where would we be without him?' And then, just as we are shaking hands on the doorstep, he clutches mine with extra force and leans forward to whisper something to me, as deliberately as if he were about to deliver a soliloquy from the front of a stage. 'Don't tell anyone, my boy,' he hisses, in a stage whisper loud enough for the people in the cheap seats at the back of the upper circle to hear, 'but we're *leaving*.'

'Leaving Jolibois? For good?'

'For ill, my boy, for ill.' Ralph hangs his head.

'But . . .' My mind races.

'I daren't say more. Olga will kill me.'

And so he shuts the door with an apologetic wave, and I stand gazing at the brass lady in the fountain opposite as the waters splash at the hem of her burnished toga, green with age. She has been here in Jolibois longer than anyone. I presume she will outstay us all, too. Where on earth shall I come now, when I need a dose of good English cheer and the Dickensian warmth of Ralph and Olga's house on winter nights? What will replace the soothing rasp of Ralph's tenor saxophone? And with whom shall I watch the rugby, when England are playing France?

Cutting through the tiny passage, barely wide enough for

a bicycle, that leads up past Ralph's house to the little square, I make my way towards the rue du Coq. The tiny *droguerie*, a time-capsule of 1950s France, is one of my favourite shops in Jolibois. Here, the Nicest Man in the Universe wears a faded shopkeeper's coat and sells seven different kinds of masking tape, a viciously noxious snake-deterrent which smells like a glue-sniffer's fart, myriad hand-made pocket-knives, a selection of cleaning products specifically for wood-burning stoves and – I have no doubt – *quatre bougies* (fork handles), too, all from a shop the size of a manhole. Most of these oddments cost only a euro or two, so the Nicest Man makes ends meet by selling fireworks to the Brits.

'You English are amazing,' he tells me, in French. 'You buy so many *feux d'artifice*.'

'Ah, that'll be because of the fifth of November,' I explain, after a pause spent rummaging for his word in my schoolboy vocab. I had almost forgotten that Guy Fawkes Night was approaching. I glance at the box of firelighters he has placed on the scratched glass counter and wonder if they really are for lighting fires, or if they will explode in a riot of coloured stars.

'No, no, it's all year round,' he insists. 'You are always celebrating.'

This is news to me: have *les Anglais* really developed a taste for celebrating their ruined-barn acquisitions with rockets and Roman candles? There may be something about being on French soil that brings out the latent pyromaniac in the Anglo-Saxon soul. I wonder if I should tell him what my firelighters are for, in case he's worried I'm planning to set fire to the *Mairie* on 5 November.

'I heard you nearly crashed that plane of yours,' he says, changing the subject. Behind me, an elderly lady I do not recognize enters the shop before I can think how to reply.

'*Bonjour, messieurs,*' she announces, with old-fashioned politesse.

'*Bonjour, madame,*' we reply in unison. She blinks nervously, perhaps taken aback at how delighted we both are to see her.

'I wondered if you had any flea-collars for cats?' she asks.

'*Non, madame,*' replies the Nicest Man, with such regret that I almost expect him to shed a tear. And then he rouses himself. 'And nor do we have any cat-collars for fleas.'

Not to be outdone by *les Anglais* with their fireworks, my neighbour Young Boulesteix is currently using his tractor to build a bonfire a few hundred yards from La Folie, a pyre which looks big enough to immolate a Viking longship. He is out there when I drive home, and I watch him from the kitchen window. How hard and fast these *paysans* work, I think to myself, as I sip my tea. While Boulesteix clears trees and scrub from the hillside, noisily taming the wild landscape like Hercules slopping out the Augean stables, I read about Diseases in Potatoes, doing my best to evade my homework for French class, which – Ralph reminded me, with a theatrical sigh – is on the subjunctive. The subject irks me, for I know I shall never use the subjunctive in anger; not when I already have enough trouble with pronouns and reflexive verbs. Mind you, I feel that way about fire extinguishers, too, or about the life jacket I wear when I fly my Luscombe across the Channel. So I struggle on with the subjunctive, wishing that I had enough land to justify buying an old red tractor like the one Young Boulesteix is using to heap up his flammable mountain of branches, bracken and scrub. It occurs to me that if I had a red tractor, I would be irresistible to women, and not just their mothers.

And then, fed up with French, I head out to the barn, to saw and chop some logs for my first fire of the year. For any chap who has been sitting for too long in front of his subjunctives, there are few things better than swinging an axe into a hefty lump of seasoned oak, and feeling the wood yield as it splits with the sound of a firework exploding. Certainly, the last time my pilot friend Jethro came to stay at La Folie, the one thing that he wanted to do was not to weed jungles, or visit local markets, or contemplate very small sheep. No, he simply wanted to chop logs.

The physical pleasure in splitting wood with an axe is akin to the satisfaction in thwacking a golf-ball straight and true with your driver, or thumping a perfect tennis serve. And there is something else, too. The father-figure in fairy stories is so often a woodcutter; an archetype of stolid masculinity untrammelled by ambition, credit-card debt, or a stressful job in the City. This may be why golf driving-ranges and tennis have become so popular in the home counties: the men of Surrey are not chopping enough logs.

Here at La Folie, the days are beginning to shrink with the cold, and it is already dark at six o'clock when I trudge in from the barn with an armful of oak, feeling far too sweaty to light the stove. The tractor's rumbling grumble is silent. Out in the chicken house, Titus and his girls will be blinking on their perches, waiting for me to come and bolt the door, to shut out the frost and the fox. Hotspur will be waiting for the dark, too, cloaking him at last from his father's jealous rage.

I am always relieved when the darkness brings an end to their feather-flying fisticuffs; to the violent games of tag, in which it is always Hotspur who is fleeing for his life, with Titus in neck-straining pursuit. I swear you can feel the ground shake as their bandy legs go pit-a-pat outside, as Titus does his damnedest to recreate one of those Greek myths in which the father kills and eats his sons. There are days when Hotspur's shrieks of terror make me put my hands over my ears. And there are days, too, when I cannot help laughing at the sight of them. For Titus and Hotspur share the same genes, so they run at exactly the same speed. And – like the figures on Keats's Grecian urn – no matter how hard he tries, nor how fast he runs, Titus never gains an inch on his squawking prey.

On the hillside behind La Folie, my seven manky Rastafarians will already be curled up for the night, each stencilling their own dry roundel on the dampening grass as the dew begins to fall. I can picture Gaston, my toothless old ram, lying a little apart from the others, drawing up what is left of his strength for tomorrow, when he must once again dance and jink to avoid the head-butting violence of his young rivals. Though I haven't the stomach to eat the rascals, I do know a field with too much testosterone in it when I see one.

Even as a neophyte *paysan*, still ignorant in the rugged ways of the genuine farmer, I am beginning to see, too, that you can never have too many women. Girls are just plain better, at least when it comes to chickens and sheep. They lay their eggs in the hay each morning. They produce their hop-skippety lambs each spring. They are always gentle and sweet-natured. It's the chaps who cause all the mayhem: endlessly charging at each other, tormenting their harems, and caterwauling about how this is their territory, so cock-a-doodle-yah-boo-sucks to you, Sonny Jim.

Switching on a couple of lamps in the gloomy kitchen, I sit down with a glass of red wine and a bowl of peanuts at the old oak table I inherited from Zumbach, its scrubbed top almost white with age. Beside my chair, Cat sits poised on her haunches, pawing the tiles like a fast bowler about to begin a run-up, before leaping on to my lap with a grunt. She has eaten so many lizards over the summer that her furry undercarriage is beginning to swing beneath her like a ram's credentials as she walks. As if guessing my thoughts, Cat begins to knead the doughy bulge of my own belly in that claws-out, insistent fashion that the French call *chat boulanger*. She has a point: a diet is in order for both of us.

Six o'clock has always been my favourite time of day. In the parallel universe of my childish imagination, my father is home from work, my mother has switched on the table lamps in the sitting-room, and the world is beginning to glow. My father swaps his grey suit-jacket for a shabby green cardigan with leather buttons, and – if it's a Friday night – opens a bottle of red wine while my mother leafs through *French Provincial Cookery* and begins to slice an onion. I watch as she slices it first one way and then, turning it through ninety degrees, the other. Nothing is happening, except everything, and there is a cosy warmth about the scene – about the way that the two of them are together – that fills my insecure child's heart with reassurance. The world feels a safer place when you can see that your parents are happy together.

Even now, alone in darkest France, six o'clock has become my thinking time, once I have finished hammering in fence-posts, or sanding floors, and the coiled spring of the day's pressures has finally unwound. Night after night, Cat and I have sat out on the terrace together, in summer and in winter, in darkness and in light, gazing out at the changing view on the far side of the valley.

Tonight, however, I have only just pressed 'play' on a CD of organ music and begun to sip my wine when the phone rings.

'Michael?'

I recognize the voice of Jethro, my pilot friend from Kent, who always announces himself in that slightly shocked tone that makes me wonder if he has just narrowly avoided electrocuting himself. Dashing and driven, Jethro is special to me because we are exactly the same age, share the same passion for flying, and the same faintly hopeless desire to meet the woman pilot of our dreams. He reminds me of myself, only with half the expensive education and twice the natural flair. 'So how's it going?' he says, in his Cockney-sparrow lilt. 'And what's that awful music?'

'It's going fine,' I laugh. 'I haven't flown the Luscombe recently, because the oil temp is running a little high, I've got too many rams and too many cockerels. Other than that, I can't complain. And it's Bach, I'm afraid. How about you?'

'Oh, you know,' he says, innocently. 'Same as ever.' I smile to myself. For Jethro, I know that business as usual means crackling through life like a forest-fire eating up a mountain-side. I wonder what new scrape he has got himself into this time.

Five years ago, Jethro and I were members of the same little flying club at Biggin Hill; two newly fledged pilots, renting worn-out Cessnas for £100 an hour, wondering if it was for this that we had worked so hard to gain our licences. Except that Jethro was different. The moment I overheard him talking in the clubhouse to a couple of other young pilots, I was electrified.

'I'm going to buy my own aircraft,' he told them, the words capturing my attention like the flash of a speed-camera on the road to Damascus. For here, in this dreary Portakabin on the perimeter of a former RAF base, here on the outskirts of Bromley, I sniffed the first, heady whiff of a dazzling possibility of which I had never dreamed. And not from some white-haired millionaire, either, but from a down-to-earth young bloke whose glottal stops and industrial haircut suggested that he was probably born with a greasy spoon, rather than a silver one, in his mouth. Jethro talked about flying in the way I had always dreamed flying would be in my Spitfire fantasies: as the source of a dazzling catalogue of heroic exploits, rather than a joylessly calcu-lated exercise in risk-management. And as I strained to eavesdrop on his conversation I knew, in my timid, suburban way, that I wanted more of the same thing for myself. Not just in my flying, but in my life.

Jethro had it all worked out. No matter that he was still a raw beginner with only a hundred hours under his belt, all of them on Cessnas. He was going to do an instrument rating, buy his own aircraft; use it to learn aerobatics and for trips across the Channel to France; go on all sorts of amazing airborne adventures; join a display team; be paid for the raw brilliance of his flying. And what struck me, listening to him, was the certainty behind his words. When the other pilots left, folding up their charts and shaking their heads at his crazy bravado, I went over and introduced myself to him; to this fearless bloke who made difficult things sound not merely possible, but a cinch.

'I heard what you were saying,' I told him, 'and it chimed with me, so I just wanted to say hello. It's a relief to hear someone talking like that, instead of just moaning about this rain, and how much it costs to fly to Compton Abbas.'

'Oh, thanks,' he said, blinking with surprise. 'Pilot yourself?'

'I've only just got my licence myself, in Florida, but I'm mad keen to do more. I just can't seem to get enough of the sky.'

'I know,' he grinned. 'What do you fly?'

'Oh, you know. The club planes . . .'

'Spam-cans.'

'But I learned on a Piper Warrior.'

'Spam-can too,' he shrugged. 'Everyone seems to think that all they can do with their precious licence is fly one of these rust-buckets to some godforsaken aerodrome, and drink a cup of tea that has cost them a hundred quid.'

'Whereas . . . ?' I wanted to hear him do his speech again, to remind me about how beautiful and exciting flying could be, if we had the nerve to make it so. But he had already moved on.

'It's Jethro, incidentally,' he said, extending his hand. 'If you like, we could go flying together some time.'

'So the tea will only cost me fifty quid?'

Jethro grinned; began packing his headset into his flight bag.

'Are you really thinking of buying your own plane?' I continued.

'Not just thinking about it. I'm going to do it. And you?' He stopped what he was doing and straightened to look at me, gazing at me with a curiosity that made me wonder if he could see right through me. 'What ambitions do you have?'

'I'm thinking about going to live in France,' I replied.

'Snap,' he said, his eyes sparkling. 'All those French chicks, eh? Except that I can't speak a word of French, and I'm not sure I could make my business work out there.'

'I was beginning to think you could do anything you wanted.'

'I can,' he laughed. 'Apart from languages.'

'And I want to fly a Spitfire,' I continued. And then I blushed, because I had never told this to anyone before. Not from the heart, anyway; and not in a Portakabin on the perimeter of a former Battle of Britain fighter station. Hearing the words come out of my mouth made me feel like a six-year-old again.

'Don't we all,' he sighed, shaking his head.

'No, but for me . . . it's more than that.'

Jethro stared at me.

'I believe you,' he said, at last. And in that moment, we became friends. We went flying together; rented a spam-can and flew it to North Weald, one of the great Battle of Britain fighter stations, where we admired the gleaming Extras, Jet Provosts and vintage aircraft basking on the apron in the sun. One of them caught my eye, with its 1940s curves and the way its nose-cone seemed to point expectantly up into the sky. Jethro had already moved on, his attention caught by a sleek aerobatic aircraft in rainbow colours, but I was arrested by the old-fashioned loveliness of the two-seater in front of me, with its gracefully tapered fuselage, high wings and an unmistakable whiff of adventures waiting to be shared.

'What is it?' asked Jethro, returning to where I was standing, peering into the plane's tiny cockpit.

'Not sure,' I replied. 'But if I ever have my own plane one day, I want it to be one of these.'

'Badge on the tail says it's a Luscombe Silvaire,' he said, slowly circling the plane as if he were doing a pre-flight inspection. 'I've heard they're dangerous; difficult to control on the ground. But it looks darn pretty, too.'

A few months later, Jethro finally bought his own plane, all steel tubes and plastic fabric, which was the ugliest aircraft I had ever seen, but climbed like a funicular railway and went a whole lot faster than its squashed-brick streamlining seemed to promise.

We both joined the Tiger Club at Headcorn, where I finally learned to fly Tiger Moths, always the basic apprenticeship for Spitfire pilots, while Jethro was looping and rolling overhead in a Stampe, already working hard at his aerobatics. The months went by, until one day, out of the blue, he emailed me with a sales advertisement he had spotted for a bright yellow Luscombe with white wings.

'What do you think of this one?' he wrote. And that was that.

Our flying careers advanced in parallel, except that Jethro was always in the fast lane and I was in the slow one, several steps behind. Our romantic lives seemed to move in step, too, somewhat in the manner of two fellow foot-soldiers crawling through a minefield beneath an artillery bombardment. Both of us, it turned out, had just emerged from long-standing relationships with lovely women with whom we somehow could not quite believe we were going to spend the rest of our lives. For both of us, something wasn't right, something we couldn't put a finger on.

But that was then, and this is now. Five years on, and Jethro and I are both single again; he in sunny Bromley, with a Porsche and a high-powered aerobatic biplane, I in darkest Jolibois with my puttering Luscombe and a Renault Espace that still smells of dead dog. Usually, when he phones, it is to recount his latest crashed-and-burned exploit with some beautiful blonde air-stewardess who turns out to be married, or how an affair with an exquisite parachute instructress whom he was convinced was The One has foundered. The last girlfriend, a stunning oriental beautician, sounded especially promising, until Jethro discovered a sheaf of his bank statements in her handbag. 'That would have been okay,' he told me, with his habitually shocked intonation. 'But then she burst into tears, and swore that she only took them to show to her mother.'

Tonight, it is flying rather than women that Jethro wants to discuss, although I sometimes think the two are interchangeable for him. 'I've won my first aerobatics competition, and I've been thinking about you and Spitfires,' he says, his voice crackling down the line to France.

'That's fantastic. Bravo to you.'

'Actually it's not that great, because I only won the Basic class, whereas I need to be winning the Advanced if I'm going to get anywhere.'

'It's a start.'

'Yes, well . . .' Jethro's voice trails off. 'Now, about this Spitfire. I've met a couple of guys who fly them.'

'That's great.' I can't believe that Jethro remembers a conversation we had five years ago.

'Yes, and the good news is that all your tailwheel experience in the Luscombe and Tiger Moths should stand you in good stead.' He hesitates. 'The bad news is that you still need to notch up at least a hundred hours on Harvards.'

Ah. I know about Harvards, the boxy two-seat workhorse on which Spitfire pilots used to train. One used to buzz the circuit in Kissimmee, Florida, when I was learning to fly, its pilot absurdly yelling 'Tally-ho' over the r/t as he came in for a run and break. 'And how much does it cost to rent a Harvard?'

'About four hundred quid an hour.'

'Right.'

'After that, if you become a top display-pilot – and especially if you have flown fast jets with the RAF – it's quite possible that some millionaire recluse will let you loose on his pride and joy.'

'Aha.'

'What many people find, however, is that if you want to fly a Spitfire, you have to buy one yourself.'

'And how much does that cost?'

'About a million and a half quid.'

'Hm.'

'And then there's the insurance on top.' Jethro pauses. 'Are you still there?'

'Yes, I'm still here,' I sigh. Although I feel a little bit as I did when the irresistibly beautiful Zara Malkin, with whom my twenty-one-year-old self had naïvely imagined he was going to spend the rest of his life, told me that she never, ever wanted to see or hear from me again. I can feel my Spitfire dream climbing away from me, into the clouds. 'Looks like I'd better start saving.'

'At least now you know what's involved.'

'Yeah, thanks, Jez,' I reply, ready to change the subject. 'And what about you, what's your latest wheeze?'

'Me? Oh, skywriting.'

'Skywriting?'

'You know, spelling out messages in the sky with smoke. For weddings, parties, advertising, anything.'

'Like in *Mrs Dalloway*,' I reply, thinking aloud, and then cursing myself for being so prim.

'Yeah, maybe. I think I saw the film.' Jethro sounds unconvinced. 'Skywriting used to be all the rage in the twenties and thirties, but nobody's doing it any more. So I thought I'd give it a go, to help pay my Avgas bill. It's a blast, but the smoke-system makes a frightful mess of the plane, and I'm really struggling with W.'

'Don't tell me: your latest girlfriend is called Winifred.'

'You know me too well, Michael,' he says, exploding with laughter. 'Hang on, got a call on the other line . . . I think it may be a babe.'

'Aren't they all?'

'I wish.'

'You'd better go.'

'Thanks, pal. Fly safe.' There is a click as Jethro hangs up. A few moments later and the phone rings once again. The babe must have hung up on him.

'Is that Michael?' says a young woman's voice, doubtfully.

'Yes?'

'Well, it's just . . . this is Amy.'

Oh, golly. It's the girl in the blue dress; Amy, whom I dared to invite on a date just before I moved to France and have not seen since.

The girl in the blue dress somehow seemed to symbolize all that I was leaving behind when I swapped the smoke and mirrors of the metropolis for darkest rural France. It was almost as if London were taunting me, that night, with the twinkling sophistication I was about to renounce; with its shadowy hint of sexual possibility; the being able to sip a gin and tonic on the banks of the Thames with a beautiful girl you have only just met, to chatter about life for an evening, and then kiss her by moonlight in the reflected glow of Tower Bridge. It was all so perfect. And it was all over so soon.

And now here she is. Amy and I have been sporadically emailing each other ever since that unexpected encounter two years ago. And to my amazement – her resistance finally beaten down by my repeated invitations – she announces that she will come and stay for a long weekend at La Folie, after all.

'It will be brilliant to be in France,' she says, in case I should think her too keen.

'Ah, good.'

'And I'll be *fascinated* to meet the chickens,' she adds.

'No other reasons for wanting to visit?' I try to imagine that I have Jethro's confidence with women. I am doing all I can to sound flirtatious rather than merely friendly, but end up sounding like Terry-Thomas.

'None that I can think of,' she laughs.

'Well, I'm really looking forward to seeing you,' I reply. And then I wince, as the words 'we'll have fun' slip unbidden from my mouth.

'Uh-huh,' she says, as if we were playing yes-no-black-white. 'Jolly good.'

Later that night, I walk outside to look at the stars, gazing up at the crumbling render on the front of the house in the moonlight, attempting to see the place through a young woman's eyes. I cannot help remembering old Zumbach's warning, even as I was signing the *compromis de vente* for La Folie at the estate agent's in Jolibois.

'I have to warn you, Monsieur Wright,' he growled, with a furtive glance at the two lady estate agents who were watching us sign, 'that La Folie is no place for a woman.'

I blinked up at him from the desk. '*Et . . . pourquoi?*'

'It's too isolated,' he whispered. 'It sends them mad.'

'But how do you know?' Wasn't it a little late for him to be telling me this?

'That,' he said, pursing his lips into a pained smile and pressing his fingers together, 'is a story for another time.'

*

The next day is 5 November, and I am woken at day-break by the sound of an entire chapter of Hell's Angels gunning their motorbikes outside my bedroom window. When I peer out to investigate, all I can see below me is a cloud of thick white smoke, as if Guy Fawkes were already beginning to smoulder on his pyre. Gradually, this disperses to reveal a single, enormous quad-bike, painted the dark green colour of an army jeep, whose rider is dismounting as stiffly as if he were wearing a full suit of armour. Pulling a pair of jeans and a fleece on over my pyjamas, I hurry down to investigate.

'*Bonjour*,' I call, flying out of the front door. But the quad-bike's rider has vanished. He materializes a few seconds later from around the side of the house, not looking at me, yet with his hand outstretched in greeting. A fiftysomething *paysan* in a khaki boiler-suit, he has the stocky build and stiff gait of a former prop-forward whose back is scrunched with too much scrummaging, and his round, bespectacled face reminds me of an old Stilton with a cheese-wire laid across it. We shake hands, and I wait for him to speak.

'*Bonjour, chef,*' he says, at last. '*Je suis le jardinier.*'

For a second I stand there, bemused, for I didn't know I *had* a gardener. And then the smoke clears. 'Aha! You must be Monsieur Jadot,' I exclaim, with a little too much excitement. It is the man who my neighbour Gilles promised me would come. '*Enfin.*'

He steps back a pace, suddenly looking nervous. 'I heard you needed some help with your *potager*. So where is it?'

'It's . . . there,' I say. I point over his shoulder at the fenced rectangle of thick jungle that has yet to succumb to the effects of approaching winter. I scan Jadot's face carefully, in search of any glimmer of encouragement. In vain. If anything, he looks quite pale as he shakes his head.

'You found the place all right, then?' I continue, changing tack, trying to sound as upbeat as possible.

'I used to shelter here from thunderstorms as a child,' he replies, grinning through his mud-spattered specs. He has the kind of round, urchin face that makes it easy to imagine, even fifty years on, how he might have looked as a boy of ten in short trousers and the very same glasses. 'In there, that's where I used to hide.' He jabs his thumb at the windows of the summer sitting-room, the soaring space which now houses my grand piano. 'Of course, it was full of cows in those days.' Then he strides off into the overgrowth.

I'm still feeling uncomfortable about having desecrated a perfectly good cow-byre with a grand piano when Monsieur Jadot emerges from the bush.

'*Oh-là*,' he says, scratching his head. And then '*oh-là*' again. He looks like he wants to sit down. '*Il y a beaucoup de travail à faire*,' he says. I don't know what to say, but his words give me a warm feeling inside. I feared I was being wimpish in enlisting outside help with my land, when the whole point of my coming to France was to learn to be tough and resourceful and independent. But a local *paysan* reassuring me that there *is* much work to be done – this is exactly what I want to hear.

'You live in this big place all alone, then?' he asks, peering up at the windows of La Folie.

I nod.

'*Pas de copine?* Don't you find it a little cold in winter?'

'*Un petit peu*,' I reply, smiling.

'I'm looking for *une copine* myself,' he continues, jutting out his elbow as if to nudge an imaginary bystander in the ribs, his eyes twinkling behind his specs. 'I don't suppose you know any nice women, do you? I'm not fussy. Even if she's *une Anglaise*. Just as long as she's not too ugly, and knows how to cook good French food. And then a little more, too.' More jabbing of the elbow; much twinkling. He seems more like a playful schoolboy than a predatory adult, and I can't help laughing at his delight in his own rakishness.

'If I think of anyone, I'll let you know,' I assure him.

'Probably you'll take her for yourself.'

'Er . . .' My mind races. In English, knowing how to respond to this would be tricky. In French, I am lost.

'How many sheep have you got?' asks Jadot, changing the subject. At least, I *hope* he's changing the subject.

'*Sept*,' I reply, and we both stand in silence, watching the dwarf Rastafarians grazing in their field behind the house, each as gnarled and black as an ancient conker.

'So . . . how many rams?' Out of the corner of my eye, I can see him chuckling to himself. This funny Englishman with too many rams is even more of a hopeless townie than his friend Gilles said he was.

'*Trois*,' I admit, sheepishly.

'*C'est beaucoup*,' he whistles, and I know that he is right, because Gilles has often told me so. Three rams is two rams too many. 'But I can only count two,' adds Jadot. 'Where is number three?'

I look again, scanning my scraggy flock for the ones with crescent horns jutting from their temples like racing handlebars. And my heart sinks, for I can see at a glance who is missing. It is Gaston, my chief ram and mighty patriarch of my featherweight flock, who has been with me almost since the start of my time at La Folie. The toothless old paterfamilias is so old that I'm always worried he is going to collapse with lumbago or gout.

Even when I bought him – to the palpable astonishment of the lady vendor, who hadn't counted on meeting anyone who knew so little about sheep – Gaston had no teeth. Gilles told me he would soon die of starvation. But Gilles wasn't reckoning on quite how soft *les Anglais* can be when it comes to caring for their animals. I haven't liked to admit to my neighbour how many sacks of expensive feed I have bought from Alliance Pastorale, just to keep Gaston and my oldest ewes going. The gummy pensioners have no chance of ripping up grass with their soft black lips. Hoovering feed from the trough is their future now, like the residents of some ovine old people's home, sipping liquidized stew from a spoon.

And now Gaston has vanished, and I can't get rid of poor Monsieur Jadot quickly enough. At last, having shaken hands and said *à bientôt* to the old *paysan*, and watched him depart in a thunder-cloud of smoke and petrol fumes, I climb the fence into the sheep-field to begin the search for my old friend.

The search is back-to-front, since I am hoping against hope that I shall not find him. The chances are that he has finally collapsed. But it is just possible, too, that the old scoundrel has escaped through one of the fences. I like to think that my fencing has improved since my first botched efforts at La Folie, but even so: I cannot forget the ease with which a lust-crazed Gaston was able to escape last autumn, after Young Boulesteix's fat white ewes came on heat in the next-door field.

I walk up to the top of the hill, scanning the pale grass for a dark shape, laid out as flat as a dog asleep in front of a fire. At the top, I turn left and stride along beside the fence, until – just behind me – I hear the crackle of bracken breaking underfoot. I am being followed.

I stop and spin on my heels. Behind me, the lone sheep who is wandering in my wake stops and looks away, too, as if she were playing grandmother's footsteps. And I know what this means. Ella is Gaston's closest companion. If the old rascal were dead, his war-widow would be yelling her head off. Whereas this silent dismay, this means that her randy consort has vanished for another spot of Bunburying once again.

My heart goes out to Ella as she stands abandoned here in

her field, gazing at me with 'So what do I do now?' wretchedness. Some of the light has gone out of her eyes.

Suddenly, a different kind of light catches my attention as, further down the valley, the dark orange flames of a bonfire laced with kerosene leap into the iron-grey sky. The tearing-cotton sound of combusting bracken mingles with the groaning of a tractor straining through the gears, and I glimpse my neighbour Young Boulesteix at the wheel, fuelling the vast conflagration of felled branches and scrub in his sheep-field with yet more tinder.

A few seconds later, on the horizon above Young Boulesteix, I spy a familiar shape. *Nom de Dieu*. Not again. Far from popping his clogs, the priapic pensioner – Gaston, not Monsieur Jadot – has only gone and tunnelled his way under my fence, and is even now galloping in the rear of a flock of perhaps a hundred ewes, all fleeing in fear for their maidenheads. This is an exact repeat of his escapade last year, only this time Young Boulesteix is on hand to watch. I'd love to reassure the ewes that they have nothing to fear, for Gaston does not appear to be carrying a stepladder. But there's no time for that now.

A glance across at my neighbour reveals that he hasn't yet spotted the lustful interloper, or the carnage he is causing. So if I can just head Gaston off at the pass . . .

Half an hour later, I am still galloping breathlessly after my love-sick Lothario, and Young Boulesteix and the two friends who are helping him with his bonfire have sat down on a log to watch the Englishman suffer.

At first I am torn between wanting my neighbour to see what a splendid effort I am making – puffing time after time up the hill behind Gaston's swaying wedding-tackle – and not letting him think that I am somehow prolonging the torment of his ewes with my incompetence as a human sheepdog. And then I become dimly aware that the three of them are pointing and giggling at me as if I were a bear with my head stuck in a honey-jar, and I know that I have nothing to worry about. No, I have just become the day's cabaret.

At last, in a distant corner of this field which is beginning to feel about as big as Biggin Hill, Gaston's battery begins to run down. Unlike Titus in pursuit of Hotspur, I actually seem to be gaining on my quarry. Sure enough, after another few seconds of head-up cantering, Gaston slows to a trot. Then the trot becomes a walk and – just as I am about to make a desperate lunge for his horns – he slowly turns to face me. We stare at each other. I take a step forward. He does not flinch. Instead, with a sigh, he gives himself up. The noble beast growls something as he allows himself to be captured, which I take to mean 'It's a fair cop, guv,' although I suspect from his sheepish grin that it may be more along the lines of, 'Not a word about this to anybody, right?'

And so I head home with my errant Don Juan, staggering half a mile across three fields and two barbed-wire fences – the second of which now sports a significant fragment of my trousers – with a sweaty black ram in my arms. I receive a round of applause from the audience on the log as I pass.

'*Merci*,' I gasp, more for letting me trespass than for clapping me home, but they find it amusing all the same. Another few years of this, I reflect, and Boulesteix and I will be best friends.

Back at La Folie, Gaston's girls gather round the old boy, nuzzling and nibbling at him, re-establishing the old intimacies of the flock. Only Ella stands apart. The deep chestnut of her wool is beginning to go grey now, though it glows red in the light of the distant bonfire. They have been together for so long that she has seen it all before. And from her wounded stance, and refusal to greet the old boy she knows so well, I cannot help thinking that, each time, it becomes a little harder to forgive.

Behind me, smoke and flames from Boulesteix's great pyre of timber and brushwood pour heavenwards, lighting up the

Bonfire Night sky. Never mind gunpowder, treason and plot. The shadows dancing on the trees behind resemble the dancers in some primitive celebration: a celebration for the safe return of Gaston, for neighbours who become friends, and for the simple act of being alive in this forgotten corner of rural France. And if I had bought a rocket from the Nicest Man in the Universe, I'd be tempted to send one up, right now.

# 4

## DECEMBER

Fog. La Folie is blanketed in icy cotton wool, Amy's plane lands at Limoges airport in forty-five minutes, and I am about to be late again. Out on the terrace, a robin hops on to the low stone wall and peers quizzically at me through the kitchen window. Good Mr Robin, I cannot explain why I do this to myself, let alone to other people. Ever since I was a child, I have done things at the last minute, from sending my list up the chimney to Father Christmas, to finishing my sheep-fencing some time after the arrival of my sheep. Late prep at boarding school became a rolling essay crisis at university; has become a series of closely shaved deadlines for national newspapers.

I think I am not very good at assessing how long anything will take. I thought I would meet some biddable mademoiselle within a few weeks of beginning my French adventure. I thought the dusty shell of La Folie would be renovated into an elegantly weathered gem almost before I arrived, just as I imagined I would feel like a tough peasant as soon as I bought my first six chickens.

For Amy's visit I have half-tidied the kitchen and winter sitting-room. I have whizzed down to Champion to buy fresh supplies of bread and wine. I have also chosen this moment to brush-cut what's left of the nettles, clean out the chicken house, take the empty bottles to the bottle bank beside the old stone bridge, and hide all the copies of *Nous Deux* magazine that I normally keep in the loo. Peter Viola assures me that these breathless photo love-stories are the best way to improve my French, but I cannot expect Amy to buy this. And I still have to make up the spare bed before leaving for the airport.

I am about to whizz out of the front door when something makes me stop. Hurrying back into the kitchen, I fling open the window and scrape the crumbs from the breadboard out on to the wall. May the robin find his tea before the Egg Squad get there first.

The engine of the Espace rattles and roars as I hurtle down hills and around sharp bends, leaning forward in my seat in an attempt to see a little further through the fog. Fortunately, I was born luckier than I deserve. So today there are no hidden nasties waiting for me to smash into them, and no hidden gendarmes lurking in the trees with their shiny boots and motorbikes. Actually there's one, in the village of Beaumarin, but two oncoming motorists flash their head-lights at me to signal that he's lying in wait.

Finally I'm there at the airport, and I can tell from the mêlée of grey souls in shabby anoraks and fleeces – each with that excited air of someone about to pick up their holiday photos from the chemist – that the daily Ryanair flight from London Stansted has yet to disembark. Here and there, smartly coiffed women and men in well-cut jackets stand out from the crowd: a flight from Paris must be expected, too. A fresh-faced damsel in a fur-lined hood walks past me and, for a second, our eyes meet. Feeling the usual questions beginning to form themselves at the back of my brain, I make a special effort to look away.

I wonder if I shall recognize Amy. I have some sort of

facial dyslexia that makes me hopeless at remembering what people look like. And I have now seen her just twice in my life: once at the rowdy stag-and-hen party where I met her, and once in the shadow of Tower Bridge, where we met for our one-and-only date, two years ago. That time, taking no chances, I arranged to meet her beside the statue of Julius Caesar at Tower Hill. Here at Limoges, there are no Roman emperors on hand to help.

Recognizing Amy turns out to be easier than I feared, however, as almost everyone else who is disembarking from the plane appears to be forty-seven or more, apart from three fat lads with shaven heads and England football shirts, gazing out into the autumn mist with faces so blank that their acne makes them appear more interesting.

And then there comes Amy, her pretty smile shyly directed at the floor, with a suitcase rolling behind her like a submissive poodle. If I had to pick the one person on the plane who I was hoping was coming to see me, it would be her.

'How are *you*?' she says, as if she were surprised to see me. She smiles elsewhere, smudging my cheek with a kiss.

'We didn't say hello yet, did we?'

'All right. Hello,' she laughs.

'Here, let me take your suitcase.'

'It's very small,' she declares, and lets me take it anyway.

'I'm impressed. I hope you're going to be warm enough.'

'If I'm not, there'll be trouble.'

The fog is now so heavy that we can see only about twenty yards ahead of us as we drive slowly back to La Folie in the gathering dusk. Haloed by our headlights in the thick mist, we are a torch moving slowly beneath a duvet.

'So where's this house then?' asks Amy with a brave stab at jollity.

This is a good question. Even as we bump up the drive, voles scurrying across our path in the beam of the headlights, it is hard to believe that there might be a human habitation hidden in this murk. I think back to Zumbach's warning when he signed the paperwork for the sale: La Folie is no place for a woman.

'You'll see it properly in the morning,' I promise, as the lights of La Folie glimmer weakly out of the fog.

Amy peers doubtfully at the dark shape looming before us, and fumbles in her handbag for the security of her mobile phone.

Next morning, the fog is thicker than ever. A dank whiteness hangs over everything, so that even the trees are hidden. It feels as if we're having breakfast in an igloo.

As I squeeze out a tea-bag, I can hear Titus crowing forlornly outside, like a foghorn to alert passing shipping. The wood-burning stove is crackling and popping; two freshly laid eggs are boiling away in a saucepan on top.

'You can't see where it stops and where it ends. It's just everywhere,' says Amy, biting her lip as she pours orange juice into two glasses. The tone of her voice – at once reedy and sweet – makes me think of a flute and oboe playing at the same time.

'Sorry I haven't got any egg-cups yet,' I say, lining a pair of earthenware cups with scrunched-up tinfoil, and perching a steaming egg in each one.

'No worries,' chuckles Amy.

'By the way, how outdoorsy are you feeling today?'

She shivers and peers out of the window, into the murk. '*Quite* outdoorsy,' she says.

'I just wondered how you'd feel about trying a bit of fence-building.'

'Michael Wright, you certainly know how to treat a lady.'

I seem to spend much of my time at La Folie building fences. There wasn't a lot of call for this in East Dulwich, but there weren't a lot of very small sheep in south-east London, either. And so Amy and I set about building a length of sheep-fence to create a new field for my Rastafarians. Or rather, I do my best to build the fence, and Amy makes fun of it, as I continue my project to reclaim the jungle left behind by Zumbach when he sold me La Folie. People described him as *un écologiste*, which makes me wonder if, sometimes, ecology is just another word for idleness.

'I thought I was coming to France for a nice relaxed time,' says Amy as we mix concrete together in an old wheelbarrow. 'And then you make me do all this rough physical work.' Usually I would borrow Fred the Viking's cement-mixer, but he is currently lending it to Douglas the Giant.

'But working is fun, isn't it? Better than whatever you do in the city, anyway.'

Amy puts down her trowel and gives me a look.

'What?' I ask, feigning innocence.

'You do want me to help you build your fence, do you?' She smiles, but it is not a smile that goes very deep.

'Yes. Sorry. I know your job in London is frighteningly powerful and important . . .'

'Stop it.'

'Sorry.'

And then we are pouring the grey gloop into a hole I have dug in the earth, around the base of a concrete fence-post that feels as if it weighs about as much as a small family car. As Amy smoothes off the surface of the liquid cement with her trowel, I tell her to put a thumb-print in it, for good luck.

'You can make a wish.'

'Is that traditional in France?' she replies, not looking up.

'I don't know. But at least I will have something to remind me of you.' I like the idea of capturing something permanent from the evanescence between us; want to have something I can touch, to remind myself of the playfulness of this delicate soul, even as I sense that she is somehow slipping away from me.

'I'm not sure it's a good idea,' she says, hesitating. Her

hand hovers over the wet concrete like a young bridegroom outside a registry office, unwilling to commit.

'Oh, come on, it's nothing,' I urge. 'And whatever happens between us in the future, you will always be able to say that you left an indelible mark on La Folie.'

'There,' she says, pressing her thumb into the grey sludge. 'Did you make a wish?'

She nods, climbs to her feet and quickly walks away.

A brighter, fogless start to the next day makes me suggest that Amy and I go flying together. The Luscombe's high-oil-temperature problem is resolved – a stuck valve has been ground and reseated, with the help of Antoine, the ace mechanic at St Juste – and the perfect winter sky seems to be calling out for aeroplanes to come and fly in it. Amy leaps at the idea. Anything is better, I assume, than building fences. And then she looks more doubtful when we arrive at the little aerodrome, and she sees the modest contraption in which we will be flying to La Rochelle for lunch.

Over breakfast at La Folie, she suggested Paris, but that's a bit far, and I'd have to remortgage the house to pay the landing fee for Le Bourget. And then there are the Parisians. Now I don't have anything against the Parisians. But the French do. They say *les Parisiens* are even worse than *les Anglais*.

'They're cold and aggressive, and they think they've seen it all,' Gilles tells me cheerily.

Viewed from London, Paris exudes a sophisticated, romantic allure. Viewed from Jolibois, it is Mordor, Gotham, Sodom and Gomorrah rolled into one, a post-apocalyptic den of iniquity where everyone is either a criminal or a politician, and usually both.

So La Rochelle gets the nod, by a whisker.

'Gosh, it looks sleek,' says Amy, visibly impressed by my aircraft, as we stand in the doorway of the hangar at St Juste, gazing at the aircraft waiting in the ghostly silence. 'It's hard to believe it was built so long ago.'

'Luscombe was ahead of his time,' I reply, happily. 'The Silvaire was the first all-metal sports aircraft. Although this one was storm-damaged in Arizona in the 1950s, and now has fabric wings.'

'Fabric wings?' echoes Amy, smiling at the thought. I hadn't expected her to be such an appreciator of old aircraft. 'And why did he put the propeller on the back like that?'

My jaw drops open, and I shift my weight from foot to foot, suddenly feeling too hot in my leather flying jacket. 'Actually, Amy . . . that one's not my plane.'

'I thought you said it was the yellow one.' Too late, I realize that she has been admiring the super-sleek Long-Eze that belongs to Pollux, a retired engineer from Limoges.

'There's another yellow one, just over there.' I point, watching her face carefully.

'Ah,' she says, as she follows the direction of my outstretched arm. For a second or two, she says nothing. And then I glimpse the tip of her tongue moistening her lower lip, as if she were about to stick her arm into a beehive. 'Gosh.'

'So what do you think?'

'Is that *it*?'

'That's it,' I reply, as cheerfully as I can manage.

'No, but I mean . . .' she giggles.

'Help me push her out of the hangar,' I tell her. 'You can save the compliments for later.'

While Amy sits in the right-hand seat, with instructions to switch off the magnetos at once if the Luscombe starts to veer out of control across the grass, I stand beside the two-bladed propeller in my gardening gloves, doing my best to start the beast. This involves standing as far from the propeller's arc as I can, and then heaving downwards on the upper blade as if I were yanking the chain on a very stiff old-fashioned lavatory. Ad infinitum. This would be, I suspect, a very good training exercise for Nordic skiers. Every so often the engine makes a reluctant cough, just to encourage me. The rest is silence.

'Maybe the carburettor is flooded,' I pant, leaning into the cockpit to pull the key out of the ignition and firewall the throttle, after two dozen attempts to swing the thing into life have failed.

'Ah,' says Amy, pursing her lips into a brave smile. 'Can I help?'

'Yes, keep your fingers firmly crossed,' I reply, over my shoulder. Now I spin the propeller backwards a dozen times, give it a single turn in the opposite direction, return to the cockpit, close the throttle and switch the mags on. 'Throttle set, contact!' I announce, largely for Amy's benefit. 'Right, this time she's going to start. You'll see.'

'Jolly good,' she says, containing her excitement.

'Please,' I whisper, under my breath, to the Luscombe's recalcitrant engine, old enough to be my father. 'This time.'

A mighty swing on the prop, and the orchestra finally calls off its strike.

*Cough-cough-whumpf-whumpf-pocketa-pocketa-pocketa* harrumphs the wheezy old engine, racketing into its familiar rhythm at last. Standing beside the shaking plane, I raise my arms in victory to Amy, who smiles nervously back at me from inside the cockpit.

Side by side, we don our headsets, and I go through the various checks of the instruments, carburettor heat and magnetos before turning to her for a final briefing on what is about to happen.

'We're very unlikely to have an engine failure,' I explain, wishing she would look at me instead of at her feet, 'and, even if we do, I will be most disappointed not to land safely in a field without bending the aircraft. But if this looks likely, I will ask you to unlatch your door and assume the brace position, like this.' I cross my arms and bury my head in them, as if I were asleep in an exam. 'All right?'

'All right,' she nods, after a split second's hesitation. But of course I am far too wrapped up with thinking about the wind direction and radio frequencies to notice her discomfort.

Our flight is an unusually silent one, considering the loveliness of the velvet landscape that unfurls beneath us as we buzz our way into the west. Being up here in the sky relaxes me; eases me out of the tautness of my earth-bound egoism, and I finally glance across at my passenger. Amy has been in a small plane once before, she says, and claims to have enjoyed it. But today the air is so bumpy as we head for the Atlantic coast, even at three thousand feet, that she has soon turned as white as the sunlit clouds.

'Are we nearly there yet?' she asks, her voice crackling in my headset over the roar of the engine.

I stare expertly down at the big lake on our left, then at the chart on my lap, and then (more surreptitiously) at the GPS. 'Maybe another half-hour,' I reply, my mind racing over our options. In an aeroplane, pulling in at the side of the road isn't one of them.

Five minutes later, Amy is the same pale green that I almost painted the shutters at La Folie, before I settled upon lavender. So we divert to St Jean d'Angély, a rural aerodrome I visited by car when I was first house-hunting in France. I remember it looked as if no one had landed there since Blériot. The aerodrome made the surface of the moon appear convivial. But at least we'll be on terra firma.

Sure enough, as we circle the grass runway, I can see that the place is deserted, and the pretty town itself – with its streets of distinctively pale stone houses, white as a nauseous passenger – is miles away.

After we have landed and taxied up to the single rusty hangar, I leave Amy to sit shivering in the winter sun and wander off to see if I can find a place for lunch. Flying always makes me ravenous. It hasn't occurred to me that eating might be the last thing on a pale green passenger's mind. There is a scattering of houses beside the aerodrome, so I ring one of the doorbells and wait. An old man comes to the door, wiping sauce off his chin with a pink napkin.

'*Bonjour, monsieur*,' I begin. 'I'm so sorry to . . .'

'Did you just land?' he asks. Thick specs, leather skin, more pink than brown, and the tottering ponderousness of a walrus standing on its tail. Probably a useful discus-thrower in his day, before his knees were shot. 'I didn't think anyone was flying today.'

'Only the mad English,' I reply. I explain our situation and ask if he knows anywhere to eat nearby.

'I'll drive you,' he says, waving his napkin and naming a restaurant in town.

'But I'm sure we can call a taxi,' I protest.

'Nonsense. It's a pleasure.' And this even before he has seen Amy, who has by now returned to her normal colour. Her appearance is greeted with a graceful bow from our new friend, and a nod-with-raised-eyebrows at me, which I take as a compliment.

So he drives us the ten minutes into town, and I'm just thinking that I don't feel like talking, because my brain is fried from flying and worrying about Amy, when she suddenly takes me by surprise. She starts bantering away with our chivalrous walrus in perfect French, far more fluently than I could hope to match. At the end of this, as we step out on to the pavement in St Jean d'Angély's main square, the man hands me a card.

'When you've finished having lunch,' he tells me, 'call me at home, and I'll come and pick you up.'

The bright white stonework of the houses, shining in the winter sun, makes me screw up my eyes. But it is Amy's French that has made me blink, too.

'You didn't tell me you could speak French like that,' I declare, rounding on her as if she had just mugged a penguin, when our friend has driven off.

'You never asked,' she replies, with one of her faraway smiles. Amy, it emerges, is a fully paid-up Francophile who has spent many months here in France over the years. So I am disappointed to find that the only place in town open for a snack turns out to be an Irish theme-pub.

While I tuck into my steak sandwich, Amy sips carefully at some Evian. Then she says she wants to find the station.

'I didn't know you were interested in trains,' I say.

'I am now.' I scan her face for the twitch of a smile, and do not find one.

Amy must be *very* interested in trains, because when the man behind the desk establishes that the fifty-mile journey back to Jolibois will involve three changes and take a full thirteen hours, she looks as if she is considering it.

Travelling up and down France is swift and easy. It's when you try to go *across* the country from east to west and back again that you run into trouble. No wonder Napoleon found it so much easier to invade Spain than Russia. Everything takes for ever, by road or by rail. You can see why the Montgolfiers were so desperate to find an alternative.

Fortunately, Amy, like them, is made of stern stuff, and opts to return to Jolibois by Luscombe, after I have assured her that the air will be smoother by now. So we ring our new friend, who comes to pick us up from the station car park.

'I've been amazed,' I tell him gratefully, as we hurtle across the flat landscape, 'by how much kindness I have experienced in this region.'

'I know. I've noticed it, too,' he says, his specs glinting in the rear-view mirror. 'I'm from Paris myself.'

Amy's three days at La Folie have flown by, and we drive back to the airport in silence. My mind is struggling with a conundrum: I have had a wonderful time with this gorgeous young woman for the past three days, enjoying a connection with her which has recharged my batteries and made me feel ready to face the oncoming winter with freshened resolve. I know I will miss her when she is gone. And my heart is not filled with sky. No voice in my head is clamouring that I should elicit some sense of her commitment to me, nor that I should pledge mine to her. She has left a thumb-print in the wet cement of my heart, and that is all.

Lovely as Amy is, there is a silence in that place where – on rare occasions in my life – a chorus of sky-borne internal voices has yelled at me that I must do something, and fast, to avoid losing this girl or woman with whom nothing would be more beautiful than the dazzling prospect of a long-term future. Nor is it generally the sex-bombs or the sirens, not the femmes fatales or the pin-up queens, who exert the most insistent pull. No, this yearning which I have felt only a handful of times in my life is something harder to put into words than that.

All I know is that one moment I am standing there, gazing at a girl in all her peachy femininity, and the next moment, a cobwebbed trap-door has opened in my heart, and I am staring inwardly into a spangled abyss, knowing that I am lost. Someone has pulled an invisible rug from under me and, whilst technically I am still standing, I can feel myself flail like a fish in a net.

Clara Delaville had this effect upon me, aged nine, at Windlesham. And for her, I would happily have sacrificed my life. Suffering in silence for year after year, I only once managed to express my love, in a Valentine's card when I was eleven. 'I know you don't love me, but I love you,' I wrote, with the same blue and yellow felt-tip pens I had used to draw the striped love-heart on the front. And then I foolishly signed it, '– – – – – – – – – – –'.

Clara showed this card to the rest of our class before an

English lesson, while we were waiting for Mr Dickinson to arrive. And Stephen Priestley deciphered the dashes.

'It's *him*!' he cried, pointing a scornful finger at me. 'Can you believe it?'

No, they could not.

To think that *I*, the swotty nerd with my NHS specs and my hopelessness at PE, would presume to admire *her*, the prettiest girl in our class, the captain of netball, the best at tennis and adored by all the staff. Burying my scarlet face in my hands, I dared not look at her. Everyone except Clara danced around me, whistling and shrieking with laughter, and this only made me love her more.

I have only once seen Clara Delaville since, in the queue for the check-out at WH Smith's in Sloane Square, a few years ago. She was wearing a bright yellow jumper that looked expensive. Our eyes met for a second, but I do not think she recognized me. Fearing the spangled abyss, I was still far too much in awe to speak.

The voices sang again, when I was at Sherborne and fifteen, for a girl called Ellen Gonn, with whom I experienced the blinding revelation of requited love for the first time, and whom I so venerated, and set upon so high an old-fashioned pedestal, that I could barely think about her in lustful terms, for fear that the grubby paws of my boyish imaginings might besmirch the grace and beauty for which I idealized her. Ellen had already decided that she was going to marry a Swiss ambassador and have five children, a green Mini and a white telephone. Besotted, I nevertheless spent a blissful term writing daily love-letters to my sainted paramour, delivering them by hand under the pretext of an out-of-character addiction to cross-country runs at which my housemaster was kind enough to wink.

'You're wallowing,' warned Mr Shelley, my clarinet teacher, when I spent the whole of the next term morose with grief at the fact that Ellen Gonn had dumped me.

'I'm mourning the end of the most perfect love I shall ever know,' I told him, with a sigh. This was my excuse for still not being able to play Weber's Grand Duo Concertante, even after weeks of lessons on it.

'You're wallowing,' he insisted. And, twenty-three years on, I think he was probably right. Yet even now, I cannot help but measure – unfairly and inevitably – the strength of my feelings for Amy with the zinging intensity of my teenage obsession with Ellen.

The same thing happened when I was twenty-one, and at university in Edinburgh. There, the voices yelled and swooned and poured out a cathedral polyphony of besotted devotion to Zara Malkin, who should have been far too beautiful for me, and yet somehow connected with me on so many levels that I felt convinced that destiny was hard at work on our behalf. We visited ruined monasteries together, listened to Mozart concertos together, won a cup for our piano duets. I was so smitten that I spent my entire third year writing love-sonnets, songs and fragments of swoony piano music to her, which would have sounded dated even if I had written them in the 1960s, but which were for me a necessary outpouring of the overpowering emotion I felt. It was as if we were separated by oceans, as opposed to sleeping in next-door bedrooms in a shared student flat on Dundas Street.

Zara Malkin and I went out together for two years, eleven months and fourteen days, and I always presumed that these years would grow into a lifetime. I wanted to believe that Zara and I were made for each other, not realizing that beautiful relationships and a sense of mutual commitment do not just fall out of the sky, any more than do green beans and perfect spuds. I was a child, playing at being in love; too young a puppet butterfly to commit myself for ever, when there were so many other breathtakingly pretty puppeteers lining up to pull my strings. Could we not split up for a while, I wondered, so that I could flit my puppet-dances else-where, and then return to Zara afterwards, as though nothing had changed between us? Her reaction to this brilliant suggestion was not quite what I had hoped: in a raging torrent of smoke and thunder, she flew out of my life and refused to speak to me ever again.

In the background to all this, like the distant tinkling of a triangle cutting through the blaze of a symphony orchestra in full flight, there had been Alice Melbury: Survival-Kit Toby's little sister, now grown into a finely chiselled siren with a smoky catch in her voice and a dimpled loveliness that could stop traffic. I spent far too much of my priapic youth struggling to summon up the courage to telephone Alice, and never dared. With hindsight, this was probably a good thing, because the day I did finally telephone her was the start of the end of a beautiful relationship that never even had the chance to begin.

After this, the sky in my heart darkened to an iron-grey overcast and the voices fell silent for a very long time.

A fledgling crush on Phoebe Yates, a wild baroque recorder player whom I came across at a music workshop and decided was the most delicious creature I had ever met, had to be hurriedly returned to its bottle, like the wrong genie, when she explained that she had met the Love of her Life the previous evening. And then there was that disastrous entanglement with Zuleika at La Folie, a year or so ago, which was positive only in the sense that it reassured me that I do still have a breakable heart, after all.

The lovely Amy, with her sweetness and perfect French, is so suitable for me in so many ways, compared with these unreachable women, that I cannot make sense of why I do not want to attempt to win her like a fairground prize. We get on so well. She speaks French. I want to want her.

Yet as I sit in the Espace, gazing at the road rushing up to meet us as we drive to the airport, the voices are daring barely to whisper. I know that the rails of our lives may run in parallel, but they do not seem fated to converge, nor do I feel impelled to bend them until they do. I feel myself wishing I could see more of Amy, and yet am not willing to bid to be with her all the time. Like a butterfly on a window-pane, I dare not ensnare her, for fear of damaging her wings.

'Will you be lonely?' she says.

'Probably for a while.'

'And then what?'

'And then I shall go back to just being alone again. I'm happy with that.'

'What's the difference?' For once I can feel her eyes upon me, as I stare blankly at the road ahead.

'Alone is what I'm used to,' I reply. 'Lonely is what happens when someone I like comes to stay, and then abandons me to my sheep and chickens.'

'I'm not abandoning you.'

'Of course you're not. But you know what I mean. At the very least, I've got a *soirée dansante* and some sheep house-building to look forward to over the next couple of weeks.'

Amy is watching the cows flash past, lost in her own thoughts. 'Is this home for you now, then?'

'I suppose it is. There's nowhere else.' During my childhood, my parents moved house eight times, including three different houses in Bogotá. So when the locals ask me where I am from, I do not know how to reply.

'I don't think I could ever live out here. Not on my own, I mean. Not like you.'

Sometimes a comment like this would make me feel proud, conscious that I am doing something almost slightly brave. But tonight it just makes me grip the steering-wheel a little tighter, and press my teeth into my lip.

Amy's plane is swallowed by the sky, and afterwards I sit at the narrow table in the kitchen, eating spaghetti with pesto from a jar, draining my glass of Languedoc, and then another, and wishing she were still here.

Next morning, frost glitters on every blade of grass around La Folie, and the fields are so white that at first I think it must have snowed in the night. The kitchen and winter sitting-room feel icy, too, but I've run out of logs small enough to fit in the wood-burning stove. And so, after marching out to feed the chickens and sheep, I set to with my chainsaw in the doorway of the barn, enjoying one of those repetitive activities that requires just enough concentration to be satisfying, yet which still leaves space in the brain for reflection.

Pulling enough metre-long timbers off the wood-stack to keep me going for the next fortnight, I heave them, one by one, on to my home-made sawhorse while the chainsaw gargles at idle at my feet. Then I squeeze the trigger and see the chain blur as the motor roars into an angry frenzy in my hands.

I am just like Jethro and all the other townie blokes who have come to stay at La Folie. I feel almost hypnotized by the gin-and-tonically perfect combination of the sawdust glitter-ing in the sunlight and the throaty roar of a manly power-tool as I attack the rough timbers. And while I work, I catch myself wondering what else in the world I would rather be doing at this moment. As Ralph the artist asked me last year: if I won the lottery and could live anywhere I wanted in the world, where would I wish to be?

I am still reeling from the news that Ralph and his wife, Olga the spy, whose cheery townhouse has always been such a haven of warmth and light to me on lonely winter evenings, are planning to quit Jolibois. I assume they miss their children, and the buzz of London, although this scarcely explains the need for secrecy – unless they owe a lot of money to the Renault garage and to the Nicest Man, who frames all Ralph's paintings for him. I am conscious that the grass has always been greener, for Ralph, on the other side of the Channel. And many are *les Anglais* who are following suit. The noticeboard at the supermarket often has a small ad or two, in English, for 'old house, partially renovated'. Two of the Brit-owned *chambres d'hôtes* in town are for sale. They say that the average stay of *les Anglais* who attempt to make a life for themselves in the Limousin is just over two years. And that was before everything began to collapse. The only English couple who have been here for ever, and look likely to remain for ever, too, are Ralph's friends Harold and Elspeth Brand: he, a dissolute ex-publisher who is still an *enfant terrible* in his eighties; she, a well-born anorexic who suffers his rages with heroic stoicism and a lot of white wine. The Brands will stay in Jolibois, because no one else will have them. But in the end, when times are tough enough, human beings just want to go home.

I must have sawn through half the pile of timbers when something moving to my right brings my labours to a halt. I kill the engine and lift my visor to see Gilles bouncing up to the house in his flashy white van, which is so thickly caked in mud that it looks like a choc-ice.

Every farmer in the Limousin drives the Citroën version of one of these mud-magnets, almost as a badge of office. Yet last year Gilles – who did his National Service in Germany, and is therefore a man of the world – splashed out on the upmarket Ford equivalent. With his retirement approaching, I was surprised at such extravagance, but he assures me that he has been promised a wonderful deal when he trades it in next year.

'*Salut, Gilles,*' I call from the barn doorway, and remove my stiff leather gloves to let him crush my hand in his iron grip. An accident with a chainsaw, years ago, has left my peasant mentor with half of one finger missing, and little

sensation to let him know how much force he is applying
when he shakes hands. So I have learned to take a deep
breath before surrendering mine to the crusher, with its
sawn-off stub jammed unintentionally into my palm.

'*Salut, Michael,*' he replies, still with a hint of shyness,
despite the two years that we have known each other. Next
will come the ritual throat-clearing, the frittering chit-chat
about sheep and chickens, the flitting bric-a-brac of Jolibois
tittle-tattle – as I wait for Gilles to say what he has really
come to say. My friend never comes to visit me without some
piece of news to impart, some offer of assistance, or some
pressing invitation to lunch in several months' time.

Gilles's wife, Josette, approaches as silently as a shadow
from the other side of the car, still walking stiffly and with
an expression of extreme concentration that suggests that
the pain in her back has not left her since the accident
with the tractor. Gilles failed to see her in front of him, holding a fence-post, and they had to send a helicopter from
Limoges. We kiss each other twice, with a peck on each
cheek, as we always do. Yet this time I notice – and not for
the first time – that Josette instinctively turns her cheek
again, even as I am straightening up.

'Should it be three kisses, then?' I ask. Even now, after two
years in darkest France, I still feel like a beginner when it
comes to the unspoken customs of daily life.

'Four is more normal, in these parts,' she replies, with a
shrug.

'You mean I've been doing it wrong, all this time?' I ask.

'*Ce n'est pas grave,*' she whispers, and she and Gilles do
something that I have rarely seen before: they smile at each
other.

'*Ça va, avec le beau temps?*' he asks, at last. Gilles always
asks me this, rain or shine; the only thing that changes is the
level of his sarcasm. Today, however, the brilliance of
the winter sunshine answers him for me.

And so we chat away beneath the rustling of the gnarled old box tree in front of the house, which sometimes feels like the most permanent thing in my life, as I wait for Gilles to feel sufficiently warmed up to impart his piece of news. And, after a few minutes, he makes me think that this moment has come.

'We wondered what you are doing for *le Réveillon*. Will you be alone for New Year's Eve?'

'Um, yes, I think so,' I concede. 'I'm going to *Angleterre* for Christmas, but I'll be back straight after.' I stroke my chin, doing all I can not to look as if I have interpreted the question as an invitation.

'In that case, would you like to come and have dinner that night in the Moulin Vaugelade?' he asks.

'*Mais oui, bien sûr,*' I reply, genuinely delighted.

And then the real bombshell comes as, without warning, Gilles changes the subject. It's almost as if my accepting the invitation to New Year's Eve was a test as to whether I could be trusted with the next nugget of information.

'I've started looking at houses,' he says quietly.

'Houses?' Though the French words he utters make sense to me, for a second I cannot grasp the meaning behind them.

'I am looking at houses. You know, to buy,' he repeats.

My mind whirrs. Gilles can't be thinking of moving from the Moulin Vaugelade, can he? No, it's unthinkable, the idea of muddling through my life as a trainee peasant at La Folie without my heroic neighbour to lead me through the muddy quagmire of spud-husbandry and the ovine reproductive cycle.

'We are only renting the old place. It's not ours.'

'But you've lived there for thirty years, Gilles. It's your *home.*'

'*Non, non, non,*' he says, sadly, shaking his head. 'We can't stay there. When I retire next year, I don't want to carry on living in a draughty old farmhouse. So we're looking at modern *pavillons*. The only trouble is, the prices have become so high, because of . . .'

'*Ce n'est pas vrai*. You can't move,' I interrupt, only half in jest, and partly because I think I know where his last sentence was heading. 'What will I do without you?'

Gilles smiles to himself; that twinkling grin that I have seen a hundred times before, especially at times when the funny Englishman has done something unusually silly. My friend nervously strokes his beard with his outstretched index finger. How I would miss that smile, and that curious beard-stroking, if he were to move.

'With any luck, we won't be too far away,' he growls, with a sad smile at the branches of the box tree swaying in the cold breeze. 'But again, everything is so expensive now. The prices are crazy, ever since *les Anglais* started buying up the region. You pay too much for everything.'

'I know, I know,' I reply, sheepishly, before quoting back to Gilles the instruction he gave me all those moons ago: 'You have to haggle.'

'*Il faut marchander*,' he echoes, with a chuckle, nodding.

'So what will happen to the Moulin Vaugelade now? Will it be sold?'

'It should be knocked down by whoever buys it, and a decent, modern house built in its place.'

'But it must be three hundred years old.'

'That's the thing about *les Anglais*,' replies Gilles. 'For you, anything old is automatically good. Whereas for *les Français*, we'd rather have a house that is warm and dry and comfortably insulated. We're not afraid of things that are new.'

'Even so –' But it's no good. I know that my old friend is right about the Brits. My love of the past, and what is ancient and unchanged, is what drew me to this part of France in the first place, after all: the desire to inhabit a world that drifts along at its own pace, several decades behind the frenetic buzz of the life I left behind in London. I am half in love with the past. It is living in the present that is more of a challenge, let alone carving out a meaningful future for myself.

I am half in love with France, too. I cherish the way rural France seems so unchanging, year after year, as the familiar rhythms and cycles of a primordial existence continue to unfold; as the old box tree adds another few inches to its slow-growing splendour.

Losing Ralph and Olga is bad enough. But if Gilles moves from the Moulin Vaugelade, I shall be losing my heroic neighbour, chief advisor, spirit guide and friend, all in one. And much as I exult in the feeling of having changed my own life in moving to France, I'm simply not prepared for the experience of having someone else, upon whom I have come to rely, doing the same thing to me.

Twenty minutes after Gilles's departure, the pile of logs is almost sawn. And as I feel the warmth of the December sun on my shoulders, I am delighted to discover that I have not been able to think of anywhere else I'd rather be than here. Here, working at this simple task in an old barn on an unspectacular French hillside, with the smell of seasoned oak in my nostrils and a clutch of chickens watching me with interest outside.

I leave the chainsaw purring at idle, and heave the final log on to the trestle. Above me, a Mirage jet thunders low overhead, then another, and I picture the intense concentration of the pilots at the controls. The one thing they are not thinking about, as they pull 5Gs in a screamingly steep right bank, is where on earth they are going to find the dream woman who will complete their life. I watch as a wood-beetle staggers along the log, and the chain carves a blur through the oak. The end of the log drops with a swishing thump on to the barn floor, like a decapitated head falling into the basket of a guillotine.

In the distance, as I wipe the grease-black sawdust from the silent chainsaw with an old rag, loosening the chain from its sprockets to allow the hot metal to cool and shrink, I hear the bells of the level-crossing ring, as the mid-morning train rattles through on its way to Poitiers, unseen as a driven hare behind the trees. This is my life, I think to myself. And I wouldn't change it for the world.

Though winter is still only just settling into its brittle stride, the Rastafarians are white with frost when I trudge out to them at first light. I am working on a wooden sheep house to shelter them from the worst of the rain and snow, but progress is slow.

My biggest problem is that – still the victim of a hopeless weakness for Useful Gadgets – I have succumbed to the impulse purchase of a laser levelling device from Lidl for fifteen euros, and now feel duty-bound to use it. If I can ever get the beastly thing level, it may even prove quite useful. As it is, standing in the freezing rain and doing my best to line up the bubbles in the various spirit-levels reminds me of the kind of annoying Christmas puzzle where you have to coax all the tiny ball bearings into different holes, and then your brother jogs you because it's time for the Queen.

And so, soaked and flummoxed, it feels good to stop work and – after putting the chickens to bed and gratefully submitting to the rejuvenating splurge of a hot shower – to head off to the Lions Club *soirée dansante*. I'm not sure how many people in history have met their future life-partner at the Jolibois equivalent of the Rotary Club ball, but you never know.

Jean-Michel – the president of the tennis club, whose flinty cheer always makes me think of a rocky crag from which trickles a thin stream of water – has invited me to join his party, even though he knows I have a match to play for the Jolibois over-35 men's second team tomorrow morning.

And Jean-Michel is a man who expects all his players, even the hopeless English one, to win.

The dance must be a swanky affair, for Jean-Michel's wife Agnès has advised me to wear *une cravate*. For the very first time in my Jolibois life, I therefore don a tie. I even unwrap a new shirt. I'm hopeless at ironing and, besides, this shirt only cost three euros in the Carrefour sale.

As I enter the Lions' den, Jolibois's finest are already sipping champagne around the dance floor. Jean-Michel and Agnès wave me over to their table. I have a powerful urge to flee. What the hell am I doing here, the lone *Anglais* and almost certainly the only single person in a room which, my scanners tell me, is entirely stuffed with French couples? And then the band strikes up, the room is a frenzy of motion, and I am also the only person sitting down, because – *sacre-bleu* – everyone else is dancing the paso doble.

This is something the Living in France books never told me. Every last man-jack knows his cha-cha from his rumba. National Service may have ended, but ballroom dancing – *danse de salon* – remains compulsory.

In vain, I gaze out over the dance floor for a dancer almost as flat-footed and pedally challenged as me. And everyone – *everyone* – can do it. A huge, portly gentleman is spinning his partner round the room with ineffable elegance and not so much as a bead of sweat upon his ruddy brow.

'*He* looks pretty impressive,' I murmur to Agnès, when she comes and flops down next to me, panting from her exertions on the floor with Jean-Michel. Her jaw drops like the bottom half of a lemon-squeezer when I tell her I really don't know how to do the two-step.

'The big dancers are often the best,' she nods, fanning herself with her hand.

'*C'est vrai? Mais pourquoi?*'

'Because they're more solid. So it feels good when they're leading you.'

I suspect that there is in this response some deep revelation of the female psyche, but there's not time to consider this now, for the band has struck up a waltz, and someone is asking Agnès to dance. And, in the midst of the whirling and the lights, I am appalled to discover that that person is me. This is about as doomed an enterprise as climbing into an aeroplane when you don't know how to fly. It's really not a very good idea at all. But I came to France to learn to be brave; to slip beneath the razor-wire of my comfort zone and off out into those uncharted regions where real learning begins. And this feels like one of them.

'Come on, Michael,' says a voice that I recognize, inside my head. 'You can do it.' And I know where I have heard that voice before: it's the one that pipes up when I am staring down the double-barrels of a six-love, six-love defeat; *une bicyclette*, as they say in France. To date, the voice has never been right. But *courage*, I tell myself, channelling my inner Cyrano de Bergerac: there can't be all that much to it.

As we stand motionless in a spotlight on the dance floor, with the music pulsing triangles in my ears and my feet refusing to move, I feel as if we are sitting in the duff bumper-car at the fairground; the one with no juice. If only there were a swarthy attendant to come and give us a push-off. I tell myself that I'll be fine once we've started, but how to start? I am Popeye without his spinach. The ballerina without the red shoes. Dumbo without his magic feather.

*One, two, three.* Grabbing Agnès as if I were dragging her out of a flaming tent, I launch off to my left. And, bless her, the startled creature manages to follow.

'How are we doing?' I pant.

'*Très bien,*' she hisses, through gritted teeth. 'What's good is that you're not too stiff, like some men.' I force myself to relax, conscious that I am clutching her hand in a kind of Vulcan death-grip, and that my shoulders are hunched like Dracula. Strange: I cannot remember the last time I was this close to a woman. And Agnès, in her blonde, curvaceous way, is undeniably attractive.

In MGM musicals, what happens next is that our hero spies the dazzling woman he really loves, dumps his dumpy dance-partner, and cuts in. Here in Jolibois, the roles are reversed. As we pass another couple, Agnès mutters whatever is the French for 'Here, I can't do anything with him', and escapes into the arms of a dashing man who has only one foot attached to each leg and can actually dance. So now, picking up the shards of what is left of my dignity, I am steering a new victim across the floor, and feeling more and more like a blind man dragging a guide-dog across a dual-carriageway. The brave woman smiles doggedly at me through her misty spectacles and would, I think, be useful in a war-zone.

'So what are you doing in Jolibois?' she squeaks, straightening her black silk dress when the music finally stops, and I release her from my clutches. She introduces herself as Sybille from the Jolibois Festival.

'Learning to be a *paysan*,' I explain. 'And, as from tonight, learning how to dance, too.'

'*Vous êtes anglais, peut-être?*'

I laugh. I like that '*peut-être*'. I like Sybille's suggestion that 'perhaps' I am English – even though the French can somehow tell, immediately I walk into a room and before I have opened my mouth, that I am *anglais*. So when she asks about my former life, I am happy to tell her about my years as an arts journalist in London, and about how I feared that my work as a theatre critic honed my ability to judge rather than to accept; to find fault rather than to look for what was good.

'But being a critic,' she says, smiling up at me from beneath a dark fringe, greying at its tousled edges. 'It need not be a negative thing. You can celebrate the positive, too.'

'Of course,' I reply, gazing into her eyes. 'After a time,

that's what I decided: I would be a positive critic. To strive harder to articulate what was good, rather than simply to excoriate what was wrong.'

Sybille smiles. 'Well, let me tell you that what I like about your dancing, is that it is very . . . enthusiastic.'

'Thank you.'

Suddenly I feel a tap on my shoulder. It is Jean-Michel, Agnès's husband, and he looks as if he has eaten a bad oyster.

'You really should be in bed, Michael,' he says, fiercely. 'You have an important match tomorrow.' It's true that I do have a match to play. I hadn't realized it was an important one. But Jean-Michel is that sort of a club president: a wolf in wolf's clothing, for whom winning is paramount, always, and at all costs.

As swiftly as he appeared, Jean-Michel slips away.

'How would you feel about helping to organize next year's Jolibois Festival?' asks Sybille, when he has gone. 'It's mostly theatre and jazz, with some dance and film, too.'

'Er . . .'

'With your cultural background, we'd be glad to have you on board. Here's my card.' And with that she fades back to her table, leaving me staring at the card, and wondering if the tendrils of my old life are threatening, even now, to claw me back from my peasant simplicity into the world I left behind, where art was more highly valued than nature, cleverness was better rewarded than wisdom, and simple was just another word for dim.

After a bleary drive through the early-morning mist, I arrive at a smart indoor tennis club just outside Limoges, where a pilot I recognize from the aeroclub raises his cowboy hat and shakes my hand.

'*C'est le pilote anglais!*' he exclaims. 'And a tennis player, too?'

'Well, not a very good one, I'm afraid.'

'Ah, but you're just saying that.'

'No, really. I assure you.' I glance at the matt green surface of the courts, which dimly reminds me of the blackboards in the high-windowed classrooms at Sherborne.

'Ah, that's the English reserve,' he guffaws, a little too loudly. 'I'll bet you win everything, don't you?'

'Not very often, actually.'

'Well, what is your *classement*?' he asks. Every tennis player in France has a classification – an index of ability – unless it is their first season, or if they are totally hopeless. I qualify on both counts.

'*Non-classé?* Ah, so you're one of *those* bandits. Then we don't stand a chance.'

I am relieved to see that my friends Maxim the boxer – who is really an economics teacher – and Claude, the electrician with the strong forehand, are playing in the match, too. They have driven down to Limoges together, and walk over to greet me like a little-and-large comedy duo: the tall, sunny one, and his glum, stocky shadow.

'*En forme?*' asks Maxim brightly, shaking my hand.

'*Ah oui, toujours,*' I respond.

As the number-three player, I am first on court.

'You must win, Michael,' Claude reminds me, punching me on the arm, his face breaking into a toothy grin. 'Think of Jean-Michel.'

The sight of my opponent gives me hope. Pascal Doutoueix has the air of a faded French rock star, with lank hair in several shades of grey, a nose like a giant gariguette strawberry, and a way of walking that makes me wonder if he has a sack of onions tucked into his baggy green tracksuit.

My tactics are simple: if I can make him run around enough, and not give him time to breathe, I might just pull off a spectacular upset. If he succumbs to a heart attack on court, I could even win.

For two blurred sets, Pascal runs me ragged. Maxim and

Claude do their best to cheer me on for a few games, before slipping away, stroking their chins. At the change-overs, I put a towel over my head and tell myself that all is not lost. I just have to hit the ball over the net. But this is easier said than done, when your confidence – shaky at best – makes you feel like a six-year-old beginner clutching a racquet the size of Poitiers. By the end, I feel as drained as if I had just run several miles, which is probably because I just have. Pascal hasn't warmed up enough to take off his tracksuit. I look around for the man in the cowboy hat, but he has vanished, too.

The reward for this inglorious defeat is that the entire team – myself, Claude, Maxim and Ja-Ja, our captain – are invited to take ourselves out for lunch at a restaurant in Limoges, at the club's expense. We never used to do this sort of thing in East Dulwich. But today is the team's last match of the season, so it is a moment to celebrate. Or so Claude assures me, slapping me on the back so hard that I cough.

Never mind that my only contribution was to play in the very last match, and lose. It is a celebration for me, too, because – almost for the first time since I arrived in France – I am finally socializing with people of my own age, rather than at least twenty years older than me. I know this shouldn't matter. But it does.

'So why did you come to France, Michael?' asks Ja-Ja, as we tuck into our *choucroute* in a cheery Alsatian restaurant that is about the only place in Limoges that is open for lunch on a Sunday at 4 pm. With its cosy lighting and its red velvet banquettes, it feels like a haven after the echoing torture-chamber of the tennis club.

'I wanted an adventure,' I reply, putting down my fork. 'And to live close to nature, to learn some stuff about life.'

'Like how to win at tennis,' teases Claude, hacking at a sausage.

'It's true that we English are expert at losing,' I laugh. 'But I might even start winning eventually.'

'And learning about nature . . . is it too foggy to do that in England?' asks Ja-Ja, with a half-smile.

'Not quite as foggy as you might imagine. But it feels as if there's a different level of simplicity here. Are you a farmer yourself?' Everyone laughs except Maxim, who yelps as a piece of Claude's masticated sausage lands in his lap.

'No, I work at a bank in Limoges,' says Ja-Ja, wincing as if I had wormed a secret out of him. 'But my true *copains* are in Jolibois.' Small, wiry and twinkling with warmth, he reminds me of one of Gilles's sheepdogs. Those flashing eyes and that shaggy mop of hair cannot disguise his high intelligence and bottomless loyalty to his boyhood friends. 'There are so few jobs in Jolibois,' he adds, fixing me with his dark eyes. 'All the young people tend to leave. Doesn't it make you miss London?'

'London is mad,' I reply. 'It's like Paris, only with narrower streets and weirder haircuts. I like the fact that it is so quiet here in the Limousin. But I *was* hoping to find a charming French girlfriend, and that's beginning to look somewhat unlikely.'

The young men look at each other.

'What about her?' asks Claude, pointing at the very pretty waitress who is just now walking down the stairs towards our table.

'*Ah, oui, er* . . .'

'Well?'

In England, I would know exactly how to respond to this friendly male joshing. But here in France, struggling with a foreign language, weary from my defeat, I just don't know what to say. I can only blush as the waitress – perfect skin, almost no make-up, fresh as a spring day – puts a basket of bread on the table and asks if we have everything we want. Because what I really want, this minute, this second, while she stands there in all her youth and beauty, her green eyes sparkling beneath her expectant eyebrows, her soft voice promising calm and contentment at the end of a long winter . . . what I really want is for her to put her arms round me and kiss me, and whisper that everything will turn out all right in the end.

Next morning, I am reflecting ruefully on the double disaster of my ballroom-dancing debut and tennis defeat, when the phone rings. It is Peter Viola, the aeroclub's resident white-haired English daredevil.

'Look, old boy, we're going to have dinner with some very good friends of ours – that delightful French couple I told you about – and they wondered if you'd like to come, too. Good time guaranteed, if you're free.' Something about the way Peter talks always transports me back to the 1940s.

I am free every night, with the exception of tennis torture on Tuesdays. And putting the chickens to bed at sun-down. And playing the organ for Mass on Saturdays. I am certainly not about to turn down the offer of my first French dinner party in months.

'Their son's about your age,' adds Peter, 'and he'll be there with his fiancée. So perhaps they'll be able to introduce you to some nice French ladies.'

Living alone is, I have discovered, a little bit like living in the desert. The conditions can be extreme, but they are survivable so long as one can find an oasis from time to time, to replenish the dusty jerrycan of the soul with something cool and sparkling. Amy's visit was one such oasis. The evening of the dinner party is another, with candlelight reflected in glowing faces, easy laughter, and something fishy in white sauce.

Bernard and Arlette, who live on the edge of a huge meteorite crater in the suburbs of a nearby town, are exactly as Peter promised: as gentle and refined as old port wine, with no edge of affectation nor sediment of gruffness.

No sooner have I arrived in their highly polished show-home, and been led upstairs into the first-floor salon, than Arlette takes me by the hand and looks so deeply into my eyes that I wonder if she is about to clutch my palm and tell my fortune. I am struck by the sadness in her gaze. And I am caught off-guard by the directness of her first question to me.

'So you are looking for a young lady?' she says in French, with the infinite pity of a priest giving the last rites to a drowned child.

'I'm sorry, Michael,' chuckles Bernard, hunching his shoulders with empathy for my embarrassment. 'That is my wife for you.'

Peter and his wife, June, are already installed side by side on a sofa. My pilot friend winks at me as I shake his hand and kiss June on both cheeks. 'Good to see you, old boy,' he whispers. He explains that June's speciality is remote viewing – finding things that are lost, by picturing them in her mind's eye. 'You name it, she can find it,' he says. 'From car keys to weapons of mass destruction.'

'Amazing. I bought a magic alligator once,' I tell him, 'that was supposed to have the same power to find lost things.'

'Oh, really?' Peter's eyes widen with interest. 'What happened to it?'

'I gave it to a schoolfriend. I think he lost it.'

Bernard pads across the room and arranges seven tiny glasses on a tray, each movement carried out with the meditativeness of a sadhu laying himself upon a bed of nails.

'Peter tells us you're looking for a wife,' persists Arlette, the skin around her soft eyes crinkling as she speaks. Her son, Roman, a tall, sweet-faced young man with a hint of James Bond about him, laughs a little louder than is strictly necessary and throws me a sympathetic glance.

'Well, I . . .' I begin to reply.

'May I ask how old you are?'

'I'm thirty-eight.' Arlette exchanges glances with her husband. I know that people tend to marry very young in rural France.

'*Ah, ce n'est pas un problème,*' says Arlette. 'How much land did you say you have?'

I blink. Everyone else in the room has fallen silent. I feel as if I am spotlit in the hot seat on *Mastermind*.

'No, really, it's not that sort of . . .' I stammer.

'A mistress, then?' asks Arlette. Another guffaw from the good-natured Roman, whom I suspect would prefer to see the conversation rippling along in shallower waters.

'*Pas une maîtresse. Une copine,*' I protest, though I'm not sure if this is quite the right word, either.

'*Une petite amie,*' corrects Bernard, whom I have heard speaking the most beautifully rounded English to Peter's wife, somewhat in the manner of a 1950s continuity announcer for the BBC. Is that what I am looking for, then: a little friend?

'And have you met anyone yet?' asks Sophie, Roman's pretty fiancée, who sparkles with such *joie de vivre* that I almost begin to fall beneath her spell. Watching me carefully, Roman reaches across the sofa to take her hand. So I tell them about how I crashed and burned on my very first attempt at inviting a French girl out, when the dazzlingly voluptuous lady in the Jolibois tourist office almost reached for the panic-button behind her desk; about my unrequited crush on the Botticelli in white wellies behind the supermarket fish counter at St Juste; and how the only woman who has shown any romantic interest in me has been a chain-smoking estate agent in Limoges, whose husband is a gendarme and whose sons are old enough to vote. Arlette chuckles and gives me a sage nod.

'The French women, it is not straightforward,' she says.

'But you have to persist. They know they must not say yes too easily.'

'I'm really not sure persistence would have made any difference in this case,' I reply.

'Peter says you have an aeroplane, Michael,' says Roman, shifting in his chair. 'Is it a microlight?'

And the conversation takes off and circles in less turbulent airspace. We move through into the dining-room, where Arlette lightly touches the back of each chair around the table, to indicate where we are each to sit.

Silver clinks on porcelain and candlelight gleams on crystal, illuminating smiling faces as if from within, like Chinese lanterns. This is my life, I remind myself, thinking back to the chainsaw in the barn, and the Mirage jets roaring overhead. Yet right now, it feels as if I have wandered into someone else's. Bernard refills my glass, yet again.

'So what sort of woman are you after, Michael?' asks Arlette, warming to her earlier theme.

'Someone who tells the truth, who is comfortable with themselves,' I say, after a pause. 'That's really why I came to France—'

'—to find a truthful woman?' Arlette leans forward in her chair. Sophie holds her nose, suppressing a giggle.

'No, no. In order to learn how to be like that myself, so that I wouldn't be always needing someone else to make my life work. If I can be happy alone, that feels like a better starting-point than if I am expecting some other person to do it for me.'

'And will she have a high-powered job, this woman?'

'I hope not,' I reply, too quickly, and hesitate. 'Not one on which she relies for her self-esteem, anyway. I'd rather find a woman who has had enough of proving herself in the rat race, or who never wanted to be there in the first place. Someone who would be happy for me to look after her, and would – in turn – be happy to look after me. It's very old-fashioned . . .'

'Well, why not?' asks Arlette, looking at Bernard. He gazes at me, lost in his own thoughts.

'Sounds like you've got it all worked out, old boy,' chortles Peter, his blue eyes twinkling as he leans his chin on his folded hands.

'Oh no, I haven't. Really, I haven't. I'm just thinking aloud.' And even as I am thinking aloud, parroting my foolish desires for all the world to hear, another voice in my head – one that I recognize only too well – is beginning to murmur its dissent. I do my best to ignore this voice, for it invariably tells me what I do not want to hear and, even more annoyingly, it is always right. And right now it is telling me I really should stop looking for the ideal woman as if I were looking for a gaudy new hen to brighten up the chicken house. Undaunted, I plough on.

'What do you reckon, Sophie?' I ask Roman's pretty fiancée, ignoring the voice. 'Do you think I shall find such a woman in France?'

'I'm sure you will,' she replies, her voice tinkling with amusement. 'But you have to go to Poitiers. There are lots of single women there.'

'Actually, I was rather hoping Roman might be willing to take me around one evening, perhaps introduce me to some people.' Roman looks as if he would rather disembowel himself with a pair of nail-clippers.

'Of course, I will,' he says, with a smile that looks like hard work, 'on condition that you agree to play the organ for our wedding in two summers' time. The church has an English organ in it, so it seems only right that we should have an English organist.'

'I should be honoured,' I laugh, amazed at their forward planning, 'although you have never heard me play.'

'Yes, but we believe in you,' he says. 'Isn't that right, Sophie?'

'*Mais, oui*,' she says, in her tinkling voice, clapping her hands in delight. '*Ça serait parfait.*' And we all sit in silence for a moment, surprised at what we have just agreed.

'One day, I bet you will write a book about all this,' says Arlette. She rises to fetch a tray of miniature coffee cups. 'And it will have a happy ending, you'll see.'

'I think that's highly unlikely,' I declare, shifting nervously in my seat.

On Christmas Eve, I drive to Limoges airport in the Espace and catch the FlyBe flight to Southampton for the first time. This feels less spirit-squashing than Ryanair, what with propellers on the wings, proper leather seats, and a stewardess who smiles at me.

My parents have both come to meet the plane, standing huddled in the terminal like Ant and Bee in their matching anoraks. I feel as if they are picking me up from boarding school at the end of term. My father even wants to carry my overnight bag for me, as if it were a wooden tuckbox filled with Butterfly yo-yos and Slime and magic alligators and a survival kit, far too heavy for his urchin boy to lift.

'It's all right, Dad, I *can* manage,' I insist, with a hint of irritation. I cringe to hear it in my voice, and hope that he does not.

'Sorry,' he says, pretending to wipe his nose. 'I forget.'

England again, and I am struck by the softness of every footstep I take. In France, the ceramic tile is king, even in the bedroom. In Britain, carpets and cushioned underlay soften the blow of living in a climate that is only marginally better than Iceland's.

My mum pays for the car park, fishing for coins in her purse, shoulders hunched, head tipped slightly to one side: just as she has always hunted for coins in her purse. The fact that I notice the snapshot image at all makes me feel a pang:

how unfamiliar the deeply familiar is becoming to me, the longer I am in France.

'Look, Spitfire,' I exclaim, pointing at a shiny white aircraft balanced on a metal spike in the middle of the main airport roundabout.

'But it only has a two-bladed propeller,' replies my dad. 'And the cockpit looks wrong.' Every Englishman knows exactly how a Spitfire is supposed to look.

'It's a replica of the prototype,' I explain. 'They flight-tested it here at Southampton.'

'Such a shame you don't see them flying any more,' says my mum.

'But you *do*,' I reply. 'It's amazing what you can still see flying – Spitfires and Hurricanes and Mustangs and Corsairs – roaring across a familiar sky.' I know this, because I have been there at the summer airshows that I miss at La Folie: at Duxford, Woodchurch, Headcorn and beyond. The past is still the present, several times a year.

I gaze out at the wintry English landscape, enjoying this feeling of being driven by my parents; taking me back.

On the front steps of their house in Farnham, looking out over the cricket pitch, they have set up the old wooden crib that my dad knocked together thirty years ago. I remember this miniature scene so well, with its tiny light inside to illuminate the three kings and the shepherds and their lambs, all moulded out of rubber and painted in gaudy colours. It looks so different to me now; now that I have sheep and straw and a full-size manger of my own at La Folie. I wonder what the three kings think of Farnham; what the shepherds make of the not-so-gaudy English weather, and how many new births lie in the stars for me this year at La Folie. Several of my ewes should be pregnant by now.

The next three days pass slow, slow, quick-quick, slow. Quick, because the time I spend with my parents feels always so fleeting; the chances for me to repay them for the years of thankless child-rearing, blighted by my tantrums, so few. Slow, because my brother Steven's wife is Romanian, her parents have come over for Christmas, and we are all striving, on both sides, to bridge the gulf of our inability to speak each other's language. So I feel at once at home and abroad, much as I do at La Folie.

Afterwards, as my parents drive me back to Southampton airport, a familiar pang in the pit of my stomach transports me back to my childhood again, and to my days as a boarder at Windlesham. I loved every minute of my time in this school-shaped playground, run by an improbably glamorous couple who charmed us into awestruck adoration with their grace and brilliance and tallness and wisdom. I always looked forward to seeing Survival-Kit Toby and the other friends in my dorm. So why did I experience a lurching, sinking feeling of abject nausea every time I was driven back through the front gates and up the long drive at the start of a new term?

# 5

## JANUARY

Back at La Folie, the temperature has plummeted and the house seems darker than ever. The Rastafarians all look snotty and disconsolate and Cat follows me everywhere, yowling her discontent, not taking her eyes off me, even for a second. I think the cold has frosted her brain. I light the wood-burning stove and, two hours later, check the thermometer on the wall. It still says six degrees.

Various messages are blinking on the answerphone, but I do not feel like talking to anyone yet: I am still enjoying being back in my hermitage, insulated from society. So I just phone back the ones I know will go straight to answerphone and leave the others until tomorrow.

On New Year's Eve, I fill my brass lantern with lamp oil, and half-stride and half-slither down the icy drive to Gilles's house, the Moulin Vaugelade, on the other side of the river. This is my first *Réveillon* celebration in France, so I am on best behaviour as I take my place in the gloomy dining-room, shrill with the sound of Josette's caged canaries, alongside Gilles's daughter Marine and her partner Daniel, who wears a baseball cap at all times, and Big Leif and Anna, the vertically unchallenged Dutch couple who drive down from Amsterdam several times a year to spend their holidays in the signal-box just across the way from the Moulin Vaugelade.

'How international you have become, Gilles,' I say, meaning to congratulate my friend, but from the way he purses his lips and only manages to raise half a smile, I'm not sure he takes it as a compliment.

Big Leif, in high spirits already, warms to this theme. 'It's because *il déteste les Français*,' he yells, in his unique French accent, which always makes me think of a German man attempting to speak Japanese. But no matter: the combination of Big Leif's 30,000-candlepower grin and the sea-roar of his infectious laughter means that in the end even Gilles himself cannot resist a nervous chuckle. 'We Dutch and English may not be able to cook good food, but at least we know how to eat it,' bellows Big Leif, guffawing with gusto. 'Eh, Michael?'

'*Tout à fait*,' I reply, feeling so unable to match Big Leif's unbridled gaiety this early in the evening that it comes as a relief when Gilles pops open the first of several bottles of champagne. What follows turns out to be a very long hiatus punctuated by the six courses of a magnificent feast cooked by Josette, as Gilles does his best to eke out dinner to take us through to midnight without too many longueurs.

I have never been in this room before. Gilles's kitchen has always served as hall, dining-room and living-room until now, so I am intrigued to have such a glimpse behind the scenes of the Moulin Vaugelade. Most of the space is taken up with a table wide enough to hold tense conferences between warring tribesmen, with a looming dresser straight out of Castle Dracula on one side, and on the other a painted metal bird-cage of such curlicued extravagance that I suspect it may be worth more than the Moulin Vaugelade itself. The room's walls and ceiling are powder blue, and someone has created the effect of a shiny brown picture-rail with a roll of parcel tape. In the corner, a cylindrical Godin wood-burner glows with a feeble heat which is sucked up and away by an icy draught long before it reaches my side of the table.

At one minute to midnight, Gilles finally switches on a radio which looks like a cat's whisker assembled from bits of sawn-up bunk-bed by POWs at Colditz. And we discover that all the clocks in the house are three minutes slow.

So we have missed the arrival of the new year, and – in the midst of my wine-fuelled wooziness – I feel myself missing the bongs of Big Ben, their sombre clangour reminding me of an England that is still there, as changing yet unchanged as the Thames in which the reflection of the great clock-tower lies shimmering every night.

They remind me, too, of listening to the World Service in Bogotá with my parents, and feeling painfully Abroad: a million miles from Clara Delaville, and Alice Melbury and the delicious mistiness of the Sussex Downs, which made me feel more at home at school than I ever quite felt at home.

They remind me of all those other New Year's Eves, at Ellen Gonn's exquisite thatched cottage in a picture-book Dorset village, where – as a spotty teenager, even more tipsy with champagne than tonight – I would sit and gawp and foolishly grin at being surrounded with so many beautiful and alarmingly sophisticated girls whom I was desperate to ravish and never dared so much as kiss. And then midnight would come, and I would have my chance to brush Ellen's cheek with my tremulous lips, feeling like Pip in *Great Expectations* as I stole a Happy New Year kiss that must keep me going for another twelve long months of torch-carrying for an adored Estella who had already moved onwards and upwards from the brief wisp of our dalliance long ago. And then I would play jazz piano duets with the head of the RAF, Ellen's neighbour, hoping that this might melt Ellen's heart, or perhaps even bring me a little closer to flying a Spitfire. And somehow it never did.

And now here I am, a billion miles from all that, watching the candle-wax dripping on to Gilles's table in darkest France, and we are making resolutions.

'My resolution is to work hard on my *potager*, to make it so good that even *you* feel proud of it, Gilles,' I tell him, and he laughs.

'Impossible,' roars Big Leif, almost falling off his chair with mirth. 'Gilles is never satisfied. Is he, Josette?' There is a thud under the table, and Leif yelps with pain, his jaw dropping and quivering as he glances accusingly at them.

I watch the various couples sitting round the table – Gilles and Josette, Big Leif and Anna, Marine and Daniel – and what I do not admit to them is that I make a second, secret resolution, too: to stop weighing up every single woman that I meet, in case she might be The One. I need to stop looking. I do not need anyone else any more to make my life work.

As I begin the slow trudge back up the hill to La Folie, shambolic with champagne, I feel relieved at the thought that I can stop living with this heavy quest always weighing upon my shoulders, as if I were an old ram, sporran swinging in the wind, driven to distraction by his hormone-heated ewes.

Next day, the snow arrives. Flakes as big as cotton-wool balls, falling in a silent ticker-tape parade, so thickly that I cannot even see the trees when I gaze out of the kitchen window. The dead ground is covered in a white sheet. Then by a blanket; then a quilt; then a luxury Russian goose-down duvet of snow.

Cat and I sit at the window of the winter sitting-room, gazing out at a scene that reminds me, obscurely, of some half-forgotten desire, and makes me want to rebel against the voice that is always right. I am a child again, peering out of the steamed-up windows of a classroom during French class, basking in the proximity of the perfect creature beside me as I watch the snow falling upon the rugby pitches, turning the grass the same colour as the H-shaped posts, their arms raised in wonder at the sheer loveliness of the winter weather. It is in moments like these that I yearn, more than ever, to share my life at La Folie with some beautiful woman whom I have yet to meet. Or perhaps I have met her already, and failed to spot that she, too, was waiting for my future.

Long gone are the days when I used to wait until the temperature in the winter sitting-room dropped below twelve degrees before allowing Cat to persuade me to light the wood-burning stove. These days it is the first thing I do, after feeding the chickens, breaking the ice on the water-trough for the Rastafarians, and flicking on the kettle for my first cup of PG Tips of the day.

In London, I could decide whether or not to go out of the house based on how hard it was raining at the time. Here at La Folie, when the sheep need feeding, and the chickens want to be released from their clucking in-carceration at dawn, the ancient processes must take place, and never mind the weather. So out I go, feeling like a polar explorer as I trudge through the snow, my boots stencilling fat exclamation marks in the powdered ice outside the barn, my breath making foggy speech bubbles in the frozen air.

The door of the chicken house groans on its frozen hinges as I drag it open, and I cannot help smiling at the head-twitching panic of the Egg Squad as they glimpse the white-out that awaits them. Several of them are contemplating snow for the first time. And – *ook!* – how chilly it feels underclaw. Meg, always the smallest in the platoon, is looking scrawnier than ever: I make a mental note to keep an eye on her.

Afterwards, stomping the snow from my boots, I return to

the stone sanctuary of the house. I make my tea, and spread a piece of toast with butter and a thin slick of my mum's home-made marmalade. Such heartwarming tastes of home must be rationed like ammo during a siege. And then Cat and I sit in silence, watching our stove crackle into life: breakfast telly.

Today, after the tea ceremony, Cat wedges herself into the deepest corner of her favourite window recess, where a slim sunbeam just manages to slant through the white-out to project itself on to her fur. I need milk and cat food and bread yet again, so I scrape off the windscreen of the Espace, my footsteps creaking in the snow, and attempt to negotiate the drive. This is slithering, more than steering. I leave the car at the bottom, and walk the mile or so into Jolibois, feeling the snow settling on my coat and hair.

Even by Jolibois standards, the town is unusually deserted. Huddled behind the counter of the *boulangerie*, Marie, a woman with the shape and complexion of an unbaked loaf, shivers as I enter. I feel a familiar twinge of disappointment. The princess whose chiselled beauty once lent an extra thrill to buying a baguette has not worked here since the summer. And then I remind myself that this isn't supposed to matter to me any more.

'Ah, this weather,' she coughs, as she reaches for the loaf of *pain aux céréales*.

'It's not too bad, is it?' We both peer out at the goat's-cheese sky.

'It makes everyone ill,' she says. 'And you don't have any heating, do you?'

'I have my wood-burning stove.'

'Yes, but for a whole house . . .'

What I can't quite explain to Marie is the fact that, because I live alone, I can happily sit down to breakfast in a woolly hat, and not feel silly. It is when there are two of you that you start to feel self-conscious about wearing survival gear indoors.

It helps being English, too; to have grown up with the expectation that houses will be cold and draughty, so one might as well make the best of it. I know that Tilly and Charles, a bluff, *bon-vivant* and hilarious pair of sheep-farmers who live a few miles up the road from La Folie, snuggle up with their dogs in their beds for warmth. Meanwhile Harold and Elspeth Brand have started hurling his collection of first editions into their wood-burning stove. 'Only the authors I don't like,' he snarled at me the other day. 'Which happens to be *all* of them.'

Agnès, whom I have not seen since the *soirée dansante*, enters the shop, shivers, and pecks me on each cheek. I make a special effort not to glance down at her thrusting embonpoint, and a mental note to self: *don't mention the waltz.*

'*Bonne année, Michael*,' she croons. 'Have you been practising your waltz?'

On the way back to the Espace, I have just caught myself staring at a sultry brunette leaning on a quad bike outside the shop of the Nicest Man, and wondering if she happens to be the one with whom I was supposed to spend the rest of my life, in the days when I was still on the lookout for someone like that, when a dark blue executive saloon, lustrous as a box of truffles, swishes to a halt beside me.

'Maurice,' I exclaim, when I recognize the white-haired driver. '*Bonne année*.'

'*Comment ça va?*' he says, extending a hand through his window. Smooth as a salmon, Maurice lives in a draughty chateau outside St Sornin-les-Combes, combines Parisian sophistication with local charm, and has been unfailingly kind to me ever since I first arrived at La Folie.

'Oh, you know,' I reply, in English, for Maurice used to live in Maida Vale, and his English beside my French is like the Space Shuttle beside a firework. We smile at each other.

'We're hunting the hare up at the chateau in a fortnight's time. Pétrus and Antoinette will be there. Care to join us, if you're not snowed in?'

Before I can reply, or ask him what he means, the sleek saloon is purring away like a well-fed cat, easing back to its lair.

Six o'clock, and I am sitting in the dark on the snow-covered terrace for my thinking time, wrapped up in my flying-jacket, with a glass of Pastis in my gloved hand. Cat is nowhere to be seen. But behind the fence to my right, my old ram Gaston stands watching me, whinnying in that rough gargle that is the closest he can get, these days, to a bleat. 'What is it, Gaston?' I ask, wandering over to him. He turns side-on to peer back at me, his legs wobbling beneath him like a pair of woodwormy trestles as he moves.

'Urgghhh,' he whinnies again, and a long filament of mucus dangles from his muzzle. Up this close, I can hear the wheeziness of his lungs, and I know what this means: his pneumonia has returned. Last time round, the vet was amazed he survived it. I can hardly hope to be so lucky again.

People still ask me why I chose France for this adventure and I have almost forgotten myself. Two years after my arrival at La Folie, my original reasons are mere palimpsests; early sketches barely visible beneath the rough brushwork I have daubed on top.

What remains unchanged is the series of charged memories of France that I have carried with me from my youth, crystallized into snapshots in my unconscious.

Aged two: a stone wall in Brittany, on which I stand, bathed in sunshine of such shimmering brilliance that I have to shut my eyes, and fall. I do not remember falling, nor the fact that Great-Uncle Jock was there, too, and caught me.

Aged seven: the uniformity of the blue-and-white numbers

on the houses in Le Touquet, each with their squat brown letterbox beside the front gate. We have come to visit one of my mum's old pen-pals. And a vile dinner of eggs in aspic – the uneatable embalmed in the inedible – puts me off gelatine, and hard-boiled eggs, for life.

Aged twelve: watching Clara Delaville and her friends, all a year older than me, set out on a day-trip from Windlesham to Dieppe, the reward for having passed their Common Entrance exams. To the child-me, my voice still a piping treble, Dieppe sounds as exotic as somewhere the Tardis might land in *Doctor Who*. Is it really possible to sail to France and back in a day? The boys come back with Opinel pocket-knives and shiny packets of petards made of cardboard wrapped in red crepe; some of the girls are wearing make-up; the teachers waft and wobble with wine and garlic. Everyone has suddenly joined a clique to which I do not belong.

Aged nineteen: I am invited by a refined English couple to teach Maths and Latin to their beautiful daughters, Alix and Sarah, who are preparing for their own Common Entrance exams, beside a pool somewhere rustically glamorous, not far from Toulouse. And this, now, is my first taste of the idyll of rural France; the bicycle rides through lazy avenues of poplars, offering their blissful shade from the raging sun; the long lunches of grilled sardines with crisp white wine, bread that is all air and crunch, coffee that jolts the soul; afternoons spent lounging by the pool, reading froth, while swallows swoop and dive overhead. I do not think I meet a single French person in this whole fortnight. Yet like a salmon about to be played long on the line by an expert angler, France has already hooked me, though I do not know it at the time.

Aged twenty-nine: I return to France, to spend a month on a rural farmstead. I meet sheep and chickens and a medieval gardener called Jean-Luc, who communicates in a series of grunts and drives a car that looks like a sugar lump. I spend the mornings writing passionate nonsense in brown ink in a series of fat notebooks, and in the afternoons I help on the land, nervously watching for rats as I turn the compost with a fork, or inhaling the leathery smell of the handful of sheep with whom my job is to wrestle while someone else trims their hooves. And I meet a wise old man from Denmark, whom I watch in the fields spending minutes that extend into hours as he gazes almost lovingly at trees, at motionless sheep and at individual ears of corn.

One day I ask him what he is doing out there, spending all that time looking at things he must have seen a hundred times before.

'I'm learning to look with my eyes, and not with my mind. You should try it some time.' So the two of us stand there for a while, staring at an old oak tree. I peer at its gnarled old trunk for a while, before it dawns on me that what I am seeing is not oak bark, but the bark of several thick tendrils of ivy that are climbing the trunk and slowly strangling the mighty oak.

After a few more minutes of this, when I am beginning to wonder how much longer I can spend counting the bumps on the edges of a million oak leaves, and my mind is beginning to wander on to the subject of the sassy Australian girl who has just arrived at the farmstead, the wise old man suddenly turns to me.

'Perhaps you don't need anyone,' he says in his deep, Danish growl, his eyes twinkling at me. It sounds as if he is answering a question, even though I have not asked one. He shrugs; smiles a penetrating smile that makes me feel as if he is X-raying me with his eyes. 'Perhaps you are enough in yourself.'

I feel stunned: rooted to the spot as if a carapace of ivy is holding me there. And although I have no idea why he is telling me this, his words will stick in my mind.

\*

No sooner was I telling Big Leif, on New Year's Eve, about the nightmare of having too many male animals, than poor old Gaston has fallen sick. Really sick. So now I am feeling guilty.

The truth is that three Rastafarian rams will co-exist as peacefully as monks just so long as *les brebis* are not on heat, though they may playfully attempt to mount each other on occasion. It's the same story in the chicken house: chaps en masse are fine until you introduce a few women into the mix. Titus and Hotspur are almost civil to each other when there are no sultry hens in the vicinity. It's only the whiff of sex that drives them bananas.

I can see, too, that rams and roosters do have their part to play, over and above their ability to look picturesque and procreate. For example, before Titus arrived on the scene, Melissa – my big white *poule de Bresse* – had become so macho that she was practically sporting cropped hair and dungarees, and doing her best to crow. The atmosphere in the chicken house was poisonous. Everyone was a bully except Silent Mary and Meg, and that was only because my two little Rhode Island Reds could find no one weedier than themselves to taunt. Fighting was rife. And some of the things they clucked at each other would not disgrace a Wednesday night session at the Jolibois *club de pétanque*.

Then Gilles gave me Titus, and the sisterhood bullied Titus, too.

But only for a day.

After that first day, I watched as Titus began to assert himself. He would dance around the girls, splaying his wings to the ground, dancing like a child playing at being a matador with a cape. Then he'd come closer and jump on them, beginning with Silent Mary and Meg, and working his way up through the pecking order. At the beginning, these frantic couplings were enough to make my eyes water. And yet – despite some disgusted ruffling of feathers – an unprecedented calm began to descend on the stormy coop. The girls began to blossom. Their posture became more upright, more haughty, like a gaggle of Mrs Thatcher lookalikes strutting to a hen night, following their haughty new leader on his worming expeditions, as they cheerily explored the wider universe to which he introduced them.

I do not regard Titus's brand of macho patriarchalism as a pattern for humanity. But it seems to suit chickens.

Today, grey old Ella is yelling in the snow-frosted sheep-field as if she were summoning a helicopter, and a high-pitched whistling is coming from the feed-trough, like the sound of air escaping from a leaky set of bellows.

This is what is left of Gaston. My venerable paterfamilias is lying prostrate on his side, and I can see his scrawny flank pulsing as he struggles for breath, as if he were a woofer pumping out a bass line in the boot of a Peckham BMW. His latest escapade, coupled with the snow and the cold, really must have been too much for him. And now his *pneumonie chronique* has returned to lay him low.

So this is what has unsettled Ella. I have heard it said that sheep can fall in love – at least to the extent of cleaving to one mate above all others. Ella strikes me as just such a one-ram ewe. She and Gaston have been through so much together. And her anxiety is a reminder that I am not the only one who is going to miss La Folie's toothless old warlord, if this is the beginning of the end.

The snowy fields all around La Folie look grey and for-bidding as the landscape of Brueghel's *Hunters in the Snow* as I gingerly make my way up to the hare-hunt at Maurice's chateau, striving to banish from my mind the nightmare image of Gaston's bony shoulders shuddering beneath my syringe. The vet has given me a course of antibiotics for my old friend, though I suspect they are intended more as a placebo for me than a rescue for him.

I have, nevertheless, made a ridiculous bet with myself. If Gaston is still alive by the time this year's snowdrops appear, then he will jolly well live to fight another day. By day three, the antibiotics appear to have boosted him a bit. But if the snowdrops don't appear soon, it will be too late.

I used to make similar bets in London, when I was waiting for trains on the Underground, in that warm, thunderous breeze which signals the imminent bursting forth of the clattering projectile from the muzzle of the buried gun. If I could walk beyond the third crack in the platform before the train overtook me, then Zara Malkin would change her mind. If I reached the District and Circle line exit before the driver shot past me in his cab, Alice Melbury would be mine.

My mood improves when I arrive at the gates of the chateau. Frenchmen with glowing faces stand around braziers in the early-morning mist, murmuring to each other as they warm their hands. I suppose it was like this before Agincourt. For my first-ever hunt, I am wearing seventeen layers of clothing, and congratulate myself on having wolfed down a full English breakfast before I came. Although, as my face stings in the cold dawn air, I am beginning to regret slapping my cheeks with a goodly splash of aftershave from Lidl, bought on a whim after I decided on New Year's Eve that I am not looking for love, after all.

More than a hundred of us are gathered by the time Maurice appears, smiling beatifically, shaking hands. I cannot see Gilles or Monsieur Jadot, or any of my friends from the tennis club. I hoped Gilles at least might be here, because his shearing barn and some of his best fields lie just outside St Sornin-les-Combes. But whilst every hunter is a countryman, not every countryman hunts. I recognize the beard of Jean-Louis who delivers my wood, and Yves-Pascal the notaire comes and shakes my hand, looking as dapper as Mr Toad in various shades and textures of dark green tweed and Goretex, all of it perfectly pressed.

'*Maurice est très sympa*,' says a burly *paysan* beside me, nodding at the white-haired figure moving amongst us in a huge green Dryzabone overcoat, shaking hands and whispering greetings. 'It's kind of him to invite us all.'

Soon, we are ushered into the half-light of a vast stone barn that feels fine enough to pass itself off as a cathedral; its timber frame immaculate, its walls white and crumbling. Here, three long tables – each the length of a *pétanque* pitch – have been laid with a gleaming array of cold meats, loaves as big as piglets, and wine in earthenware flagons. Suddenly that full English doesn't seem such a bright idea, after all.

'Ah, Michael,' booms a familiar voice behind me. I feel a heavy paw on my shoulder, as if I'd just been grabbed by a polar bear, and turn to see Pétrus, Maurice's son, grinning down at me. 'It is good that you are here.'

'You, too, Pétrus,' I reply, shaking his hand. 'It's good that *you're* here.'

'I don't think my father would have been very amused if I'd stayed in Paris this weekend,' he says, grinning at the thought. 'But it's great fun, you'll see.'

I am fond of Pétrus. A burly teddy-bear of a man, often wreathed in cigar smoke, he has a beery geniality about him that makes me think of medieval feasts, whole roast oxen and libations to Bacchus poured from butts of sack. I suspect he would be useful in a joust, if one could only find a suit of armour big enough to fit him. And because he was born in London, he is the only Frenchman I have ever met who understands Marmite. It is a private bond between us.

'*À tout à l'heure*,' he calls, disappearing into the throng.

We sit on rough oak benches, forty to a table. There are perhaps half a dozen women in the group of 130. Antoinette, Pétrus's sister, waves at me from a little further down the table, and I blow her a kiss in return. No flirting, I remind myself. Besides, Antoinette's boyfriend is here, too, a reluctant banker who writes comedy sketches for French television and is a black belt in the martial art of golf.

Every man but me now pulls out a well-worn pocket-knife, and sets about hacking himself a manly hunk of bread, a few virile slices of *saucisson* and a macho slab of roebuck-liver terrine. The man next to me peers at me, making a question-mark of his eyebrows.

'Not hungry?' he asks.

'Yes, but I have forgotten my knife,' I lie. For I do not really own a pocket-knife at all.

'Try this,' says the man, and at first I think he is going to hand me some blood-stained hunting-dagger that has been passed down through his family since the Revolution. And then I see what he is directing me towards.

Shrinking like a character in a Bateman cartoon, I reach for one of the comedy knives provided for the handful of ladies present. Flimsy, and with translucent pink plastic handles like National Health specs circa 1979, these are not intended to help women to cut meat. They are designed to teach chaps like me a lesson. There's certainly no danger of any of them being stolen. I really must buy myself a decent knife from the Nicest Man, next time I visit his shop.

After the terrine come slabs of wild boar, roasted on the embers outside. And then more wild boar. And then a little more. And then cheese. If I am ever invited to hunt the hare in France again, I shall go on hunger-strike beforehand.

Standing on a bench, after Pétrus has whistled for silence, Maurice gives a little speech.

'Now that hunting the fox with hounds has been outlawed in *Angleterre*,' he bellows, 'it is all the more important that we celebrate our ancient rural traditions here in France.' He pauses, allowing the hearty applause to subside before continuing. 'It is quite possible that we will not find any hares today,' he says. 'Even if we do, they have a very good chance of evading the hounds. And you will perhaps have a chance to witness the wonderful elusiveness of the hare; of the amazing ruses and stunts it can pull, as part of the struggle to survive.'

Outside, a dozen of the *echt* huntsmen, immaculate in their cream tweeds, form up in an arrowhead on the grass with their backs to us, the black bells of their instruments raised. Lifting their coiled brass horns to their lips, they blast out a series of farted fanfares in a honking triplet rhythm. Later, in the field, these will tell their comrades the latest news ('Still no sign of the hare, Pierre has ripped his breeches and it's two–one to Marseilles'). It is a blazing racket: crude, spirited, faintly lavatorial, like someone playing the trombone inside an oil tank.

At last the wiry-looking *piqueur* releases his bloodthirsty hounds from their trailer, and we're off, striding behind the streaming pack, their tails swaying like antennae, noses hugging the ground as closely as the machine that paints the white lines on a football pitch.

I yomp over frozen fields, through streams, woods and thickets, trying to keep up with the wagging tails and flagging tweeds. Two gleaming roe deer gallop headlong across my path, and a wild boar comes squealing from a coppice like a baby stegosaurus. There is a splashing, howling, shrieking turmoil in the river, as the hounds attempt pursuit and are somehow driven back, as much by the strength of the current as by the desperate cries of the huntsmen snapping their whips. I can feel the adrenaline surging inside me, as I silently cheer on the cornered boar, who turns out to be a young pregnant female. Beside me, a wiry little man who makes me think of a friendly Niebelung on day-release from the mines explains that since today's hunt is for the hare, the hunters have no right to kill her. I nod, relieved. And the boar, though visibly wounded with a series of scarlet gashes in her flank, staggers upstream to live another day.

Sometimes, amid the wild and undulating woodland, I

lose sight of the hunt, but regular blasts from the *piqueur's* horn – *taa! taa!* – bring everyone back on track.

All these men, striving so hard to find and corner the object of their quest, elusive as a rainbow's end. *Quaerite et invenietis.* I really didn't think hunting was my thing, but I am enjoying this. It feels good to be doing something so primitive, with 130 close friends whom I have only just met; to feel at one with this wild French landscape which is all new to me. I don't even mind the hounds too much, despite that tussle with the wild boar, for their excitement is palpable, as they revel in their dogged pursuit. And what Maurice said in his speech was right: the chances of catching a hare today are beginning to seem wonderfully slim.

After a couple of hours, the dogs enter a dense wood. No one seems to know where they have gone, and we all wander around, feeling lost and unloved, like the drugged lovers in *A Midsummer Night's Dream.* I find myself alone in a thicket. Then there's a horn-blast not far away from me. There it is again: *ta-ta-tum! ta-ta-tum!* They have picked up the scent of a hare. I can hear the hounds baying, somewhere off to my left, and the excited *piqueur's* triple blasts: *Ta-ta-tum! Ta-ta-tum!*

They're coming straight for me.

My pulse racing in what feels like triplet rhythm, I stand motionless, holding my breath. And there, out of the corner of my eye, I see something streak out of the undergrowth and zing from left to right, twenty yards in front of me, about as fast as a low-flying jet plane.

All I glimpse is a smudge of grey-brown, barely breaking the surface of the fallen leaves with their sugar-frosting of snow. And I wish I hadn't seen it. Because this vision – a blur of mortal terror, distilled into headlong flight – this changes everything. Suddenly hunting isn't fun any more. Not because it is cruel for hounds to follow their natural instincts and chase a hare, but because now I can see inside the mind of their panicked prey, flying for his life.

Four seconds later, the first two hounds come galloping from my left, on the same flight-path as the hare. But my human smell must have blurred the scent, for they stop to mill and snuffle around, frustrated and uncertain.

I freeze, as fearful of being bitten as of giving any clue as to where the hare has fled. The rest of the pack arrives, closely followed by the *piqueur*, who gives me a long, stern look. I smile and shrug, and I have the uncomfortable sense that we understand each other perfectly. I know that he knows that I know something that he does not.

And then everyone dashes off again, on the wrong path. The thrill, I can see, is in the chase. And I decide that I do like hunting quite a lot, after all.

# 6

## FEBRUARY

Ever since Cat and I first arrived in darkest France, and the panicked twitching of her ears drew my attention to a whirring insect soundscape that I hadn't even noticed until she pointed it out, I have been prodding myself to notice the changing of the seasons: to witness spring exploding into high summer, summer being burnished into autumn, and autumn crisping before it grimly shrivels into winter.

Time after time, these changes pass me by. It is like when I swore that I would watch all the little number-wheels slide round from 199,999.9 to 200,000.0 on the dashboard of the Espace, and then I was lost in the suburbs of Paris at the time, and I forgot to look. If my favourite ram's life had depended on my noticing all those zeros creeping into place, perhaps I would have taken more trouble, just as I am taking great trouble to keep an eye on the spot where the snowdrops are due to appear, conscious that they may be about to flower any day now. I have the snowdropping-zone under constant surveillance. Day after day, as I rumble up or down the drive, I scout the place where *les perce-neige* are sure to appear. Day after day: not a *saucisson*.

But looking and noticing, I am beginning to discover for

myself – seeing what is there in front of my face – is an advanced game, trickier than I ever guessed.

In London, where the topsoil is almost entirely composed of concrete, the change in the seasons is easy to recognize, perhaps because there are only two of them. Winter is when everyone wears black and a scowl. Summer is when they wear black and a smile, except on the Underground, where the scowls, interred, persist.

Only at my local gym, just behind Sainsbury's on Dog Kennel Hill, did I ever detect evidence of another season, a month or two before the summer, as the mirrored, flock-carpeted torture-chamber grew busier in the run-up to the bikini season. Suddenly a new batch of pale, lardy forms would arrive to pound away on the treadmills and puff out reps on the bench-press, hoping to show rippled muscle and lithe limbs in place of the uncooked pastry with which they arrived.

One morning, Didier the postman winds down the window of his little yellow Clio and leans across the passenger seat to hand me a stiff white envelope.

'*Une invitation, peut-être?*' he fishes.

'*Peut-être*,' I reply, chuckling at his curiosity. I scrutinize handwriting that I recognize from long ago. 'At least it's not a bill.'

'Ah, all these bills,' he says, shaking his head, and jerking his thumb at the box of mail on the seat beside him. 'It's not much fun delivering them, I can tell you.'

We wave at each other, and he roars away.

I sit at the kitchen table, take a swig of tea, and open the envelope.

My spirits go up, down, up like a house-painter's roller as I read the card. It's a wedding invitation: up. Phoebe Yates, the wild baroque recorder player, is getting married: down. And I feel so happy for her, that she and Tor have finally decided to make the magic leap: up.

So Phoebe Yates is getting married. I lay the embossed invitation carefully on the table; take another swig of tea. One more of the dazzling damsels on my old and slightly foxed list of what-if-just-possibly-maybe-one-days – of girls with whom I could imagine happily spending more than a hint of my life – has found the secret of happiness with someone else.

Fine.

I am relieved to discover that I feel no jolt of jealousy; no bolt of indignation that I was not consulted first. On the contrary, the universe seems just that little bit more ordered, that tad less chaotic, when two friends promise to spend the rest of their lives together. A note from Phoebe asks if I could bear to play the organ for the wedding, which will be in a little church in Devon.

I scribble a reply, attach a blue stamp for *Angleterre*, and leave it by the door to give to Didier on his next visit.

Gilles drops by, out of the freezing fog of a February dawn, to take a look at Gaston for me. And for the first time ever, I notice that he always wears exactly the same blue-and-grey checked shirt, every time I see him. Perhaps Gilles is like Einstein, I reflect, with eight identical outfits in his wardrobe, to reduce the mental strain of having to choose between them. I do not tell him about my bet with the snowdrops.

'*Ça caille*,' I tell him, with a shiver, as we shake hands and he jams the bony stub of his middle finger even harder than usual into my palm. I'm not sure exactly what this phrase means, but I have heard the locals muttering it in the steeliest depths of winter. And they always giggle at each other whenever I come out with it myself.

Gilles does not giggle. '*Ah, tu parles*,' he says. 'Down at the Moulin Vaugelade, it's at least three degrees colder than it is up here.' We both gaze at the thick fog lining the depths of the grey valley; suds in an old tin bath. Somewhere in that white murk is a dank old farmhouse, and Josette scrubbing floors. It's hard to imagine the pair of them growing old down there. Yet it is unthinkable to picture them anywhere else.

I tell Gilles about the hunt, and he seems pleased that I was invited; glad that I went. I want to ask him why he wasn't there, but something about his faraway smile discourages me. I am beginning to discover that relationships in the countryside are complex. Easy for me, the funny Englishman whom no one can quite pigeonhole, to flit like a butterfly from group to group, clique to clique and class to class. Not so easy for a Frenchman like Gilles, who has lived in Jolibois for only thirty years. Because he originates from a village that lies almost ten miles away, he will always be an outsider here.

Gaston is standing in the shadows of the barn, head lowered, when we wander over there. His snotty muzzle still resembles some cheap candle that has been burning beside an open window, sending rivulets of molten wax everywhere. And his back legs are drawn in behind the front ones as though he were trussed. He is fast becoming an outsider, too.

'*Ah, oui,*' sighs Gilles, sucking air through his teeth.

'So what do you think?'

'*Ce n'est pas bon,*' he mutters, shaking his head. 'I'm afraid he won't be long in dying.' This is not what I want to hear. Not today.

'But you said that last year, Gilles,' I remind him, 'and he's survived until now.'

'Yes, until now. But this time . . .' He smiles at the earthen floor, lost for words.

Gilles can say what he likes. I venerate my neighbour for his wisdom and experience, and for the generosity with which he has shared them both with me. But Gaston has given me something similar, too, in the indomitable, silent way he has already endured the brutal winters beside me, each year's chestnut fleece a little more threadbare than the last. He is the shaman, elder statesman and paterfamilias of La Folie. And I am not about to let him go lightly. No, in my stupid, sentimental way, I am not ready for him to die.

Gilles drives back down into the murk, and I picture him switching to flying on instruments, like a light aircraft descending into cloud. I sneak back to the vet; request another bottle of overpriced medicine; continue to squirm as I puncture Gaston's bony shoulders with my merciless syringe, praying that my wiry pensioner, his nostrils trailing fronds of swampy green goop, can somehow battle his way through to the dawn of another spring. But how long until the snowdrops come, white-uniformed outriders racing ahead of the peloton of spring?

Next morning, Didier the postman draws up outside the house again, and I scamper out with my reply to Phoebe Yates's wedding invitation.

'Have you seen them?' he says.

'What?'

'*Les perce-neige.*'

'The snowdrops? They can't be . . .' My heart leaps and sinks. Did I really miss them again?

'*Ils sont arrivés.*' He points down the drive. 'But they're late this year, *non?*'

Cheerful as he sounds about his discovery, Didier looks as surprised as I am by my own response to it. Grabbing the sheaf of URSSAF bills and Netto pork bargains from his hand, I race down the steps and run in a vast circle, beginning with the snowdrops – for there the blooming blighters are, beside the drive, as clear as beer-froth on a gendarme's moustache – and ending with the barn. With a wave over my shoulder at the departing Didier, I charge inside. Gaston, startled, doesn't move: I think the shock of my sudden arrival may have stopped his heart.

'It's all right, old boy,' I murmur, watching him nervously. I pour a heap of his favourite granules into the feed-trough. 'You're going to live.'

Gaston, lying in the straw, looks unconvinced. Yet from the way he struggles to his feet to nuzzle at his breakfast, I sense that he has turned a corner at last.

Snowdrops aside, spring does not actually spring, even in darkest France. No; it sidles up to you, like a lady with a clipboard outside Champion. I used to think that spring was hop-skippety lambs, and budding saplings bursting out all over, and everything green as Amy in a Luscombe. But now I know better.

Now I know that spring is an old ram, braced against the rain. It is hail on fresh leaves. It is tight clusters of stinging nettles, tiny as daisies, in places where you least expect them. A few days later, and Gaston, slowly shrugging off his pneumonia as if he were an old man struggling to clamber out of a swimming pool, comes and snaffles a little stale bread from my hand. And then he retreats again, horns lowered like the barrel of a tank. I take this as an encouraging sign: his old fight-or-flight responses are beginning to return.

Spring follows the same pattern. I spot a few buds on the trees, and there is a glimmer of sunshine, so – being *anglais* – I decide to sit outside with my wine tonight. And then the snowstorm starts again: the kind of howling blizzard that makes me want to quote Captain Oates, when all I am going to do is check on the chickens. Cat, curled up into a tight ball of disgust beside the wood-burning television, appears to want to cut out the middle-man. *She* is waiting for summer.

Life suddenly becomes a struggle at La Folie. As the snow melts, the river at the bottom of the hill bursts its banks. Rivulets of water seep through the rear walls of La Folie, lending the dark place the dank ambience of a leaky submarine. Heavy earthworks are required, to shore up the waterlogged hillside that is slowly sliding and burying it. Is La Folie itself sliding, too? Some of the floors slant at a crazy angle, like a fairground haunted house. But the foundations are built on solid granite. So I can only assume that it is France itself that is slowly sliding east towards China. I cannot afford to have this fixed right now.

Next comes a bombshell from Peter Viola: he and June are leaving, too, going back to England along with Ralph and Olga and the rest.

If the snowdrops were one false promise of winter's passing, the cranes – *les grues*, the quintessential French harbinger of spring – are another. Several times this week I have dashed outside at La Folie, drawn by the mournful bugling of these birds. Each time, I expect to see spectacular formations of them heading north, only to witness a ragged squadron of a dozen misfits, struggling into the wind towards Poitiers. Spring may be coming – but it appears to be going elsewhere.

In its place, more snow arrives, falling as silently as the eyelids of a sleepy child, marooning us in Ice Station La Folie once more. One day, I witness a cruel sight: a single crane standing in a white field like a downed Dornier, hoping for rescue.

A day later, and everything changes. The sun melts the snow. The fields gleam. I throw open the back door of La Folie, allowing light to flood into the place as if I were a Victorian archaeologist opening an ancient tomb. Peter Viola gives an impromptu flying display in his Thruster above La Folie, making me laugh out loud at the way he seems to hang motionless in the strong headwind, hovering like a helicopter or a kestrel, before he dives, roaring towards the earth at a speed calculated to make me hold my breath. At last he wheels away, rocking his wings in farewell. And Doris, bless her, lays herself down behind the house to produce my first lamb of the year: a tiny male, who looks like the sort of thing Valerie Singleton used to make out of pipe-cleaners and sticky-back plastic on *Blue Peter*.

Doris is out there now, whinnying to her lamb in a low murmur which is, I presume, the sheep equivalent of a bed-time story. Her sisters watch from a respectful distance. It will be their turn, soon. And then, overhead, like a Battle of Britain fly-past roaring over Buckingham Palace, comes a sight I had not dared hope might come. The cranes. And it is cranes en masse, too: a vast V-formation the size of several football pitches in the sky – perhaps five thousand birds, beating their wings in time, arranged in a family tree of so many generations that it might almost run back to William the Conqueror, or Abraham, or the fossils. It is as if Peter's display were merely the warm-up act, clearing the path for these mighty aviators. Their trumpeted calls, plangent and heartrending as bagpipes after a massacre, make my eyes prickle, as I stand and marvel at their airmanship. Despite the yearning pathos of their music, I feel so happy and relieved. For the lone crane, downed in a field, muscles himself into the sky to join his brethren. And I know that all this, now, finally, means that spring has come, even at La Folie. And for once, I noticed it arrive.

My mother phones. 'It's wonderful that you're going to be self-sufficient, Michael,' she says.

Well, yes, it would be, if I were. And I know what this means: it means they're showing repeats of *The Good Life* on BBC2.

'My motivation for creating the *potager* is not some dream of self-sufficiency, Mum,' I explain, 'any more than my Rastafarians are intended for turning into lamb chops.' This comes out rather more piously than intended, and I feel guilty for the silence on the other end of the line.

'We're just impressed that you're having a go,' she says at last, treading as carefully as if she were stroking a cat that may lash out a claw at any moment. 'Impressed, and just a *little* bit surprised.'

I am about to rise to this, and stop myself. For my mother is right, even if she does sometimes seem to be on a private mission to plug me in at every opportunity. But today I make a special effort, reminding myself that it is not her fault that my buttons are so easily pressed.

'I'm surprised, too,' I reply. 'I know it's out of character. Which, of course, is why it matters.'

'What else are you going to plant, besides potatoes?' she asks, moving swiftly on. 'Have you decided yet?'

To be honest, I haven't a clue. But I am not about to tell my mother this. So I reel off a list of all the vegetables I can think of, including Jerusalem artichokes, purple sprouting broccoli and chard. Then I wait for her to tell me that most of these will be quite impossible to grow at La Folie considering the pH of the soil, the prevailing wind and the overriding incompetence of the fellow who runs the place. But, all credit to my mother, she is making a special effort, too.

'Gosh, you *will* be busy,' she says, kindly. And my heart goes out to her, for I know that all she really wants is to have a warm connection with her son over the phone, because she sees him far too rarely. And because we both know that she will not be there on the phone for ever. So who am I to waste these precious moments, while they are still ours?

Besides, my mother has a point. Last year, my attempt at creating a respectable *potager* was, frankly, pathetic. I spent a lot of money on fence-posts and chicken-wire, to protect from the Egg Squad all the miracles I was about to grow.

Then I bought fifty kilos of potatoes to plant, because no one told me that this would yield enough *patates* to feed Belgium. Even now, Gilles never tires of recalling my gaffe, giggling until he has to dab his eyes with his hanky.

'But what you don't understand, Gilles,' I plead, still attempting to defend myself, a year later, 'is that *les Anglais* eat a lot of potatoes.' I'm not about to confess to him that I somehow thought each small new potato planted in the spring would become a big potato in the autumn. It turns out that the little blighters multiply underground, though I still find this very hard to believe.

I suppose I was caught off-guard by just how *fast* nature starts working in the spring. It was all I could do to keep my encroaching jungle at bay, let alone add to nature's ammo by planting anything new. So even my intended fence was never built. The potatoes rotted in the barn. The land went to seed. It was, as I could tell from the way Didier the postman would glance witheringly at it every time he came up the drive, a shambles.

This time round, I am determined to do better, which is why I am pleased that Gilles has enlisted Monsieur Jadot to teach me. Willingness is all very well, but experience does the job better in half the time.

And here he comes. Cat goes rocketing out of the cat-flap at the sound, which evokes the primordial rumble of tectonic plates, mingled with the piccolo tinkling of my wine glasses trembling on their shelf. I have never seen a tractor like Jadot's, except in Expressionist daubings of strapping Soviet peasants ploughing their fields for the greater glories of the mother country. The beast looks about two hundred years old, and may or may not be green beneath all the oil and soot in which it is coated. Jadot rattles up the drive in a cloud of smoke on his engine-of-war, dragging a plough upon which I am alarmed to see a small person crouching, like a charioteer behind four mighty stallions, their nostrils flaring as they pound the dust of the Circus Maximus. I am even more amazed when the small person turns out to be a lady, clinging on for dear life.

Grinning at me, Jadot sets his tractor to rattle at idle, leaps down from his seat, winces at the impact, and helps his charioteer to unclasp her whitened knuckles from the metal of her mount.

'Here's my new *copine*,' he whispers to me, over his shoulder, while the lady in question – a slim mouse with a kindly, well-scrubbed face and a pleated skirt that looks like the sort of thing that air-stewardesses wore in the 1970s – wanders towards the box tree, upon which she leans, her shoulders rising and falling as she takes several deep breaths.

'Is she all right?' I ask, unsure whether to feel anxious or appalled.

'*Ah oui, ça va, ça va*,' he replies, waving his hand as if he were polishing a brass doorknob. 'It's good that I teach her how to work. And with the melting of the snow, the earth will at last be soft enough to plough. We should have done this months ago, you know, but better late than never.'

Half an hour later, Jadot has ploughed the cold grey earth of my *potager* into a perfect black concertina, with furrows deep enough for a fat man to take shelter from a medium-scale artillery barrage. Just like that. I think how long and hard I have worked to transform my life at La Folie, and how the state of the *potager* has felt like a relief map of my capacity for idleness and procrastination.

And now Jadot has come and fixed it, just like that. I am tempted to ask if he could fix me a flight in a Spitfire and find me a beautiful *copine*, too, but I fear he might take me at my word.

'It's important to know how to grow food, before you can cook it,' chortles Jadot, amused at my awe. Offering his wrist for me to shake, he prepares to drive away.

'Yes, it's—' I begin.

'Not you – *her*,' he interjects, jabbing his thumb at his new *copine*, who smiles back at him so beatifically – two parts Mona Lisa to one part Widow Twankey – that it occurs to me that there must be more, much more, to old Jadot than meets the eye.

Besides prodding myself to notice the changing of the seasons, I am also working hard at La Folie to live in the here-and-now, as opposed to the there-and-then. As I haul out strokes on my rowing machine, always striving to turn my soft suburban body into a hard rural one, it is still a battle to concentrate on each breath I puff from my lungs, and not upon what the sheep are up to outside, their black silhouettes jostling like smoke particles in Brownian motion under a microscope.

I know that I must learn to live in the present, because of the hold that the past has upon me. But I miss travelling on the tube beneath London in the morning, and seeing all my fellow hamsters scampering on their wheels, fiddling with their make-up, twisting at their cuff-links, frowning at the lurid tittle-tattle in their newspapers as they prepare to start another day.

I miss meeting the glance of a beautiful young woman before she looks away, and then looks back again, to re-assure herself that I am not staring at her. Let alone dreaming, there and then, of a future together.

I miss my friends at the Oval gym, where our motley band of tubby non-cricketers would heave away at the same rowing machines that stretch my sinews now at La Folie. We none of us were sportsmen, but for those forty-five minutes, I could dream myself an athlete, sweating towards success. Every Sunday morning, we would meet at the bandstand in Battersea Park at 7 am, and run and run until our legs were jelly. And then, feeling fit and healthy and deserving, we would drive to one of the cafés on the King's Road, eat a full English breakfast and drink a lot of hot chocolate, and feel a whole lot better. I still think of Peter and Stephen and Harry and Anita on Sunday mornings at La Folie, because I know that the bandstand in Battersea Park is exactly where they will be. And this helps to coax me back on to the dreaded rowing machine, for another five-thousand-metre slog.

I cling to the delusion that muscular arms and a stomach like a Roman centurion's may one day be enough, in the eyes of a woman, to make up for the fact that I am not a film star or a footballer; not an astronaut or a fighter pilot; that I am not quite the heroic figure whom I always intended to become when I was a little boy at school. It helps that I have a particular motivation just now, for next month I am starting evening classes in ballroom dancing here in Jolibois, and there is no knowing whom I may meet.

'What on earth is that?' asks Serge, the heroic stonemason who periodically comes and smashes another hole in the windowless walls of La Folie. He has just spotted my rowing machine, gleaming like a modernist sculpture in the *maison des amis* at La Folie. I can tell that he is suspicious about the fact that I am wearing gym shorts, even though it is eight in the morning, and it's raining.

'*C'est un rameur*,' I confess, sheepishly, miming with my fists the action of someone rowing.

Serge labours five days a week, without tea-breaks, sweating and straining with rocks and chisels and his bare hands. In the evenings and on Saturdays, he takes other jobs, to feed his three children. And his expression as he contemplates my townie time-machine designed to allow a fellow to turn the clock back a few notches by wearing himself out without heaving any cement, ploughing any fields or doing anything remotely useful, reminds me of one of those speeded-up films of clouds billowing over the desert, or of a cartoon rabbit in the split-second after he has whacked his toe with a sledgehammer. The worthy stonemason wrings his hands, bites his lip and cocks his head to one side, like a chicken attempting to make sense of a helicopter, before limping off into the workshop beside the barn, where we store the sacks of cement and lime. When he emerges, he shins straight up a ladder with a seventy-pound bag of cement under one arm, as casually as if it were a feather pillow. I think the sight of my rower has given him the willies.

Exercise is different in rural France. Cycling is the national obsession, and no one goes to a gym, because all the men are already getting quite enough exercise with their chainsaws and sledgehammers, thank you very much. French women, meanwhile, stay magically slim thanks to something in the water and (according to Serge) by eating nothing but oranges for one day a week.

'*Non*,' declares Marie-Claude, when I try out Serge's orange theory on her, during my weekly lecture from the scariest cleaning lady in the west. She glares alarmingly at my shorts, and then at Serge's dusty boots as he passes the back door with another seventy-pound bag of cement, daring him to cross her pristine threshold. 'It's because what we eat is *équilibré*.' With this, she straightens her apron and brushes her hands down her front, in case I hadn't noticed how trim she is.

# 7

## MARCH

'The trouble with this place is that it is so dark.' Ariane, the comely wife of Yves-Pascal the notaire, sleek and un-compromising as a moon-rocket, gazes around herself, shaking her head. The pair of them have very sweetly come round to show me how to prune my wisteria, even though Ariane insists that I should have done this in January. And now they are giving me tips on how to beautify La Folie.

We have not even stepped inside La Folie yet. No, Ariane is still standing outside the front door, frowning at the ring of pine trees that surrounds the *fosse septique*, and at the various overgrown shrubs, trees and bosky monstrosities that crowd in upon the house. As far as I can tell, it is not the house that is too dark. It is France itself. Ariane waves her arm. 'This must go.'

'Which one?' I ask, nervously, peering at my beloved trees. I know I have no talent for making things grow. So the idea of chopping anything down, when it has already done the growing part all by itself, fills me with dread.

'All of it.' Ariane fixes me with a stare so penetrating that I can feel it going straight through me and burning a hole in the grass.

'Well, maybe not quite *all* of it,' coaxes her husband, Yves-Pascal, quietly dousing the smouldering vegetation with his tones of gentle conciliation. He makes a shape in the air with his hands, as if he were a potter throwing a spherical pot on a wheel. 'Just some of the trees, here and there.'

'All of them,' repeats Ariane, more firmly. Yves-Pascal and I wince at each other. He always makes me laugh, even when he is beating me at tennis.

'Even the box tree?' I gulp.

'Of course not the box tree,' she snaps. 'But everything else. You need to open this place up; make the best of that beautiful view. Surely you don't want always to be staring at Christmas trees and that horrid car?'

I glance at the Espace, hang my head, and know in my heart that Ariane is, as usual, absolutely right. Not everyone sees my little paradise as I do. There is always more work to be done.

After I have thanked them profusely for their ruthless decimation of my wisteria, I kiss Ariane goodbye, and Yves-Pascal and I shake hands.

'*Bon courage*,' he murmurs, with a weary smile of such perfect understanding that it makes me feel better at once.

Accepting that one is likely to be alone for eternity is one thing. Convincing other people that this may be a survivable disease is quite another. Thank goodness Kiki, the twice-divorced *femme fatale* with whom Le Grand Mermoz – who runs the local hardware store – has been trying to set me up ever since we went skiing together, has now found lasting happiness with a sewing-machine salesman from Poitiers. For Mermoz and the rest of our skiing group are coming to dinner in a week's time, and I am already steeling myself for another ribbing about my love-life.

Four days of perfect sunshine finally persuade me to drag all the wisteria cuttings – long straight shoots, stiff as electrical flex – down to a clearing near the gate. I am just about to set fire to them, when a violent hailstorm appears from nowhere. Two more balmy days, and then – just as I am bestirring myself again, armed with my box of matches and a plastic bottle of *alcool à brûler* – an afternoon of horizontal rain makes bird's-nest soup of my bonfire. These sudden squalls are known as *les giboulées de mars*, and are apparently so normal for the time of year that they merit barely a shrug of despondent recognition from the locals.

Didier the postman rattles up the drive in one of the hailstorms, and looks more than usually grateful as I dash out to meet him in my habitual pyjamas-and-waxed-jacket combo.

'A lady, perhaps?' he asks, handing me a pink envelope that he takes the trouble to sniff.

'*Je ne sais pas,*' I shrug, genuinely clueless, feeling the hail begin to melt and trickle down my neck. Didier's curiosity still makes me laugh. When he arrives with a parcel, he will shake it and ask what it contains. When he delivers the box with my pods of espresso coffee, he invariably announces, 'You can relax now. *Le café est là.*' I always make sure to give him a tip at Christmas.

Armed with my pink letter, I dash inside. Who can it be from? I do not recognize the handwriting, which manages to be at once bulbous and spiky, feminine and feisty. It is postmarked in Coventry: the English Limoges.

'Dear Michael, I read with amusement your column yesterday and pondered on it overnight,' it begins. Oh, golly: I'd forgotten that I'd wheeled out that piece last week, written long ago, about my search for a dishy *copine*. 'I am looking for a partner and your photo is quite nice so I thought I'd offer my services to you. I'm 44, single with two beautiful kids aged 11 and 9, live in Cornwall, used to farm but now live in a small town. I have been single for about three years, mainly because the locals just do not have anything at all to offer. I would love to come and join you in rural France. It sounds amazing and we are looking for a life change!'

How wonderfully fearless, I think to myself, to write such a letter. And then I flinch at the idea of two fatherless children running amok at La Folie, torturing the cat in revenge for their mother running off with a younger man with a rubbish backhand and a leaky house in the middle of nowhere.

I have never wanted my own children, let alone someone else's. But I cannot help noticing that almost all the sane and semi-attractive girls whom I coveted at school and university have already gone forth and multiplied. So perhaps I must accept – if I want to meet a soul-mate who is my equal, rather than a predatory nymphet prowling for a sugar-daddy – that any potential love-interest may indeed come with strings attached, in the shape of pre-existing sprogs. This is the price I must pay for leaving love so late. And my stomach flips with panic at the thought.

In response to the weather, the Rastafarians are in and out of their little sheep-shelter like the shepherd and milkmaid on a weather-clock. All except Gaston who, though his wheezing has ceased, still lingers in the shadows like the milkmaid's ageing grandpa, only rousing himself from his armchair when the porridge is already on the table.

There are many good things about Ouessant sheep. They are sturdy little blighters, almost small enough to count as Ryanair cabin-baggage, yet wild and rugged enough to stand up to the rigours of a French winter without any pampering. The breed originated on the tiny isle of Ouessant, where – in the eighteenth century – their black wool was said to be highly prized by the womenfolk, many of whom were almost permanently in mourning for husbands and sons lost in fishing expeditions at sea. These days, black wool is worth even less than white wool, but I still keep three bags full of the stuff in the barn, for sentimental reasons.

More important to the trainee peasant is the fact that Ouessants look after lambing all by themselves. Not for me the sleepless nights, with a torch, a pessary and a pair of rubber gloves always at the ready that Gilles and Josette must endure. No, with Ouessants, each lamb tends to pop out like a sweet from a Pez dispenser in the middle of the night, with no need for hot towels or stirrups or birthing pools. Nature takes care of the whole business.

This is why I am watching Daphne very carefully today. So heavily pregnant that she looks like a Space Hopper in an astrakhan coat, the poor dear has been staggering around since lunchtime. My sheep books tell me that this is quite common when a sheep is close to giving birth. But as I watch from a safe distance, I know that something is not quite right.

Daphne stares back at me, bleating like a car-alarm. Time after time, she takes a few knock-kneed steps and sinks back to the ground, craning her neck to the sky, her eyes wide, her black lips strained with pain to reveal a set of perfect white teeth. I wince as I watch.

An hour later, and something protrudes from Daphne's back end: a hoof perhaps, or a tiny snout? Aha! So everything is going to be fine because, after all, Ouessants look after lambing all by themselves.

Now comes more rain, hammering on my shoulders like the fingertips of an annoyed masseur. It rains so hard that the landscape is obscured behind a filthy grey curtain. I can hear the water splashing out of the broken guttering behind the house; picture it soaking into the stonework like sherry into sponge. The other Rastafarians scarper for cover beneath the trees. Daphne just lies there in the wet grass, pushing for France. That tiny hoof is still just visible, but it isn't coming any closer. Neck and legs stiffly extended, Daphne looks like a broken rocking-horse. And then she lies as still as if she were dead.

'Something is not right,' I murmur, helplessly, to myself. Besides the tiny hoof, I can see pink, too, as I approach, as if part of Daphne were coming out, rather than an inky lamb. I am still a few paces away from the stricken sheep when she staggers to her feet and flees, with a pair of miniature hooves clearly protruding from her back end.

'No, Daphne, no,' I shriek. And I might as well be remonstrating with a pilotless plane that has jumped its chocks and is threatening to fly.

I have been resisting phoning Gilles, because he is in the middle of lambing himself, and has already been up to La Folie once this week, to help me castrate Doris's lamb. But this is an emergency.

Twelve minutes later, we are kneeling side by side in the wet grass behind the house, with the rain streaming down our faces. Gilles has rolled up his sleeve, grits his teeth and begins to feel around inside Daphne. I feel like an extra on *All Creatures Great and Small*. This cannot be my life; it must be a film. And I wish the special-effects people would switch off the storm. A flash of lightning makes the grim landscape flicker, and then comes a double drumbeat of thunder, bouncing back at us off the far side of the valley.

Daphne is weakening fast. Gilles says there is not much time.

'There's no head,' he roars, his lank grey hair pressed against the dripping black sponge of Daphne's flank.

Teeth clenched, I hold Daphne's head and shoulders while Gilles winces and puffs and mutters to himself, desperately searching for the lamb's tiny head buried inside the crushing panic of her womb.

'Stop pushing, damn it,' he barks.

'Sorry,' I cough, swiftly releasing my weight from Daphne's shoulders.

Gilles chuckles. 'Not you. *Her*.' I push Daphne down again as she makes a weak attempt to flail free. Streams of blood and jelly trickle in rivulets down Gilles's forearm. Even by my own standards, I feel helpless. 'She's crushing my hand,' he says. I know that Gilles is beginning to suffer from arthritis in what is left of his fingers. And from the way he gasps and screws up his face, I can only guess at the pain.

At last, my friend draws something out of Daphne that looks like a wet black sock.

'*Ah, c'est un petit mâle,*' he says, gently.

It seems impossible that anything so mangled and puny and slicked with blood and mucus could be alive, let alone have a gender. Daphne emits a low bleat, like the sound of a dying electric razor, and Gilles lays the wet sock beside her, so that she can see what she has done.

In her exhaustion, Daphne begins to lick the wet corpse. I can hardly bring myself to watch. And then I blink, open-mouthed, as the corpse raises its head and emits a wavering cry, as if an asthmatic old woman were attempting to play the oboe on her deathbed. Gilles seems quite unmoved by this tumultuous event, which makes me want to do a double-back somersault. Who needs children, I think to myself, when they can have lambs?

'What would have happened, Gilles, if you hadn't done what you did?' I ask.

'It would have died inside her in an hour or so. And she would have died, too.'

Later, I wander out to the sheep-shelter, to see the new lamb's tail whirring like a propeller as it sucks at Daphne. I can't help clenching my teeth at the violence with which it head-butts her undercarriage to let down the milk. But how good it feels, to watch a new-born creature feed.

I have decided to name the little blighter Gilles. And I do not suppose I shall tell Gilles this, any more than I shall tell anyone, ever again, that the wonderful thing about Ouessants is that they look after lambing all by themselves.

*

Next morning, little Gilles Junior is prancing and tottering in Daphne's wake as she does her best to graze with a toddler in tow. And I have a little of the same feeling myself when I trudge out to feed the Egg Squad, and Martha, my favourite, comes scampering along beside me, measuring her jaunty footsteps to mine. Black and gold and gorgeous as if she were costumed for the Venice carnival, Martha is the chattiest of chickens, now that Mildred, bless her, is no longer with us.

'I'm off to dance class tonight, Martha,' I tell her, as we march, side by side, from the barn. 'I'm not much good, but I think it's the physical contact that I like more than anything.'

'Coo-co-co-co-co-coo,' replies Martha happily. I often forget that she doesn't speak a word of English.

Some sounds are international, however, and as I dig the feed-scoop into the sack of grain in the chicken house, peering carefully at little Meg, who looks weaker than ever, I hear a scream. Behind me, Martha is hopping in circles, hooting with pain. A trail of bright blood soaks into the saw-dust on the chicken-house floor. Oh, Martha. What have I done?

I have only gone and crushed one of her toes, that's what I have done. The hooked claw is squashed and ripped, with a slow drip-drip-drip of Martha's scarlet life-force leaking from it. And I know from my brief experience of killing chickens that she has not a lot of this to spare.

Leaving Martha bravely standing on one leg, I race down to the vet. I can at least *ask* him for advice about a chicken, even if I am wary of humiliating myself again by turning up with one under my arm.

The vet's surgery happens to be next door to the gymna-sium where – following my fiasco at the Lions Club *soirée dansante* – I am belatedly learning how not to be a ballroom dancer. As I sit and wait my turn in the surgery, surrounded by yapping mongrels, I wonder if treading on my favourite *poule*'s toe is a sign. For even after my first lessons as the lone *Anglais* amid a group of sixteen wannabe Fred-*et*-Gingers, I still feel like the only fellow in rural France who doesn't know his paso doble from his *petit déjeuner*. Actually, that's an exaggeration: Jean-Louis the woodsman is almost as bad at the paso as I am. But we have also established my inadequacy in the waltz, tango, polka, madison, Texas stomp and something called *Hrroquenhrrol*, which turns out to be rock'n'roll.

This, despite the best efforts of Renée, a lady basketball player who always dances the man's steps, and her assistant, Cécile, tiny and sparkling as a fairy on a Christmas tree, who smiles serenely when I tread on her toes. For once it is my good fortune to be the only single man in the room, for this means that I get to dance with Cécile again and again. Not only is she the best dancer in the room after Renée, but she happens to be the prettiest, too.

Renée is not like most of the Frenchwomen I have met. She is built differently for a start, with an ampleness of figure that makes one think of late-summer ripeness rather than the wintry nip favoured by many of the pared-down ladies of Jolibois. She is captain of the local women's rugby team, and she is also one of the softest and gentlest creatures in the world. When she dances, she is as light on her toes as a pebble skimmed across a lake. She must be about my age and – when I take her in my arms for my approximation of a waltz – holds me with a gentleness that reminds me of the way Martha would cradle her chicks in the early days, stretching out one wing to encircle them in her feathery warmth.

'*Tout le monde* knows the paso,' she assures me, as if I am just being stubborn and English and weedy by not mastering it at once. 'If you forget about the twiddly bits, it's just the same as a walk.'

I am worried because there is another *soirée dansante* coming up and I am not sure I can handle another humiliation like the last one. Renée says that if I panic at the dance, I should simply walk round the room, pushing my partner in reverse. But whenever I do this to poor Cécile, I just feel like Clint with his .45 up the bad guy's credentials.

'*Ce n'est que de la marche*,' repeats Renée, as if walking across a crowded dance floor in a stiff clinch with an attractive stranger were as easy as planting spuds.

'*Ah, oui. Mais . . .*' I stammer. Sometimes my French feels even clumsier than my paso doble. And then there are the twiddly bits.

'*Ouverture, deux, trois, quatre*,' I mutter, before launching Cécile, in all her delicate loveliness, into my blunt interpretation of *les Ciseaux* (the scissors), or *le Carré* (the square, but more of a rhombus in my case), or *le Huit* (the eight, once you round up the decimal point). Then there is something called *l'Élastique*, which feels about as elastic as wisteria, not to mention *le Lasso*, which strikes me as downright dangerous in a crowded room.

All these moves are tricky enough with the petite and lovely Cécile, who – rather like a Spitfire – instinctively knows where you want her to go even before you touch the controls. With the other ladies, several of whom are bigger than me, I feel more like a rookie pilot attempting to land a Hercules on an aircraft-carrier in a Force Nine gale. I know the bloke is supposed to lead, but what if your rudder is shot and your hydraulics have failed?

In a municipal gymnasium in darkest France, the schmaltzy music pumping out of Renée's ghetto-blaster begins to weave its spell. I know I am supposed to have left all this behind. But a thought lodges itself at the back of my mind, and begins to nudge its way, with growing insistence, towards the front. What if I were to ask Cécile if she would like to accompany me to the *soirée dansante*, or even simply to meet me for a drink one evening? Enough time has passed since my disastrous attempt at chatting up the *femme fatale* who works in the local tourist office for my wounds, if not my pride, to have healed. And the pink letter from Coventry has reminded me that I need to start being brave again. It would not be a date, exactly, but Cécile is so pretty and must be about my age. It would be fun.

I tell myself that I shall ask her, at the end of this tango, if nobody else is listening. *Lent, lent, vite-vite, lent.* We dance to the lilting beat, she light on her tiny feet, I shuffling like Steptoe. Perhaps I am too old and crabby for her, I think to myself, as she smiles over my shoulder at my classmates struggling with their *pas de chassées* and *ouvertures.*

At last the music stops and, while Renée riffles through her CD collection for a Texas stomp, I take my courage in both hands. Cécile and I are still in tango hold and, before she can slip away, I let my words tumble out.

'I wondered what you were doing this weekend,' I begin.

'Oh, I'm—'

'Because I wondered if . . .' And my courage runs out, for she has already begun to answer.

'*Oui?*' Her eyes widen, and she beams at me, urging me to continue.

'No, no, you say first,' I beg her, feeling my palms growing moist. I wonder if I can let her hand go without it seeming too obvious.

'Well, it's my fifty-seventh birthday,' she declares, her eyes sparkling with delight. 'So my grandchildren will all be coming round, and my husband is taking me out for a special surprise.'

'Ah.'

'But I interrupted you. You wanted to ask me something?'

'Not really, no, no.' I gaze around the room, just in case someone has scrawled on the walls the way you are supposed to explain to a married grandmother why you are not planning to invite her out on a date. 'I . . .'

'*Oui?*'

And the sheer warmth of her sparkle helps me over the ridge of my embarrassment.

'I'm just a little nervous about this *soirée dansante* on Saturday,' I confess, 'and I couldn't help wondering if you might be there.' And as I cough my excuses, I resolve to face the music alone.

The kindly vet – too young for his grey hair – pulls a sad smile when I explain the tragic case of Martha's Toe, and fetches a small white box from which he pulls a bottle approximately the size of a cigarette-end. The only difference is that this cigarette-end costs fifteen euros, or roughly three times the price of a chicken.

'I was actually wondering about the . . . purple spray,' I tell him. I saw Gilles using an aerosol of this magical stuff at the sheep-shearing last summer, whenever the shearers nicked the animals' skin. I have no idea if it worked, but at least the lurid purple colour meant that the blood did not show.

'Ah, *oui*, the purple spray.' He nods, approvingly, returning to his store-room. 'That's an even better idea.' He thumps the aerosol down on the counter. '*Trois euros.*'

And Martha – one foot white, one foot dyed bright purple – pulls through. True, that purple toe still sticks out at quite the wrong angle, but at least she can cling to her perch without falling off. And we are still friends. As the *soirée dansante* approaches, I take this as another sign – and a deeply reassuring one at that – that treading on a girl's toes need not necessarily be fatal.

That night, as I sit at the kitchen table with Cat and a glass of cloudy Pastis, having my six o'clock think, I cast my mind back to my schooldays, and to the many things I learned for which I cannot imagine ever finding a use. Things like how to solve quadratic equations, the formation of ox-bow lakes, and the German word for 'waste-paper basket'. Against these, I must set all those things I learned which I assumed would be useless, yet which have actually turned out to be highly beneficial: French irregular verbs, Pythagoras's theorem, and how to make a mitred joint spring to mind. And then there are all those things I *didn't* learn at school, but which I dearly wish I had, because it now strikes me that they would be very useful indeed. The care of animals (to include chicken ailments, lambing lore and advanced tactics for capturing very small sheep). Plumbing. The night sky. How to make conversation with a French lady over lunch. The paso doble. And how to build a decent fire.

You'd think that, by his late thirties, a fellow would know how to build a decent fire. Building fires – like fixing electronic devices by bashing them hard on a table, or spraying water everywhere when attempting to replace the washer on the cold tap – is something that we chaps take pride in knowing how to do. It is an atavistic donné, a nugget of primeval folk memory handed down to us from Prometheus via Nero, Baden-Powell and Pudding Lane. Me um man, me build um fire.

Strangely, however, the gift appears to have passed me by, such that my potential as an arsonist is roughly on a par with my promise as a tennis player in the Jolibois over-35s league. This becomes embarrassingly clear when I invite Gilles and Josette to dinner and – since summer has not yet shown the slightest sign of y-cumen in – I make a fateful decision to light the fire. Not my trusty Godin wood-burning telly, but a big medieval fire in the fireplace proper, with industrial quantities of kindling, logs a metre long, and much choking of smoke and pumping of bellows.

With rare foresight, I opt to ignite my blaze well before Gilles and Josette arrive. This should give the fire plenty of time to establish itself. It has not occurred to me that the smoke might have the very same idea.

'Ah, I see you've lit the fire,' says Gilles, choking into his handkerchief as he is enveloped by the acrid fug that billows around me when I open the back door.

'Come in, come in,' I cough, even though what I really want to say is 'Chim-chim, cheroo'.

We shake hands and I kiss Josette – four pecks, two on each side – noticing, too late, that I have left her with a fetching black smudge on each cheek.

'*Bof, c'est pas comme ça,*' roars Gilles, with some annoyance. Panicking, I am about to apologize to him for defacing his wife when I realize that he is not jabbing his finger at me. He is remonstrating with my fire. Or, more accurately, with my smoke.

There have been many epiphanies in my life at La Folie, and this is one of them. Gilles tuts at the way my smouldering logs are balanced on a wire grill that Monsieur Zumbach left among his discarded *trucs* when he sold me the place, and which reminded me of a grate. I thought the important thing with fires was air from below – as much of it as possible – whereas it turns out that the rules for open wood fires are as different from the ones for stoves as the requirements for a lasting marriage are different from the requirements for an exciting fling. According to Gilles, it is having a good layer of embers that counts, so the thick layer of ash that I have been attempting to brush aside like the memory of an embarrassing tennis defeat is actually integral to the thing.

'And don't keep poking it,' he snaps, undermining another of my treasured male beliefs as he grabs the poker from my hand. 'Just make sure you have plenty of contact between the logs and *les braises*, and leave the fire to it.'

Two minutes later, the smoke has cleared and the fire is blazing away as if it were in a costume drama. Amazed, I tell

Gilles what I was thinking about earlier; about all the gaps I have discovered in my expensive education. 'I feel so lucky to have been able to come here to La Folie,' I explain, 'and to have learned so much from you and Josette.'

'*Bof*, I left school when I was thirteen,' he chuckles, puffing out his chest. 'Everything I know, I learned outside. That's the trouble with the young today: they're trying to learn in classrooms what you can only learn in the fields.' We stand in silence, gazing at the flames as we bask in the difference between our two worlds. 'Now, what are all these other things you want to learn about?'

'Plumbing,' I reply, hopefully. 'And the night sky.'

'Ah,' he nods, with a shy grin at Josette. 'Me, too.'

I have learned not to give Gilles rice or avocado, that he has a weak spot for squintingly acidic flavours and a hint of the exotic, as long as this doesn't involve hot peppers, and that – in the countryside – the way to honour one's guests is to serve them plenty of good lean meat. Vegetables are optional. Vegetarian lasagne, *nul points*. So tonight we have prawns in a lime dressing to start, and then – continuing the citrus zest-fest – sweet-and-sour pork with noodles. Josette has brought a pear tart for dessert. After supper, as she sips her coffee, and Gilles gazes searchingly into his glass of red wine, I ask how they are feeling about their impending retirement. There is a long silence.

'I have no choice,' shrugs Gilles. 'I've had my turn, and now – *hop* – it's over.' He mimes a chopping action with his hand, as if he were beheading a chicken.

'But surely you won't stop just like that, will you? I mean, you'll wind the farm down gradually.'

Gilles shifts uneasily in his seat and reaches for the bottle of wine. 'May I?' he says. It is the first time he has ever asked to help himself at La Folie.

'They've sent me the letter,' he says, at last. 'On this date: *hop*.' Gilles prepares another hapless chicken for the pot.

'But what will you do?' I glance at Josette beside him. She quickly looks away, biting her fingernails.

'I've worked hard,' says Gilles, smiling to himself. 'I'm ready for a rest.'

I gaze at my friend. I am struggling to imagine what it is like to spend forty-seven years working from dawn until dusk with the animals in your care; to live in accordance with the seasons, the sun and the moon; to be intimately connected to the earth and its capacity to sustain life. And then to stop, just like that, because a man in a suit says you must.

'It will be a big change, though, won't it? I mean, won't you miss the life?'

'Oh, *bof*,' he shrugs, grinning at Josette, shifting uncomfortably in his seat. I notice that she does not return his smile.

'But seriously: what are you going to *do*?'

'I shall go on walks,' he says.

'Will that be enough?'

'I am going to buy a bicycle, too.'

'And you, Josette. What will you do?'

Her mouth opens and closes. She purses her lips, glances up at me from behind her fringe, then stares at the table, shaking her head. I can see that it is time to change the subject. But my mind is blank.

'It's not easy,' says Gilles at last. 'The way prices are going . . .'

'Food has become so expensive,' I nod.

'Not food,' he continues. 'Houses.'

'So why don't you just give up the land, and keep the house?' I ask.

'We have to move,' says Gilles, shaking his head. I look at Josette, who by now is staring, expressionless, into the fire. 'Le Moulin Vaugelade is rented. And we can't keep paying out every month on the tiny pension I'll receive.'

I puff the air out of my cheeks. 'How far are you planning to go?' I ask.

He shrugs. 'That depends on what we can find. We've started having a look around Jolibois, but there's nothing we can afford.'

I know what is coming next, because I have heard Gilles say it before. But that does not make it any easier to hear. 'It is because of *les Anglais*,' he sighs. 'The way they have pushed up the prices around here, it's impossible for us locals to compete.'

'I'm sorry,' I offer. We both know that, according to Gilles, I did not bargain hard enough with old Zumbach when I bought La Folie. But Zumbach and I understood each other: I had not the heart to steal from him.

Gilles smiles. 'Not all the *Anglais* are to blame, Michael. It's not *your* fault, personally, what's happened in the Limousin.'

'I'm as much a part of the problem as anybody else,' I say. 'But if it weren't *les Anglais*, it would be the Germans, or the Dutch. Europe is one big housing-market now.'

'Except that England isn't really part of Europe, is it? You still have *la livre sterling* and everything. And for the locals, that makes the whole thing even harder to swallow. It just doesn't seem fair.'

I do not know how to reply to this. It doesn't matter if Gilles's argument is right or wrong; the local resentment to which he alludes is real enough. So I don't try to reason with him, because it doesn't seem important just now.

'I can't believe you're going to leave the Moulin Vaugelade,' is all I can bring myself to say.

Next day, the rising sun wakes me, glaring out of a sky of such severe clarity that transparent shapes float like ghosts across the jelly in my eyes as I stare out at it. Perfect flying weather: the air dense; the wind calm; the visibility endless.

CAVOK weather, pilots call this: Ceiling and Visibility OK. Such skies must have been what made men first dream of flight.

Though I know I should be working on my book about personal romantic failure, or practising the 'Arrival of the Queen of Sheba' for Phoebe Yates's wedding in a few weeks' time, I cannot resist the lure of such a blue serenity. A few steep turns above the Monts de Blond will do me good.

Naturally, the aerodrome at St Juste is deserted, just as you would expect on a dazzling Sunday morning with the best flying weather in weeks. I am not complaining about the silence, however. Whilst I do miss the fun of flying out to neighbouring airfields with Jethro and my other pilot friends back in Britain – dropping into the Squadron at North Weald for a gleaming cooked breakfast with all the trimmings, or down to the Tiger Club at Headcorn to watch the aerobatics and the parachutists and the aero-modellers, all sharing the same airspace in hold-your-breath proximity – there is something magnificent about having a French air-field entirely to yourself, too. I suppose it was like this for Blériot and the pioneers. And it means I can wear my khaki flying-suit without feeling like too much of a poseur.

And then I hear footsteps crunching on gravel behind me, and for a nasty moment I think it may be Marcel with his dank cigarillo, come to blight my day. But instead it is Jacques the flying schoolteacher, who has just nipped into the clubhouse to book one of the Robins for next weekend.

'I'm flying to La Ro*chelle* with Richard Ruther*ford*,' he says, with jolting emphasis, and a quizzical glance at my flying-suit. 'You must know him. He's another *Anglais*.'

'To be honest, Jacques,' I reply, 'I mostly do my best to steer clear of *les Anglais* out here.' I am half-expecting him to smile. But his response pulls me up short.

'You're the second English person who has said that to me, Michael,' he says sternly, wagging his finger at me as if

I had just cut in on short-final. 'And how do you think it makes us French feel?' He leaves a schoolteacher's practised pause: just long enough for me to see the error of my ways, yet too short for me to formulate a response. 'Should *we* be avoiding *les Anglais*, too?' he continues. 'Is there something *wrong* with them?'

I hang my head, conscious that he has a point.

'Nice suit, by the way,' he says, turning to go.

As Jacques drives away, and I unlock hangar three, I ponder his words. My official reason for not hanging out with *les Anglais* is that this would make it much harder to become integrated with the locals. The unofficial reason is that they remind me – in a hideous, Dorian Gray-type way – of myself. And Jacques is right: it is time I grew out of my brittle isolationism. Who am I trying to kid?

The sun comes streaming in as I thunder back the hangar's vast metal doors, bringing the Luscombe's gleaming surfaces to life. I still cannot shake off the childlike sense that owning your own plane is something that millionaires do, rather than people like me. There is a reassuring whiff of leather and oil and the 1940s as I lay my charts and headset on the seat.

Wheels chocked, brakes on, stick tied back. 'Throttle set, contact!' Out of habit, and the sheer Biggles pleasure of the words, I call them out to the deserted apron. Then I haul down on the propeller, and feel a surge of happy outrage as the engine splutters into life first time – huffing and puffing and straining and clattering before gradually settling into its familiar rhythm, like a rock drummer at the end of a very weird solo.

'How come you only do this when there are no women around?' I yell out loud, staring in disbelief at the blur of the prop spinning happily at one thousand rpm.

A few minutes later and I am climbing into the sky, en route to Brive. There is no purpose for this trip, except that

I have never been to Brive before, and I want to discover what is there. Even from 2,700 feet, I can see for twenty miles. The towns far ahead of me stand out like speckled chalk on the green baize of the landscape. Navigation, like life, becomes a whole lot simpler when you can see into the future.

The runway at Brive is enormous; big enough to land a 737. But the futuristic control tower is dark and the place looks as deserted as St Juste: Sunday lunchtime in France. In England, there would at least be someone sipping tea in the office, waiting to collect the fifteen-quid landing fee off you in exchange for the privilege of rolling their bumpy sod with your Goodyears and extracting a cup of scalding instant from a Klix machine. Here at Brive, everybody is clearly far too busy eating foie gras with their families to go flying. This is a blow, for it means there is no one to witness one of my all-too-rare perfect landings, which doesn't dislodge my sunglasses or anything.

I am just taxiing to a parking space on the vast, empty apron when an English voice crackles in my headset. Shortly afterwards, a gleamingly graceful plane, painted Ferrari red, taxis to a halt beside me. I watch as a man and a woman in matching maroon fleeces emerge from the perspex bubble of the cockpit, like twin moles from a hole. The English have landed.

Part of me wants to run away. But I still have the words of Jacques the schoolteacher echoing in my mind: 'Is there something *wrong* with them?'

'Beautiful Falco,' I remark, wandering over. 'Did you build it yourself?'

The man looks up, smiling. I tell him about an eccentric Albanian millionaire who once took me for a thrilling Falco flight, zooming low through the river gorges of the Creuse.

'Ah, yes – James,' laughs the man: tall, stooped, brushing his hair from his eyes. 'Quite a character, isn't he?'

'Small world,' adds the woman, and we all introduce ourselves. Phil and Jean turn out to be British schoolteachers,
who renovate ruined houses in France for light relief.

I almost suggest that we inhabit parallel universes, until it
emerges that La Folie is not half as ramshackle as I thought:
Phil and Jean have no water or electricity, and can see the
stars through a hole in the roof of their bedroom.

'That's deeply rugged,' I say, impressed.

'Yes, but you've done it alone,' says Jean, 'and that's
harder.'

'Is it?' I reply. 'I sometimes think that a bit more hardship
would be good for me.'

'It's how we like it,' she nods, her eyes sparkling.

I feel as if I have just bumped into a couple of old friends.
It is no surprise that they have come across Harold and
Elspeth Brand, Jolibois's most infamous *Anglais*, because
everyone knows Harold and Elspeth. But they even know
Jethro.

'The aerobatics whizz?' asks James, grinning with recognition. 'I used to race bikes against him.'

I must look confused, because he laughs and continues.
'He was British champion. Road bikes. At least until he
smashed up his knees.'

'I had no idea.' My friend Jethro is a man full of surprises.

'Isn't he doing skywriting now?' asks Jean. 'I think we saw
him doing it at Goodwood. The Os and the Ds were all right,
but he really struggled with the W.'

I smile at the recollection; picture unbookish Jethro, with
all his driven perfectionism, desperately trying to master his
handwriting in the sky.

'Did he happen to draw a heart, too?' I ask. I know
Jethro has been working on this, to impress his latest love-
interest.

'I guess that would be impossible with a single aircraft,'
replies Phil. He traces a shape in the air with his hands, like

a child mimicking an aerial dogfight. 'But he was pretty darn impressive all the same.'

Together we wander into Brive's ghostly airport building, whose high windows and strong pong of floor-polish remind me of being back at boarding school, until we come across an unlocked side-door. Propping this ajar with a pebble, we clamber over a fence to freedom. Well, at least into one of those lunar landscapes of squat grey boxes – Monsieur Bricolage, Darty, Decathlon – which lurk on the outskirts of French towns. Walking in line abreast, we are a trio of visiting astronauts from the planet *Angleterre*. Perhaps I should not have worn my flying-suit, after all.

We eat lunch together in the neon ambience of a Buffalo Grill – two *salades de chèvre chaud*, and an entrecôte – and it feels the most natural thing in the world to be here together, as we talk about French eating habits and Spitfires and plasterers, and why nobody else is flying on a day like today. I had almost forgotten how much I like the English.

It feels like a simple, perfect moment of serendipity: this chance occurrence of arriving with like-minded souls in a deserted nowhere at the same time, which seems as unlikely as electrons colliding, and yet which is the kind of happy collision that somehow makes sense of the universe for a while.

Later, over a glass of Pineau on the terrace at La Folie, with Cat kneading a painful game of *chat boulanger* on my lap, I tell myself that this is why I am still single; still alone on this lush hillside whose beauty makes me feel almost guilty at keeping it all to myself. That chance occurrence has not yet happened, of meeting the right person, at the right time. Clara Delaville, Ellen Gonn, Alice Melbury, Zara Malkin: either I was not yet ready for the wonderful girls whom I loved, or else they were far from ready to appreciate me.

Behind me, Gaston and Ella, the toothless grandparents of

my flock, stand side by side at their fence, unable to munch the rich spring grass that is sprouting all around them. The other Rastafarians tear at it with violent relish. Undaunted, they nuzzle each other with their grizzled muzzles, their eyes glinting in the evening sun.

The next morning is another perfect day for flying, with everything crisp and glittering and renewed with dew. Yet this morning I must stay at home, for Monsieur Ducroux the plasterer is coming to give me a quote for plastering several of the breeze-block walls that old Zumbach erected inside La Folie.

First impressions can be mistaken, I fail to remind myself, as Ducroux emerges from an expensive-looking van in a fake leather jacket and a cloud of plaster dust. I know better than to judge a man from his appearance, so I wait at least until I've shaken his hand before pre-judging him. His hand feels as cold and hard as a feed-bucket at dawn. It doesn't matter that I know nothing about plastering. The less one knows about a trade, the more one attempts to judge a tradesman from the glint in his eye. And Ducroux hasn't got one.

'*Ça va?*' I shiver.

'*Oui, ça va,*' he replies, as if he were a gouty pall-bearer who had just been entrusted with the coffin of a big, big woman. His shaggy grey hair makes me think of a battleship that's been through a garlic press, and I cannot help noticing the fastidious care with which he tiptoes around the edge of the hearth-rug. Fussy misanthropist, I decide; mid-fifties, lives alone, avoids sunlight and has a vast collection of porcelain thimbles.

'Seven hundred euros,' declares Ducroux, glancing at the walls to be plastered, 'or thereabouts.' No measuring-tape, no ruler, no nothing.

I gulp. 'Couldn't you do it for a bit less?' I ask. He looks taken aback.

'I . . . I might be able to.' He takes a deep breath. 'I'll have to see.'

Next day, I solicit a quote from another plasterer, who studiously measures everything with a laser, and comes back with a quote twice the size of Ducroux's.

And so, just before eight on Monday morning, I greet Ducroux as he arrives to start work. He has already started preparing the walls, with much bashing and crashing, by 8.01 am.

Every hour or so, his footsteps clump heavily on the stairs, and he comes down to fill up his bucket of water in an uncomfortable silence.

'The water pressure's not very good, is it?' he comments, speaking for us both as the pitch of the water in his bucket rises with inexorable slowness.

'Coffee?' I ask. 'Or perhaps a cup of tea?'

'*Ah, non*,' he replies, horrified at the suggestion. 'I never stop.' It occurs to me that I have never known a British workman refuse a cup of tea. Ever.

After the first few buckets, however, Ducroux and I begin to chat. About life and work, and how it is all changing. And the chasm that divides us begins to narrow.

'*Oh là là là là*,' he says, before adding, for good measure: '*Oh là là là là là là*.' He shakes his head slowly, like Gaston at the water-trough. 'I've had a good life. But it's no wonder the young do not want to learn a trade any more.'

'I've heard that in France they all want to be civil servants,' I reply.

Ducroux laughs, and his eyes sparkle. 'Oh, I don't know about that,' he says. 'But they're all so busy sitting exams and amassing qualifications. What they don't have is *this*.' He holds out his hands, as if they were unconnected to him, and we both stare at them.

Two grey-white hands, encrusted with dried plaster. Two open palms, lined with age and experience and hard manual labour. Ten fingers, trembling ever so slightly, which tell more of a story than I could ever write.

Already feeling shabby and unworthy at having misjudged him, I ask Ducroux what he does when he is not working.

'I look after my grandchildren,' he says, his eyes twinkling at the thought. 'That's the greatest pleasure in the world. Do you have children, *monsieur*?'

'*Non*,' I reply, trying to imbue the word with as much neutrality as possible, hinting at neither regret nor relief.

'You will, if God wills it.'

And we stand in silence for a moment, thinking about this.

'I also fly microlights,' he adds at last, reading my thoughts. 'I share ownership of a ULM with René, who runs the *chambres d'hôtes* just up the road.'

'What, the one on the way to St Juste?' This must be Myriam's place, where I stayed on the last night of my old life, before I received the keys to La Folie. And dry-as-dust Ducroux is an aviator. Once again, I am lost for words; silenced by my own false assumptions.

By the time Monsieur Ducroux's work is finished, I have decided to increase his fee to seven hundred and fifty euros. But he will not hear of it.

'No, six hundred euros is all I will take.'

'At least let me pay you the seven hundred on which we agreed,' I beg. But he shakes his head.

'Six hundred euros is more than enough to live on. And perhaps we will meet in the air one day. I hope it will be as friends.'

'I hope so, too,' I reply, wringing my pathetically soft English hands. 'But you have worked so hard.'

He smiles at me. 'That is what it takes, *monsieur*.'

A few minutes later, the phone rings. It is Marie-Claude, my formidable cleaning lady, who has transformed my ramshackle French life by cleaning and polishing and scrub-bing the parts of La Folie that I didn't even know existed.

'*Monsieur Wright?*' she says, quietly.

'*Oui?*'

'*C'est pour vous annoncer que je ne viendrai plus.*'

Harrumph, she won't be coming tomorrow, I think to myself. And then the meaning of her words sinks in.

'You won't be coming any more? But why?'

'A lady in town has offered me extra hours with her.'

'But surely . . . ?'

'And so I had to cancel something else. *Et c'est vous . . .*' Her voice trails off.

For a moment I sit in silence, feeling like a marquee after a bunch of schoolboys have loosened all the guy-ropes.

Sacked by my own cleaning lady. People in the rue du Coq will point and stare. The check-out girls in Champion will be unable to serve me without giggling. I shall be blackbouled by the Pétanque Club. Even the Mushroom Society is liable to take a very dim view.

The truth is that Tuesday afternoons have become a high-light of my week. Marie-Claude's silent-but-deadly approach to cleaning has transformed my life like the mice in *The Tailor of Gloucester*. I would be lost without her.

More than this, Marie-Claude is one of the very few people in Jolibois who is not too polite to correct my French, subjunctives and all. I have learned many other things from her, too: that tomatoes should never be stored in the fridge, cabbages should be wrapped in foil, spiders are evil and *courants d'air* are deadly. She it was who told me how many hooks for brooms and mops I needed under the stairs, and just how ashamed I should be of the state of my flower beds. I have even become attached to her caustic generalizations about *les Anglais*. From her, I have learned that we are rude, thoughtless, talk too loudly and never say hello when enter-ing shops.

'Are you angry?' she asks, in a whisper.

'*Que . . . deçu*,' I reply, settling for merely disappointed, although devastated might be nearer the mark. I had grown accustomed to her face.

'*Déçu*,' she corrects me, emphasizing the acute accent.

I try to work out what I can have done wrong. True, La Folie was a shock to Marie-Claude when she first arrived, what with the spiders and everything. But she no longer goes through that whole eye-rolling, *ooh-là-là* performance with which she first demolished my pride in the place. Each week I would tell her how amazed I was with the miracle she had wrought, until she huffed '*c'est normal*' and that she distrusted compliments. So I stopped telling her.

Then there was the time I asked her to clean the *maison des amis* in midwinter, and she insisted on taking a thermometer with her. I thought she was just being flirtatious, but perhaps five degrees *is* a little chilly for dusting.

And I don't think she liked it when I teased her about her fixation with locking her car, even though La Folie is miles from the nearest car-thief. 'It's a good idea to lock it,' I told her, 'because I have been teaching the chickens how to drive.'

'*Ah, ça c'est l'humour anglais*,' she replied, doubtfully.

On the phone, today, there is another silence before she says, 'I can give you someone's name, if you want a replacement for me.'

'*Merci, je voudrais bien*,' I say, without conviction. I have never been on the rebound from a cleaning lady before.

And so, a week later, Pauline arrives, and I can tell immediately that this is going to hurt. Stocky, combative and with her mouth permanently set at twenty past eight, Pauline reminds me of a belligerent scrum-half outraged at being booked for dissent.

'*BONJOUR, MONSIEUR*,' she shouts, as if she were checking me into a retirement home.

'Marie-Claude used to vacuum first,' I murmur, coughing, as she lays waste to the floor of the *salon d'hiver* with a stiff broom.

'*JE NE SUIS PAS MARIE-CLAUDE,*' she yells at me, from the centre of a cat-hair dust-storm, three feet away. '*JE LE FAIS COMME ÇA.*'

I take a step back. I always thought it was an English speciality to shout at foreigners who are slow to understand, but Pauline demonstrates that it is international. 'That will be fine,' I say quietly.

With Marie-Claude, I sometimes barely noticed she was here, yet always I knew she had been. With Pauline, it is the other way round. She makes me long to hear the sweet sound of fingernails scraping down a blackboard. Strange, how the same vacuum-cleaner can sound so much noisier in someone else's hands.

'AM I BETTER THAN MARIE-CLAUDE?' she bellows, after her first visit.

'*Vous êtes . . . différente,*' I tell her, with a sigh, as I shut the front door behind her and lock it, twice.

There are some people who, when they leave a room, leave it feeling emptier. A tangible gap remains in the place where they once were, as if their absence has its own presence, like the hollowed-out spaces in the lava at Pompeii which map where people once were. The imprint of a head on a pillow; a leather seat-cushion, worn to a shine; a hat-stand flowering with the hats that an absent friend used to wear. And there are other people whose departure lights up a room, as a glow of peace and tranquillity descends like balm on the benighted air.

So it is in the silence after Pauline has left. Cat emerges from her hiding place upstairs, and the two of us sit staring at each other, wide-eyed, at the kitchen table.

I open a bottle of red wine and begin to slice an onion, because I am not sure what to have for supper, and this is usually a good place to start. But in the midst of slicing the onion, something unexpected takes place.

As I feel the knife-blade hissing through the translucent layers, and breathe its pungent zing, and blink, for my eyes are beginning to smart, I suddenly have one of those rare moments of preternatural clarity when things drop into place, as if all the melons or cherries on the reels of a slot-machine had suddenly fallen *click ... click ... click* into line. There is no bumper pay-out; no tinkling torrent of coins gushing into an open drawer. I simply feel, in this simple moment, an awakeness that transcends my standard daily torpor.

After I have sliced the onion in one direction, I turn it through ninety degrees, and – carefully holding all the slices together – cut it the other way. And a simple thought occurs to me.

*I am truly happy with my life. I do not need anyone else, for all my needs have been met. I can therefore stop searching, and seek instead to see what I can give.*

I sip my wine. The moment of presence has passed. But the imprint of the realization remains: I have crossed a bridge. I am ready to move on. I can finally stop looking for someone to fill the void that Clara Delaville and Ellen Gonn and Alice Melbury and Zara Malkin opened in my soft young heart, because I do not need anyone else to complete my life, after all.

# 8

## APRIL

At dawn or thereabouts, I am woken by the roar of an aircraft engine just outside my bedroom window. Not again. Stumbling downstairs in my pyjamas to investigate, I can see Monsieur Jadot's immense quad-bike parked just outside the back door.

Is today the day when we are finally going to plant vegetables; when I am to climb another rung on the ladder towards becoming a true *paysan* and cement my connection with the earth? Dashing back upstairs, I get dressed in yesterday's clothes, before heading outside to search for him. I know Jadot thinks I am lazy because I do not get up at six o'clock, and I also know that I am the only *Anglais* he has ever met. So I feel like an ambassador of sorts.

Ah, there he is: in the *potager* already, jaw set and shoulders hunched as he makes neat furrows with his *pioche*. And Madame is here, too, in her pleated skirt and pained smile, politely watching him. It occurs to me that I have never seen anyone using a mattock before, if we discount Grumpy and Sneezy, and people building railways in cowboy films. But Monsieur Jadot used to work as a ditch-clearer for the Jolibois public works department – I have looked up *cantonnier* in my dictionary – and he wields his magic wand with the precision of an artist, using every edge and surface of the *pioche* to dig, scrape, smooth and push the earth as if he were daubing paint on to a canvas. After two minutes, he has created a perfect *sillon* twenty feet long. It looks like a miniature Viking burial mound, or a barracks for moles.

'May I have a go?' I ask.

'You better had, because I might not be here next year,' he chuckles, with a wink at Madame that she pretends to ignore.

'Oh, are you thinking of moving abroad for a while?'

'That's right,' he says, tipping back the brim of his hat, and leaning on his mattock. 'To the cemetery.'

I feel as if a large black lorry has just pulled out into the road in front of me. Jadot seems too cheerful to be telling me about a terminal illness. I gamble that he is just indulging in some black humour, and smile at his joke. Gilles did warn me that he is a bit '*spécial*'.

'There's plenty of space there, you know,' he continues, cheerily.

'Enough for all of us, then.'

Jadot appears to find this uproariously funny, although not nearly as funny as my battle with his mattock. My laborious interpretation of a *sillon* resembles Mont St Michel after an earthquake.

'A little more practice required,' says Jadot, his eyes bright behind his grubby specs. 'Now, potatoes first,' he instructs, and I dutifully sprint up to the barn to bring back my three punnets of seed potatoes, already sprouting with noodle shoots.

He shows me how to make a hole for each potato with the butt of the mattock-shaft, and how to press each beige tuber into place, shoots upward, as gently as if it were a grenade. I still cannot imagine how these things are going to multiply.

But no matter: we are planting my first-ever crop of spuds, so I feel I must have grown in some way, even if my potatoes never do. Madame watches from a safe distance, at least until Jadot beckons her over with a shout.

'Here,' he says. 'You can sow the beans, while he does *les patates*.'

'But I want to learn about beans, too,' I protest, glancing up at Madame, who thanks me with a weary smile.

And so she and I follow Jadot as he uses his mattock to carve a line of perfect pockets in the soil, into each of which he bids us place a quartet of brown beans, glossy as cowrie shells, and to hide them from the birds with a scraping of earth.

Besides the beans and potatoes, we also plant onions, garlic, shallots, leeks, broccoli, cauliflowers, cabbages, peppers, aubergines, tomatoes, lettuces and melons. We sow green beans, white beans, carrots and radishes. But it is the spuds that really matter to me. I cannot wait to tell my mum.

Jadot looks at me blankly when I ask him the difference between sowing and planting. His expression is more shocked than pitying, as if I had just asked how to distinguish beef from beetroot. Call me a cucumber, but I never knew that sowing is what you do with a seed, and planting is what you do with something that is already small and green and leafy.

I see now why people say that gardening is time-consuming. I feel obliged to make regular trips to gaze at my furrows in awestruck wonder, as I wait for glory to sprout before my eyes. For secret treasures lie buried beneath this ploughed and planted soil like ghosts of the past; ancient artefacts, waiting to be rediscovered by an anorak with a watering-can. And still it requires an act of faith to believe in the transforming miracles that lie ahead. Mind you, even if nothing grows at all, I do at least have a trainee vegetable patch of which a man can feel almost proud at last.

*

The following afternoon, I am standing in silent admiration of my *potager* – which may have been created largely by Monsieur Jadot, but still feels like a perfect evocation of the rich new possibilities that have entered my life since I arrived at La Folie – when the phone rings in the house. I catch it on the sixth ring.

'Would that be you, Mike?' asks a deep growl.

'Blimey,' I pant. I'd recognize Survival-Kit Toby's voice anywhere. 'Toby Melbury, as I live and breathe.'

'Oh, you guessed,' he says, pretending to sound crest-fallen. 'You all right, mate? Any snake problems to report?'

Snake problems? But of course: it was Toby, the jungle specialist, whom I instinctively phoned when I found a viper wrapped around the bathroom taps in my first summer at La Folie.

'None recently,' I laugh. 'And if any come to call, you'll be the first to know.'

Toby is not one to phone simply for a chat and, sure enough, he comes straight to the point.

'Actually it's about my homesick little sister,' he says. 'Do you remember her stick-collecting at Windlesham?'

Alice Melbury. My heart misses a beat, although I am not about to give Toby any inkling of that.

'Of course I do. Why?' How odd to be talking about Alice Melbury on the telephone of a ramshackle farmhouse in the middle of darkest France, all these years after our last, disastrous meeting in Sloane Square. Even now, when I revisit London, I cannot ride the District and Circle line westbound from Victoria without the twitch of a cringe at the memory.

At Windlesham, in my early rustic phase, Toby and I built camps together in the woods, using branches and bits of old timber that we persuaded his little sister to run and fetch for us. Alice was only nine, and we were both almost thirteen, so she was desperate to be included, a little girl in a red velvet hairband and a dimpled smile, puffing and panting as she trotted up with another armful of sticks, little imagining that we would never let her into our camp, once it was built.

What Toby does not know about is the torch I carried for his sister for years, smitten as I was by the dazzling creature she had turned out to be; about the number of times I sat flicking through the pages of my address book, daring myself to telephone her, and never quite summoning up the courage to do so, just in case Toby answered; about the time I did finally telephone her, and then spent the rest of my twenties regretting it.

'It's just that she's learning to fly, and doesn't really know any other pilots. So I thought of you. I think she's finding it hard to land the thing, or something. Would you mind if she emailed you?'

'It would be a pleasure,' I reply, my mind whirring.

So Alice Melbury is learning how to fly. I shall not forget my own struggle to land a plane, when I was a student pilot myself: that sensation that my brain was melting; its over-worked neurones short-circuiting in a shower of sparks, as I struggled again and again to bring down a small plane that would respond to a command only after it was already too late, and gave no hint of wanting to return to earth. And then it would suddenly change its mind, belly-flopping on to the runway with a frightful bump, and a stereo yelp of alarm.

I remember, too, how it helped to know that I was not alone. I met a girl called Flying Helene at my Florida flying-school; a pretty civil servant who had mortgaged her future for the sake of bumping a rusty Cessna 150 around the circuit at Kissimmee, and who was just as tormented by the nightmare of trying to land the beast as I was. Both of us had young Indian instructors with a disarming habit of murmuring prayers to themselves as we descended on short-final for another bash on the tarmac. In the evenings, our brains fried, we would sit and commiserate with each other over supper and a Budweiser about how hard it all was. And even now, I feel as if it was Helene who, by keeping me sane with her vegetarian chilli and her cheerful tales of aerial disaster narrowly averted, really taught me how to fly. True, my landings are still a long way short of perfect. But I do not tell Toby that.

'You're a pal, Michael. Thanks.'

As soon as I have put the phone down, I email Flying Helene, whom I have not thought about for months. It would fun to see her again, so I invite her to come and stay at La Folie. And, two days later, an email arrives from Alice Melbury.

I stare at the name in my inbox: Alice Melbury, the little girl who came up with the worst knock-knock joke of all time. Alice Melbury, with whom I rode the ghost train on Brighton Pier, when Toby invited me on a rare day-out from our boarding school. Together he and I raced up to our dorm to change after Sunday-morning chapel, and then waited excitedly to be picked up from the wooden benches outside the front door, en route to the Big Wide World.

I remember that Toby's mum came to meet us in a rented car that smelt of carpets, and that she seemed rather cross about something, although I never found out what it was. I didn't mind that she wasn't *my* mum, or that she was cross. I could tell that she was kind, too, and at least she was somebody's mum, and I wasn't spending another Sunday at the half-deserted school with all the other left-over children whom nobody had come to fetch. Here was a chance to break out of the bubble; to explore the universe beyond. And from the moment we drove out of the school's towering front gates, we were in unknown territory; excitingly abroad. Nowhere was more exciting than Brighton Pier, with its grubby penny arcade and its rickety old funfair.

Toby and I went on the bumper cars, while Alice rode with her mum. After that, we slid down the helter-skelter on doormats, and span the tea-cups until we were dizzy, and staggered across the wobbly floors of the haunted house. And then there was just the ghost train, and the man said that all three of us could ride in one car. So Alice clambered in to sit in front of me, almost on my lap, and the safety-bar came down and the siren hooted, and we went clattering and jerking through the saloon doors into the dark. I cannot say if there was a spider in a cotton-wool web, or a skull that glowed, or a plastic skeleton jiggling on an elastic rope. All I remember is that I was almost alone with Alice Melbury. And it felt special and beautiful and precious until – wham – the saloon doors shot open again, and the three of us rattled laughing and blinking and squinting into the sunlight as if we had just come out of the best film in the world.

'Was it awful?' asked Toby's mum, grinning at us.

'Yes!' we lied.

Several years later, Alice Melbury was one of the handful of names with an asterisk beside it in my blue-and-yellow-striped address book: Especially Desirable Girls to be invited on dates in moments of unusual fearlessness brought on by extreme desperation. And when I finally summoned up the nerve to phone her, I discovered that the gap between her quicksilver urban sassiness and my bookish suburban plod was so yawning an abyss that even the things we had in common – such as her brother, and Windlesham – seemed far less significant than our differences. She was cool; I was square. And that was it.

I open the email. I do not know what I was expecting to read, but it was not this: the homesick little girl who used to pick up sticks for us is working in Baltimore. She has now metamorphosed into an intensive-care nurse in one of the top hospitals in America, and is learning to fly a

Cessna 172 in her spare time. She sounds scarier than ever.

'I think you must be the only pilot I know, so I thought you might understand,' she writes. 'Send flying stories when you have a moment.'

I open a bottle of Kronenberg from the fridge, to savour the beautiful strangeness of the moment. The small, square choirboy whom Alice once knew, with his collar-length hair, tinted NHS specs and brown 1970s flares, and his nose buried in a book of Latin and Greek irregular verbs, is now a small, square trainee peasant with sheep and chickens and manly power-tools, gazing out from a ramshackle farmhouse on the side of a French hill that local people call the end of the world. Strange, that my childhood should have tracked me down, here at *le bout du monde*, all these years since I threw those hateful flares into the bin.

So I reply, telling her about my Luscombe, and about how I would like to follow my friend Jethro into aerobatics. As I write, I keep trying to stop myself thinking about that night when Alice and I finally went on a date together. I can feel myself beginning to blush, even as I suppress the snapshot images that flood my brain. Don't think about that now: the cringe-factor is too great. And besides, there are more important things to consider, such as how to judge your height above the runway in the final seconds before touch-down, and the perils of porpoising as a result of pilot-induced oscillation. More important still: out in the *potager*, the first weeds have begun to appear.

These sneaky interlopers look just like neophyte vegetables to me, but Monsieur Jadot sets me straight: action is required. And the French don't go in for anything as weedy as weeding. Here, you rip out the naughty grasses, which is a far more tough and manly pursuit.

Obeying orders, I rip out the naughty grasses; every last one of the blighters. It takes me almost three hours to finish the job. And Monsieur Jadot says I haven't finished yet. He says I must do this *every day*. I think Monsieur Jadot is having a laugh. Nevertheless, I begin to have a quick rip three times a day, so as to give the naughty grasses no respite. And for the first week at least, I appear to have the rascals on the back foot.

'How much should I pay you?' I ask Jadot as he climbs into his van one day.

He recoils from the question like a snail prodded by a toddler with a twig. I suspect I could not have wounded him more had I asked if he were from Paris.

'Do you think it was for this that I chose to help?' he asks, a cloud passing across his habitually sunny expression.

'No, no, I know it was done out of kindness and neighbourliness,' I reply. 'But even so . . .'

'You do realize, don't you, that there are still people who do things with no thought of reward or recompense?' He pauses. 'Not many of us, admittedly. But we do still exist.'

'I'm sorry, I'm so sorry. Thank you. I just wish there were something I could give you in return.'

'*Bof*,' he says, scanning my property with his gaze. Now I am worried he may ask me for Gaston. Or Martha, perhaps, whose limp has almost gone. But, to my surprise, Jadot suddenly points at the rusted, twisted agricultural roller I discovered months ago, when I hacked my way through the rainforest of brambles outside the chicken house. '*Ça*,' he declares. 'Do you want it?'

This would be an easy question, if only I had not inherited my father's hoarding gene. In Dad's case, this means that all mechanical detritus that might – just conceivably – prove useful in the future must be squirrelled away in the garage, where his treasures include several boxes of electrical fuses from the 1950s, assorted bakelite handles, various curtain-tracks, two partially dismantled Goblin Radio Teasmades and enough misshapen pieces of timber to build a passable replica of a Viking longship. 'Everything comes in useful in the end,' my father likes to declare whenever my mother threatens to tidy him up. I am not quite that bad, but still struggle to throw things away, especially if they are connected with ex-girlfriends or aviation. Nevertheless, gritting my teeth, today I shake my head.

'In that case, may I have it?' Jadot grins. 'I need a roller for my field.'

I look again at the rust-encrusted object, which looks as if it has been dragged up off the *Mary Rose*. Is he serious? From the way Jadot strokes the venerable object like a favourite labrador, I think he must be.

'You're missing a wooden steering-bar.' He points to a rusted socket on top of the roller. 'Have you got it some-where?'

I pat my pockets. No, I don't think I have. Perhaps the roller is an old friend from his childhood, I muse; from that time when he used to hide from the storms at La Folie. I know how it tugs at the heart to rediscover something you thought you had lost a long time ago.

Days pass; days of weeding and waiting and watching things grow. In learning to grow my own vegetables, I am learning something for the first time. Yet I have the strangest sense that I am simply re-learning how to do something that I must have known all along.

Take potato plants, which I never even knew existed. Here they are before me: dark green leaves, each the shape of a spade on a playing card, nestling in a tight crown on the surface of the soil. Large fries, coming up. How many other people, I wonder, have gone through life without ever having watched a potato grow?

Alice Melbury writes again, to tell me that her flying-school is close to Chesapeake Bay, at an aerodrome shared with the military. 'The naval cadets here are soloing in about two minutes, which makes me feel hopelessly slow at times.'

I know the feeling: according to his log-book, my grand-father, Pa, flew solo in an unstable Tiger Moth after about five hours' training in 1938. It took me a plodding twenty-five hours to achieve the same feat, sixty years on, despite days of intensive flying lessons in a docile spam-can about as twitchy as the *Queen Mary*. And hundreds more hours after that, before I felt confident enough to launch a Tiger Moth into a spin above the white cliffs of Dover myself.

At the end of the email, I smile. For here is a line which I have been quietly hoping to read: 'It would be lovely to see you in France, and meet your plane one day.'

And so our correspondence begins, and Alice and I write to each other about how hard it is to land until you get the knack; about carburettor icing, and spin recoveries, and the differences between learning to fly in America and Europe. I learned to fly in America myself, sweating on the apron of an aerodrome near Disney World as I did my pre-flight checks on a Piper Warrior whose cockpit was so hot that you could have baked bread in it. I remember doing my best to keep my legs, white as Wensleydale, in shadow under the wings, to spare them the furnace intensity of the Florida sun. They called this learning to fly; it felt like learning to fry.

We write about England, too, and how much we miss the feeling of home, 'wherever home is', as Alice puts it. I tell her about Phoebe Yates's marriage next month, and how much I am looking forward to seeing the Devon countryside, rather than simply revisiting the seething cauldron of London.

'God, I miss London,' she writes, one day. 'I came to Baltimore because my boyfriend lives here, but I was born and bred in Islington, so I suppose it's in my blood. Do send my love to the place, when you're passing through.'

I sip my Pastis, and allow myself time to digest this news. Fortunately, I had not allowed myself to dream of a long-distance romance. No, I have no illusions about the fact that

I crashed and burned with Alice Melbury almost twenty years ago, on a long evening that made me realize that the simple fact of finding someone devilishly attractive is not a recipe for a delightful dénouement. And she, on the receiving end of my clumsy, post-adolescent admiration, undoubtedly felt the same.

A day later, and Monsieur Jadot returns, perched on the bicycle seat of his ancient tractor. He appears to be carrying Madame over his shoulder. And then I see that his burden is in fact a stout tree-branch, roughly hewn. Looking at the tractor, I can see why Jadot wants my ancient roller. The rusted fossil will make his smoke-belching transport look almost up-to-date.

'Are you sure that's a good idea?' I shout, over the sound of the engine, as he wedges one end of the tree-branch into a barnacled socket on top of the roller, drills a bolt through it, and attaches the other end to the back of his tractor.

'Of course,' he yells. 'It's acacia. Very strong. Won't break.'

His house is two miles up the road. And he wants to drag an eighty-year-old horse-drawn roller up there, crunching along on a pair of hand-made iron wheels, attached to his ancient tractor by a tree-branch. When I am old, I hope I meet more people like Monsieur Jadot, and fewer people like myself.

Chickens scarper in all directions as Jadot heads off in a cloud of dust and smoke. The noise is incredible, like a suit of armour being chewed up by an escalator. I hold my breath, barely able to watch. The wheels of the chariot waggle and wobble as they bump over the rocky drive.

But the thing holds. Part of me wants to cheer and laugh out loud. And part of me is silenced by the nobility of the scene: by the sight of this gentle old peasant atop his medieval tractor, dragging away a lump of machinery that I had written off as a broken relic, but which for him is filled with usefulness and life. I cannot help feeling a sense of awe at Jadot's faith and ingenuity. And my father is right: everything does come in useful, in the end.

# 9

## MAY

Dangerous as it feels to turn my back on the naughty grasses, even for a couple of nights, today I am back in Britain for the weekend, driving down to Devon to play the organ for Phoebe Yates's wedding. And England feels like another country.

I am struck by the gentleness of the road-signs pointing the way to Exeter. That lower-case, primary-school font is somehow friendlier and more mellow than the shouted, hectoring capitals of French signs. But English driving is terrifying: I feel as if I am in a video-game. And then I remember that I should really be driving on the left, and this helps.

At the motorway services, I begin to question English washing-powder. Most young women appear to be wearing shrunken T-shirts that do not quite reach their trousers, exposing the blue-whiteness of their doughy midriffs to the chill morning breeze. This worries me. Have English girls not heard of the dangers posed by *courants d'air* of which Frenchwomen live in mortal fear?

On hot days, I leave the doors open at La Folie to allow a breeze to circulate. But never on Tuesdays, when Shouty Pauline comes to clean. Shouty Pauline will not work in a *courant d'air*, even when the sun is shining. It is just too risky. The only reason she would expose her midriff on a chilly day would be a suicide bid.

By the time I have driven past all the shops selling karma crystals in Totnes and reach Dartington, I am getting used to England again. It seems only natural that there should be a bald man, stripped to the waist, practising his t'ai-chi in the church car park. And when a shiny convertible draws up and a Bunterish fellow in shades and tweeds leaps out, I am quite prepared to hear that he has come to feng shui the flowers.

'Hello,' he booms. 'I'm the vicar.'

If England has changed since I have been away, the little church at Dartington remains just as the Victorians left it. The air still smells of hymn books. Sunlight still streams through stained glass on to oak pews worn smooth by the buttocks of generations of parishioners, all wondering how much longer the sermon will last.

An elegant lady in a straw hat is arranging flowers in a vase. I want to believe that she has been standing there, lit by that sunbeam, for a hundred years.

'Hello, you must be Michael,' she says, smiling.

'Have we . . . have we met?' Don't tell me she is the local medium.

'I'm the bride's mother. Phoebe's told me all about you. How are the sheep?'

'Golly,' I reply.

No disrespect to Cat, but I had almost forgotten what a relief it is to be *expected*. Whenever I arrive at Limoges airport – at any airport, actually – I always scan the waiting faces and look for someone holding up a sign with my name on it, just in case. But there is never anybody there. And now here is this beautiful lady, and she knew I was coming.

After a quick music rehearsal with Gavin the trumpeter, I don my one-and-only suit, pleased to find that the moths of La Folie have yet to develop a taste for English wool. No one wears a suit in Jolibois except the man who stands in the doorway of the suit shop at the top of the rue du Coq, glum as a mannequin.

And then the church is filling up, and the bride enters to the strains of me straining to play the 'Arrival of the Queen of Sheba'. The organ's radiating pedal-board, shaped like a fan, feels alarmingly different from the grid-iron on which I have practised in Jolibois. My feet are all over the shop. No wonder Phoebe, reaching the altar, looks set to burst into tears. Gavin the Trumpet, sitting just below me in the choir-stalls, turns and gives me a worried smile.

But there is no time for self-recrimination, as the vicar is already announcing the first hymn: 'Dear Lord and Father of Mankind'. Though I am concentrating hard on playing the right notes, I sing along, too, grateful that Mr Charles the headmaster made me learn all the words as a punishment after he caught me snogging Amelia Blunt in the language lab at Windlesham. Forgive our foolish ways . . .

And then a supermodel in a gold silk dress is reading the lesson, and I am flicking through *Hymns Ancient and Modern* all in a palaver, because the next hymn is 'Love Divine, All Loves Excelling', there are two tunes, and I forgot to ask Phoebe which one she wants.

'Does any man know of any lawful impediment why these two should not be married?' declares the vicar.

Amid the awesome silence, I clear my throat. In front of me, Gavin the Trumpet flinches.

'It's not a *huge* problem. But I am a bit worried about the next hymn.'

This is what I want to say. But I am distracted by two swallows that have flown into the church, and miss my chance. Phoebe throws me a nervous glance.

'How does "Love Divine" go, Gavin?' I whisper, leaning forward to show him the two tunes in *Hymns Ancient and Modern*.

He hums a snippet of the one I first thought of. So that settles it.

'We now sing the hymn "Love Divine, All Loves Excelling",' declares Rev. Bunter, and – deep breath – I launch into the introduction and wait for the singing to start. Except that it isn't singing at all. It is that strange mumbling drone that people make when they are trying to join in with the sound of someone else's childhood, and don't know how it goes.

'I think it was the other one,' whispers Gavin over his shoulder, helpfully. I dare not look up, for fear of being struck down by Phoebe's flashing glare.

And then everything changes. For now the Rev. Bunter is leading the bride and groom through their vows, and I feel transported by the perfect Englishness of this scene, in which two young lovers promise to have and to hold one another in a sunlit country church, while a pair of swallows flits amid the roof timbers, a trumpet soars over 'Praise My Soul the King of Heaven' – the singing raucous as a rugby crowd, Gavin's cheeks purple with the joy of blasting it to the rafters like a burnished sunbeam – and nubile damsels in straw hats and summer dresses quicken the pulses of strapping young men in rented morning suits, so that they, too, may be standing before an altar next year.

I had begun to doubt that such an England still existed; feel proud and deeply heartened that it does. La Folie is a thousand billion miles away as, in the midst of everything, the red, white and blue sallies of the bell-ropes suddenly fly skywards in the tower, and a jangling peal of bells rings out across the countryside: out, out over the churchyard and Tor and Phoebe smiling with relief; out over the fields and the children playing cricket and the ruminations of the black-and-white cows; out over the friendly road-signs and the dangerously bare midriffs, and on, on, towards France, where sometimes I miss England so much that it hurts.

*

On the flight from London Stansted to Limoges, people are exchanging worried glances. The pilot has already announced that we will be routing around the thunderstorms in our path. Now flickers and flashes begin to illuminate the horizon like distant artillery, the fasten-seatbelts signs light up with a ping, the aircraft shivers and lurches, and the stewardesses park their buffet trolleys to sit out the buffeting.

'You think we crash?' asks the French girl next to me, in English. We are sitting in one of the emergency-exit rows. Slim and chiselled in a white lace cardigan, she looks old for her youth; her skin sallow, her fingers yellowed with nicotine.

'No, absolutely not,' I reply. 'The plane is very strong. It is used to this.' Even so, I glance up at the red handle of the emergency exit; remind myself to pull the door inwards, rather than shoving it outwards, if I must.

Suddenly the plane bucks beneath us, then drops like a brick, checks itself – *oof* – and all the lights go out. There are a few muffled shouts of protest before the lights come on again, and the noisy silence returns. But the atmosphere has changed. I glance at one of the stewardesses in her jump-seat, and she is no longer joshing with her colleague. Tight-lipped, I can see her eyes darting as she runs through the training she never expected to have to use.

'You are not fearing?' whispers the French girl.

I shake my head, and smile. I have frightened myself in aircraft before, certainly. But only when I am at the controls; only when I know that I am on the outside edge of my own competence and the aircraft's ability to stay in the air. Lost in clag, inbound to Chartres. Whipping a Tiger Moth into a spin, and sensing for one alarming moment that it may flip inverted. Hearing the overheated engine of my Luscombe labour, as a tree-lined ridge looms to meet us. Here, in this computer-controlled cigar – the fastest way to a place called

Abroad, as Miss Dembinska once told me – there is so little I can do to affect my fate that I cannot find it in myself to feel afraid.

'This is normal?' asks the girl, eyes wide, as we rock from side to side and, with a hefty clunk, the undercarriage drops into place on final approach.

'Quite normal,' I reply, and feel her hand slide into mine. It feels cold and wet with perspiration.

'And this?' There is a sudden roar as the pilot adds a burst of power. We must be coming down too fast.

'Still good,' I nod, giving her hand a squeeze. Now the pilot reduces power and we hang in the air for a second, with the blue runway lights flashing past us. I hold my breath; can almost hear Anand, my old flying-instructor, yelling 'Sinking! Sinking! Sinking!' a split second before there comes a hell of a bang, several of the overhead lockers fly open, and we are down.

'This normal, also?'

'It is for this airline,' I chuckle. I can't wait to tell Alice about that arrival. The French girl smiles at me, embarrassed, as I gently release my hand from her rictus grip. 'Thank you,' she says, wiping her palm on her cardigan.

As I emerge from the baggage hall at Limoges, I scan the faces of friends and relatives waiting for their loved ones to arrive, just in case someone is here for me. Cat, for example. For a second these strangers smile back at me, and then – like bored television viewers, channel-surfing with the remote control – their attention flicks to the next trolley that comes clattering through the sliding doors, like one of the skull-shaped cars emerging from a fairground ghost train.

I feel a tug on my arm, and the French girl is smiling beside me.

'*Maman*, this is the kind man I told you about.' I shake hands with her mother, and mumble a greeting.

'What a relief to hear someone speaking French,' replies *Madame*, in a whisper. 'I was starting to think I was in London.'

English thunderstorms used to make me want to stand outside, just for the hell of it. The French equivalent makes me want to dive for cover. The one waiting for me outside the airport terminal is the full King Lear: the sky lit up with shafts of burning magnesium; the thunder exploding with the roar of a bunker-buster aimed straight at the front door. So much rain has already fallen in such a short time, gushing off the roof in torrents, that I could swear the drive up to La Folie is steeper tonight than it was before I went away.

The house is in complete darkness. Strange. I know I left various lights on when I left, and that Monsieur Jadot – who promised to feed the cat, the Egg Squad and the Rastafarians – specifically requested not to be entrusted with a key.

Telling myself not to be afraid, and almost managing to comply, I tiptoe and stumble into the black silence. I am not too bothered about the contents of the freezer as I flick blindly at the switches on the fuse-box, but I cannot help clenching my fist and letting out a 'yes!' of pleasure at discovering that my wireless modem has – against the odds – not been fried.

As I fire up my PC, I open a bottle of red wine, hack myself some bread and Camembert, and sit and reflect on why it should matter so much, now that I am home, whether an intensive-care nurse in Baltimore should have sent me a message or not. Alice Melbury has a boyfriend, lives three thousand miles away, and the chances of any romantic interest between us conclusively fizzled almost two decades ago, when Jean Anouilh was still alive, Rick Astley was almost hip, Pat Cash was Wimbledon champion, Mathias Rust had only just landed his Cessna 172 in Red Square, British Airways was still rejecting female pilots and the drilling of the Channel Tunnel had yet to begin.

Nevertheless, I cannot help feeling a flutter of pleasure whenever I see her name on my screen; a glimmer of brightness amid an inbox black with spam.

I take a sip of wine and glance at the message she has sent today.

From: Alice Melbury
To: Michael Wright
Monday, 16th May
I'm coming home in July to see my family, and Toby said he and I should come and see you at La Folie. We wouldn't stay with you, but in a local B&B if there is one. It would just be a couple of days, as I haven't got much time. But perhaps you'll be away then?
Love A XX

After reading this message twice, I take another sip of wine. I wander to the back door; gaze out at the storm. But the sky has already cleared, and there is a bright moon glittering on the wet earth. Unscrewing my oil lamp, I light the wick with a match and wander outside to shut up the Egg Squad for the night.

It really doesn't bother me, either way, whether Alice and her brother come to visit me at La Folie, I think to myself, swinging my lamp, my boots squishing on the muddy earth. And then, with a hot flush of embarrassment, I think back to our date in Sloane Square. Not just the vague, cringing outline of that forgettable night, but the indelible details I have tried to forget. I groan, aloud. In the chicken house, my familiars blink back at me from their twin perches, one above the other, nervous and expectant as if they were waiting for their starter for ten on *University Challenge*. No, I decide, as I slide shut the bolt on the chicken-house door: their visit will not affect me in the least.

Wednesday, 23 September 1987. In China they were said to be watching a solar eclipse, but I remember the evening sky was as murky as an old milk bottle as I left the four-square Georgian house in Vauxhall where my parents lived, just beside the old Unigate Dairies factory. How invincible I felt in my grey winklepickers, my corduroy drainpipes and a dark grey bomber-jacket covered in straps, my latest mistake from Mr Byrite at Oxford Circus.

No one could touch me as I danced across the football-pitch-wide junction that funnels the stream of vehicles entering the metropolis from the south. The streetlamps were haloed with yellow mist, and the sky glowed faded orange, like a sunrise glimpsed through the canvas of a dirty tent. It is a four-minute walk to the tube station from here, but that night it took me three, because my whole life was ahead of me, and tonight I was going on a date with the irresistible Alice Melbury, whom I had known since I was twelve years old.

The trees in Sloane Square looked gnarled and ghostly, and there was a neon glow above the gold awnings of the Oriel Café: *Breaking the Code*, starring Derek Jacobi, was playing at the Royal Court. Inside, a waitress showed me to a table in the middle of the black-and-white marble floor.

'Are you eating?' she asked, bored.

'Probably,' I replied, before glancing down at the prices on the menu. 'Not.'

And then Alice Melbury arrived, and she was all powdered and beautiful, with a smoky catch in her voice and hair as glossy as a brand-new LP. I felt my legs wobble as I kissed her hello.

Alice was not like the girls I had met in my first year at university, with their denim jackets and their defiantly greasy hair. No, she was already the finished article, even though she was only seventeen, in a charcoal skirt and tights, and a cream cashmere jumper that caressed her curves. I felt like I had won the pinball high-score: a date in Sloane Square with the girl of my dreams. At least until all my confidence went rolling away from me, like a pocketful of marbles spilled on the black-and-white checkerboard floor.

Just be yourself, I told myself. But it's so hard to be yourself with someone else, when all you can think about is the tragic unlikelihood of a snog.

'Right, what shall we have?' giggled Alice, grabbing the menu with a playful light in her eyes. And from that moment on, I was running to keep up: pressing too hard with my questions; trying too hard with my jokes.

We drank cold white wine; smoked too many Marlboro Lights. Alice was into the B-52s, she said, and I thought she meant Boeing Stratofortresses. No, it's a band, she said. So I told her I was into Wagner, expecting her to be impressed. And she pretended she was, which made it worse.

She was a natural-born princess, skiffling along on a cloud of her own unforced charm; winking at the waitress; pretending not to notice me bumming another cigarette. And I sat there like a peasant, fixated on her dazzling eyes and lip-glossed lips, trying not to let my gaze stray south. For all I could think was: what do I have to do to get closer to this girl than that cream cashmere jumper and charcoal skirt are right now? How do I break the code?

Alice said we should split the bill, and I was too young to know that this was a bad sign. It was beyond me to twig that, with no chemistry between us, the chances of anything physical or biological happening were nil. Lust is blind. I knocked over a glass as we rose to go.

No nightingale sang as we stepped out into Sloane Square, shivering at the nip in the ten o'clock air. I tried to put my arm round her. She froze. And still I persuaded myself that if I could just manoeuvre us into the vicinity of a bedroom, this princess for whom I had yearned might drag me in there and ravish me. I was far too ashamed of my own lust to dream of making the first move.

Neither of us had eaten, and we were both too broke to

do so in Chelsea; two glasses of wine each had cleaned us out. She needed to head north, back to Islington; I back to Vauxhall, south of the river. Yet I urged her to come back to my parents' house with me, for something to eat, and she was too polite to say no. So we sat swaying on the tube, staring up at the notches on the yellow line as we thundered to Victoria, and then at the notches on the blue line, as we rattled south through Pimlico to Vauxhall.

I tried to take her hand as we ran across the football pitch of the seven-lane junction, dodging the night buses, but she was too quick for me. We tiptoed into Grove House, where my parents and my brothers were sleeping upstairs. And then we stood in the kitchen eating jam sandwiches. God knows what Alice Melbury thought we were doing there, whispering in the dark. I waited for her to give me a sign. She waited for me to drive her home.

So we drove all the way back to Islington in my 2CV, and we had to grind out small-talk for another half an hour. I think it ran out around Blackfriars. We had already established that what we had in common was not enough for two hours in a wine bar, let alone a tube ride, jam sandwich and car journey home.

In Belitha Villas, she leant across to peck me on the cheek and leapt out of the 2CV like a kidnap victim, without so much as a see-you-around. I watched her walk into number three, betting myself that she would turn around to wave. And she never did.

A week after playing the organ for Phoebe's wedding, and my return to La Folie, I am standing in my wellies and the warm fug of Gilles's shearing barn in St Sornin-les-Combes, just opposite the perfectly manicured garden of Monsieur Boudin, a retired soldier. It is hard to imagine how this place must have looked when it belonged to Ralph the artist and Olga the spy, in the days when they were still having their bash at being trainee peasants like me, rather than centrally heated townies in the heart of Jolibois.

Today, we are shearing sheep. Actually, Gilles's regular shearers, Cool Hand Luke (whose real name is Fabrice) and a fleshy, red-faced ox of a man, are shearing sheep. Hubert, a kindly old shepherd with a face like the Pyrenees, is picking out each victim from the baying mêlée for his strapping son to manhandle into the barber's chair. And the funny *Anglais* is scrabbling around on all fours, gathering the wool. My job today is also to make sure that none of the sheep leap over the fence into Monsieur Boudin's perfect garden.

After last year's sheep-shearing, I received a rare compliment from Gilles.

'Not everyone takes so much trouble over gathering the wool, Michael,' he told me. 'And you were particularly good at removing the poo.'

'*Merci, Gilles*. That's one of the nicest things anyone's ever said to me.'

Glowing with pride, I asked him how he felt about promoting me to the altogether more tough and manly job of manhandling the sheep this year. I had a feeling that wool-gathering was for wimps.

I now see that this was me thinking like a rat-racing townie, more interested in promotions and proofs of manhood than on getting a job done. Since then, I have spent another twelve months alone on my desolate hillside, chopping wood in the darkness to keep out the cold, watching animals dying and animals being born, trudging a mile into town to buy a loaf of bread when the car was snowed in. I have watched the locals living simply on very little, each content to make their small contribution, gruffly content with their lot. I am not aware of having changed, especially, beyond my new-found acceptance of living my life alone, and of not needing anyone else to make me happy any more.

But when Gilles asked me what job I would like at this year's shearing, I found myself saying that I should like to gather the wool, after all.

Rain is lashing from the sky again, so Gilles has shut up all his sheep in various barns within a half-mile radius, like troops billeted on a town.

'I bet it's hard to get started, isn't it?' I ask, as we stand in the shearing barn, contemplating the day ahead. The two shearers are grimacing out at the rain streaming off the roof. Shearers hate bad weather, partly because wet sheep do not shear well, and partly because the men shearing them have a nasty habit of being electrocuted during thunderstorms.

'Until you find your rhythm, yes,' says Cool Hand Luke, sucking on a roll-up. His eyes look weary, and the creases on his face do not match his smile.

'It's always harder without the sun,' adds the burly ox, whose mane of grey hair somehow makes me think of Odysseus.

And then we are off. With a sigh and a muttered *allez*, old Hubert uses his crook to hook the first animal by the leg, and the barn is filled with the buzz of the shears.

Gilles says sheep are stupid animals, unlike cows which – he assures me – understand French. But this is not my experience of my Ouessants. People misjudge sheep because they are easily frightened and do not like to make their own decisions. I have just scraped a fleece up off the shearing-rug, and am pulling the warm *crottes* of dark-green poo from its edges with my fingers when, out of the corner of my eye, I see Hubert's son Manu do something unexpected. He punches the struggling ewe he is holding – hard – in the face. And then he laughs, grinning at his father.

'What the hell are you doing?' I shout, racing over to Manu.

He grins back at me, nonplussed.

'It's so unnecessary,' I continue. 'You're bigger and stronger than them, so why do you have to hit them?'

Manu shrugs and stares at his feet. Everyone else becomes very silent. I have, I think, crossed a line. But it is not always easy to see where the lines are drawn when you live in a foreign country.

Every couple of hours, Gilles and I trudge off up the hill with his dog, Rose, to fetch another fifty-odd animals. The sheep come trotting down the road behind their master's chest-out strut, with Rose and the funny Englishman bringing up the rear. Meanwhile Hubert and the shearers wait at the bottom, to herd them into the barn. But when we are all feeling mellowed and strengthened by a lunch of *gigot d'agneau* and men's wine at the Moulin Vaugelade, and there are just eighteen ewes left in a distant field to shear, Gilles announces that he will bring them down by himself.

During the hiatus, the shearers oil and clean the combs of their shears, and I chat with them in the fetid shadows of the barn.

'It must be a tough life for you,' I say.

'Earth is not hell,' shrugs Cool Hand Luke, smiling. '*Et je gagne ma vie.*' I have heard this expression often in France, usually accompanied by a shrug that combines pride, humility and acceptance. I earn my living, is what we'd say in English. But I prefer the literal translation: I win my life.

'Many shearers are city people who wanted something different,' adds the burly ox. 'Like this, we are free.'

'And today we ate a good lunch,' adds his comrade, smiling.

Too late, as I stand day-dreaming in the shade of the barn, wondering how long it will be before I can go home and check my emails, I hear the rattle of hooves on the road outside. Oh, lordy. And I'm meant to be out there, beneath the storm-clouds. There is only old Hubert to stop the sheep from galloping off down the road to Jolibois or – worse –

leaping over the neatly trimmed hedge into Monsieur Boudin's garden. Best to stay out of sight, and hope that Hubert prevails.

Cool Hand Luke's puppy, a vicious-looking ball of fluff roughly the size of a gerbil, who is tied up just outside the barn, now begins to bark. Up until now, he and Rose were almost beginning to make me think that maybe dogs aren't so bad, after all. But not any more. The eighteen terrified sheep, who do not wish to spend their afternoon at the *coiffeur* after all, scarper on past the barn, and off in the direction of Paris. And the noble Hubert, no spring chicken and a stout carl for the nones, lumbers off in hot pursuit. This is a sight to gladden the heart. Even from behind, I sense Hubert's amusement at the ridiculousness of it all, as he does his best to catch up with the galloping escapees and his lost youth. Arms flailing, head tipped back, our man's running style reminds me of Eric Liddell in *Chariots of Fire*. It's just that his dungarees are several times bigger, and you could safely time him over the 110-yard dash with a sundial.

'Aren't you going to help the old man?' murmurs a voice behind me, and I turn to see Cool Hand Luke's sly grin, framed by a smoke ring he has just blown at me.

Hubert is puffing like a steam train by the time I overtake him at a sprint. Wellies flapping, I race in a wide arc around the eighteen sheep so as to head them off in the trees. A couple of minutes later, the pair of us are herding them back towards the barn, exchanging grins of relief at a disaster narrowly averted, when Cool Hand Luke's puppy suddenly starts shrieking again. For a second the sheep stand motionless, ears pricked. And then, with the hideous rending sound of an inlaid wardrobe being crushed by a hippo, they all pile over – or through – Monsieur Boudin's beautiful hedge.

Within seconds, Boudin's neatly clipped topiary is toast. Next comes the lawn: smooth as a snooker table one moment, ravaged as Biggin Hill after a Stuka attack the next.

This must be how the place looked when Ralph and Olga lived here with all their cats. And then come the flower beds. Oh God, not the flower beds. No, today the flowers are spared, because the Jolibois Eighteen have already spotted the young lettuces in Monsieur Boudin's vegetable patch. I cannot look. I feel like Joyce Grenfell watching a riot at St Trinian's. In the door of the shearing-barn, Cool Hand Luke and the burly ox are bent double, their glistening shoulders shaking with laughter.

Gilles's anger at our ineptitude is something to behold. His face darkens and he does not so much shout as roar, tearing at his hair with his fists, making great howling 'OHHHHH' sounds like some wronged king ululating in a Greek tragedy. This absolutely is not and should not be funny, I tell myself, feeling my lip beginning to go. But sometimes laughter is so deeply and completely inappropriate – my face is starting to tingle, my stomach muscles to hurt – that it takes the law into its own hands, and begins to generate itself. Through my tears, I can see the shearers doing their best to wipe their eyes with wool-greased wrists, as they wait for the storm to pass. Hubert leans thoughtfully on his stick, his face creased into a Bacchic mask, his shoulders shaking with sublimated hysterics. I hold my nose and pinch myself, hard, in the leg because I know I absolutely must not let out so much as a snort. And Gilles, affecting not to notice, goes stomping off up the hill in his own private thundercloud.

I think it is probably a good thing I did not go for that promotion, after all.

# 10

## JUNE

As the would-be vegetables and the naughty grasses in the *potager* continue their breathless power struggle, my simple male brain is finding it hard to multi-task. I cannot imagine how I ever found the time to do a Proper Job in London, when all the bits in between are already colonizing my day like the weeds in a row of carrots.

Weeding fills my life, and other *devoirs* are beginning to fall by the wayside. My French tax-return is overdue. The Luscombe has an oil leak. Flying Helene, my old friend from flying-school in Florida, is coming to stay in a fortnight's time. On top of everything else, there is the small matter of this year's Jolibois Festival, for which I appear to have volunteered in a big way.

Volunteering is different in France. In England, you volunteer for things by putting up your hand. The French version is rather more subtle. Someone – perhaps a bespectacled lady in a black silk dress, still breathless and hobbling from your attempts at waltzing with her – will buttonhole you at a *soirée dansante* and invite you to come along to a meeting, with what sounds like a flattering offer. 'I thought you might find it interesting,' she will purr, 'to see what the festival committee does.'

This is the moment to have your oarsmen stop their ears with wax and lash you to the mast. But the siren-song of Sybille catches me off guard. So I turn up for the meeting – just as an observer, you understand – because, as Sybille says, I may find it interesting. And a stern lady with a clipboard immediately tells me that I am making beds.

'*Mais . . . mais . . .*'

'Do you have a problem with that?' she snaps (early fifties, spiky white hair, expensive clothes definitely not purchased from the Jolibois boutique). She points her clipboard at me, as if it were a loaded harpoon-gun and I a helpless turtle.

I have opened my mouth to speak, but no sound comes out.

'*Non, non, pas de problème,*' I manage at last.

'*Bien.* I've put you on duty with Sandrine, who is very pretty, so you won't mind that, will you?'

'*Non,*' I squeak, to titters from around the room. Even Franck, the festival's unsmiling artistic director, who wears nothing but black Armani, allows himself a mild smirk. And then the lady with the clipboard informs Franck that *he* is on bed-making duty, too, and – as I watch his chiselled jaw drop – I feel a whole lot better.

I feel better, too, when I return to La Folie and find the answerphone blinking with a message from Jethro. Jethro has a new girlfriend. He describes Karen as 'crazily amazing', so she is certainly his type. And now he wants me to meet her, at a weekend house-party they are throwing at the vast, partially renovated chateau that belongs to Karen's brother-in-law, another pilot.

This will coincide with Flying Helene's forthcoming visit to La Folie. And though I am loath to leave my *potager*, even for a weekend, it feels like an ideal opportunity to kill two birds with one stone. Although I am not sure that Helene will see it that way.

*

Sitting in the right-hand seat of the Luscombe, Flying Helene is looking nervous. I remember her complaining in Kissimmee that the rusting, thirty-year-old spam-cans on which she was learning to fly were old planes. Whereas now she is squeezed into a flighty little two-seater that is twice that age. Not only that, but she is about to set out on a long cross-country flight with a pilot who, she may recall, is not the most naturally gifted airman on the planet. Right now, that same pilot is drenched in sweat, hauling and hauling again on the Luscombe's two-bladed metal prop, to no avail. As I have come to expect whenever an attractive young woman is occupying Golf-Zulu-Alpha's right-hand seat, the engine will not start.

'Okay, let's try this one more time,' I gasp, leaning into the cockpit, switching off the magnetos, and pushing the throttle wide open. 'Maybe she's flooded.'

'Is there anything I can do?' calls Helene, holding the stick back between her knees to keep the Luscombe's tail down, in the unlikely event that the donkey fires. I begin to wind the propeller clockwise, to blow out any excess fuel from the cylinders.

'A few prayers might help.'

And at last we are off, flying east across the beige table-cloth of central France towards St Étienne. I can feel the stiffness ebbing from my aching muscles, and my problems slipping away, as the engine roars, and a nudge on the control-column allows me to feel the surging resistance of the air through which we are carving an aircraft-shaped hole at a hundred miles an hour. Slowly we climb above the scattered clouds, and the Luscombe's cockpit is filled with brilliant light. Helene takes the controls, swooping left and right as she gets a feel for the skittish little aeroplane's delicate handling.

'You can relax,' I chuckle, over the intercom. She is

gripping the stick so tightly that her knuckles are white, and her smooth skin has turned to stone with concentration: lips pursed, brow furrowed, eyes flickering between the compass and the horizon like the flashing headlights of an angry driver.

'Sorry,' she giggles. Dropping her hunched shoulders and unclenching her jaw, she sighs with relief. 'It's such a long time since I last flew.'

'You're doing beautifully,' I tell her. 'It's not an easy plane to fly.' Helene always was a better pilot than me, I reflect, enjoying the feeling of being a passenger again, flown by my old friend. For as long as I have known her, she has been in an on-off relationship with a bloke called Tom, whom she clearly adores. Just now they are in one of their off-phases. Yet I know from the kindly shove she gave me when I kissed her goodnight yesterday evening that other dalliances are off limits, too.

Jethro meets us at a misty little aerodrome on the flat plains near St Etienne. With his shaved head, flying-suit and wrap-around shades, he looks like something out of *Top Gun*.

'Nice landing, me old mucker,' he says, giving me a hug as I climb down from the Luscombe.

'That was thanks to Helene,' I reply, introducing her as she steps under the wing.

'Charmed,' says Jethro, with a broad grin. And then, turning to me, he whispers, 'You lucky bugger. Fancy finding a bird that flies!'

'Actually . . .' I reply, but Jethro has already started pushing the Luscombe back towards the fuel bowser. He introduces us to Karen, his new girlfriend, and Benj, a handsome engineer who says he fixes jumbo jets for a living.

'I don't suppose you fix Luscombes, too, do you?' I ask, shaking his hand.

'It has been known,' he grins. 'Although we don't have too many of them in the Virgin Atlantic fleet.'

Jethro was right about Karen being crazily amazing. A tall, crackling figure with an infectious laugh and a manic smile, she kisses Helene and me as fondly as if we were her children, and orders Jethro to sit in the back of the Jeep while she drives us back to the chateau. Her driving is not fast, but it is terrifying, all the same. The engine screams in protest, and – clenching my teeth as we round each blind corner – I am inclined to agree with it. Helene and I exchange nervous glances, like kidnapped hostages.

'Why didn't she change out of second gear?' I ask Jethro when, against the odds, we arrive at the monster chateau, and have gawped at its lack of doors and surfeit of windows.

'As far as Karen is concerned, all cars are automatics,' he shrugs. 'I've learned not to comment.'

The weekend turns out to be a spectacular fireworks display of raging emotions, tiffs, tantrums, stand-offs, rows and sulks. And that is just Jethro and Karen. I have always known that my friend was instinctive, passionate and reactive. Unfortunately, in Karen he seems to have found someone who is exactly the same. It must be like seeing a reflection of himself warped in a wobbly fairground mirror.

Helene maintains a brave smile throughout, at least until midnight on the Saturday, when we are all sitting shivering in one of the chateau's three kitchens, wondering what on earth has happened to Jethro. He vanished about an hour ago, after yet another blazing fire-fight with Karen, which ran the full crescendo from whispered to screamed. And then the door of the kitchen flies open and Karen charges in, holding a shotgun.

'Oh, golly!' exclaims Helene.

'Have you shot him?' I ask, quietly.

Karen roars with laughter and spins round. Lucky I don't

want children, I remind myself, when I see where the gun is pointing.

'Did I scare you?' she drawls.

'*Yes*,' comes a muffled voice from behind the sofa. 'I think it would be a good idea to put the gun down, Karen,' continues Benj, with a coolness that I covet. Emerging from his hiding place, he stands, takes the shotgun from her and, breaking open the stock, removes the cartridges. Beside me, Helene's eyes widen.

'I think I'm ready to go home now,' she whispers.

'I'm so sorry,' I mouth, in reply.

Next day, I am woken early by the sound of gunfire, and race downstairs in my pyjamas. But it is only the local hunters.

Karen is nowhere to be seen, and Jethro, still in his shades, is muted as we say our goodbyes. It feels a relief to climb back into the sky once more.

'Will he be all right?' asks Helene, as we set our course across the mountains to St Juste. 'I can't believe that gun was loaded.'

'Jethro will always be all right,' I tell her. 'That's the amazing thing about him: he always comes through in the end.'

On my birthday, I stroll down the old cart-track to Jolibois. I am taking Gilles and Josette out to lunch at the Cheval Blanc, for a small celebration. And, on my way, I am surprised to see a little girl sitting on a bank all alone.

I glance around, wondering where she has come from. We are at least half a mile from the nearest house, which happens to be La Folie, and I cannot imagine why she is here. Her hair is jet black; her skin dark; her eyes flash with a kind of malevolent beauty, as if she is destined to be either a bank robber or a film star. In her jeans and T-shirt, she looks about ten years old, although her frown and air of intense concentration lend her several extra decades of maturity.

'*Bonjour, mademoiselle*,' I say.

Barely looking up, she casts me a sidelong glance and tosses aside the daisy she has been twirling between finger and thumb, as if she had been waiting for me. I am about to walk on by, but something about the scene disquiets me. My curiosity piqued, I stop and ask what she is doing here.

'*J'effeuille la marguerite*,' she says, with a shrug, as if it were obvious. What else does one do with a daisy, except pluck its petals, one by one?

I take a step closer, and – unfazed by my presence – she picks another.

'Is it a game?' I wonder, aloud.

Silence.

'Maybe for you, *monsieur*,' she replies, after a while. '*Mais pas pour moi.*'

For a moment I feel I should retreat; that I am encroaching; an adult predator in the dreamworld of a child. But I am transfixed by the simplicity of the scene. Especially when she starts all over again, almost as if I were not standing there, interloping. A gypsy child, perhaps? I notice that her top is stained and grubby around the sleeves. Again, I glance left and right. But there is no one else in sight.

One after another, she removes the petals from the tiny flower in her hand. I can see her lips moving as she does so, though no sound comes out. When there are just two petals left, she stares at them for a moment, and I see her shoulders fall. Then she tosses the flower aside, and picks another. I do not think she is playing to the crowd, for she seems as wrapped in her own little world as a bouquet in cellophane. Though now she murmurs, loud enough for me to hear.

'*Il m'aime bien*,' she says, to the flower, as she pulls off the first petal.

'*Il m'aime un peu . . .*' She pulls off another with finger and thumb, as though she were drawing an invisible needle through a fragment of silk. '. . . *Il m'aime beaucoup.*'

Then she peers more carefully at the daisy, before taking the next petal, extracting it as delicately as if it were a tiny angel balanced on the head of a pin.

'*Il m'aime à la folie,*' she whispers. And then, her face hardening, she plucks out the next victim, like a slug from a salad. '*Il m'aime pas du tout.*'

And so it goes on: '*Il m'aime bien . . . un peu . . . beaucoup . . . à la folie . . . pas du tout.*'

'May I try?' I ask quietly, fearful of breaking the spell. I still cannot decide whether to go or to stay – and feel I somehow need her permission to do either.

The girl looks up at me, without interest. She squints a little, for the sun is bright on her face. She doesn't reply; merely shrugs. So I bend down to pick a daisy, kneel beside her, and begin to pick off the petals.

'He loves you,' I say, in English. 'He loves you not . . . he loves you . . . he loves you not.' I stop for a moment, and glance across at her. '*En anglais*, there are only two choices,' I explain. But she pretends not to be listening.

'He loves you . . . he loves you not . . .' I slow down as I approach the last few petals, until there is just one left. 'He loves you,' I say quietly, not looking at her.

'*Non, il ne m'aime pas.*'

'Yes, he does,' I reply, offering her the daisy with its single remaining petal.

'*Il m'aime,*' she murmurs, doubtfully, as she plucks the last white strand of silk from the rim of its dimpled yellow head. And then she smiles for the first time, as if a fresh thought has struck her. Glancing up at me, she adds, almost in a whisper, 'But perhaps he doesn't know it yet.'

And because there is nothing more to be said, I stand, nod my head in farewell, and continue my walk into town.

\*

A day later, and I am making up beds. Really quite a lot of beds, as it happens. A group of jazz-playing *manouches* from Eastern Europe is performing at the Jolibois Festival, and – up at the local *lycée* – I am doing my allotted stint with a pile of sheets and blankets and Sandrine, the comely daughter of Yves-Pascal the notaire, so that the musicians can stay the night.

I watch while Sandrine makes up the first bed.

'Aren't you going to help?' she asks.

'I thought I'd better see how it's done, in case you make beds differently in France.'

Sandrine giggles, but I can tell that she is secretly impressed by my hospital corners. And then we are folding down the top-sheet together, silently synchronizing our movements, and I decide that it is really rather fun making beds with someone else.

Afterwards, she puts a pillow under each mattress.

'Aren't these meant to go on top?' I ask, holding up one of those sausage-type bolsters that serve as pillows in French hotels, but which are only really comfortable if you are a stone knight sleeping on a tomb with a dog at your feet.

'We have no pillowcases,' she shrugs. 'So the pillows must go underneath the mattress.'

I learn something *nouveau* every day.

Back at the festival office, the lady with the clipboard is waiting for me. She looks worryingly like Cat does, when she is waiting to pounce on a baby lizard that has disappeared under a rock.

'You will go and clean the cabaret bar next, won't you, Michael?' she purrs. I remember this from Latin: *question expecting the answer yes.*

'Er . . .'

'You're not busy, are you?' she continues: *question expecting the answer no.*

'Er . . .'

And once again, without uttering a word, I find that I have volunteered.

In the evening, I return to the cabaret bar, to listen to the gypsies play their drab jazz. Hearing them, I half wish I had made them all apple-pie beds.

'What do you reckon?' asks Ja-Ja, who captained me in the tennis match and still reminds me of one of Gilles's sheepdogs. Tonight he is serving *demis* behind the bar.

'I don't think I have ever known this place so well swept.'

He laughs. 'You're a good volunteer, Michael. We'll both be busy at the end of the week.'

'How come?'

'Because of organizing the tennis tournament, as well.'

'I haven't volunteered for that.'

'Yes, you have,' says Ja-Ja.

'But I never . . .'

'You came to the tennis-club meeting, didn't you?'

'You don't mean . . . ?'

Ah, but yes: he does.

# 11

## JULY

Hot, hot, hot. Here at La Folie, the thermometer's thin red line has hit the thirty-eight marker. Even the lizards are sweating.

Whoever invented the phrase 'cool as a cucumber' clearly never ventured south of Bognor, let alone Poitiers. I have just sliced a cucumber, fresh from the *potager*, and was surprised to find, as I put the slices into my mouth, that they were still hot. Warm tomatoes, straight off the plant, I like. But warm cucumber is unsettling, like warm yoghurt or a blue fried egg.

Outside, the overheating Rastafarians hide beneath the trees, dreaming of snow in winter and cool wet grass. I pity the chickens. The Egg Squad pad around beneath the Espace, beaks open, wings held away from their bodies in the manner of Bible lecterns. Poor old Meg is still not right, and stands apart, motionless beneath the Lone Pine. I wonder if she knows that this is where her sister, Silent Mary, is buried. The cat lies in the shade of the sumach tree in front of the house, the pink tip of her tongue hanging out of her mouth like a tap-washer stuck in the slot of a vending machine. The grass is so brown and frazzled, it is almost white.

'How do you bear it?' asks my mother, on the phone. Mum is about as keen on hot weather as she is on air travel, spiders or Labour prime ministers.

'Well, I suppose it makes a difference that this is France, not Farnham, Mum.' One expects a bit of dry-roasting, this far south of Cleethorpes, in a country where the words 'Warning: Contents may be hot' are marked on the packaging. So I find myself accepting the furnace heat rather than resisting it, which is what I might once have done in England.

It helps that the walls of La Folie are as thick as thieves (i.e. two very fat burglars, strapped together). So even if I cannot quite bring myself to emulate the locals by keeping the shutters closed all day – as if I were Master Colin in *The Secret Garden*, or a Turner watercolour – I do now keep the doors shut against the oven-blast of the daytime air, so that I can have the illusion of coming into somewhere cool when I have finished ripping out the naughty grasses in the *potager*, or replacing the goldfishes' dark green water yet again.

I think I am in love with my *potager*. I am as hooked on the buzz of watching it grow and flower as I am on the endorphins I whip up in my brain as I haul out strokes on my rower. Each week brings another milestone. Eating the first peppery radish I have grown in my life. Washing the first home-grown lettuce; slicing the first courgette; snapping the tips off the first green bean. Seeing the first tomato begin to blush, the first melon begin to swell. Miracles, miracles all.

And then, with due aplomb: the day of my destiny. The moment when I pull up my first ever spud. As I press my fingers into the warm, crumbling earth, the shock of its smooth skin hits me as if I were a rescuer stumbling upon a living creature buried in an earthquake. Gentlemen, please be seated. I could not be more proud of this potato if I had delivered my own first-born child. The little fellow even looks a bit like me: pale, squat and tubby, with a merry twinkle in his eye. I have yet to decide what to call the young scamp, although Michael Jnr has a certain ring to it.

The significance of this moment dawns upon me only gradually. Potatoes are vegetables, just like lettuces and beans and courgettes. The difference, however, is that man cannot survive a winter on courgettes, though he can on spuds. That first plant I dig up yields a dozen potatoes, many of them as big as one of Melissa's eggs. There must be more than a kilogram of prime carbohydrate in that handsome bunch of Walter Raleigh's finest. And I have planted 250 such plants.

Unwittingly, in other words, I have taken my first step towards self-sufficiency. My mother will be amazed.

Later come my first broccoli, first shallots, first green pepper, aubergine and cauliflower; first ripe tomato, still warm from the sun as I slice it and shove the pieces into my mouth, almost sniggering with pleasure as the sweet juice dribbles down my chin.

Unfortunately, at this early stage of my transformation into an expert gardener, I am quite convinced, like any new parent, that *my* first-born tatties are better than anyone else's. And this has led me to do something deeply foolish. I have only gone and challenged Le Grand Mermoz, the uniquely competitive forty-nine-year-old who runs the higgledy-piggledy hardware store, to a potato competition.

I really didn't mean to. I still don't know quite how it happened. There we were, chatting about our hopes and dreams for our spuds as we watched Ja-Ja playing an interminable match at the Jolibois tennis tournament, when I suddenly came out with it: let us have a potato contest, Mermoz.

I blame this rash act on my background as a serial plant-killer, and my awestruck disbelief at the ever-increasing gap between past disasters and present success. Tomorrow, then, back at the tennis tournament, the big man and I are going to be crossing swords – well, spuds – at dusk. The rules are brutally simple. The biggest, meanest, baddest *pomme de terre* wins.

Next day, after lunch, I gaze out over my serried ranks of *pommes de terre* like a general inspecting his battalions. The *potager* is looking alarmingly dry: it feels like weeks since we had any rain. Nevertheless, choosing the stoutest *pied* I can find, I grab its half-dozen stems in both hands, and pull. There is a sound of tearing velvet, and the golden-skinned troops rise slowly to the surface. One warrior spud stands out, towering like Hector over the Trojan line. Ha! Mermoz doesn't stand a chance.

At the tennis club, a match is in progress, and I could swear a murmur goes through the crowd when I stride through the gates, holding up Hector for all to see. *Tuber mirum spargens sonum!* People stand aside to let him pass, and the umpire of the tennis match has to make angry *shhhhh*-ing noises to silence their laughter. Awe sometimes expresses itself in unexpected ways.

Seated on a bench behind the court, I see Mermoz turn and smile. Then he glimpses Hector in my raised palm, and bursts out laughing. Nervous laughter. Beneath his bluff exterior, I can see the blood draining from his face; beneath that carnival grin, I sense the grimace of pure horror, as if Caesar were receiving the final dagger-blow from Brutus, or as if I had just aced him with my second serve. Well, perhaps that is a slight exaggeration. But he does look a *little* concerned as he makes his way around the court to me.

'*C'est ça?*' he asks, his shoulders shaking with laughter. He points at Hector. '*C'est tout?*'

I nod, standing my ground. But Mermoz fails to produce his challenger. Anyone would think he was not taking the competition seriously.

'I'll be back,' he says, striding out of the gates.

Mermoz is gone a long time. He is gone for so long that I cannot help wondering if he has gone to Champion in search of the biggest spud money can buy. Either that, or else he is digging up his entire *potager* in search of a *patate* to rival Hector.

He returns with a monster. If I was hoping for Patroclus, he has brought Achilles. Pink and knobbly, his prize spud resembles the clenched fist of a nightclub bouncer, and must weigh more than Barbra Streisand. Eat it? It looks as if it could probably eat me.

'I think that makes up for the Olympics, doesn't it?' laughs Mermoz, brutally raising his vast Achilles side by side with my shrimp-like Hector; a watermelon beside a Brussels sprout.

'It is a clear victory for France,' I concede. 'But Mermoz . . .'

I am not finished yet. I have been mentally counting up the different vegetables in my *potager*: tomatoes, peppers, aubergines, cabbages, courgettes, broccoli, cauliflower, onions, garlic, and shallots. Yup, that should do it.

'*Oui?*' he says.

'Does the name Daley Thompson mean anything to you?'

I write to Alice, though not about my humiliation in the potato competition. I had been so looking forward to our going flying together in the Luscombe, yet my oil-leak persists, and my Armstrong starter problems – the fact that it sometimes takes forty hefty swings on the prop before the tiny Continental finally coughs into life, and I invariably climb up into its leather-lined cockpit drenched with sweat – have forced me to take drastic action: I am finally going to replace the aircraft's ancient breadbox magnetos with a pair of Slicks. 'And while I wait for the new parts to arrive from Belgium,' I write, 'the little yellow plane is grounded until further notice.'

A few days later, Alice and her brother, Survival-Kit Toby, finally arrive at Limoges airport. I am not sure which of them I feel more nervous about seeing again.

I spot Toby first, towering over the thronged airport lobby with an outsize rucksack slung over his hulking shoulders. The twelve-year-old tearaway I once knew has turned into something out of one of Ovid's scarier *Metamorphoses*: a giant figure with a face hewn from solid rock, and a Bacchic twinkle in his mischievous eye. As he gazes round about him, at *les Anglais* in all their holiday glory, Toby wears an expression of quizzical contempt. And then, when he sees me, I am relieved to see him break into a smile as broad and sparkling as the river at the bottom of the drive.

'Wotcha, mate,' he growls, enveloping me in a friendly hug.

'Hi, Toby,' I reply, glancing over his shoulder. 'Did you come alone?'

'Don't worry, Al's just coming,' he says. 'It was kind of you to invite her, too.'

'No worries. I'm just glad you could both make it.'

And then Alice herself appears, looking even prettier than I remembered, in a pink T-shirt and white three-quarter-length trousers. As she shuffles towards me in her suede ballet pumps, dragging her bag on wheels behind her, my mind whirls. Speech will feel unnatural, after so many emails and all these years. I am hoping she will speak first, for I have not the first idea how to begin.

She smiles, a smile that crinkles her eyes and dimples her cheeks in a way that is strangely familiar. For a second she hesitates. And then, at last, she utters the very first words I have heard her speak in the eighteen years since we last met.

'Gotta pee,' she whispers to us both, as she dumps her bag at our feet.

Toby and I grin at each other.

'It's so great to see you again,' I tell him.

'Amazing, isn't it?' His eyes are shining, and he stares at me for so long that I begin to wonder if I have spaghetti stuck to my face. 'How many years is it now? I'm longing to see your place.'

'The house is still a bit of a building site, I'm afraid. But it's getting there.'

'Dinky little airport, isn't it?' he replies, gazing up at the terminal's polished wooden ceiling, not really listening. 'I can't believe I'm in France. I haven't heard a single French voice. Even on the plane, the announcements were all in English.'

'The invasion is in full swing. They've only just built this new airport, and already it's too small. No one could quite imagine how many Brits would want to come.'

'Doing what you're doing . . . fleeing the sinking ship.'

'Oh, it was never that for me,' I reply, with a laugh which comes out at a higher pitch than intended. 'I love England. But I wanted to have an adventure . . .'

I stop in mid-sentence, for Alice has returned to join us. And it is hard to describe the impact of the arrival of a beautiful young woman in a chap's local airport and, by extension, his life – even a chap who feels whole and complete in himself, thoroughly at one with his manly power-tools – when that life is usually filled only with walnut-faced peasants, garrulous chickens and very small sheep. I feel much as I did when my grandparents first took me to the RAF museum at Hendon, and I saw a real-live Spitfire for the first time. Back then, aged six, I screamed. Today, aged thirty-nine, I hold my breath.

'Hello,' she says, shyly, as we brush each other's cheek with a kiss.

'Hello, at last,' I reply, the small pocketful of my confidence evaporating. Her bashfulness is contagious, and I suddenly feel almost too shy to look at her. 'I'm so pleased you made it here,' I mumble. And then, in case this sounds too keen – too far removed from the joshing-with-a-couple-of-old-school-chums that I should be doing – I hastily add: 'Both of you.'

Out we wander, the sliding doors of the terminal parting like theatre curtains to reveal the next act. I am surprised at the weight of Alice's bag, which looks as big as a canoe, and must have enough clothes inside for both of them, for a month. And then we are squinting into the throbbing sunshine, the heat bouncing off the tarmac so powerfully that it seems to come at us from below, like some giant barbecue.

The one time I truly appreciate this French furnace heat is whenever I am picking up friends at the airport. For the superheated brilliance feels like a visceral sign that we really are in France. So their visit has already been worth it, now that they have felt this momentary waft of being palpably Abroad. Abroad is good, when you are British, because Abroad is everything that is not the mundane grey rasp of home.

Toby sits beside me in the front seat of the Espace, with Alice lodged just behind.

'Sorry about the smell,' I mutter, as we set off on the half-hour drive back to La Folie.

'I didn't know you had a dog,' replies Alice, coughing.

'I don't.'

'But you've had sheep and all sorts in the back of this car, haven't you, Michael?' asks Toby, helping me out. 'Cor, look at that,' he adds, jabbing the window with his finger. 'Sixties cows. You need a haircut, mate.'

'Do I?' I ask, surprised at his tone, before it dawns on me that he is giving fashion tips to one of the long-haired bovine rockers in the field to our right. Alice breaks into a peal of delightful laughter.

'I trained her to laugh at my jokes years ago,' explains Toby, and I hear a tinkling giggle echo his guffaw just behind me. This pattern is repeated throughout our journey back to

La Folie. Roughly every seven seconds, Toby spots some-thing new to delight his magpie mind, yells something witty at it, whether it is a lamb or a lamp-post, and Alice falls about laughing with such infectious delight that it makes me think that the steering-wheel is unusually wobbly today. I feel as if I am driving the tour bus of a comedy double-act, and I don't want the road to unwind.

La Folie can be hell in the company of urbane townies like the man I used to be; for stress-junkies struggling with the silence and the lack of distractions for their busy, buzzing minds. But it can be heaven, too, when the sky is huge and blue, and friends come who are happy to dance to the simple tunes of the countryside. Alice and Toby somehow chime with the place like a pair of musicians jamming along to an old song, instinctively knowing the key in which La Folie is set, and finding their own ways to harmonize with it.

Except Cat. Alice and Toby visibly shrink when Cat arrives to inspect them; she leaping up from her chair to avoid becoming an occupied lap; he curling his lip with exuberant disdain.

While Toby basks like a lizard in the sun, sipping a milky Pastis and almost purring with contentment as he lounges in a garden chair so rickety that even the woodworm have abandoned it, Alice sits in the shade, smiling to herself as she watches the chickens having their dust-baths beneath the Lone Pine.

'It's a weird sight, isn't it?' I murmur, as I wander out from the kitchen with a bowl of pistachios and a glass stuffed with a bundle of breadsticks. I gaze at the bathing chickens, as they flop on to their sides and splay and convulse their wings in the pale earth, showering soil over their plumage as if they were commandos embedding themselves for a night attack. 'The first time I saw one of them doing that, I thought she was dying. They just look so contorted, as if they've been in some horrible accident.'

'I think they look blissful,' she replies, 'digging themselves into the cool earth. Pastis, how lovely, thank you. It probably won't be long before posh hotel spas are offering dust-baths, too.'

'Chicken digger massager,' announces Toby, in an Indian accent. 'We used to have a chicken ourselves, in Malaysia. A great big cockerel; terrifying bugger. He used to chase us round the garden, until Mum whacked him with a spade, and he was never the same after that.'

'Wasn't he called Triangle?' I ask, a shard of memory cutting through the mists of time.

'Isosceles,' laughs Alice, correcting me. 'How amazing that you remember that.'

'Toby talked so much about your time in Malaysia, while we were at Windlesham, that I almost feel I lived there myself. I was always so impressed that Toby lived in his own mud hut.'

'No, he didn't,' she replies, turning accusingly towards her brother.

'This is the life, eh, Michael?' interjects Toby, changing the subject, not opening his eyes. 'I don't know how you put up with it.'

'It's not always as lovely as this, you know.'

'No, it must be hell when we're not here,' he chuckles, his shoulders rising and falling like Muttley in the *Wacky Races*.

'Let's go and pick beans,' I announce, changing the subject.

So we all pick beans in the *potager*, and Toby wants to pick everything else that is growing, too – even the melons, which are only just the size of tennis balls, and the red peppers, which are still, like well-meaning traffic lights, resolutely stuck on green.

A little while later, Toby announces that he is going to cook roast lamb for dinner. Alice looks suddenly nervous, as if he had announced that he was planning to construct a small nuclear device using found objects. I am beginning to wonder if she knows something about her brother that I don't. Even at thirteen, he did have a wild streak.

'Perhaps Michael has already decided what we're having,' she warns him.

'No, no, roast lamb sounds great,' I reply, yanking the cork out of a bottle of red wine far more expensive than my usual Lidl parafino. 'I have bought a whole *gigot*, which I was planning to cook at some point over the weekend. It might as well be now.'

'As long as it isn't too pink,' says Alice, voicing a thought that I didn't dare utter myself.

'*Tout à fait*,' I reply.

'*Veni vidi vici*,' responds Toby, not to be outdone.

'But I do think we should make the cooking a joint effort,' says Alice, before I can say it myself.

'Haven't I got enough Michelin stars for you?' asks her brother. His smile is playful, but I can tell that he is beginning to feel rattled, too. In the end, after a long and passionate diatribe about how he was once hired as head chef of a Soho restaurant without any culinary training apart from the domestic science lessons we had at Windlesham, where we learned how to cook beef casserole and brandy snaps in the domestic science lab beneath the Girls' Wing, Toby relents, and agrees to take us both on as his sous-chefs. So while Alice scrubs my miracle potatoes and Toby devotes himself to creating a mountain of washing-up using the crash-bang-wallop wall-of-sound technique, I prepare a pot of home-grown white beans with onions, lardons and white wine.

The first bottle of red wine leads to another. Unfortunately, the oven at La Folie is a primitive beast that runs off a gas cylinder stashed inside it, and – although it is only with Toby's arrival that I discover this – if you slam the oven door violently enough, the gas flame blows out. So the lamb is cooked in instalments. And by 1 am, after the three of us have raucously sung our way through the entire Flanders and Swann songbook and most of *Grease* at the piano, it is almost ready to eat.

'The great thing about *haricots blancs*,' I announce, 'is that you don't have to make gravy.'

Too late. Fifteen minutes, five pots and two saucepans later, with lamb fat sprayed over every surface not already covered with dirty washing-up, Toby has made gravy.

Alice peers doubtfully into the jug. 'Were you inspired by The Hippopotamus Song, Tobes?' Her brother pretends not to hear.

'Now don't tell me *that*'s too pink,' he says, bringing the lamb to the table on an antique tea-tray that I have always cherished, and giving the oven door one last, mighty slam which will undoubtedly be reported as an unusual earth tremor in *Le Populaire* in a couple of days' time.

After I have carved the meat and we have all toasted our own culinary brilliance, there is silence for a while as we tuck into our food with that bleary, bottomless hunger that comes from drinking a surfeit of red wine on an empty stomach.

'So, Michael,' says Toby at last, 'are you ever planning to settle down? And what are you looking for anyway? Perhaps the bachelor lifestyle suits you?'

I stare at my plate, hearing the same questions that I have asked myself so many times now being put to me by my old friend. People sometimes tell me off for my own tactless directness – let's cut to the chase, I think to myself; let's talk about what really matters – but I am somehow relieved when the same approach is used on me.

'You know what?' I reply, putting my knife and fork together. 'If you'd asked me that question a few months ago, I would have told you how desperate and lonely I was. I went flying by myself one afternoon, and I gave myself a fright. I really thought I was going to crash and die.'

Alice looks up, suddenly interested.

'Oil temp off the scale,' I explain. 'And I was over forested hills at the time. Really thought it might be curtains.' She nods, and I continue.

'Anyway, it bothered me that no one would have known about it, if I had. It made me realize how isolated I have allowed myself to become, here on this windswept hillside. The locals call it the End of the World.'

Toby leans forward in his chair, rotating the stem of his wine glass between finger and thumb, staring at me with X-ray eyes. Alice is pulling fragments of wax off the candlestick, and feeding them into the molten pool beneath the flaming wick above.

'And then came a chain of events that I can't quite explain. I was sawing up logs in the barn, and this Mirage jet flew over . . .'

'One of the delta-wing jobbies?' interjects Toby.

'No, I think it was a more recent model than that.'

'Shh, Tobes,' says Alice, wrinkling her brow at her bro.

'Anyway, somehow I sensed that for as long as I needed someone else to make my life work – for as long as I was looking for someone else to make me happy – then I would never have a wonderful relationship. You know: a life relationship, as opposed to a sparky romance. I'd always be needy; on the take, not on the give. So I decided to stop looking; to stop needing. I worked on being happy in myself. I grew my first-ever crop of potatoes. And I can truly say, now, as we sit here today – if we discount the small matter of flying a Spitfire – that I have everything I want.'

'Yes, but you're a bloke, come on,' says Toby, splashing more wine into my glass, like an interrogator attempting to elicit a confession. 'You're not thinking of becoming a monk, are you?'

So I tell him about Amy, the girl in the blue dress, and the delightful time we spent together at La Folie. I tell him about some of the other women who have been to stay at La Folie, lightening my hermitic isolation, and about the generous-hearted readers of my column who have sent bikini-shots of their daughters and nieces for my delectation.

'You're *joking*,' says Toby, with more than a hint of Basil Brush.

I shake my head. 'But it's odd,' I add. 'One of the things I appreciate about the dance classes I attend, with a bunch of local ladies almost all of whom are considerably older than me—'

'Oh, here we go,' roars Toby, 'the Jolibois gigolo, doing his foxy foxtrot with Fifi the sheep—'

'Toby,' hisses Alice, giggling.

'. . . No, but seriously, I'm almost surprised to hear myself saying this, but I really do enjoy the physical contact.' Toby is still chortling to himself as if over a private joke. 'I'm surprised at myself, but that's the truth. I even feel it when I go to have my hair cut by the pretty lady who works in the local *coiffeur*.'

'Good God, isn't there a massage parlour in Jolibois you can go to?'

Laughing into my lap, I plough on.

'I suppose I still dream that I might, one day, meet a woman with whom I immediately want to spend the rest of my life, but I'm not holding my breath. I can't help feeling that, if it was going to happen, it would have happened long ago. Don't you feel that?'

'Still pining for Clara Delaville?' he chuckles, not rising to the bait.

'You remember her?'

'I remember you wouldn't stop talking about her.'

'I do think of her, every now and then, as it happens. Because she's a kind of yardstick of how I would need to feel about a person to want to spend my life with them. That excitement . . .' I turn to Alice, and she nods, but she seems lost in her own thoughts, '. . . that yearning to be close to someone who is everything.'

'Oh, don't ask Alice about that,' interjects Toby.

'What do you *mean*?' she asks, smiling but indignant.

'Well, you're the original frog-kisser, aren't you, Al?'

'You had a French boyfriend?' I ask, innocently. They both collapse into raucous laughter.

'No, Toby means that I've kissed a lot of frogs in my time,' says Alice, with a wounded frown at her brother. 'You know, hoping that they might turn into princes. And to be fair, he's right: most of them were frogs.'

'Well, maybe that's what I'm talking about, Toby,' I continue, too bound up in my own contorted logic really to listen to what she is saying. 'Just idly fancying someone a bit foxy and having a bit of a laugh together wouldn't be enough. It would have to be everything, or it would be nothing.'

'Yes, but come on,' he says. 'It's not too late to meet someone like that. There must be lots of gorgeous French ladies in Jolibois.'

'It's not that the women of Jolibois are not gorgeous. It's just that they're all either fifteen or fifty.'

'Where are all the others, then?'

'In Paris or Lyon, I believe. Or else they're married, and slaving over a hot tractor.'

'I know what you should try, mate.' Toby sloshes more red wine into his glass, and then into Alice's. I attempt to move mine out of his reach, before he can refill it, and he sloshes wine all over the table. 'Internet dating.'

'Really?' Alice and I exchange glances.

'Mate, I've met some *amazing* birds online. You just put up your details and a pic, and wait for the replies to start flooding in. The only trouble is knowing how to weed out the nutters. And half the pictures they send of themselves are of Cameron Diaz.'

'So have you had any actual dates?'

'Oh, plenty. Loads of nutters. And a couple of real diamonds. The one I'm currently seeing – Linda – caught my eye because she said her hobby was bog-snorkelling. And somehow that called to me.'

'I'm not sure I'd have the nerve to go down that route,' I reply. And then, as innocently as possible, I ask, 'So what's the web address of the best of the bunch, in your experience?'

Toby begins to answer, but I do not hear a word of what he says. Because at this moment, with the shock factor of a dormouse scampering up my trouser-leg, I feel a slender ankle press against mine. At first, I think I must be imagining it, or that perhaps it is Cat. And then I wonder if I have been teleported into someone else's body. Because this is not the sort of thing that happens to me, *anywhere*, let alone beneath a scrubbed wooden table in the oak-beamed kitchen of a ramshackle farmhouse in darkest France. And I have the strangest feeling, once I have sneaked a quick peak beneath the tablecloth to check that the ankle is not Toby's, that my life is about to take an utterly unexpected turn.

Next morning, the three of us visit the little Saturday market in Jolibois, with its two vegetable stalls, a lady selling fearsomely expensive cheese and a van selling freshly plucked chickens still with their sleepy heads and butter-yellow claws attached. Then there's a man who has set up a plank of wood on a couple of trestles, and lined up a dozen jars of foie gras like targets at a rifle-range. Alice shudders.

'Delicious as it is,' she whispers, 'that's one thing I can't bring myself to eat.'

'I'm the same,' I reply, 'ever since I saw one of the gavvying machines they use to feed them. It was like this big wooden corkscrew with . . .'

'All right,' she says quickly, touching my arm. 'I think I've heard enough.'

Toby buys three pieces of cheese from the cheese lady, and limps back over to us with a pained expression, staggering as if he has been shot.

'Are you all right, Tobes?' asks Alice, alarmed.

'I think I need to sit down.'

'Where does it hurt?' I watch her switch into nurse mode, her face serious, her voice suddenly firmer and calmer than the girlish breathiness, always on the brink of a giggle, to which I have grown accustomed over the past twenty-four hours. Only four words, and already I feel we are in safe hands.

'I just paid twenty-three euros,' gasps Toby, clutching his heart and gazing heavenwards, like a mannerist painting of the Virgin Mary. 'For three pieces of cheese.'

With a snort of annoyance, Alice shoves him away and wanders off to look at chicken claws.

'Oops,' murmurs Toby to me, his shoulders shaking with contained laughter. 'I think I'm in Nurse Melbury's bad books.'

'That's *Sister* Melbury to you,' sniffs Alice, grinning over her shoulder.

Later, I take them to visit my friend Jérôme's lake, its icy waters watched over by nine terrifying kelpies: a herd of hefty Fjord horses, which Jérôme swears are tame. They probably would be, if anyone ever came and rode them. I cannot help noticing the wild glint in their mascara'd eyes, and sensing a pack mentality that makes me think of a gang of whispering street-kids with honey-coloured skin and bleached mohicans, cruising for trouble.

Nevertheless, fringed with towering oaks and sweet chestnuts which make a natural amphitheatre of the scene, the oil-smooth surface of the lake shimmers invitingly in the sun. In front of us, a rickety wooden jetty extends a few yards from the grassy bank that serves as a beach, as if to turn the lake's capital O into the letter Q.

'Are you sure you don't want to swim?' I ask Alice, who shakes her head.

'I haven't brought my costume,' she says, sitting down on a rock. 'But it's okay. I'll just watch you and Toby.'

Until this moment, living alone on the outskirts of a small town where people are too busy eking out a living to worry about beauty or style, where nobody visits a gym and where blue serge overalls are the preferred daily wear of the average peasant, I would have said that I have lost all traces of self-consciousness about how I look.

But this; this is different. As I slowly remove my trousers behind an oak tree, keeping a weather eye out for marauding Fjords, it occurs to me that Alice is going to be appalled. I just know she is. Why haven't I spent more of my mornings hauling out stroke after stroke on my dreaded ergometer? Would anyone notice if I just did a few press-ups, right here, behind my tree? It is all very well cosying up and chatting for hours in the half-light of a darkened bedroom, but here – beneath the harsh spotlight of the Limousin sunshine – I cannot help fearing that the beautiful girl with whom I shared a whisper of intimacy last night may bitterly regret it once she spots the similarities between my exposed waistline and one of those cardboard tubes of Pilsbury cookie-dough that explodes into a ball of white stodge when you tear it open.

And so, as I emerge in my swimming trunks from behind the oak, I face a dilemma I had almost forgotten existed: how am I to hold in my stomach just enough to look passably athletic, yet not so much that Alice can guess at my ridiculous vanity?

The obvious answer is to sprint.

And, in a moment of rare insight, as I dash down the jetty, I opt for a comedy leap into the shimmering brown waters rather than attempting a graceful dive.

The zinging chill of the lake blitzes my self-consciousness

the moment I hit the water, and I rise slowly to the surface like an aspirin fizzing in a glass; reborn; happy to be alive. As I wipe the water from my eyes, I catch sight of the svelte figure in a cream-coloured top and short khaki skirt sitting on a rock just a few yards in front of me, and I think to myself: let this perfect moment be the start of the rest of my life.

A few more such perfect moments later, and Toby emerges from behind his personal oak tree, and I am almost relieved to see that he is carrying a little extra tonnage above the water-line, too. In my head, we are both still children. But in the flesh, we are both spreading like oaks towards middle-age.

I am almost dressed by the time Jérôme wanders down to the lakeside from the house, his eyes twinkling as he catches sight of Alice.

'I am so pleased you could come,' he says, clasping his hands together to express his delight, 'and I can see that Michael has the most exquisite taste.'

'Ah, actually Jérôme, Alice and Toby are old friends of mine from school,' I reply, blushing at his insinuation. On cue, Toby emerges from behind his oak tree, still buttoning up his 501s.

'*Bonjour, enchanté, et comment allez-vous?*' he says, extending his hand in greeting without missing a beat.

Jérôme beams. '*Je vais très bien, merci,*' he replies, with a low bow. 'And all the better for having such enchanting guests at Les Sablonnières.' He gazes sweetly at Alice, and then at Toby, and then back to Alice again, before entreating us all to come to dinner when he returns to the Limousin with his wife next month. I explain that my friends will be flying back to London tomorrow.

'In that case, you must just come by yourself,' says Jérôme, smiling at me. 'But it's too bad.' He winks at Alice, with a wistful shrug. Even at the age of seventy-nine, and after fifty years of marriage, Jérôme has not lost his eye for the ladies. '*Vous parlez français, Alice?*' he adds.

There is a silence, and for a second I consider leaping into the void, to rescue Alice from the panic that I can see in her eyes. I already feel unusually protective of her; sense a beguiling vulnerability behind her easy charm and breezy appetite for working multiple twelve-hour shifts on the trot.

'*Un . . . petit peu,*' she replies, in a perfect French accent.

Bravo, I think to myself.

'*Ah, c'est formidable!*' exclaims Jérôme, glancing approvingly at me, as if I were her French teacher. 'And when are you coming back to see Michael again? *Ça va être bientôt, j'espère.*' It has not occurred to Jérôme that Alice has almost certainly just exhausted the only three words of French that she knows.

'Er . . . er . . .' She turns to me in a panic, searching my face for subtitles, before turning back to Jérôme and settling for the Spanish: '*Qué?*'

So now Jérôme repeats his question in Spanish, and everything begins to go *poire*-shaped. I am vaguely conscious of Toby standing beside me, making no attempt to stifle his giggles.

'It's not fair,' wails Alice afterwards, as we drive home in the Espace. 'Toby can't speak French either. Yet somehow he has this incredible confidence just to go wading in, and words come out, and people seem to understand what he's saying.'

'I *can* speak French,' says Toby, sounding aggrieved. 'It's just that I prefer speaking English.'

'Are you really a Sister?' I ask Alice, catching her eye in the rear-view mirror, and relishing the split-second moment of connectedness that sparkles in her private smile, before I add, 'In nursing, I mean?'

'Ooh, Matron,' interjects Toby. 'At Bart's they were all

terrified of Sister Melbury clopping down the corridors. Scarier than Hattie Jacques, she was.'

'Nonsense, Toby,' she giggles. 'And I'm not a Sister any more, because the grading works differently in the States. But to be honest, just working in the intensive-care unit at Johns Hopkins feels about as good as nursing gets. The hours are horrendous, but it's a close-knit team, and there's a buzz about the place that keeps you going, knowing that everyone else is working flat out, too.'

'Sounds fun,' I say, keeping my eyes on the road.

'Sounds knackering,' says Toby.

'It's amazing, actually,' she says, leaning forward, 'because it's probably one of the best hospitals in the world. And everyone is so brilliant at their jobs that I felt quite out of my depth at first. The protocols are different in the States, and all the drugs have different names, so it was as if I was having to learn a whole new language. And in intensive care, when things go wrong, they can go wrong very, very fast.'

'It's like *ER*, isn't it, Al?' asks Toby.

'Apart from the shouting,' she says, laughing to herself. 'And we don't have George Clooney, either, although some of the surgeons would disagree.'

'Do a lot of people die in intensive care?' I ask, and immediately regret it, because the mood changes. Alice does not reply at once.

'We're dealing with very sick people,' she says. 'So sometimes we do have to take them down to the morgue, yes.'

'And what's that like?'

'It's not what I went into nursing for. I don't like going in there. And you never go alone.'

I stare at the straight road ahead, and at the ancient forest of oaks and chestnuts through which we are passing, dappling the road with flecks of brilliant sunlight. I have never in my life seen a dead body, although I did once see the leg of a deceased tramp poking out from under a bush in

Edinburgh. And here is Alice Melbury, the little girl with whom I rode the ghost train on Brighton Pier, dealing with the inevitability of death every day. I try to hold both pictures in my mind: the serious little girl in long socks and a velvet hairband, and the intensive-care nurse at work in a Baltimore hospital, tending to the sick, helping to save patients as they negotiate that narrow margin between death and life, like tightrope-walkers wobbling across an abyss. And my mind falls short; it is too much to imagine.

'Does it affect you, Al?' asks Toby, swivelling in his seat. 'I mean, it can't be easy, having people dying on you all the time like that.'

'It's not all the time,' says Alice. 'We're there to make people better, not to wheel them off into the wings. The idea is for them to spend as little time in intensive care as possible.'

I sit in silence for a while, reflecting on my former life as a theatre critic, and my new life as a trainee peasant, and wonder if I have ever done anything, ever, that was as hard, or which had as much impact on people's existence as what Alice Melbury is doing, every hour of every day.

'Sounds like quite a job,' I say, at last.

'I wouldn't change it for the world,' she says, brightening. 'And I get to learn to fly, too. You couldn't do that on a nurse's salary back home.'

'You must be joking,' groans Toby.

'Flying is the most amazing thing, isn't it?' I reply, grinning into the rear-view mirror.

'It's amazingly *hard*,' she harrumphs.

'How are your landings?'

'Hard, too.'

'They'll get better.'

'I wish.'

'I just think of all the things on which I've ever spent money in my life,' I continue. 'And learning to fly was the finest of them all.'

'Snap,' says Alice, gazing dreamily out of the window at a pair of buzzards that are wheeling in the sky.

By the time we get back to Jolibois, Toby and I are both feeling those chilled hunger-pangs which tend to follow full-body immersion in icy water, so the three of us sit eating *steak frites* in the Crêperie opposite Ralph and Olga's house, marvelling at the sunny good humour of the young couple running the place, who remain unflappably cheerful despite being completely run off their feet.

'That's what happens when you're in a good team,' says Alice, watching them.

'Or when you're on good drugs,' adds Toby, drily.

I cannot remember when I last felt so glad to be alive, nor when I was last with two people with whom I felt so exquisitely at home. Yesterday was fun, but everything about today is wreathed in a kind of sparkling aura of gold and purple, because last night Alice and I stayed up talking into the early hours about everything under the sun, and I experienced a hint of connectedness that ever-so-slightly transcended my trundling tangos and paso dobles with Renée and Céline and the other good ladies who light up my dance-class of a Monday evening.

I am not kidding myself that this connectedness will lead to anything. On the contrary, I am conscious that it can have no future, even though Alice quietly explained last night that she and her boyfriend are no longer, as she put it, an item. A night of talking after lights-out in darkest France is one thing, but I have known ever since our disastrous date in Sloane Square, eighteen years ago, that Alice Melbury is way too cool for me for this to go any further. And besides, Alice's urbane world is three thousand miles away, and she has people's lives to save in big-town America, while I must continue to scratch away at my little vegetable patch in darkest France, dreaming of spuds and Spitfires and the finer points of wool-gathering at shearing time.

So why do I feel so light, sitting beside this beautiful woman whom I met so long ago? Why, when nothing has changed in my life, does it feel as if a switch has flicked, and something is subtly different today?

Through the window of the Crêperie's kitchen, I can see Éric cooking flat out amid clouds of steam. I watch his face break into a smile as his dazzling wife delivers another sheaf of orders, and touches his lips with a kiss; glimpse the pair of them blow each other another kiss before she returns to the fray, with her heart replenished and three laden plates carefully balanced on each arm.

Alice Melbury has shown me that it *is* possible, even at my age and with my degree of hermitic isolation, to meet someone who stops me feeling alone. I think I never expected to hear the voices in my heart, silent for so long, begin to sing again. And she has given me hope that I will meet someone after all, somewhere, in the end.

'Aren't you two going flying together?' asks Toby, as we sip our coffee outside the Palais café at the other end of the street, watching the world go by. I wave as good Monsieur Ducroux the plasterer drives up the road in his white van, and then at Raphaël the priest, who saunters past on foot, on his way down to the presbytery.

'How I wish we could,' I reply. 'But I'm waiting for a new set of magnetos for the Luscombe, so sadly the one thing we can't do is go flying together.' I smile at Alice, and then at Toby, who appears to have no inkling that anything has changed between us, if indeed it has. 'You'll have to come back again for that.'

Back at La Folie, I fill a paper bag with lumps of stale baguette and give it to Alice and Toby, so that they can feed it to the sheep. For my little Rastafarians, stale bread is like chocolate. They cannot get enough of the stuff.

'Won't they bite us?' asks Alice, doubtfully, until I reassure her that these are the sweetest sheep in the world – especially snorty old Gaston, despite having the scariest horns in the flock. Not to mention the dangliest mucus.

'And what about my shoes?' she asks, peering down at her suede ballet pumps.

'What about them?'

'Don't get her started on that, mate,' chuckles Toby, who has already leapt over the fence into the sheep-field, sending the hungry Rastafarians scarpering in all directions; shrapnel from a grenade. 'Every single pair of Alice's precious shoes is kept in its own special box and stored in a high-security, humidity-controlled environment at precisely fifteen degrees Celsius. Except on Tuesdays, when all the shoes are taken out for a special spit-and-polish, even if they haven't been worn since 1980.'

'Toby!' exclaims Alice, archly.

'Is this true?' I ask, laughing.

'Well, I'm not *that* bad. But I do believe in looking after my things. When you live on a nurse's salary, you have to. I saved for weeks and months for some of those shoes. So yes, I do polish them quite regularly. Maybe it's a bit silly.'

'Maybe it's very silly,' corrects Toby, whose own shoes look like a pair of ransacked bird's nests transformed into footwear by a desperate cobbler.

'No, no, it's excellent,' I reply. 'If only I polished *my* shoes more often, they wouldn't be so cracked and split and leaky. So look: if you want to borrow some wellies, I've got some that are probably only about four sizes too big for you.'

'But there isn't even any *mud*,' snorts Toby. 'It can't have rained since Domesday.'

'I'll manage,' says Alice bravely, clambering over the fence.

So Alice and Toby administer the stale bread to the Rastafarians, while I take photographs, pretending that I am taking snaps of both of them while the camera, apparently with a mind of its own, lingers over Alice with a prurience that verges on cheekiness: her slender, bronzed limbs, emerging from a khaki miniskirt that is long enough to look more stylish than saucy; her irresistibly exquisite eyes and nose and mouth and cheekbones and ears and eyebrows and lips and teeth, all somehow conspiring to make me feel as if I am tumbling headlong into a shimmering lake of distantly forbidden bliss.

'Who's this one then?' asks Toby, pointing to an especially greedy ewe. 'And why haven't you fed her since January?'

'That's Daphne,' I reply. 'Pretty, isn't she?'

'I think I'll pretend you didn't just say that.'

'And here's her sister, Doris, who is just as greedy, but not quite as pushy. I have to give her an injection later – it's the end of her antibiotics.'

'Alice will do that for you,' says Toby, airily. 'Won't you, Al?'

'Well, I suppose I *could*. If injecting sheep is anything like injecting humans . . .'

'Search me,' I reply. 'But the needles for the sheep look pretty scary, considering how small the poor creatures are.' I buy my heavy-duty syringes from the ladies at Alliance Pastorale, and feel relieved that nobody is about to jab one of their needles, thick as a broad italic nib, into my own bony shoulders.

Whenever I am the one injecting my Rastafarians, they stagger and writhe with pain. Today, I stand and gape as Doris gives me her gummiest grin, succumbing to Alice's expertly wielded needle as happily as if she were being tickled behind her ears.

'You've done this before, haven't you?' I ask Alice, bemused at her effect on my wild sheep.

'Once or twice. But never on a sheep before.'

'Are you quite sure the needle went in?' At this, she throws me a look that makes me laugh and back away, sharpish.

I feel as if I am in a stalling aircraft that is threatening to spin, as I watch this trainee pilot who doesn't mind giving injections to Rastafarian sheep and is palpably comfortable in her own skin; who happens to be beguilingly pretty, and whom I have known since I was a small child in my NHS specs and 1970s flares. A safe-cracker with a stethoscope might detect the well-oiled pinions of a combination lock noiselessly falling open, one by one.

Another night of deep excitement follows, after Toby has gone to bed. Sleep feels like a waste of the short and precious time that we have to spend together. Instead, Alice and I talk and talk, our thoughts enmeshed as we lie in the darkness of my bedroom, gazing out at the moon.

We talk about flying light aircraft, and about the wrung-out brain-fried paralysis we both experienced during our early attempts to land them. We compare flying instructors we have known, and establish that all young male flying instructors, everywhere, develop the same swagger, as if they have just shot down several Messerschmitts, or been wearing their straps a bit tight.

We discuss our memories of Windlesham; the awe in which we held the headmaster, a brilliant classicist who was as tall and dark and glowering as a thundercloud, and his equally formidable wife, a bluestocking bombshell, who has left us both with a deep-seated belief in the value of reading, and a disproportionate fear of ever being heard to utter the word 'nice'. Alice tells me secrets from the forbidden kingdom of the Girls' Wing, such as the fact that they were allowed a bath once a year, on their birthday, and that in the showers they, too, had to request special permission for rinsing: 'Do I pass for soapiness, matron?'

We recall the struggle to write a compulsory letter home each week, and how we would always start our letters with the identical filler: 'How are you? I am fine.'

'Even now, whenever my dad sends me a postcard, he always starts it HAYIAF,' she giggles.

We discuss which types of 1970s chocolate were our favourite for Sunday Grub – the one time in the week when we were allowed sweets at school. Mine was a Mars Bar, a Milky Way or a packet of Minstrels – anything beginning with an M, in fact, except a Marathon, because that had nuts in it – whereas Alice was a nut-glutton for Marathons, Lion Bars and Topics.

I am relieved to discover that we agree about the pleasures of Toffos, Creme Eggs, Wagon Wheels and Refreshers. We argue over the relative merits of Fruit Gums and Fruit Pastilles, before agreeing that Curly Wurlys always tasted stale, Space Dust was disturbing and that a real Cadbury's Flake is far more delicious than the furled cardboard that you get in a so-called Flake '99 from Mr Whippy.

'Oh, God, that was my absolute favourite,' sighs Alice. 'Even now, in Baltimore, I hallucinate about Flake '99s.'

We discover that we both have parents who made us cut our Mars Bars into slices, to make them last longer, and that we both have an older sibling who had an annoying ability to make their Mars Bar last at least a month longer than anyone else's, and who would still have bits of their chocolate Easter egg left in the fridge in July.

And then I ask Alice about what her absolute favourite chocolate treat used to be, and am surprised when she names a Terry's chocolate orange – 'milk, not plain, of course' – because this was mine, too.

'The one you had to tap on the table to separate all the segments,' I remind her, unnecessarily. And then I'm about to tell her that my other favourite thing was a bumper tin of Quality Street at Christmas when she adds:

'Yes, and at Christmas, a huge tin of Quality Street.'

'No way,' I blink.

'Yes way.'

'I used to spend months looking forward to the opening of that tin,' I tell her, 'planning which ones I would eat first.' It is beginning to dawn on me that this is the kind of conversation it would be tricky for me to have with a French *copine*, no matter how dishy.

'I expect our mums both learned at Mother School that that's what they should provide at Christmas.'

'You mean they went to the same Mother School?'

'All mothers do. It's where they learn how to sew on name-tapes, how to wrap very small presents for Christmas stockings, and pick up that annoying habit of constantly reminding you about things you haven't yet forgotten.'

'But it was odd that my mum bought such a big tin of chocolates,' I muse, 'because she can't actually stand sweet things herself.'

'Nor can mine,' shrugs Alice.

There is a pause, as we listen to the crickets fizzing in the long grass outside. I wonder if Toby can hear all the noise we're making. And then wonder why it matters so much to me that he can't.

'Space Dust,' says Alice, in the silence, and again we explode into childlike giggles.

'Do you remember that time in the eighties that I invited you out on a date, in Sloane Square?' I ask her, reckless amid all the hilarity.

'What the hell was that?' she replies, suddenly gripping my arm.

'Well, you know, we met for a drink . . .'

'No, I mean, what was that noise? Up there.' In the darkness, I can see her pointing up at the great oak beams of the ceiling far above us.

'Ah. You mean that loud crash and all the scuttling. That will be Georges.'

'Who . . . is . . . Georges?' she says, suddenly sitting bolt upright in bed.

'He's a *fouine*. I mean, he's a friend.' And then, anticipating her next question, I explain that a *fouine* is a marten.

And that a marten is something like a weasel or a stoat. And that there is nothing to fear, because they only eat the rotting flesh of the small animals they have been storing in the roof for months.

'Oh, right.' There is a pause, and I can sense her re-arranging thoughts and fears in her mind; cogs turning, as she struggles to adapt to her wild surroundings. 'Anyway, tell me about this date we had.'

'You really don't remember?'

'I'm sure I do,' she says, hurriedly. 'Just not very clearly.'

'But why would I want to remind you about it, when the whole story just makes me look like a complete plonker?' I feel as if I have just climbed up on to the high diving-board at the pool, and am ready to clamber back down.

'Oh, go on. Please tell me.'

I hesitate, take a deep breath, and fling myself off the end of the board. 'Well, I'd seen you at a Windlesham reunion a few weeks before, and thought you looked incredibly pretty and delicious. I think it gave me a certain warped encouragement when you started snogging some bloke, right in the middle of the dance floor.'

Alice snorts; sits upright in bed again. 'I did *what*? And why did that make a difference?'

'It made you seem . . .'

'Easy, you mean?' She sits as still as a mannequin; gazes at me with cold eyes.

'No, no . . . more like, er, spirited.'

'So what happened?' Her body stiffens, and there is more clicking and whirring of cogs spinning in the darkness, as though she is preparing herself for bad news.

'A few weeks later, I somehow summoned up the courage to ask you out. It was touch and go, because I kept expecting Toby to pick up the phone.'

'He'd have been pleased.'

'He'd have teased me to death. And anyway, at the time I

was convinced that lust was a guilty secret that you had to try and hide from everyone. You were meant to like girls only for their personalities.'

Alice giggles again, enjoying my discomfort just a little too much.

'I blame my biology teacher at school,' I continue. 'He persuaded us that women don't reach their sexual peak until they are thirty-five. And that, until then, boys are just annoyances with grubby desires way out of kilter with the chasteness of the maidens they are bent on ravishing.'

'And what happened?'

So I tell her the story of our date at the Oriel café in Sloane Square; of my failure to summon up the courage to make a pass at her.

'It's lucky you didn't, because if you had, I wouldn't be here now, would I?'

'Because you'd have been so appalled?'

'Probably,' she replies, teasingly. 'You've already told me you were a frightful square.'

'Whereas you liked the B-52s, and I hadn't even heard of them.'

'I can't stand the B-52s.'

'You could back then.'

'I thought I was the bee's knees.'

'And were you?'

'Hardly. But I'm glad you didn't try it on, because that would have changed everything.'

I think about this for a while, and it dawns upon me that Alice is right. Timing is everything. Back then it was all too soon; the line-graphs of our lives were still miles from inter-secting. Even now, accidents of geography and the incompatibility of our chosen paths mean that they do not come close to meeting up. We are two planets whose trajectories have brought us into an unusual conjunction, just for this moment, before we spin off into outer darkness to sit out the next few millennia alone.

'But now I've found you again,' I continue. 'And this time I've somehow made it happen that I did end up kissing you, after all. And I'm not letting you go again.'

'That's good,' says Alice, softly.

'Alice Melbury,' I repeat to myself.

'What?'

'I'm just reminding myself that I really am here. And that you are here, too. The same person, the very same, with whom I rode the ghost train on Brighton Pier a quarter of a century ago. And here you are, beside me, at La Folie.'

'And tomorrow I fly back to England, and then to America.'

'I know. And let's not think about that right now. Because for now, just having you here is perfect.'

'That's good,' she whispers, again.

And I lie there in the moonlit silence, feeling utterly amazed. I gaze up at where Georges must be settling down for the night. And for the first time in my life, I find myself hoping that he is comfortable in my roof.

Next day, I drive my two old friends back to the airport, conscious that something has changed between the three of us, and unable to put my finger on quite what it is. Mind you, the large red bump on my forehead, sustained when I walked slap-bang into the rusty padlock-hasp on the barn door, is somehow symbolic of how topsy-turvy I suddenly feel.

This time Alice sits next to me in the front of the Espace, and Toby – still unaware that the universe has been rearranged beneath his nose – sits just behind. I hope he cannot see the way I brush her thigh each time I shift up into fifth gear; the way our fingers touch when I haul up the hand-brake at traffic lights.

As we make our goodbyes, I am still keeping up a stupid pretence that nothing has happened between me and Alice.

'Goodbye,' I tell her, with a kiss and a hug. 'It was so lovely to have you here.'

'Mate, it's been massive,' says Toby, giving me an even bigger hug of his own. 'We must do it again soon.'

'You bet,' I reply, doing my best to ignore the pang that is making me want to grab Alice all over again, to smother her in kisses and prevent her from climbing on to her plane. And then thankfully she takes things into her own hands by slipping into my arms for another hug. As we cling to each other, I glimpse Toby gazing at me, over Alice's shoulder, grinning like a lighthouse, as if he'd just come up with the funniest knock-knock joke in the world. For a split second our eyes meet, and the way he reacts makes me blush as if I were a prawn caught shoplifting: Toby winks.

Cat is waiting for me when I return to La Folie from the airport, and even she looks a little bereft at Alice and Toby's departure. I pick a handful of beans from the *potager*, thinking how much less fun this is as a solo activity. And then I eat cold lamb for supper, gazing at the chair where Alice sat, and trying to imagine her still sitting in it now. I even peer under the kitchen table, at the point in empty space where her ankle brushed mine, and the world suddenly started spinning a little faster.

This room has never felt so empty before.

Before she left, I slipped a handwritten letter into Alice's luggage, for her to find when she unpacks in Baltimore. And now I send her an email, too. 'I think I must have a delayed teenage crush on you,' I write. 'But at least you can return to the US knowing that you have established an international fan-base in France.'

And then I go upstairs to make the bed in the room where she slept, and lie down beside the imprint of her head on the pillow. I take a deep breath, and the bed still smells deliciously of Alice Melbury. It smells of vanilla and strawberries and clouds and rainbows. So perhaps I will not change the sheets quite yet, after all.

Out in the chicken house, the two ranks of the Egg Squad are sitting on their perches, waiting to be shut up for the night. I know they want to sleep. But I want to talk about Alice Melbury. And now that Cat has vanished into the night for a spot of mousing, there is no one else for me to tell. No one else who has actually met her, anyway, if we discount Daphne and the other Rastafarians, who have never been great conversationalists. So I sit on the window-sill in the chicken house, leaving the door ajar to allow a slim shaft of moonlight to outline the shapes of my surprised listeners. And I tell them all about Alice.

One of my wilder aspirations when I first came to La Folie, I explain, was to find myself a dishy French *copine*; some sultry local girl, perhaps, with a gift for vegetable production, lamb castration and the trimming of a cockerel's spurs. Either that, or at the very least a country-minded French-speaker from *Angleterre*, an ace at apple crumble, happy to exchange the comforts of home for the icy isolation of La Folie. I imagined she might be a novelist or a knitter; someone good at finding ways of diverting themselves from the harshness of the winter and the domestic limitations of the man of the house.

So there I was, seeking a French-speaking rural-minded domestic goddess with advanced farmyard skills. And somehow I have managed to fall for a self-professed City Girl who lives in some distant US metropolis, works twelve-hour shifts in her dream job as an intensive-care nurse at a cutting-edge hospital, can't cook for toffee, owns many glossy pairs of expensive shoes (and not a single welly), goes for a manicure once a week, and has been heard to speak just three words of French.

As I rather expected, the chickens are speechless at my news. Even Martha, my chatty favourite, makes no sound. Perhaps she is jealous. And so, having discovered that I do actually yearn for a conversation about Alice, and not just a soliloquy, I phone Jethro to tell him my news.

'It's not exactly official yet,' I explain, 'and I can't see how anything can come of it. But even so . . .'

'You lucky bastard,' he laughs. 'It's the grail quest, isn't it: a babe who's into flying? And snap, incidentally.'

It emerges that Jethro split up with Karen soon after the weekend at the chateau, and has now found himself a gorgeous woman who is mad-keen on aviation: an air-stewardess called Sasha who works for Cathay Pacific and moonlights as a yoga teacher in Acton Town. I have never heard him like this before: he sounds seriously smitten; swears that this is the real thing.

'Anyway,' he concludes, 'Sasha and I are taking things a day at a time.'

'A day at a time? Whatever happened to the old Jethro approach to courtship?'

'Michael, Michael, Michael,' he says. 'This one is special. I'm sure of it.'

He has amazing news on the flying front, too; says he has landed a paying gig with a display team.

'You mean, a *flying* gig?'

'I'm not just making the sandwiches, if that's what you mean.'

Even by Jethro's standards of making things happen, this is astounding. It feels as if it was only a few months ago that both of us gained our pilot's licences. And while I am still puttering around the skies over rural France in an antique plane whose top speed is slower than that of most modern cars, Jethro is about to be paid to fly aerobatics in front of crowds at air displays.

'But that's fantastic, Jethro. I mean, I knew you were

good. But I didn't know you were *that* good. Don't tell me: it'll be Spitfires next.'

'Thanks, mate. I feel the same about your news. And I can't wait to meet her.'

'You must think I'm crazy, if you think I'm going to let you work the Jethro magic on her,' I reply.

'No, but seriously,' he chuckles, 'you've done something in moving to France that I'd love to do, too. But I just don't have the nerve. You've taken the risks. And you deserve all the good things that come to you. Like this pilot babe. You've made your own luck.'

After I have put down the phone, I reflect on Jethro's words. I attempt to track back through the twists and turns of pure chance and coincidence that happen to have linked my life with that of Alice Melbury.

And the more I think about it, the more I think that, no, Jethro is right: now and more than ever before, I have begun to create my life for myself and in the shape that I want it at La Folie, as opposed to waiting for it to happen to me. I have begun to make my own luck. Yet I have a sense of foreboding, too. And with a mixture of excitement and dread, I cannot wait to see how it will all unfold.

# Part Two

# 12

## AUGUST

At the aeroclub in St Juste, the sun hammers down so hard that even the wings of the aircraft parked on the sweating tarmac look as if they are beginning to droop. In the cool of the maintenance hangar, I stand on a plastic chair to strip the engine cowlings and baffles off my Luscombe, in preparation for fitting the shiny new magnetos that have at last arrived from Brussels. Antoine, the club mechanic, is supervising my progress with one watchful eye, while he works on his own project at the bench in the corner. This appears to involve micro-surgery on a fillet of balsa wood, although Antoine is adamant that he is rebuilding the wings of a biplane designed by a Russian taxi-driver on the streets of Paris in 1917.

Wonderful things, magnetos. Some relationships rely on external stimulation to keep them alive; in others, the simple act of doing things together supplies the buzz. Thus, in a car engine, the spark is provided by the battery, which is kept topped up by the charge supplied by the alternator. In an aircraft, as soon as the propeller is swung, the spark is mechanically created by the magnetos. And as the propeller spins, it continuously generates the very ignition that combusts the fuel that drives it.

Unfortunately, my original Bendix magnetos have become as old and worn as a greying husband and wife, sitting in their matching Parker Knolls watching repeats of *Poldark* on a black-and-white television. The spark is still there, flaring as dimly as the two-bar electric fire that colours the monochrome scene with a hint of pink warmth. And so their worn-in, worn-out relationship continues to toddle along, as haltingly as their own footsteps down the corridor, on their way to their separate beds. Yet the spark that keeps an engine going is different from the spark that first brings it to life.

Hence my purchase of a new pair of Slick magnetos, each with an impulse coupling designed to supply a *coup de foudre* when you swing the prop: an especially bright spark to ignite the fuel vapour that waits in the cylinders as expectantly as a single man who has somehow never met a woman with whom he could quite imagine spending the whole of the rest of his life. If all goes to plan, once these Slicks are fitted, my Luscombe should start on the very first swing. Every time.

The big old Bendix breadboxes are squeezed between the backplate of the engine and the firewall of the cockpit. Antoine gently indicates to me the various nuts and levers and attachments that I must remove to provide access to this confined space. At one point, this involves removing an inspection cover from the top of the firewall, lying upside down on the cockpit floor with a torch attached to my head, and reaching my hands through the narrow gap.

'All this,' I gasp at Antoine, who is smiling at my contortions, 'just to create a spark?' I happen to know that Antoine could remove the nut I am struggling to loosen in about five seconds flat, with his eyes shut.

'It will be worth it, when it is done,' he chuckles, 'you'll see.' Except that I can't see, because a drop of blood from where I have cut my wrist on the sharp aluminium has just fallen into my eye, and I growl with annoyance at my own ineptitude.

'Come, let me help you a little,' he says, relenting. At last.
'Wouldn't it be quicker and simpler if you just did all of
this yourself?'

'*Bien sûr*,' he shrugs. 'But how would you learn?'

'By watching you?'

'It is not the same,' he says, shaking his head, and giving
me a grave stare.

With his white hair, his impressive girth and his genial dis-
position, Antoine always reminds me of Father Christmas.
For all his bonhomie, however, there is a sadness about him,
too; a sense of wistful longing that I recognize only too well,
as the badge of a kindly man who has never found the right
woman with whom to settle down. Antoine also happens to
be the best aircraft mechanic I have ever met, though his
arduous day-job keeps him stapled to the machines at the
local paper factory.

I could tell at once that Antoine knew his stuff, the very
first time we met. I had landed at St Juste after a short local
flight in the Luscombe, and Antoine wandered over, his
white hair blowing in the prop-wash. I assumed he was an
anorak plane-spotter, surprised to see such an old American
plane in France. After I shut down the engine, he jingled the
change in his pockets, put his head on one side and
commented that it was making a sound that I hadn't even
noticed myself. I shrugged, quite used to receiving un-
solicited advice from Marcel and the others, most of which I
had learned to ignore. But Antoine was different: he insisted
we investigate. So I unscrewed the cowlings. We chatted
about this and that. And, unable to find anything amiss, I
went off to have lunch with Peter Viola and Jacques the
flying schoolteacher at the Toquenelle café, where they make
the best crème brûlée in town.

On my return, Antoine was still examining the Luscombe,
his head deep within the engine compartment, like a well-fed
cat investigating a washing machine. He had removed

various inspection panels and the heat-exchange boxes from the exhausts. Everything was neatly arranged on a large sheet of cardboard on the hangar floor, with all the screws, nuts and washers sorted into numbered plastic pots. And he pointed out to me what he had found hidden beneath the cabin heat-exchange box: a hairline crack in one of the exhausts. I was stunned. Unchecked, this might very soon have proved catastrophic.

'How do you know about this stuff, Antoine?' I asked him. 'I thought you said you worked in the paper factory.'

'I do,' he replied, glancing across the runway at the twin chimneys of his factory, as if to double-check that they really had given up smoking for the weekend. 'But I had a different life once, a long time ago.'

Two years on, I know from the long hours Antoine spends at the aeroclub, tinkering on his projects, or just gazing up at the distant drone of an aircraft engine in the sky, that he is passionate about aeroplanes. He has even built his own aircraft: a sleek red, white and blue machine constructed not from a kit but from his own imagination – proof, he once told me, that you do not have to be rich to fly. Except that Antoine never flies any more. It seems so sad that anyone so talented should be condemned to supervising a production line spewing out the packets for corn flakes and cat food, while the dazzling plane, with its cranked wings, sits and waits.

'So why don't you give up the factory job, and do something in aviation?' I ask him, handing him the spanner I have been using to wrestle with the seized nut behind the firewall. There are so many old aircraft still flying; so few old-school mechanics gifted and experienced enough to maintain them.

He thinks for a moment before replying to my question. 'Because I promised myself that I wouldn't, until the time was right.'

I blink. Antoine must be in his early fifties at least. From his calm acceptance and steady manner, one would not guess that he is hungrily preparing himself for a brighter future. 'So, when do you think the time will be right, Antoine?'

He looks down at his grease-blackened fingers. 'I'm waiting for a sign,' he says, 'before I can fly again.' And then, hauling himself up into the Luscombe and kneeling on the cockpit floor, he reaches his hands through the hole in the firewall and, working blind, unscrews the nut with which I have been wrestling for fifteen minutes, in less than fifteen seconds.

'*Voilà*,' he says, kindly. 'It *was* a little stiff.'

Back at La Folie, I have just woken from a nightmare in which a phalanx of green snakes slithered out from under my bed and threatened to attack me. This is very frightening, especially for Cat, who becomes momentarily airborne as I sit up in bed with the force of a trebuchet. And then, as I fumble for the bedside lamp, I realize that those were not snakes at all.

They were green beans. Oh horrible, most horrible!

Even more than Alice Melbury, about whom I day-dream roughly fifteen times a minute, in those rare moments when I am not composing emails to her, or struggling to imagine how a city-slick intensive-care nurse who speaks not a word of French could possibly adapt to darkest Jolibois and the long winters at La Folie, green beans rule my life just now. If I am not picking them, I am topping and tailing them. And if I am not topping and tailing them, then I am staring ashen-faced at the rising piles of freshly picked *haricots verts* that surround me, blocking out the light. Though I am a novice at all this, I suspect that other bean-fanciers will be familiar with the symptoms: a soreness in the lumbar regions; a constant throb in the tip of the right thumb, just under the nail; and a growing sense of the hopelessness of it all.

Nor is it just the beans, either. There are the courgettes,

swelling from cigars into cruise missiles while my back is turned. For the first time in my life, I have even started looking up courgette recipes. I always assumed that courgettes were designed to be bought, allowed to slush at the bottom of the fridge, and then thrown away. It never occurred to me that I might one day feel a sense of culinary obligation towards a zucchini.

Then there are the tomatoes in their hundreds, flicking from green to red faster than a traffic-light when you are already running late. And the radishes: ah, pity the radishes, whose pink, misshapen corpses lie even now in the unmarked grave of the compost heap.

How I wish Alice were here now, to share my treasures with me.

As far as I can see, the hardest thing about growing your own vegetables in rural France is finding people to give them to. Every self-respecting Frenchman in the region has his own *potager*. And everyone else has gone to spend August with the in-laws in Bordeaux. I have phoned them all: Le Grand Mermoz, Maxim the boxer, Claude the electrician with the strong forehand, Grillon who works as a guard on the night-trains to Rome and Venice, Yves-Pascal the notaire, Blaise and the Proustian Madeleine; all gone.

Meanwhile the countryside fills up with Parisians escaping the big smoke, and *les Anglais* still house-hunting for second homes. Fred the Viking's wife, Émilie, tells me that the market is slack but, when I walk past her office on my way to the *boulangerie*, there is still no lack of shell-suited Brits gawping at the details in her window. Spying that she is busy with a client, I duck inside and leave her a large bag of courgettes before she can say no.

Across the street, Olga the spy is arranging black rubbish bags outside her front door and looks embarrassed to see me.

'Is Ralph in?' I ask her, before she can scuttle inside.

'I think he's practising his *saxophone*,' she says, pronouncing the word as if it were a black rubbish bag filled with seething detritus. 'But he's *meant* to be sorting his books.' So I go up and see Ralph in his study, where every wall is piled high with books. His face, dripping with perspiration, lights up at the sight of a distraction.

'*Ah, c'est le grand pilote anglais!*' he exclaims, in his best Inspector Clouseau accent, as he lays down his saxophone. Beside him, on a chair, is a huge cardboard box with about three slim paperbacks at the bottom of it. 'Did I ever tell you I once had a flight in a Harvard?'

Ralph often tells me about his Harvard flight with the university air squadron, and I always love hearing the tale, partly because of the schoolboy relish with which he tells it, and partly out of sheer anorak envy for his experience. We both know that flying a Harvard is only one step down from flying a Spitfire. But today, conscious of Olga pacing about downstairs, I feel guilty in indulging him, as he seeks distractions from his distractions.

'Looks like you're doing really well with these books, Ralph,' I tell him, peering into the cardboard box.

'It's a nightmare, my boy,' he wails. 'Letting go of the past, I mean. There's so much I shall have to leave behind. My paintings alone will make up a car-load. I know they're awful, but they're all I have: these fragments I have shored against my ruins. Ah, my poor, dear Rembrandt: so many memories, so many happy times here in Jolibois. Do *you* want any books? I've offered them all to Harold and Elspeth up the road, but I know he'll just burn them in his wretched stove.'

'Actually, Ralph, I was rather hoping you might let me buy one of your paintings before you go.'

He stops, frozen to the spot.

'Buy?' he asks, staring at me, aghast. 'A painting of *mine*?' And then he begins to weep. 'I'm so sorry, my boy,' he says, slumping down into a chair with his hands over his eyes. 'I'm just not used to hearing those three words in the same sentence. Ah, my poor Rembrandt. But of course you shall have a painting. I shall be proud to give you one.'

'No, Ralph,' I tell him, firmly, as I turn to go. 'I want to pay you for it.'

Jérôme, in whose lake Toby and I swam, is back at Les Sablonnières. He and his wife, Jacqueline, are opening up the house in preparation for the arrival of their nine grandchildren, and invite me to dinner. Just before setting out from La Folie, I phone to see if I can offload some of my produce on them.

'May I bring you some *haricots verts*?' I plead.

'Er, we've done all the shopping,' says Jacqueline, apologetically. And then, relenting, adds, 'But we did forget tomatoes for salad.'

'Ah, I have so many ripe tomatoes. I'll bring some over.'

'No, no. They mustn't be too ripe, for salad,' she remonstrates, shocked at my ignorance. 'Ripe tomatoes are for cooking. For salad, they must be less ripe. In Spain they eat them almost green.'

'*Pas de problème*,' I reply, hastily. 'I have so many less-ripe tomatoes, too. I'll bring a selection.'

'Not too many,' she begs. 'We'll be returning to Paris soon. And isn't it time that you were going away yourself?'

'*Ah, les animaux, c'est l'esclavage*,' I reply, borrowing a line I have often heard Young Boulesteix mutter. This is a slight exaggeration in my case – there is very little slavery in keeping seven Rastafarian sheep, nine bilingual chickens, two goldfish and one sarcastic cat – but somehow it feels more acceptable to claim that my animals cannot do without me than to admit that several thousand green beans have me under house-arrest. Or that I am quite happy to stay in France, when there is an outside chance that the prettiest student pilot in Baltimore might just fly out to visit me, some time soon.

The possibility of her presence comes as a relief, for Alice's absence is beginning to interfere with the smooth daily running of life at La Folie. Not because every dew-darked flower, moonlit landscape or sunlit vapour trail that I see makes me wish that she could see it, too. No, it is more prosaic than that. Feeding the sheep has become a hurried inconvenience, since it prevents me checking my emails for almost five minutes. And I feel obliged to take the phone with me when I go to muck out the chicken house, in case it should ring.

At the aeroclub, I hold a large spanner to imply that I am working, while Antoine adjusts the timing on my gleaming new magnetos, gently nudging the propeller with one hand while with the other he makes fine adjustments with a screwdriver. It is dusk, everyone else has gone home, and we have switched on the strip-lights in the ceiling of the hangar so that we can see what we are doing, and so that every moth and mosquito in the Limousin will know where to come. Behind us, Antoine's red, white and blue aircraft gleams in the shadows. I cannot think of a better opportunity to ask him the question I have been burning to ask.

'So why did you stop working in aviation, Antoine, when you are so passionate about aircraft?'

Straightening up and polishing an imaginary speck of grease from the propeller with his fingers, the man who looks like Father Christmas examines the screwdriver in his hand as if it were the first time he had ever set eyes on such an extraordinary tool.

'*Pourquoi?*' he asks, perhaps hoping he has misheard.

'*Oui, pourquoi?*' I repeat.

Without replying, he toddles towards the front of the hangar, where the twin chimneys of the paper factory are dimly silhouetted against the apricot-coloured sky. And then he begins to haul shut the huge metal doors that hammer and clatter on their rails like the cars of a fairground attraction. At first I think he is worried about being over-heard. Then I wonder if he is shutting up shop because I have offended him, and that my magnetos will now never produce the absurdly bright sparks of which I dream. And finally it occurs to me that a gentle breeze has begun to blow across the apron, and Antoine is closing the hangar doors to keep out the dust and leaves.

'I had my own aircraft-maintenance shop,' he begins, his voice low, his kindly face almost smiling at the memory. 'It was a successful business with several employees and I was doing what I loved. I even had a girlfriend . . .'

'It's not true,' I joke.

'No, really.' He raises his eyebrows. 'She was very beauti-ful, an aerobatic display pilot, and we were very much in love.'

'Sounds perfect: a woman who flies.'

'Exactly. I know nothing is perfect. But she, she really was. And we were happy together; we were going to get married.'

'So what went wrong?'

Antoine gazes at me: a long, gentle stare, as if I were a child and he were trying to guess what I would really, really like for Christmas. And then he says, very quietly:

'What went wrong is that she crashed her plane in the middle of a display. They say she burned to death.'

He pauses. 'Unfortunately, I was the last person who worked on the aircraft.'

There is a long silence. Antoine picks at the tip of the screwdriver in his hands. My heart goes out to him, and I do not know what to say.

'But the fact that she crashed,' I murmur at last, 'it doesn't make you responsible.'

'The police came and took me away in handcuffs,' he says. 'They tore apart my workshop, looking for evidence.'

'But what did they know?'

'It doesn't really matter, does it? The woman I loved was dead, and everyone was telling me it was my fault.'

Antoine explains how he was still under arrest when a fragment of cotton rag was found in the crashed aircraft's hydraulic system, and that he was finally able to prove that this could not have come from his workshop, where only paper wipes were used.

'At last, I was a free man. But that was the moment when I decided that I must leave aviation, leave flying behind, because it was too painful for me.'

Little by little, he tells me, he is picking up the pieces. He likes to help out when he can, on small projects such as replacing a Luscombe's magnetos, or doing anything he can to help make an aircraft safe for flight. He still dreams of meeting another woman, a pilot perhaps, with whom to share his cat and his lonely life. He would love his own maintenance shop again one day. Yet he cannot go back to working in aviation, he says, until the time is right. He cannot even fly his own plane. The beautiful red, white and blue machine, with its cranked wings, must languish in the shadows, unflown.

'And how will you know when the time is right?' I ask.

'I will just know,' he smiles.

The night is dark by the time the Luscombe is finished, but we roll open the hangar doors, push the aircraft outside, and attempt to fire up the engine even so. As Chekhov said, you must not bring a gun on to the stage unless you are going to fire it.

With a torch on the seat beside me, I sit in the cockpit whose leather smell I know so well. The stainless-steel stalk of the closed throttle gleams in the moonlight, as does the tip of the pitot-tube protuding from the leading edge of the wing. The luminous paint on the instruments has long since ceased to glow, and there is no electrical system in the plane to supply any light. After Antoine has pulled through the propeller a few times, to prime the cylinders, I hold back the stick, crack the throttle, and wait for him to give me a torchlit thumbs-up before clicking the key into the ignition and turning the magneto switch to 'Both'.

'Contact!' I yell.

There is a jolt, as Antoine swings the prop with all his strength. And then, with barely a cough of apprehension, and in an invisible shower of star-shaped sparks, the four cylinders of the vintage Continental engine suddenly explode into life, as if all four of the recalcitrant stallions attached to a chariot had – for the first time in years – suddenly decided to bolt at once.

Peering out at Antoine, a hunched silhouette in the hangar door, I raise my fist in triumph and amazement. It worked! First time! Antoine, it's a miracle! And he, Father Christmas, for whom the complexities of the internal combustion engine are as nothing compared with the inchoate mysteries of the human heart, quietly nods.

Time begins to pass very, very slowly as I wait for Alice's next visit. I am praying that this may light up the end of August, if she can only swap some of her night-shifts with her colleagues at the ICU, and squeeze in a quick flit to La Folie as part of a trip to England to see her family. I would fly to Baltimore myself, except that Alice still shares a house with her ex-boyfriend, and neither of us feels quite ready for so bracing a ménage-à-trois.

In the depths of my heart, I sometimes wonder if those night hours that Alice and I spent together a month ago, holding hands in the darkness, talking until dawn, were just a flight of whimsical fancy; something I half-imagined and she will already have begun to half-regret, now that she has returned to the intensity of her working life in Baltimore, calmly saving people's lives while I worry myself silly about the length of a cockerel's spurs, or the snottiness of an old and toothless ram.

Once upon a time, Peter Viola used to upbraid me for leaving the aeroclub early on weekend afternoons, just when the old boys were getting properly stuck into their tall tales and hangar flying. But I had to get home, I explained, to feed Cat and the sheep. I was worried about the Egg Squad, and the risk of losing them to a fox if I didn't shut up the chicken house on time.

Tonight it is a different motivation that makes me hurry home from a dinner with Yves-Pascal the notaire and his wife, Ariane. I want to hear Alice's voice again, before she heads out to her night-shift at the hospital. I think my hosts are probably relieved to see me go, now that my conversation has become as repetitively glued to one subject as an old vinyl record with the needle going *click-click-click* in the groove.

Back at La Folie, a brown-paper parcel is leaning up against the front door, and a message is blinking on the answerphone when I dash into the kitchen. I can feel my heart beating in my chest as I press the button, longing to hear the sound of America calling.

'Michael, it's Jethro,' crackles an excited, faraway voice.

I press the pause button; purse my lips; smile at my own silliness. Then I rearrange my jangled emotions as if I were tucking in my shirt, and press play again.

'There's this competition to win a flight in a Spitfire,' continues Jethro, sounding breathless. 'It's in a mag called *Warbird* or *Air Display* or something. I'd send you a copy, but I'm off to Australia for a month with Sasha first thing in the morning. See if you can find one. Got to be worth a shot, eh? Cheers. Jethro.'

Win a flight in a Spitfire. My heart lifts at the thought, and I can feel my pulse beginning to race, until I hear the bleep-bleep-bleep that announces No More Messages, and my shoulders slump: no word from Alice Melbury tonight.

Then the phone rings, a second later, and it is her.

'Is it too late?' she asks.

'It's never too late,' I reply. 'You can ring any time, day or night. It helps me to get through the next few minutes without you.'

'Aw, that's so *nice* – sorry, Mrs Charles – I just wanted to hear your voice, too, before I dash off for my shift.'

So I tell her about the Spitfire competition, and she sounds excited. And then she says that her instructor thinks it won't be long before she flies solo herself.

'But he's wrong,' she adds. 'I'm not ready. I'll *never* be ready. I must be the slowest learner in the world.'

'You couldn't be any slower than me,' I assure her. And I want to tell her about Antoine, and what happened to his girlfriend; I want to tell her to be careful, even as I know that I must not. So I change the subject, and instead we talk about chickens and sheep, and how Titus must be the most handsome cockerel in the whole of the Limousin, which is Alice's suggestion and makes me adore her all the more.

We must have a hundred such conversations over the course of a single month, chatting away about very little for the simple pleasure of feeling connected by the stream of electrons pulsing up and down the thousands of miles of copper wire and fibre-optic cable that lie between us, our idle banter bounced back and forth through the atmosphere by the silent satellites floating in space, amid the scrambled desires and longings of all the other long-distance lovers dotted over the planet as thickly as the sugar-dusting on a doughnut.

All I want, right now, is to be close to this woman who has put my heart into a spin.

Many times, when practising spins in the cockpit of a Tiger Moth, I have felt the adrenaline rush of powering vertically towards the earth, with the fields and trees blurring in a wild rotation as if someone were twirling a huge green flag in the middle of a tornado. Yet such spins always feel dangerous and counter-intuitive. Whereas with Alice, I feel as if I am flying out from beneath an iron-grey overcast, into the kind of sunlit cloudscape that looks like heaven in the old movies, and makes even non-pilots want to take to the sky.

With a start, I suddenly remember the parcel outside the front door. Fetching a knife, I slice through the heavy cord with which it is tied. I recognize the painting inside at once: Titus, as painted by Ralph. There is no message.

I had almost forgotten all the photographs Ralph took of Titus last summer. He told me he was fed up with painting chefs and their pots and pans. He said that he wanted to paint something beautiful, just once.

I will phone Ralph in the morning. Yet as I gaze at the vivid greens and reds and blues of his gorgeous painting, I know that he and Olga will already have left.

It is after midnight by the time I walk out to the chicken house to put the chickens to bed. The sky is so clear that more and more stars appear as I gaze above my head. I can even see the gauzy luminescence of the Milky Way stretching away from me like the wake of a magic carpet as big as a galaxy.

The days when I used to lift the Egg Squad on to their perches, training them out of their battery-bred habits of cowering in their own muck on a cement floor, are long gone. Instead, as dusk falls, young Hotspur leads his teen-harem to the barn where all my logs are stored, at the far end of the house, while Titus and the girls strut into the chicken house proper, flap up on to their perches, and wait for me to come and shut out the night. Ever since Mildred was taken by a fox, Titus has stationed himself on guard-duty closest to the door.

Each night I wander out into the moonlight, swinging my oil lamp and muttering 'Ten o'clock and all's well' to convince myself that all the scufflings and scamperings in the swaying bushes are on my side. I collect the eggs, murmur a few sweet nothings, and bolt the chicken-house door behind me. The scene reminds me of a school dormitory after lights-out: everyone pretends to be asleep when matron does her rounds with a torch, yet I can tell from the suppressed tittering that the pillow-fights will re-start as soon as the coast is clear.

Tonight, however, as I do my own rounds, something is not right. In the barn, there are only three chickens – young Hotspur and two of his floozies – waiting for lights-out. Normally there would be a quartet. No matter, I think to myself. One of them must have decided to have a sleepover in the chicken house.

I am not worried. Not yet. But the population of the *poulailler* is strangely depleted, too. And I can see at once who is missing.

Titus.

Now I am worried. Chickens do not simply go AWOL, just like that. Instead, like beggars and commuters and transatlantic flights, they turn up in the same place at the same time, day after day after day. And on the day when they don't, you somehow know that they are dead. Even before you have found the trail of golden feathers leading into the scrub.

I peer out into the blackness; scan the swaying branches of the trees; double-check the barn, in case Titus is hiding in there, with a view to assassinating his young rival, Hotspur, in the dark.

I have searched everywhere. There is no sign of the big fellow.

Reluctantly, I slide shut the bolt on the chicken-house door, as if I were crossing out an aircraft registration on a blackboard with a stick of chalk, or sealing a bulkhead on a sinking ship, leaving a shipmate on the other side to drown. No chance now for Titus to find sanctuary if he should stagger home, wounded, in the night. No place on the perch for the cockerel who dallied. But if a fox is at large, and I leave the door open, the killing-spree would be short and swift and complete.

I wander back past the front of the house, gazing up at the branches of the ancient box tree, so pale in the darkness, leaves shivering in the wind. The crickets are silent tonight. Even the stars appear, quite suddenly, to have vanished. And then I head back inside, into the summer sitting-room. I put Ralph's painting of Titus on the music-rest of the piano and stare at the keys, no music in my head.

He was only a chicken.

Yet losing Titus is not like losing any old chicken. He was not just another bird, to be plucked and laid out on a tray with his yellow claws still attached, like all those sad specimens at the Saturday market. No, Titus was altogether grander and more important than that: like the flash of red amid the greens and browns of a painting by Constable, he was the focal point of the entire landscape of La Folie.

So now I feel like a mariner on some ancient galleon, waking to discover that the ship's figurehead has fallen off in the night. Titus has been with me almost since the start of my time at La Folie. His crowing is part of the sound-track of my life.

'Doesn't he ever shut up?' asked Alice, when she and Toby were here, and we were attempting to eat lunch on the terrace to the accompaniment of a strutting rape alarm with combs and wattles and spurs attached.

'I love the noise he makes,' I replied, crestfallen on behalf of La Folie's strident mascot. 'I swear you can sometimes hear him from the centre of Jolibois, if the wind's in the right direction.'

This was an exaggeration, but Titus's *cocorico* is still a thing of rare splendour; a burnished trumpet-blast that dazzlingly evokes the Platonic archetype of how a true cockerel should sound.

'Yes, but what is he *for*?' asked Alice, unconsciously testing my devotion, in the closest thing to a romantic tiff we have ever had in the short span of our secret non-relationship. 'I mean, at least the girls do something useful, laying their eggs. Whereas he just totters around, showing off.'

Wounded on his behalf, I did not know how to explain that Titus doesn't have to do anything useful. Like Nelson Mandela, Jelly Tots and the Leaning Tower of Pisa, he just *is*.

'What a waste,' says Toby, when I tell him the news about Titus over the phone the next day. I am dying to talk to him about his sister, too, but it still feels too early to say anything about that. Everything and nothing has happened between us, after all.

'I know,' I sigh, grateful for his understanding.

'I always pictured him with a couple of rashers of streaky slapped on his chest in a hot oven.'

'Toby Melbury, you have no heart.'

'I mean, it's not like when a dog or a cat dies, is it?'

This is a statement that only someone who has never kept chickens could make. Whereas a cat will walk by itself, humouring humans only to the extent that they serve its purposes, chickens are interactive creatures, unstinting in their curiosity, and hilariously unpredictable in their responsiveness.

With Titus vanquished, the whole rhythm of life changes at La Folie. Gone are the days when I would see the girls scampering happily after their chief as he led them off on another expedition to some distant and exciting field, leaving me feeling as if I could get on with my day once the clucking children had taken themselves off to school. Now the Egg Squad mooch around, tormenting Cat and getting under my feet, each in her own solitary daze: seven sad old widows, window-shopping for things they do not want, picking at food for which they have no appetite, struggling to remember the good old days.

Vainglorious, Titus may have been. Sexually aggressive, and callous with it. A trumpeting show-off, who liked nothing more than to stand himself on a five-bar gate and let you know that he was there. But I could always relax when he was crowing away because, from what Titus would have me believe, at least one creature at La Folie had everything under control.

Except that it wasn't under control, after all. Beautiful plumage is no guarantee of immortality, any more than a strident trumpet is proof against a silent death. There is always a snake, or a fox, in the grass.

Two days later, I am disconsolately wandering out to the barn to fetch a new sack of granules for the sheep, when I see a familiar shape silhouetted on the old gate. I stare. I blink. I stare again. *Titus*?

For a second, my heart leaps. Holbein's Henry VIII is back in town! Long live the King! And then the cockerel opens its beak and lets forth a strangulated, hooty greeting that I know only too well. My shoulders slump, and I let out a sigh.

Hotspur hops down from the gate and scampers off, followed at a distance by Martha, Melissa and the girls, in the footsteps of their new leader. Strange, how he seems to have grown in stature, now that he is head of the household at last.

I hang Ralph's painting of Titus in the winter sitting-room, just beside my desk. Part of me feels a pang that Martha and Melissa should, so soon, forget. And part of me thinks how lucky it is for chickens that, unlike me, they do.

\*

I want to phone Alice, to tell her about Titus. But she should be in England by now, spending four days in Norfolk with her mother and her cousins, before catching another flight from Stansted to Limoges. So whilst she is now closer at hand than ever, she feels further away, too.

At least when she is in Baltimore I can phone her if she is awake; email her if she sleeps. Whereas now that she is in Blakeney, she is as out of reach as if she were on the far side of the moon. And then the phone rings, and here she is.

'Can you talk?' she whispers.

'Yes, but it sounds as if *you* can't,' I reply, taking the phone out on to the terrace. 'Where are you?' The dusk is already dimming towards night. Hearing my voice, the Rastafarians set up a frantic clamour, groaning for their granules. With the grass frazzled, I am having to spoil them with food from a sack every night.

'At the Blakeney Hotel. I've slipped out between courses at dinner; I'll have to be brief. I just wanted to hear your voice, but mostly I can hear the sheep.'

'I just wanted to hear yours, too. I think the sheep want you back. They remember all that deliciously stale bread you fed them. And how dishy you looked in your miniskirt.'

'That's nice,' she giggles. 'I mean, lovely.' She says she has been drinking champagne with her family, sixteen of them, on a high balcony, watching the sunset over a coastline so flat that the horizon is the longest she has ever seen. I try to picture the landscape – like something out of *Peter Grimes*, perhaps – but, all around me, the grey contours of the steeply sloping hillside at La Folie cloud my imagination.

'I can't wait to meet the rest of your family – all your cousins, and everyone,' I tell her.

'I know,' she laughs, still in a whisper. 'And they can't wait to meet you, because then at least they won't have to keep hearing me going on about you.'

'Poor things. Have you told your mum about us, then?'

'She laughed and laughed. She thinks it's hilarious.'

'In a good way?'

'What do *you* think?'

'I hope so. She seemed rather cross with me, last time we met.'

'But that was in the late seventies.'

'Perhaps she has a long memory.'

'And you?' she asks. 'You sound weary. Are you all right?'

So I tell her about Titus, and the lack of grass, and how difficult it is to pursue my quest to live in the present when every cell in my body is so desperately excited about her visit, which is still three days in the future.

'If it's any consolation, it's the same for me,' she whispers.

'You won't forget my Spitfire magazine, will you?'

'Don't worry, I know that's the real reason you're looking forward to my visit. And now I've *really* got to go. I'm having twice-baked cheese soufflé next, and I can see Mum waving furiously at me from down the corridor, so it must have come.'

'*Bon appétit.*'

'What's that? I mean, *merci*. I mean, oh, *you* know what I'm trying to say.'

'Of course I do,' I laugh. 'Have fun.'

And as I do my best to picture Alice tucking into her twice-baked cheese soufflé with sixteen members of her family in a hotel dining-room on the Norfolk coast, I sit at Zumbach's old table in the kitchen at La Folie, and light two candles. England feels so near, yet still so far away. At least until Monday: on Monday, she will be here.

And with this dazzling thought briefly lighting up my life like a flare above a battlefield, while Bach's Schübler chorale preludes play in the background, I pour myself a glass of red wine, and tuck into my microwaved home-grown baked potato with tuna, sweetcorn and a glug of olive oil. And I honestly think that no spud has ever tasted as magical as this one of mine tastes tonight.

Monday at last, and I am on my way to Limoges airport in the Espace. This is a drive I have made so many times before, and the warm, fuggy smell as I open the car door – still that ancient whiff of dead dog – is as familiar to me as the smell of school used to be – floor polish, maths books and vinegar – on the first day of term. Yet today's journey feels different from all the others.

Today, I feel as if I am driving off on holiday, with the same breezy anticipation I felt as a child when we drove up to Scotland for our annual feast of fresh air in a world at once familiar and strange. Scotland meant sailing on the glitter of a loch at dawn, clambering up heather-carpeted hills beneath a cold white sun, cramming my mouth with sugary lumps of melting butter-tablet, and failing to catch trout in a river whose rapids seemed too torrid for fish. That rough landscape stimulated all my senses. And there was a romance about the place, too, that made me just want to lie in the heather and hug the entire country to myself.

Alice Melbury is all these things and more. She is the first cable-car up the mountain after a night of fresh snow; a hot shower after splitting half a tonne of logs. She is Mozart after Mahler; a double rainbow after thunder; she is Venice after Rome. And she can turn a simple paragraph into the purplest of prose.

I am still eight minutes from the airport, lost in the blur of these thoughts and the roaring bluster of an unstreamlined car bowling through the French countryside with all the windows open, when I spot the pipe-shaped silhouette of what must be an airliner on its final approach into Limoges.

As I watch, the three black splodges of its undercarriage

drop into position beneath the wings and nose, and I attempt to make out the emblem on its tail. A flash of blue and yellow tells me all I need to know: I am about to be late for the most important meeting of my life.

'Please,' I mutter to the Espace, 'help me to get there in time. Just this once.' I press my foot to the floor, and the roar that comes from the engine in response comes as such a shock that at first I think the exhaust-pipe must have fallen off. I am not sure that we actually go any faster than usual, but – patting the dashboard in thanks – I do feel reassured by the infernal din.

In the airport car park, taxi-drivers stand open-mouthed as I roar past them in a feverish cloud of smoke and decibels. There is no time for proper parking; I simply leave the Espace tucked diagonally against a tree, sprint away from it as if it were wired to explode and – against all odds – reach the prison-style fence beside the airport café just as the blue-and-yellow 737 is beginning to disgorge its passengers from the front and rear doors.

The tarmac shimmers in the midday sun, the plane's polished surfaces glinting like flash photography as I move along the fence for a better view. And there, stepping down the last few stairs at the back of the aircraft, is everything I have ever wanted in my life: one small person carrying a brown bag as if it weighs half a ton.

Delirious as a puppy, I am about to call her name. And then I stop myself, for the small person will never hear me, seventy yards away, above the scream of the engines of an Air France jet, about to take off.

Besides: I am transfixed. I have never seen someone so close to me at this distance before. I have never had the chance just to watch this woman, as if she were a stranger, or a tiger in a zoo.

Will she look down at the ground, or up at the slate-grey ice-cream cone of the control tower? Will her head turn to watch the other bag-wheeling passengers engaged in that secret race for the terminal, in which everyone wants to be first, without being seen to hurry?

Slim and trim in a tight beige skirt and a dusky pink top, she is fiddling with her iPod, its white headphones still slung around her neck after the flight. Alice Melbury. For a second my life loops back on itself, and she is nine years old again: a little girl in a red hairband, Toby's little sister, skipping off the red-eye from Singapore at Heathrow with a satchel on her back and Paddington Bear under her arm. And then she is here: the beautiful and able woman she was always destined to be, spending night after night bringing light to the death-shadowed bedsides of men and women clinging to the future by their fingertips; spending her days in cool, clear air, learning to fly.

How could I ever have imagined this future Alice then, any more than I can now picture these graceful curves and grown-up sassiness belonging to the nimble little urchin whom Toby and I would send off to collect sticks for our camps in the woods; dank sanctuaries, carpeted with leaf-mould, from which she was always banned.

The prim girl's shoulders are hunched now; strained from one too many twelve-hour night-shifts. Her weary head is bowed. And as Alice Melbury slopes along in her flat shoes, struggling beneath the weight of a bag full of more or less unsuitable clothes, she is unquestionably the loveliest girl in the world.

An air-stewardess in a violent blue uniform turns to follow her with her gaze as she passes, as do two burly baggage-handlers in high-vis jackets.

Did you see that, I want to ask the leather-jacketed man standing next to me, as the woman we must all be watching reaches up with one hand to push back the glossy strand of hair that has fallen momentarily over her eyes.

*

'Is this what you wanted?' asks Alice, as we kiss amongst the crowds in the gleaming terminal.

'You bet,' I reply, kissing her again.

'No, silly,' she laughs, '*this*.' And she holds up a magazine with a picture on the front that has almost the same effect upon me as the sight of a petite intensive-care nurse from Baltimore walking across the apron of an insignificant commercial airport in darkest France.

'Win a flight in a Spitfire!' The words leap out at me as if they have been hurled from a mountain-top by an Old Testament prophet.

'Thank you, thank you, thank you,' I blurt, resisting the urge to sit down on one of the terminal's black-and-chrome benches to read the magazine from cover to cover. I will win all right. I *have* to win.

'I can see it matters to you,' she says, raising her eyebrows.

'It does,' I nod, taking her bag from her shoulder, and hearing her breathe a sigh of relief as I do. 'But not as much as you.'

As we drive back through the parched countryside to La Folie, Alice tells me about the brutally competitive rounders she has been playing with her cousins on the beach in Norfolk, and I tell her the story of my Spitfire affliction.

From the age of six, my life's dream was to fly a Spitfire. I was quite convinced that I had flown in the Battle of Britain, and if someone would kindly lend me a Spitfire, I would bag myself a brace of Me-109s before breakfast. While my classmates' heroes were Kevin Keegan and Bruce Lee, mine were Douglas Bader and Stanford Tuck. I wrote to *Jim'll Fix It*, forced my dad to build all the Airfix kits, and almost wept with joy when I first saw and *heard* a Spitfire overhead at Biggin Hill.

'I wrote to *Jim'll Fix It*, too,' she says.

'To ask if you could visit the L'Oréal factory?'

She chuckles, and pokes me – harder than I was expecting – in the ribs. 'Funnily enough: no.'

'So what did you want Jim to fix?'

'I wrote and said I wanted to follow a letter.'

'You mean in the post?'

'I just find it impossibly romantic that I can write a letter to my sister in Australia, and put it in a box, and that somehow that sealed envelope with my words inked upon it can find its way round the world, and then into another box, right outside her house. It's a little miracle, and I always want to know exactly how the letter I've written is getting there.'

'Not often enough, in the case of your letters to France.'

Again, that tinkling laugh. 'Well, what do you expect? You're the writer. You've sent me such beautiful things. I just feel I can't compete.'

'But you don't have to write anything especially beautiful. It's the same with all writing, whether it's a letter, a novel or a gas bill. You just have to write the truth, or as close to it as you can manage. In your case, just send me a blank page with a few kisses on it. And if you want to follow the letter yourself, in person, and preferably without Jimmy Savile in tow, that would do nicely, too.'

Alice smiles out of the window at the sheep and cows that stand disgruntled in their parched fields, staring balefully at each other as they dream of lush grass, juicy with chlorophyll. 'I'm just glad I'm here now,' she says.

'And if you could have any wish, what would it be?'

She replies without missing a beat. 'I'd wish Digby were here with me, too. Except that he can't stand cars.'

'Digby?' I ask, feigning ignorance. 'Is he your ex?'

'You *know* he's my dog,' she laughs.

'I know he sleeps on your bed.' I hesitate. 'So what do you think he'd make of France?'

'Digby in France?' I can see her smiling to herself, as she

juggles with the enormity of this paradox. 'I think it would completely freak him out.'

After the exuberance of my first weekend with Alice and Toby, these next three days – in which I have Alice Melbury all to myself for the first time in my life – take me by surprise. Despite the dazzling sunshine, offset by the free air-conditioning of a westerly breeze, the atmosphere feels unexpectedly charged. It is as if we have unconsciously finished the knock-up, and are now beginning to play the match itself. There is an unmentioned sense of how much is at stake; of not wanting to put a foot wrong. Over the hills in the distance, thunderclouds are beginning to tower.

It probably does not help that I take Alice on a romantic date cunningly disguised as a geography field trip. I blame this on my Surrey upbringing, in which a chap soon learns that one must Go Out And Do Things with visitors, rather than simply allowing them to relax and enjoying their company. So – having discovered that we are both cold-weather people, who love crisp winter days more than anything – I drive Alice through a heat-haze to visit the tiny village of Magny-Senlac, a few miles from La Folie, and allow her to flash-bake in the vertical sun.

Even by my standards, this is an inspired choice of diversion for a self-confessed city girl, who left London for Baltimore, not Dartmoor; whose idea of experiencing the depths of the English countryside is going for a pedicure in the smart market town where her mother now lives; and whom I am struggling to convince that the rue du Coq in Jolibois is in many ways really just as bustlingly cosmopolitan as Upper Street in Islington.

Unlike Jolibois, which is stuck in the 1950s, the village of Magny-Senlac is consciously stuck in the early 1900s, complete with sooty house interiors strewn with rusted farm implements, and a schoolroom full of gnarled little desks and a blackboard inscribed with a short treatise on the proper function of women, most of which seems to be about mangles and obedience. I begin translating this for Alice, and then stop, because she is not laughing.

'So what did you think of Magny-Senlac?' I ask, as we drive home in the superheated Espace, pretending not to notice the smell. I am worried at Alice's silence. Either this means heat-stroke, or else she is reconsidering her relationship with the local landscape.

'It was all right,' she says, with a shrug. 'I liked the pig-sty.'

'I'm so sorry it wasn't your thing.' I pause, pulling down my sun-visor against the blinding sunset. 'But I do love the way you're happy to admit that, rather than pretending for the sake of the cameras.'

'I don't play games,' she nods. 'And that's what I like about you, too.'

'That's good. Even though I know it was really my snazzy wheels that hooked you, wasn't it?'

Alice is about to stroke the dashboard of the Espace but, examining her clean hands, thinks better of it.

'I know a winner when I see one,' she says, peering up at the moss growing out of the black rubber seal along the top of the windscreen. And we both laugh as the French countryside streams past us, and I cannot help imagining that the sheep and cows are cheering our progress on either side.

On the second day, we drive to St Juste. It happens to be market-day in the humming medieval town, but the purpose of our trip is to introduce Alice to my aircraft. We still cannot go flying together, for the Luscombe's permit has expired, and I need a mechanic from England to fly out and renew the paperwork. Benj from the chateau has said he can do it, once his schedule at Virgin makes it possible. In the meantime, we can at least sit in the cockpit together and make *brrm-brrm* noises.

Thankfully the aeroclub is deserted when Alice and I arrive, although Antoine's little Peugeot 205 is parked in the shade of a row of poplars, and I can tell from the dank crackle of sublimated misanthropy that hangs in the air that old Marcel cannot be far away.

'Golly, it's quite primitive, isn't it?' exclaims Alice, examining the instrument panel as we squeeze, side by side, into the Luscombe's narrow cockpit. 'But I love it. I absolutely love it.'

'Thank goodness for that. I'm so looking forward to going flying with you.'

'Same here,' she says. 'But you'll have to do all the flying, because I'm still completely hopeless.'

'You may be surprised,' I laugh, 'at just how much we have in common.'

For a moment we sit in silence, enjoying the feeling of being inside the snug cockpit together, enveloped in its leathery purposefulness.

'Knock knock,' I say.

'Who's there?'

'Cabbage.' I search Alice's face for a grin of recognition, but she looks blank.

'Cabbage who?'

'Cabbage *Jones*,' I announce, as if this were the cleverest punch-line in the world. I remember her brother Toby pronouncing it with similar relish, in Marlborough dormitory at Windlesham in 1978.

Still Alice is puzzled, unable to recall a piece of nonsense that she made up when she was eight years old, yet that I have nursed and cherished for all these years, hooked by its surreal bluntness, and by the way it connects me to the girl I once knew. My epiphany, it emerges, is her ephemera. It mattered to me, so I remembered. It meant nothing to her, so she forgot.

'Am I supposed to understand?' she asks, waggling the

Luscombe's control-column like a child riding the rockets at a fair.

'It was your joke,' I reply, grinning. 'I was rather hoping *you* could explain it to *me*.'

Two days later, Gilles has agreed to act *in loco parentis* for the animals of La Folie, while Alice and I sit next to each other on a blue-and-yellow 737 bound for London. At Stansted I have booked a rental car, so that I can drive her to Heathrow for her flight back to Baltimore. Living as far apart as we do, every extra moment we can spend together feels precious. Especially as there is still something that I need to know; an answer that I need her to give. And it has nothing to do with Cabbage Jones.

'May I ask you something?' I turn to face her, holding her hand in mine, as a thunder-browed stewardess in a blue uniform brushes past. For a moment, we both watch her push her trolley up the aisle. She looks as despondent as Sisyphus cresting the hill for the umpteenth time.

'Of course,' says Alice. 'And no: I don't want any scratch-cards, fragrances or gift items, in case you were offering.'

'It's just that . . .' I stroke the back of her hand, noticing how slender and perfect are her fingers compared with mine, whose nails are bitten roughly to length.

'Come on,' she says, squeezing my hand. 'You're making me nervous.'

'I suppose I'm not quite sure where we stand.' I hesitate, searching for the right words. 'I mean, this isn't quite like any other experience I've ever had with any other person. We seem to have become so close so quickly.'

Again, she squeezes my hand; says nothing.

'Any rubbish or empties?' says another lady in a blue uniform, shaking a plastic bag in front of Alice's face.

'I was just wondering,' I continue, when the shaking of the plastic bag has passed, 'if you were now already, or if you aren't yet, whether you would be willing, officially I mean, to be my . . . to be my actual Girlfriend.'

'Your *actual* Girlfriend? As opposed to . . . ?'

'If I didn't know you better,' I declare, 'I would say that you were enjoying my discomfort just a little too much.'

So many switches have been flicked at once. Every throttle-lever of every engine has been pushed through the gate to full war-boost power. I am screaming down through the clouds at close to never-exceed speed, and if I do not pull up soon, it will be too late. So I would like to know where I stand, please. I want a certificate, or a receipt or some sort of acknowledgement at least, that whatever is happening between me and Alice Melbury is real; that it has been reg-istered, somewhere in the annals of the universe; that it adds up to more than just three days of passionate dalliance in the foothills of darkest France.

'Yes, please,' she says, smiling at me, as if she can see all the cogs and pinions whirring away in the double-escapement of my mind. 'Of course, I'd love to be your girlfriend.'

'Well, thank goodness for that.' I let out a deep breath.

'I'm just not quite sure what being an Actual Girlfriend involves.'

'What do you mean?'

'I mean, can you show me the job-spec, so I know what it entails?'

And I am not sure, but I *think* she might be serious.

# 13

## SEPTEMBER

On Battle of Britain day, 14 September, I gaze up into a cloudless sky, shut my eyes and visualize a Spitfire. For a second, the drone of a distant engine almost makes me think one is on its way. And then Didier the postman comes rattling up the drive in his yellow Clio, sending chickens flying in all directions. I stand on the front step, holding my completed entry for the Spitfire competition, as he pulls up beside me, his window descending even before he has drawn to a halt.

'*Et voilà*,' he says, handing me a bundle of bills, bank statements and flyers from Carrefour and Weldom. 'None from America today,' he adds, cheerily, as I hand him my envelope. 'Perhaps tomorrow?'

'Perhaps,' I chuckle.

'*Mais* . . . there is *this*.' He riffles through the box of letters beside him, draws one out and – like a magician pulling a rabbit out of a hat – proudly flourishes it in front of me. '*L'Australie!*'

'*C'est pour moi?*' I ask, peering at the unfamiliar handwriting.

'*Bien sûr*,' he replies, delighted at my surprise. I don't

know anyone in Australia. Alice's sister lives in Sydney, but surely *she* wouldn't be writing to me, demanding to know if my intentions are honourable? Didier is still waiting, perhaps hoping that I will tear open the letter and read it aloud.

So I thank him with a wave, and turn back into the shadows of the winter sitting-room. To my surprise, the letter is from Jethro, who absolutely does not write letters. And this one is no exception. Saving money on a postcard, he has simply scrawled a few words in felt-tip pen on the back of a flyer for an aircraft-hire company in Western Australia: 'CAVOK on all fronts: she is The One,' he writes. 'PS. Have sorted you a Harvard flight at Shoreham. Phone the club and ask for Stuart. *Bon courage*, J.'

I blink at the words, as amazed at my friend's ongoing capacity to surprise me as at his talent for romantic conviction. I read the message three times. I cannot quite believe that I am going to fly a Harvard, a pilot's final step on the route to Spitfire glory. And a thought that has been niggling at the back of my mind suddenly makes me pick up the phone.

'Hello, is that *Warbird* magazine? Yes, I know it's Battle of Britain day. I just wanted to check whether I am allowed to submit more than one entry to your Spitfire competition.'

Tingling with new resolve, I walk out on to the terrace, and gaze up at the perfect sky. Ceiling and Visibility OK, just as in Australia for Jethro, just as on this day overhead Kent and Sussex in 1940. There is a rustling from the wisteria, and Martha leaps off the window-sill, toddling over to peck at my shoelaces.

'*Puck puck puck puck puck*,' she announces, in cheerful greeting.

'I am going to win the Spitfire competition, Martha,' I tell her, gently stroking the gleaming feathers on the back of her neck. 'My luck is in right now, and this could be my only chance. There is nothing else for it. I simply must.'

'*Puck puck puck*,' she replies, head cocked to one side, unconvinced.

A week later, I am peering up at the ancient oak timbers of the barn, wishing they could tell me how they feel about the constant drip-drip-dripping of rain through a leaky roof, when the telephone rings with a quite different voice from the past.

'Monsieur Wright, I have been thinking of you,' growls old Zumbach, in a *basso profundo* rumble that sounds like the grinding of tectonic plates.

'*Quel plaisir*, Ludo,' I reply, because I am always happy to hear from the friendly ogre who sold me my future, on a cold spring morning that I remember as clearly as the day when Alice Melbury walked back into my life.

'For me, or for you?' he asks, his voice shaking with amusement. And then he tells me that it is imperative that I come to Limoges.

'To your house?' I have never visited the place Zumbach bought after he sold La Folie. All I know is that there had been a painful split with his wife, and he moved to Limoges, while she decamped south, towards Toulouse.

'No, to the guild of master craftsmen, where I work. Our chef is about to cook *la tête de veau* for all the guildsmen, just the same as he cooked for the president last year, at the Élysée Palace. You *need* to be here.'

My stomach lurches like a learner driver's hill-start. I want to tell Zumbach that friends do not behave like this in England. We do not invite each other round for gizzard, or testicle, or brain. We are a peaceful nation. We play cricket. I want to participate in every aspect of local life in rural France, really I do. But talking a fellow into eating the stewed head of a calf is simply not in the spirit of the game. On the other hand, I have always wanted to visit the home of *les Compagnons*, the guild of master craftsmen where

Ludo works as the resident guru of beaten copper and cauldron-making. And I so very much do *not* want to eat a plateful of mashed-up calf's bonce, that somehow I know I must.

And so, just before midday on Friday, I walk up the steep cobbled street that leads behind the great cathedral in Limoges, through the inky shadows of a medieval gateway, where I am met by the timeless figure of Zumbach himself, built like a menhir, bearded like a fourteenth-century king, and grinning like one of the stone gargoyles that gaze down from the cathedral roof hundreds of feet above our heads.

'*Monsieur Wright*,' he says, his eyes shining, making a formal bow.

'*Monsieur Zumbach*,' I grin, bowing in return. 'And I wish you would call me Michael.'

He leads me to a small, dimly lit bar that is crowded with men straight out of a Brueghel painting of a feast; joiners, metalworkers, stonemasons and their apprentices; men with lived-in faces, and hands that feel like coarse-grade sandpaper; men who exude that profound self-confidence and measured calm that comes of having eaten *tête de veau* before, or else from labouring to create beauty in the old ways; with sweat, craftsmanship and hours of intricate toil with their bare hands.

'These artisans are the best of the best,' explains Zumbach. 'Their masterworks are in the museum here. And they come together every Friday, to talk, to share ideas, and because this is the way it has always been, for the last seven hundred years.' I glance from face to face, half-expecting to see Serge, my mason hero, or Monsieur Ducroux, the pilot plasterer, among them.

Zumbach is anxious to know all about life at La Folie; how the acacias are doing, and the old box tree, and whether the Lone Pine has yet outgrown the tower of Limoges cathedral.

'You're not going to believe this, Ludo.'

'*Oui*,' he whispers, handing me a glass of undiluted Pastis. 'It's not about the septic tank, is it?'

I watch as he tips back his head and drains his own shot of Pastis in one gulp.

'You must drink it like this,' he announces. 'It is the only way to protect yourself against the wine we are about to face.'

I gulp down the aniseed draught; feel the cold liquid burning inside me.

'*Encore*,' says Zumbach, turning towards the bar.

'No, no, let me get these,' I insist.

'All right,' he shrugs, twinkling. 'But don't ask Jean-Claude for Pastis; ask him for *deux jaunes*. It's time you learned some real French.'

Once again, Zumbach clinks my glass with his, and we drink.

'Now,' he says, 'tell me your news that I am not going to believe.'

So I tell him about Alice; about how, against all the odds, I appear to have found someone who is the answer to all the questions; the granting of all the prayers; the grail at the end of the quest.

Zumbach listens, eyes shining, his empty glass pressed to his lips.

'It is not possible,' he says, at last, wiping his eyes. 'It is too perfect. And Monsieur Wright, Michael, I am so happy for you. It is a true-life fairytale: *Alice au pays des Merveilles*. But I am sorry – you remember what I told you long ago: La Folie is no place for a woman.'

I study his face, to see if he is joking. I know from experience that with Zumbach, the tragic and the farcical, the sacred and profane, empathy and insult, are always inseparable.

Yes, he may be joking. But he is deadly serious, too.

'*Les femmes*, they tell you they love La Folie,' he continues. 'And then they go crazy there.' He taps the side of his head, as if to prove the point.

I want to ask him the question that has intrigued me for so long, about what exactly went wrong between him and the whole of womankind at La Folie, but a loud '*ho!*' from the doorway cuts me off: the seven dwarfs are home.

Actually they're not: lunch is served.

In the echoing dining-room of *les Compagnons*, we sit on benches at long oak tables, shoulder to shoulder, waiting to be fed. My neighbour is a grey-haired, softly spoken man in his early thirties, who says he makes stained-glass windows. I listen, rapt, as he laments the way his craft is misunderstood: people are always obsessed with how a new window will look, he says, yet they have no understanding of what kind of light it will throw.

'A good window is like a good woman,' mutters the man opposite me, a burly carpenter with a broad, lined forehead that looks as tough as the hide of an armadillo. He specializes in building twisted church steeples, he says; in spirals pointing at heaven.

'Is there much demand for that sort of thing, then?' I ask, innocently.

'I'd say we build one perhaps every two hundred years,' he replies, with a shrug.

I feel as if I have waded into a slow-flowing river whose gushing source is located deep in the past, as we all slurp our vegetable broth and *les Compagnons*, all of them touched with the same combination of hearty cheer and resigned melancholy, set the world to rights. No one asks me if I am English, or why I came to France. There is no small-talk. Everything that is said is either wry, or profound, or both.

More than anything, I am struck by how at ease I feel in this beery den of rugged masculinity. When I first arrived at La Folie – my insecurity cloaked in sly cynicism, my confidence steeped in book-lined self-consciousness – this raw, male scene would have filled me with panic. I would have felt unmanly and unworthy; I would have been lost for anything to say. But my life has changed since then. I have grown my own food; made friends in a foreign language; seen lives begin and end before my eyes. I have learned to be happy, abroad and alone.

'I can't believe you never brought me here before, Ludo,' I tell Zumbach.

'Until now you weren't ready,' he says, beaming, as if he has noticed the change in me, too. 'Do you like it?'

'I love it. I wasn't expecting to feel so . . . so at home.'

'The things men have in common are always more profound than our differences. We all laugh, love and die.'

'Even the English?' I ask, and then regret it, for Zumbach thinks this is so funny that his soup goes up his nose.

Despite his ready laughter, I ask him about the hint of sadness that seems to hang over the cheery scene; wonder if he can sense it, too. He leans forward, resting his thick forearms on the massive table, and glares at me.

'What do you notice about this group, Monsieur Michael?'

'That a lot of you have beards?'

He chuckles. '*Oui, mais* . . . there's something else, too. Something even more obvious.' He searches my face and, finding it blank, answers his own question. 'There are no women here. So there is no light.' He leans back, stretches his arms wide. 'When we work together like this, we achieve exceptional things. But the price we pay is that we live in such darkness, that we might as well be underground. Have you not discovered this yourself, at La Folie, that the quality of the light has changed, now that Alice in Wonderland has appeared?'

I blink, think hard, and wish I hadn't drunk that second *jaune*.

'The view across the valley is different . . .'

'*Oui, oui*,' he says excitedly, his eyes blazing.

And now I feel a sense of darkness of my very own, as if a great shadow had passed across the face of the sun. For the *tête de veau* has arrived in a vast dish, borne aloft by the beaming, sweating chef. We all clap as he does a lap of honour around the dining-room, with the serving dish held high above his head.

Narrowing my eyes, I peer down at the inert matter on my plate. I am not sure what I was expecting, but it was not this. I think I pictured a whole cow's head, or perhaps a neat pile of brains, foamy as frogspawn. Whereas this – this – this heap of grey swarf looks like what is left over after a tricycle has been dragged through the propellers of a Dakota, or like someone just blew up a catfish.

I think it is fair to say that the *tête de veau* tastes quite a lot worse than it looks. Vulcanized rubber would be easier to chew; a toxic oyster easier to forget.

'Have some Men's Wine,' says Zumbach, his eyes twinkling at my struggle as he pours black liquid from a carafe.

I thump my chest with my fist. '*Moi, homme. Vin, bon*,' I grunt, and the carpenter and the stained-glass window-maker explode with laughter. I blink. And it is the strangest thing, but I feel as if I have just wandered through the back of a wardrobe and stepped out of it into the sixteenth century. I suddenly picture these same men laughing in exactly this same way, at this same table, in this same den of rugged masculinity, five hundred years ago. I say this to Zumbach, and he beams at the idea, even when I add that the menu doesn't appear to have changed much, either.

Then everyone smokes Men's Cigarettes and – although I gave up years ago – it feels like part of the occasion to puff on a filterless Camel (nasty) followed by a filterless Craven A (very nasty), which I could have sworn they stopped

making some time in the 1960s. We talk about craftsmanship, contentment, love, Poland, Chopin, and the difference
between the soul and the spirit. After this, the conversation
moves on to women, in a general tone of awed mystification.

'You understand that women are impossible, Monsieur
Wright,' says the carpenter, wreathed in tendrils of blue-grey
smoke. I am beginning to think that Zumbach may have
brought me here for group therapy. Especially when the
stained-glass window-maker takes up the theme.

'They give themselves to us,' he sighs, 'and then they
expect us to know what to do about it.'

'But how can we?' roars Zumbach, slapping his hand
down on the table for emphasis. 'Seneca was right: men are
beasts who love making mistakes.' And with that he slams
his wine glass down on the table so hard that it cracks.
'*Merde*,' he mutters, as if suddenly transported back to the
twenty-first century. 'Everything is so fragile these days.'

Around the table, the other men nod solemnly to
themselves. If the art of love is really this complicated, I
think to myself, I can understand the appeal of twisted
spires.

As the afternoon drifts on in a cloud of acrid smoke,
Zumbach proposes that he and I go back to his flat for *un
digestif*. Though I cannot face any more alcohol, I am
curious about where he lives. So I agree to accompany him.

It is a chilly afternoon and he coughs as we walk; a deep,
gut-racking cough that sounds like a series of explosions in
the engine-room of a supertanker.

'But Ludo,' I ask, when he welcomes me into the tiny
salon of his ground-floor apartment, apologizing for the
mess, 'do you never open the shutters?'

'*Jamais*,' he roars, shaking his head.

The place is as dark as a boarded-up church. Only a thin
slab of pale sunlight penetrates the gloom in each small,
bare room. It is the same in the hallway and kitchen;

we might almost be in a basement, sometime after dusk.

I cannot imagine what it is like to live here, in this gloomy crepuscular cell, after the fresh air of La Folie, with its tree-studded hillside, its swallows and woodpeckers, its sunlit terrace looking out over a wide river valley.

'Michael,' murmurs Zumbach, half-filling two large tumblers with Polish vodka. 'When my wife and I split up, all the light in my life was taken from me.' He hands one of the glasses to me, raises his own, and slumps down on to one end of a faded blue sofa. 'And now I prefer to live in this darkness.'

'To punish yourself?'

He shakes his bowed head. 'It is because the light reminds me of her.'

I do not know what to say to this, so I sip my vodka, wince at the fire on my tongue, and then take another sip. Eventually he rises to his feet, puts on a CD, and slumps back into his chair.

'Cecilia Bartoli,' he growls, as a Mozart aria brings a glow of warmth and colour into the cold, grey room. 'My only consolation.'

An hour and a half later, Zumbach opens a second bottle of vodka.

'I've read that book of yours, you know, *C'est La Folie*,' he says, leaning towards me. 'I know you call me the Ogre in it; that you think I didn't care for La Folie.'

'Ludo—'

'Oh, it's all right, no need to apologize,' he says, waving his hand, dabbing his eyes. 'I just thought you should know that I sent it to my wife, too. She might even write to you, one day.' And then, at last, he tells me the story of how he came to buy La Folie, and how it ultimately spelt the end of his marriage.

Zumbach's wife was an artist from Lille, he says, who had seen the house while out walking in the hills above Jolibois.

She had immediately fallen in love with the place and persuaded him to buy it, though he warned her that it was an uninhabitable ruin, and too far from civilization for comfort.

'I tried to explain to her what it would be like,' he says, staring into his glass, shaking his head at the memory. 'The terrible isolation she would feel, especially in winter. But no, no, she protested: she trusted the advice of the trees. And she thought it was perfect.'

Month after month, Zumbach worked on the ancient house, trying to turn La Folie into a comfortable home for his young wife, while the wind and the rain and their two young children howled in protest. She, meanwhile, grew thinner and thinner, and more and more withdrawn, as she mourned the life she had lost. And one day, she simply vanished, leaving him a note. 'She wrote that the house was an uninhabitable ruin,' he says, with a mordant chuckle. 'And too far from civilization for comfort.' Zumbach never saw her again, until the meeting at the notaire's office when I bought La Folie from them, and she quietly handed me the keys. I remember her as a slight, birdlike woman, with a poise and dignity at odds with her tiny frame.

'That was the second worst day of my life,' he tells me, draining his glass and slamming it down on a side-table so hard that the glass cracks. '*Merde*,' he mutters. 'So damn fragile.'

We have listened to Zumbach's entire collection of Cecilia Bartoli recordings, the second bottle of vodka lies upside down in the waste-paper basket and my head feels as if it is being slowly spun inside a tumble-drier filled with drunken bluebottles. Somehow I have to get home.

Zumbach and I shake hands for a long time, for I am conscious that I am an astronaut returning to earth, and he the last man in the space-station, abandoned in his lonely orbit for eternity, or until the oxygen cells run out.

And then I walk back towards the cathedral, keeping my eyes on the outsize marlin spike of its tower. Is it twisted, I ask myself? The sun is beginning to set, though I feel as if it should be beginning to rise. A brightly lit supermarket appears on my right and – suddenly ravenous, and lured by the gleaming neon lights – I stumble into its café and order a plateful of *tartiflette* from the pretty girl behind the counter. I am hoping the cheesy, greasy stodge will soak up some of this vodka that is sloshing in my veins like water in a storm-drain.

Then I eat a second *tartiflette*, lay my head on the red formica of the café table, and everything goes dark. I am hacking my way through a jungle teeming with wild beasts, when I come upon a little church. Inside, above the altar, is a beautiful stained-glass window of the Virgin Mary, who – when I look more closely – turns out to be Alice. A priest who looks a lot like Zumbach invites me to take communion. But instead of giving me a wafer, he offers me a wriggling sliver of *tête de veau*.

I am woken by someone prodding me. Raising my sore head, I see that it is the pretty serving girl, waving a set of keys in my face.

'We are closing, *monsieur*. I'm sorry, but you really have to leave.'

And all I can think is that I wish Alice were here now, to help me home.

Six o'clock, my thinking time, and – two days after my visit to Limoges – I still cannot face a Pastis. Nevertheless, Cat and I are sitting on the terrace at La Folie, striving to make the best of it as we gaze out at the familiar view across the valley.

Strange, how this view changes. Like watching the sea or a thunderous cloudscape, I think I could look at it for ever, and I would never grow bored. I think of Zumbach looking

out over it, too, from his gloomy little one-bedroom apartment, tracing his way back through the unlit corridors of his
memory to the sunlit days before the darkness fell.

This evening, even the far distance looks near, now that
late summer has fleshed out the trees – grey as vegetarians –
into green obesity. Caspar David Friedrich has been over-
painted by Henri Rousseau.

I do my best, nevertheless, to keep my eyes focused on the
distant sheep-fields, largely because it stops me having to
confront the foreground, where the *potager* is sprouting
weeds with such shameless abandon that I have begun to
cringe whenever Didier the postman bowls up the drive. It
may be a coincidence that I have stopped weeding it, now
that I have an actual official Girlfriend. I play the piano less
often, too, as if rehearsing my peacock skills no longer
matters, now that a dazzling pea-hen has already begun to
frequent my nest.

Strange, how the quality of solitude changes when one
imagines it may one day come to an end. Everyday
experiences such as chasing down a lamb for ear-tagging,
picking courgettes that have turned from gherkins into
Zeppelins while my back was turned, buying a single
entrecôte from the butcher, or slipping on a freshly laid
dollop of chicken poo just when I have my hands full of
freshly laid eggs, all feel new and different, now that I can
almost picture myself sharing them with someone else.

When I first came to La Folie, I was in awe of the gulf
between the slow rural tumble of my life here and the complicated urban spin-cycle I had left behind in East Dulwich.
Three years on, that vertigo has gradually worn off as I have
begun to find my feet. But the familiar sensation returns
when Alice phones, and – from my silent eyrie at the end of
the world – I am suddenly thrust into the life of a hard-core
intensive-care nurse midway through a twelve-hour shift
in a hospital on the other side of the Atlantic. Here, the

shadows of the trees are lengthening. There, patients wired up to ventilators and drips and computers are fighting for their lives.

'Are you sure you're all right to talk?' I ask Alice, when I phone her back. I can hear the insistent *beep-beeper-beep* of massed electronic monitors in the background. Alice's working environment always sounds to me like the Pentagon must sound, in the middle of a missile attack. She herself sounds preternaturally cool, as if everything is under control. I'm the one who feels a sense of mounting panic, as the beepings steadily intensify.

'Fine for a minute or so,' she says. 'I've only got one patient for now, and he's stable.'

'I can hear an alarm,' I say, alarmed. I am getting used to this, and still it sends a shiver up my spine. Three thousand miles away, on the other side of the Atlantic, someone I have never met is in trouble.

'It's not one of ours.'

'Shouldn't you get it?'

'It's someone else's, and they already have,' she replies, patiently. 'But I have to go soon, because they need me for the leeches.'

'*Leeches?*' I thought America was advanced. Next thing, she will be telling me they're trepanning someone's skull to release a demon.

'We do still use leeches occasionally, after reconstructive plastic surgery,' she explains, her speech accelerating. 'They help to promote blood-circulation in newly grafted skin. But I seem to be the only nurse on the unit who's willing to touch them. Gotta go. Bye.'

I log this information: good with leeches. One of my least favourite jobs at La Folie is unscrewing ticks from Cat's neck. And I figure that anyone who can apply leeches to humans will not flinch from removing fleas and other unwanted guests from feline flesh.

Quite often, when we are talking, Alice is called away to help move a patient. This is America, so two nurses are not enough. Nor are four, or six. It can take eight of them to move some of the really well-hamburgered ones.

'Luckily there's a modern aquarium nearby,' says Alice, sounding slightly out of breath when she comes back to the phone.

'Weren't you just moving a patient?'

'Yup.'

'So why do they need an aquarium?'

'Because the really big ones won't fit into our hospital scanner. So we ship them down there.'

'To lose weight by swimming with dolphins?'

'No, because they have a whale-scanner at the aquarium. We scan them in that.'

'You're joking.'

'I wish I were.' *Beep-beeper-beep*. 'Gotta go. Call me later? Bye.'

Gradually, as Alice describes her life on the unit, I begin to build up a vivid mental picture of her there. I see a glowing figure, moving softly among the transplant patients and third-degree burns victims with their spaghetti-tangles of electrodes and tubes, only stopping for a moment or two to update her charts from the digital vital-signs monitors and computerized ventilators that hum beside each fully motorized bed. I picture her doing her drug titrations, inserting lines into veins – some of the patients have to be tied down, she says, to stop them ripping out their lines in a delirium – changing dressings that cover open wounds. Sometimes the doctors will leave a patient's abdomen open, she says, if there is further surgery to come, or not enough skin to cover the void. I think of Nemo, my tiny black lamb who was killed by a badger, his stomach ripped open, his entrails spread like greasy noodles upon the grass. This was nothing compared with what Alice must see, week after week. Yet even seeing that knocked me for six.

In my mind's eye, I watch her running, too, when someone yells that their patient – someone's dad, some mother's child – has arrested. Now the whole team of nurses and doctors, surgeons and nurse-practitioners suddenly fuses into a single, desperate organism, its eyes focused, its tendons taut, its energies focused as a Formula One pit-crew upon jump-starting the infinitely complex machine that has stalled and is about to be out of the race.

Sometimes Alice tells me that one of her patients is sick. Sometimes, in a softer whisper, that they are really sick. And at first I do not understand, because is sickness not intrinsic to being in intensive care? And then I discover that this is her code for single or multiple organ-failure; for the fact that her patient may not live out the night, and she will have to face the long corridor that leads to the lift-shaft for the morgue.

I begin to feel daunted at the sheer level of human experience of the woman behind this soft voice on a telephone; begin to feel unworthy of the dedicated, un-flagging ICU nurse who has not even the time for a tea-break, let alone a lunch-break, yet who will find a few seconds here and there in her shift to listen to my sweet nothings from three thousand miles away. I thought my life at La Folie was earthy and strong. But I am beginning to feel like a vapid dilettante, next to her. Here am I, an insignificant English blot on the landscape of darkest France, feeling as if I have learned some-thing valuable because I discovered happiness with a cat and a glass of Pastis on a silent terrace; because I now know the difference between loneliness and solitude; and because I have wept whilst burying a sheep.

One day, I ask Alice what are the very worst things with which she has had to deal; which are the patients whose suffering affects her the most, whose suffering she finds hardest to leave behind and forget at the end of her shift. I am expecting her to say the cancer patients, slowly being killed by the chemotherapy drugs that are supposed to be saving them, or the recipients of long-awaited organ transplants which, slowly and surely, their bodies decide, in their wisdom, to reject. Perhaps it is the patients whose faces have been eaten away by necrotizing diseases, or those whose pain goes beyond the scope of painkillers; the untreatable sufferers whose screams could penetrate a tomb. Yet Alice's answer, when it comes, takes me by surprise.

'The very worst?' she says, after a pause.

'Yes.'

'It is the ones with no family,' she says, quietly. 'To know that there is no one there for them, no one who will come. That is the very worst thing, when I nurse someone. Here they are, clinging to life by their fingernails, and even if they pull through, I cannot help thinking that they have no one to come and take them home.'

I begin to explain to Alice how differently I feel about being alone at La Folie, now that I have met her, when another alarm sounds.

*Beeper-beep-beep*. The beeps all sound the same to me, but not to her.

'Gotta go.' She hangs up before I can make her swear never to put the leeches on me.

It is evening, half an hour before dusk. In the field just below La Folie, a lamb begins to bleat. I cannot see the creature, but it sounds anguished. A few seconds later, I hear a low, distinct *baaaaa* from the midst of the vast flock of sheep across the valley. A single white smudge staggers to its feet and trots hurriedly in this direction. Nature's alarm system is a sophisticated one.

And so, while life and death are being weighed in the balance three thousand miles away, I wander out to the field behind La Folie to watch my own sheep. Sometimes I wonder why I keep the Rastafarians, with all the hassle and heartache that this entails. But not tonight. Tonight Gaston, my old black ram, gazes into the distance, dreaming of fat white ewes. Behind him, Doris, Daphne and Claudette munch away at the grass, ripping out one tuft before stepping forward an inch or two and ripping out another. Grey-haired Ella stands apart, with a watchful glint in her eye. Each of these wild creatures stands little more than two foot high, yet their shadows are twenty feet long in the setting sun. A day is ending. The Baltimore day still has hours left to run. And far away in the future, I can already picture an entirely new day, about to begin.

On the deserted apron at Shoreham aerodrome, a T6 Harvard in US Navy markings stands gleaming in the morning sunshine. This was the hulking machine from which young RAF pilots would graduate to Spitfires or Hurricanes. I walk around it in silent awe. Even the barbed pitot tube jutting from the starboard wing looks big enough to harpoon a shark.

Brisk footsteps announce the arrival of Stuart, my instructor for the day. We chat for a while, about Jethro and Luscombes and why I moved to France, and then he shows me how to clamber up into the vast rear cockpit. This is so far off the ground that I feel as if I am climbing into a large bathtub via an upstairs window. Once inside, I feel more like a small child at the controls of a tank.

In the front cockpit, Stuart runs through the start-up procedure. There is a high-pitched *kiff-kiff-kiff* as the heavy prop begins to turn, and then we are enveloped in smoke as the 600-horsepower Pratt & Whitney's nine cylinders fire into life and the seat beneath me begins to vibrate as if a train were coming.

Beside me, an invisible hand advances the throttle and the landscape blurs in my peripheral vision. The huge control-column swings forward as Stuart raises the tail and now we are accelerating hard, the sun glinting on cobalt wings, as we head up, up and away, into the wide blue yonder and 1941.

Towns and villages may expand; roads may be widened; Jolibois has a new bypass. But the sky never changes. I know that what I am seeing now is what young pilots saw, back then, as we cruise past the old Belle Tout lighthouse, Beachy Head and the white cliffs of Dover.

'You have control,' announces Stuart over the r/t.

'I have control,' I reply, my right hand gripping the control-column and my left reaching for the throttle-lever.

'Make some turns,' he continues. 'Get a feel for the plane.'

We are skimming low over the countryside as I bank left and right, struck by the Harvard's smooth responsiveness, as much as by how far I have to push the outsize control-column to make the turns, as if I were stirring a vat of porridge for an entire squadron.

'It's a very gentle aeroplane to fly,' says Stuart, subtly reminding me to ease off on the controls. 'The handling is beautiful, but if you get too slow, it'll bite you.'

We climb for some aerobatics, and I watch the quivering needle of the airspeed indicator creep towards 180 mph as Stuart dives us towards the White Cliffs. Then we are pulling up, up and I can feel the flesh of my cheeks pulling down, down as we climb through the vertical and over the top, with the sky at our feet and the sea above our heads, waiting for the upside-down cliffs to whip behind us.

'Ready to try a loop yourself?' he asks.

'You bet,' I reply, feeling as if someone has piled rocks on my shoulders as we soar skywards.

'Great. Superb. Brilliant,' lies Stuart. 'Now what about adding a roll to that, too?'

I push the stick hard over to the left, and we are upside down before I remember that I have never flown a roll in my life. Perhaps I ought to let Stuart know? A split second later and we are the right way up again, with me blinking and gulping like a canoeist after an unexpected capsize.

'Great. Wonderful. Superb,' fibs Stuart.

All too soon, he brings us in for a graceful wheeler landing, and I am taxiing us back to the apron, swinging the nose left and right with the huge rudder-pedals, praying not to crash into anything too expensive.

The engine clatters to a halt, and I sit for a moment in the silence, blessing Jethro as I listen to the whirr of the gyros still spinning behind their instruments.

'Ah, the Harvard grin,' laughs Stuart, hauling himself from the front cockpit and turning to face me.

'Did I do okay?' I ask, not looking up.

'Yes,' he replies. 'You did fine.'

And as I picture a young man of half my age, sitting in this very seat more than half a century ago, I know that he, too, would have struggled to wipe such a smile off his face.

Back at La Folie, I start to prepare my extra entries for the Spitfire competition. I know I must maximize my chances of winning. Yet with each entry I prepare, I become more convinced that they will not be enough. In the end, I pootle down to Intermarché to photocopy the entry form, and then drive all the way to the Zone Industrielle Nord on the outskirts of Limoges for a box of envelopes.

'Do you really think it's going to work?' asks Fred the Viking, when I tell him my plan. He says that he, too, made all the Airfix kits of all the Spitfire variants, from the 1A to the photo reconnaissance Mk XIX. But, unlike me, Fred grew out of his obsession.

'It's a labour of love, Fred,' I reply. 'I've spent my whole life dreaming about this. I may never get another chance.'

At La Folie, meanwhile, tractors come, and tractors go. This morning Jean-Louis, the farmer with the beard that makes it feel as if he's talking to me through a hole in the hedge, rumbles up the drive with another ten cubic metres of splintered woodland.

'*Ça va, Michael?*' he growls.

'*Et toi?*' I reply. 'How are the dance classes going?' Our eyes meet, and I can see the weariness in his, though his bosky smile remains as undimmed as the moon shining through the trees.

The first time he came to La Folie, Jean-Louis told me that he had had it with selling firewood, because it was too much work for too little return. But that was two years ago, when life for sheep-farmers was tough. And things have become a whole lot tougher since then. So Jean-Louis has turned up again, to unload his trailer laden with seasoned Limousin oak, laboriously split and sawn into one-metre lengths, in a great cloud of dust and thunder. And then we drink a cold beer on the terrace, and have our annual discussion about how this year has been even worse than last year for the farmers. The only good news, as far as I am concerned, is that Jean-Louis has increased the price of his firewood at last.

A day later, and Gilles arrives with a bale of barley straw on the fork of his tractor. The Rastafarians disdain common-or-garden hay, and I'm hoping that this canary-yellow roughage may be more to their taste.

'How much do I owe you for it, Gilles?' I ask, beckoning my heroic neighbour inside for a drink.

'*Rien,*' he shrugs. 'I was given it by a friend who owed me a favour.'

'But . . .' And I make yet another chalk-mark at the back of mind, in the column that records my unpayable debt to my new old friend.

The more the sun shines at La Folie, the more I think about Alice. And the more I think about Alice and her meticulousness – the way she folds her clothes, just *so*, into her suitcase; her vacuuming habit; her insistence upon washing up, even when there are only two mugs and a teaspoon beside the sink – the more I begin to spot little things that are untidy or unfinished about the place.

At one end of the barn is a space I call my Workshop. This long, dark cattle-shed is littered with jars of noxious chemicals, viscous brown liquids that reek of concentrated Prep School, and various rusted tins, scarily encrusted with Marmitey goop. But the real nightmare lurks on the perished floor above, which I am hoping to convert into a couple of extra rooms. Here, balanced on a parade of woodwormy beams, festering like a swamp, lies a rotting, apocalyptic heap of ancient hay, roughly the size of China.

This hay has been there since I arrived at La Folie, three years ago. Now Zumbach lived here for twelve years before me, and he never farmed the land. And the house was derelict when he moved in. So the stuff must be a minimum of twenty years old, and probably at least thirty. Rain trickles into it through the chinks in the barn roof. Cat has been up there to take a look, and come sharply back down, spooked and wide-eyed. It is the baddie in a psychological thriller; the place in the horror movie where the children are warned never to play.

Motivation comes, as so often in rural France, in the shape of a small white van chugging up the drive. Out of it steps the friendly shape of Serge the mason, his ruddy face lightly powdered with cement dust. He explains that he will shortly have a free week between two jobs, so he can finally come and build the pair of rooms above the Workshop that we first discussed a year ago.

'*Ah, c'est très bien, Serge,*' I say, my heart sinking.

'Let's climb up and take a look,' he says.

'*Mais, mais . . .*' Too late. Serge is already halfway up the ladder.

'*Ah, il y a du foin,*' he says, whistling. His baseball

cap flops over his eyes as he scratches the back of his head.
And then I hold my breath. For Serge is climbing on to the
hay.

To my surprise, Serge is not swallowed alive, nor does he
spontaneously combust. Instead, coughing and sneezing,
he tells me how many *lambourdes* and how much *béton* to
buy, and threatens to come back in a fortnight.

'*Ah, c'est bien,*' I lie, amazed at his fearless heroism. I peer
at the dusty mountain range and wonder how the hell I am
going to shift the Pyrenees in fourteen days.

The evening is so still that the trees on the far side of the
valley, already fading towards autumn, are shapes in an old
photograph, frozen in time and space. As I gaze up into a sky
as diamond-clear as optical glass, unscratched by contrails
or misted by cirrus, I bless the day that I found this house,
this valley, this France. I am in love with it all.

The only sounds are the low buzzing of the mason bees in
the wisteria above my head; the white noise of the crickets;
the occasional yaffle of a green woodpecker, invisible in the
trees. In this almost-silence, I could be anywhere, anywhen.
I have lived here at La Folie for only three years, and already
I feel as if I have been here for ever; a forever that somehow
dates back to long before I was born. And perhaps I shall
stay here for ever, too; until my end, and then for centuries
beyond.

I wish Alice would phone. Usually we speak to each other
four or five times a day, but it has been two days now, and
still no word. Have I been too pushy? Too keen? Was it a
mistake to admit to her that the first LP I ever bought was
*The World of the Organ*? The only phone calls today have
been one from my mum, asking me how my Marmite and
PG Tips supplies are holding out, and one from Raphaël the
priest, telling me that my organ-playing services will no
longer be required at the regular Saturday Mass in Jolibois,

because this service has now become a movable feast, touring the outlying parishes buried deep in the boskier depths of the region.

So my days of blasting out Widor from the gleaming pipes of the Jolibois organ are done. My future now lies as an itinerant hurdy-gurdyist, accompanying the Kyrie and the *Gloire à Dieu* on moth-eaten harmoniums or dusty electric organs that sound like amplified Stylophones. Either that, or else accepting the alternative fate of heaving my fifteen-year-old electronic keyboard – a polyphonic synthesizer, bought in the days when I was going to be Rick Wakeman if I grew up – with all its cables and amplification into the back of the Espace, and carting it down the twisting lanes of Haute-Vienne as I strive to make my menial contribution to local life.

Cat and I sit on the terrace, reflecting on the timelessness in which we float here at La Folie, adrift in the pea-green boat of our own imaginations. And I ask myself whether everything is moving too fast. Not for the parishioners of Jolibois, but for Alice and me. Not to mention Cat.

In all sorts of ways, we hardly know each other. Yet already I cannot help wondering where she is going to live and work when she returns to Europe from Baltimore, after her contract ends in March. She says she does not know; that she has not had time to think. But what is there to think about, when you have met your soul-mate?

There is a world of difference, I tell myself, between meeting someone amid the chatter and flutter and glitter and clutter of London – shouting at each other over drinks in a Soho bar, sitting next to each other in the thumping darkness of a cinema, and generally attempting to shoe-horn the delicate flowering of a relationship into the time left over after work – to meeting them when you live in the middle of nowhere in darkest France, where there are no distractions except chickens and sheep and old hay.

With unusual self-restraint, I have not yet suggested to Alice that she simply move straight out to La Folie. She may not have had time to think, but I have. Lots. And I can already think of a hundred reasons why coming to live at La Folie might be an unwelcome prospect for her. I have only just found her again. I dread that she be scared away.

Leaving aside the heat, the cold, the damp, the draughts, the language, the flies, the dust, the chicken poo, the *tête de veau* and my tendency to leave muddy shoes and wellies all over the shop, there is the isolation for starters. And even when one strikes out across country, towards the bright lights of Jolibois, it is fair to say that the town one encounters has a little less to offer even than Westbury, where Alice's mother lives, let alone the West End.

Zumbach's words still ring in my head: 'La Folie is no place, Monsieur Wright, for a woman.'

Moving to France would mean Alice giving up a top job as part of a close-knit team of motivated experts, and an income on which she can afford to learn to fly, with no realistic prospect of finding any paid work at all in down-at-heel Jolibois.

She would have to exchange the zinging buzz of city life for the unremitting slowness of the French countryside, where people queue for a chat at the supermarket check-out, and buying a stamp at the post office takes almost as long as it takes for a letter to arrive in London. She would be cut off from her friends and family by the English Channel. And she would have to learn to speak French, a language as familiar to her as Swahili or Tagalog. Either that, or run the gauntlet of the English ghetto, and be forced to listen to her fellow British immigrants moaning, without irony, about how the problem with Britain these days is that it is full of bloody immigrants.

I have one tiny reservation of my own, too, which emerged last time we spoke, when Alice dropped a bombshell. Now, in itself, this bombshell was really no bigger than any one of the sand-coloured pebbles on the terrace. I should have been able to take it in my stride. Yet such a pebble, lobbed into the still waters of a lake, sends out ripples like a nuclear shockwave viewed from space. Cat and I were forced to cling to the sides of our pea-green boat in a panic, as we bobbed and lurched beneath the moon.

Even now, I can feel my whiskered familiar following my movements with one suspicious eye, as she pretends to be asleep on the window-sill. Cat is no fan of Alice, and no wonder. For Alice has decided that if she does ever return to Europe, she cannot possibly come alone.

No: Alice will return to Britain with her D–O–G. Digby has already had his rabies jab, she says. So the seven-month process of applying for his pet passport is under way.

'What's he like, incidentally?' I asked her, just as we were saying goodbye.

'Digby? Oh, he's *adorable*. Everyone says he's the handsomest labrador they've ever met. It's just his personality that's a bit . . . well, have you seen *Marley & Me*?'

'I've read the book.'

'I'm afraid he's worse. He's more like the Emperor Nero, or Caligula.'

'Ah.'

'Exactly.'

Tonight, while Cat sits beside me, casually pushing needles into a wax effigy of a golden labrador, I turn over in my mind the worry that irks; attempt to dislodge the pebble in my shoe. Why should it matter that Alice comes with a dog? Being savaged by a slavering beast strikes me as a reasonable price to pay for the woman of my dreams. So it must be the commitment that D–O–G spells that makes me afraid. If Alice comes alone, and we do not get on, she can leave on the next plane. Whereas if she comes with a dog, she is stuck.

Considered from this point of view, Digby would be doing me a favour.

I remind myself that Alice and I have spent only *six days* together in our adult lives. Yet we have also known each other for twenty-six years. And the truth is that I have never felt so clear about anything in my life.

I have been in love before. Or perhaps I was in lust. Certainly I was in need. But I have not been in love like this: with my eyes open, comfortable in my own skin, and with that quiet zing of physical confidence that working in the naked world of La Folie has begun to engender. And not with Alice Melbury; with a girl I have known since I was twelve years old, with someone who makes me feel – even at a distance of three thousand miles – as if I had just touched down at my home aerodrome, after a long and bumpy flight through the fog.

I pick up the phone, and dial Alice's home number.

'How would you and Digby feel about coming to live with me at La Folie?' I ask, as soon as she answers. 'As in permanently, I mean.'

There is a long silence on the other end of the line.

# 14

## OCTOBER

My entries for the Spitfire competition are complete. There is no slogan to compose; no tie-breaker to complete. So I write a letter of explanation instead, telling them why it matters so much that I win, charting the course of my Spitfire passion, which has remained undimmed though my body has lost its childhood elastic, and my boyhood grin has crinkled into an adult smile.

After I have composed the letter in rough, I make a fair copy of it on my very last sheet of sky-blue Japanese writing-paper, hand-decorated with birds and bamboo, bought in Kobe a week before an earthquake destroyed the city. And then, just as I am about to leap into the Espace to drive to the post office, I phone *Warbird* magazine.

'May I please just double-check that it's all right to enter the Spitfire competition more than once?'

'Yes, there's nothing in the rules against that, sir,' says the nice lady on the other end of the line, in a voice like a hot buttered tea-cake. 'Have you done a couple, then?'

'Slightly more than that.'

'You mean more than ten?'

'More than that, too, I'm afraid.'

She begins to chortle. 'Don't tell me you've gone and done a hundred?'

'I've done . . .' I pause, and clench everything. 'I hope you don't mind, but I've made a thousand entries.'

There is a long silence on the line. I think perhaps the metaphorical tea-cake has stuck in her throat.

'A *thousand*?' she says, at last, in a horrified whisper, as if I'd just told her how much Betty from Number Eighteen had won down the bingo last night. 'You're very keen, aren't you, love?'

Leaning on a petite gardening fork, I contemplate the upper storey of a French barn which is almost entirely filled with a festering heap of hay, its surface pockmarked with rat-holes. My task is to clear this by the end of the week, which may be why I have spent the morning mowing the grass in the field at the far end of the house. I have also mucked out the chicken house and paid the *taxe foncière*. I even had a stab at tidying my desk. But I have now run out of displacement activities, and it is time to face my destiny.

Stiffening my sinews, I cheer myself with the thought that old hay is not just old hay. No, Old Hay also happens to be the name of one of my favourite private airstrips, its crossed runways making a grassy X in the depths of the Kent countryside. A half-forgotten Luscombe Silvaire, covered in dust and straw, lurks at the back of the barn there like some hibernating animal. Battered and broken, this was the first Luscombe in which I ever sat, amazed at how cramped and primitive and perfect the tiny cockpit felt.

I wish the barn at La Folie were filled with old aircraft. But as I set to with my fork and much grunting, the only things that become airborne are about a billion dust particles and a finger-four of sleepy moths. I haven't managed to shift any hay, exactly, but my dust-cloud must be visible from Kent.

Next I begin to scoop away at Asthma Central with my

gloved hands. I cannot see a thing, for the barn is dark, my flying-goggles have steamed up, and the air is thick with itching powder. I do my best to hold my breath as I hurl arm- fuls of the matted matter out through a hole in the west wall. I make a pyre and set light to it. The crackling is vicious, and I think of Ridley and Latimer as the flames shoot high into the October sky.

Still no sign of rats. And then, on the third day, something in the hay catches my eye: a whiskered creature, curled into a ball. I freeze. They are here. They're waiting to eat me, starting with my toes. And then I look more closely; see that it is in fact a beautiful young dormouse – *un loir* to the French, *Glis glis* to the Romans – fast asleep. My instinct is to scoop up the rodent and release him far, far from the house. But Alice would want me to give him the best possible chance of survival. Even from the other side of the Atlantic, this woman is beginning to influence my life. So I leave the *loir* where he is for the moment, and wander outside for a slug of fresh air.

I thought I would feel catharsis at burning all this hay, but instead, I feel terrible. The feeling is worst when, here and there, I come upon the odd complete bale, still bound up with tight cords of hemp rope. Though Gilles insists that the hay is far too old for my Rastafarians to munch, to gaze down at those hand-tied knots still causes a pang of regret.

I imagine the peasants sweating on the hillside behind La Folie, sixty-odd years ago, at the end of the war. They made this hay; tightened this twine; tied these knots with weary, blistered fingers. I think of them scything the same grass that I blithely mulch each summer with my ride-on mower, so that their beasts would have food through the winter. I try to picture the Massey Ferguson hay-rake I found in the brambles being dragged behind a couple of cows, their shoulders straining against the yoke that now hangs from a beam in the kitchen, while liberating Spitfires roar low overhead. It is all so far away, and yet all so close, too, as I watch the red-gold sparks fly up into the dusk.

My mind is made up. Returning to the barn, I gently wrap the slumbering *loir* in a sleeping-bag made of hay, and tuck him behind the giant bale of barley straw that Gilles has given me for the Rastafarians.

'Sleep well,' I whisper, which is more than I will be doing at night when he starts to munch the roof insulation above my bed.

Cat and I are woken by a telephone call at 6.30 am.

'I can't do it,' blurts Alice, as soon as I pick up the phone. She must be in the middle of a night-shift.

'What do you mean, you can't do it? Is it your landings? Or the leeches?'

'I mean I can't come to France, to be with you. I miss my family too much. It's too alien, too soon. I don't speak a word of French. I'm so sorry. It's impossible.'

'Impossible is just a word,' I murmur, into the silence.

'I love you,' she continues. 'God knows, I want to be with you. But I've been abroad for so long already. I want to come home.'

'I love you, too,' I reply, feeling as if the ceiling of the bedroom has just come crashing down upon my head. Picking my way through the dust and rubble, I instinctively reach out to Cat, to cuddle her to me. Clawing herself free, she springs off the bed, hungry to be fed. And I gaze at the twin lines of bright blood on my forearm: a message of faithless love.

Alice is silent, and I can hear the *beep-beeper-beep* of the alarms in the background. I have never heard her sound so tired. I wish we could rewind the tape of our lives by fifteen seconds, and start this conversation all over again.

'It was just an idea,' I attempt to explain. 'I didn't mean to pressurize you.'

'You haven't pressurized me. It's just that I can't do it. I miss England too much. And besides, even if you could put up with me at La Folie, there's no way you could put up with my dog.'

I ask her where this leaves us both. She says she does not know. Until two minutes ago, our relationship was still in the phase of its initial climb, with both engines at full throttle. Now I am wondering if it has just disappeared from the radar screens of the controllers in the tower. They must be blinking at each other in panicked disbelief as, somewhere over the Atlantic, a starburst of charred hopes, twisted dreams and stray life-jackets floats to earth like so much redundant confetti.

When I am not obsessing over hay or Alice Melbury, I have been making regular trips to the aeroclub at St Juste, doing my best to fix yet another mechanical problem on the Luscombe under Antoine's patient supervision. A few days ago, Alice forwarded me a new set of piston rings from a supplier in Fresno, and Antoine is showing me how to fit them. This is the simple part. The hard part is coaxing the piston into its cylinder, which feels a bit like attempting to squeeze a champagne cork back into the bottle from which it has just popped.

I am tightening the sleeve to compress the rings once more, when I hear footsteps shuffling on tarmac. I recognize that slouching gait, I think to myself, as Marcel, the aeroclub grouch, appears in the doorway of the maintenance hangar in his beige anorak and familiar scowl.

'*Bonjour*,' he says, almost cheerfully, raising his habitual *basso profundo* growl into a gravelly baritone. Stunned, Antoine and I exchange glances. Even Marcel's soggy grey cigarillo is missing from his lower lip, and his face twitches into an almost-smile.

'*Salut, Marcel*,' we chime. 'Are you all right?'

'*Ça va, ça va,*' he replies, softly, watching what we are doing from afar. 'Those new rings should do wonders for your compression.'

'You want to come in?' asks Antoine, wiping his hands. I know he cannot stand Marcel's constant streams of criticism and unfriendly advice. But he, too, has noticed that something is different about Marcel today.

'*Merci,*' says Marcel, shaking his head, 'but I'm with someone today.' My eyes widen: so Marcel found someone, after all.

He whistles. And then Antoine whistles, too, and I cannot help laughing as Marcel's new friend – a bright-eyed white poodle, with a red ribbon in its hair – comes trotting into view.

'Meet Toutou,' growls the old grouch, squaring up to our derision. 'She can't cook and she smells a bit,' he adds, leading her away to the grass. 'But at least she listens to me, which is more than I can say for all the rest.'

At last the bottle is stopped: the piston, with its four oiled rings, is safely housed inside its cylinder. And the next day is such a burnished, blazing Saturday that of course it makes me long to try out my improved engine – to fly it hard, to seat the rings – in the big French sky. Yet it is also the allotted day for the people of Jolibois to give blood. And since flying and phlebotomies don't mix, the Luscombe will have to wait.

I have only given blood twice in my life. This is weedy of me, I know. But I have always been squeamish about needles, and was so jabbed and stabbed last time round by a nurse who had missed her vocation as a tea-bag perforator that it quite put me off. That was my excuse, anyway. Yet Alice has made it quite clear that this is not acceptable: do I have any idea how much other people's blood I might need, if I ever undergo major surgery? Besides, after all the injections I have given poor old Gaston, it seems only fair that I should be on the other end for a change. Many of the locals tell me they think *les Anglais* only really come to France for the healthcare. So it is time I made amends.

'*Donné du Sang*' reads the sign on the door of the Tribunal, converted for today into a makeshift hospital. I expected the place to be deserted, yet it feels as if *le tout Jolibois* is here. I hold the door open for Jeanne, Le Grand Mermoz's wife, and come face to face with Marie from the *boulangerie*, on her way out. She still looks reassuringly pink.

'*Ah, Michael, tu es là? C'est merveilleux. Merci!*' exclaims Jeanne. And for a second I'm so busy feeling moved by my own altruism that I forget to repay her thanks.

Jeanne, herself a nurse, shows me how to fill in the various forms that are stacked on the table. Do you suffer from the bubonic plague? Have you had a heart attack today? When were you last mauled by a rabid dog? Is your reflection visible in a mirror? And then, the googly: Did you spend time in *les Îles britanniques* between 1980 and 1996?

I take my form to the glamorous lady behind the desk. In her starched white uniform, she looks like a nurse in a *Carry On* film.

'Is this going to be a problem, *madame*, that I have ticked this box?' I ask.

She flutters her eyelashes over my form, and nods. I won't be able to give blood, she says, because it is the minister who decides these things. I show *madame* my NHS blood-donor card. I point to the boxes on my form which indicate that I do not have Munchausen's by proxy, Stockholm syndrome or housemaid's knee.

'*Quand même,*' she says, with an apologetic shrug.

'Because I may be a mad cow?'

She blushes and nods, before inviting me to help myself to a drink and a biscuit, even so. I mumble my thanks and head out into the open air.

At first, this seems like a bit of a result. I have been spotted making an effort by people who know me, without having to give up any of the precious red stuff. There was no pain. And I shall be able to go flying today, after all.

And then I think about it some more, and feel unusually deflated. For I was all psyched up, ready to do something useful. And it dawns on me that my looking good is not going to help anybody at all.

'*Bravo, Michael*,' says a man sitting just inside the exit, who turns out to be Jean-Michel, the president of the tennis club. '*C'est bien, ce que vous avez fait.*'

'*Non, je n'ai rien fait*,' I explain with an embarrassed shrug. 'They didn't want my English blood. I haven't given anything at all.'

Sometimes I think that it was my love of the Spitfire, and the reassuring certainty of its gracefully elliptical wings, that piloted me safely through my childhood. And now, amid a different kind of turmoil, it is a relief to think about Spitfires once again. I phone the nice lady at *Warbird* magazine to check that they have received my entries.

'Ooh, hallo, love, it's you,' she says, as if I were an old friend, or perhaps just a nutter. She stopped calling me 'sir', I noticed, as soon as I confessed to my thousand entries.

Yes, yes, they have received my box of entries, and someone read aloud the lovely letter I wrote, explaining why I thought I should win. And in total, she tells me when I ask, they have received six thousand entries for the Spitfire competition.

'*Six thousand?*'

After I have put down the phone, I run my hands through my hair, tugging distractedly at the roots. So I have only a one in six chance. A single roll of the die. If I'd known that, I'd have done twelve thousand.

The perfect flying weather holds for two more days, so I

work the Luscombe hard, flying to aerodromes all over south-west France. The new piston rings will take time to bed in, and running the engine at close to full throttle on some long trips across country is just the thing. Besides: I have some decisions to make. I need to think about France; about Alice; about La Folie.

On Sunday evening, I have descended to fifteen hundred feet and am about to rejoin the circuit at St Juste from Sarlat, when I make a snap decision to extend my flight.

Instead of landing at St Juste, I head north, towards the water towers of Jolibois. And there, clinging to a hillside just a mile or two south of the town, stands the low grey shape of La Folie, with its mottled peach roof and its fields scattered with what looks from up here like a pocketful of chestnuts, but which I know to be my hungry Rastafarians.

Once, twice, I circle my little kingdom, with the Lone Pine as the compass point upon which I centre my arc. I pass over the railway cutting through which four trains rattle every day, and the Moulin Vaugelade, where Josette's washing is still hanging on the line. She and Gilles will be leaving here soon.

I gaze down upon La Folie; upon this ramshackle farmhouse that I love so much, and which has changed my life, teaching me like a trusted and inspirational old friend.

This is my life, I think to myself, remembering the beetle that crawled through the blur of the wood-dust as I chainsawed my logs, and the Mirage that roared overhead, all those months ago.

This place, I swear, is the source of anything and all that is good in me. It is where I learned to give and live alone; to grow out of that needy incompleteness that made me always be searching for someone else to make my life whole.

Zumbach told me he was merely looking after La Folie for me. And now I am looking after it in my turn, for someone else yet to come.

It is too soon. I am not ready.

My heart feels heavy as I peer down at the centre of my universe: at the house at the end of the world. Thank you, I mouth, as I roar overhead; thank you La Folie, earth and sky.

'Don't leave,' cluck Martha and the rest of the Egg Squad, cricking their necks through ninety degrees to peer straight up at the noisy yellow bird in the sky.

'Stay, stay,' bleat the sheep. 'St-a-a-a-a-ay.'

My mind is made up.

Squeezing the throttle and hearing the engine note rise, I push the stick hard left, add a dab of left rudder, and swing the Luscombe's nose in a half-circle, through the dazzling blaze of the setting sun, until it is pointing at the low ridge and St Juste.

Surprised to find myself wiping my eyes, I put it down to the brightness of the vanishing sun.

# 15

## NOVEMBER

Alice is crying softly down the phone. This is not what I was expecting.

'But you *can't*,' she says. 'It's not right.'

'Yes I can,' I reply, 'because I love you. And so I must.'

'But it's your whole life. And what about the chickens, and the sheep. What will they do?'

'I can sell them, or give them to Gilles or Monsieur Jadot. It's not a problem.'

'But La Folie – it's *you*. You've put everything into it, I know you have. And it just makes me feel terrible, that you would do this for me. It's too beautiful. I don't know what to say.'

'Then don't say anything,' I say, quietly, urging my own voice not to crack.

Even now, with my mind made up, I cannot help fearing that I might be making an irreversible mistake. Because yes: La Folie is everything to me. I have been happier here in this wild old place than I have ever been, anywhere, in my adult life. Thanks to my adventures here, I feel as if I have almost caught up with the good man I always hoped to be, before I became swayed and disoriented by the bright lights of the city.

But all that changed when I met Alice Melbury again. For she, too, inspires me to be that better man, in new and different ways. And I would – I will – give all of it up for her. Weaving its natural magic, La Folie has done its work: it has shaken me out of my stupor; taught me lessons I should have learned years ago. And it has brought a brave and true and shining woman into my life. I will not lightly let her go.

'Just stop,' says Alice, her voice pleading. 'Please just wait, because I have to think. I don't want you to do anything foolish or hasty. I'm not going anywhere, you know. I want to be with you as much as – maybe more than – you want to be with me.'

She hesitates, like a diver on a high board, and suddenly I am aware of all the alarms bleeping in the background of her life; that here I am, sitting in my peaceful kitchen in rural France, with Martha watching me from the window-sill, and I am talking to a woman on a battlefield in Baltimore, surrounded by carnage. How she manages it all, even without my distracting her with traumatic phone-calls, is beyond me.

'And if that means I have to come and live in France, then so be it,' Alice continues. 'I'll do it. You just convinced me.' By now, I cannot quite tell if she is still crying, or laughing. It sounds like a bit of both.

I try to explain that this isn't what I wanted; that I wasn't making some mighty sacrifice and then challenging her to match it. I love the fact that her family is so important to her; am relieved to discover that, like me, she still thinks so much of England. All I want to know is that we may yet have a future together; somewhere; anywhere.

'Everything is going to work out just fine, somehow,' she tells me at last. 'You'll see. Just don't do anything hasty until I see you, promise?'

'I promise.' And a great cheer goes up in the control-tower of my heart, and the controllers are all hugging each other with relief, because the radar trace has reappeared: the flight is still on track.

After I put the phone down, I sit in silence for a few moments, gazing at Martha on the window-sill. How on earth did I become so lucky, that this extraordinary woman has flown into my life?

A few minutes later, the extraordinary woman phones back.

'You're not going to believe this,' she says. 'You know how I said my contract at Hopkins ends in March?'

My mind races. Please let her not be about to tell me that she has got the wrong March; or that she has agreed to extend her contract by another three years because the people of Baltimore cannot do without her. What about the people of La Folie? *We* can't do without her, either.

'Let me finish,' she giggles. 'They've just told me that I have twenty-seven days in lieu, for all the extra shifts I've worked. So I won't have to do any more work after the beginning of January.'

'You're joking. So in January you fly back to England, and we can be together at last, even if it means zipping ourselves into a sleeping-bag at your mum's?' I wave at Martha on the window-sill, give her a jubilant thumbs-up. Martha, ever the most cynical of chickens, blinks with disdain.

'Um, not exactly,' says Alice.

As so often before, Martha's insight is spot on. For there just happens to be a great big, drooling, furry, four-legged fly in the blasted ointment. Alice is going nowhere fast, because of a ball and chain marked Digby that is manacled to her shapely calf. The vile beast cannot enter Britain until April, to allow a six-month gap after his rabies jab and blood test.

'So I'm afraid I'll have to stay here until then,' she explains, doing her best to sound cheerful in the face of the mounting thunderclouds of rage and exasperation that she must sense on the other end of the line. 'But at least that'll give me a bit more time to scare my instructor into letting me fly solo. And perhaps you might be able to come out and visit.'

'Of course,' I reply, unenthusiastically. I can feel my blood chilling in my veins, as I picture a fat labrador sprawled on Alice's bed, flicking through the sports channels on television, and languidly being fed lumps of biltong from her perfectly manicured fingers, while I sit pining and desperate at La Folie, waiting for my future to arrive. And all because of a beastly, blasted dog.

'*Oh là là, ça penche,*' declares Le Grand Mermoz, the hale fifty-year-old sportsman who trounced me in the spud-growing contest and runs the best hardware store in the Limousin. Mermoz has dropped round for an *apéro* and, as we sit outside on the terrace, is gazing up at the roof of La Folie. I can see him tilting his head to straighten the chimney in his mind's eye, as if he were a golfer peering after a hooked drive.

Yes, Mermoz, it leans. Worse than that, the chimney now teeters so far beyond the vertical that the masonry has actually started to curl, like the corner of an old sandwich. It wobbles when you touch it, too, at least according to Monsieur Duruflé the tiler, who hauled my grand piano up the drive all those years ago and does not share my fear of falling off roofs. This would not matter – I'll bet parts of the Parthenon wobble, too – except that the chimney in question is located slap-bang above my bed, and on the side where Alice is likely to sleep. That can be Digby's side, I decide.

And so, when Serge the stonemason arrives to crash and bang and install windows in the new rooms at La Folie – the house is growing lighter all the time – I wonder aloud if he would mind coming to crash and bang the errant *cheminée*, too. Serge's response is a classic of rural forward-planning.

'*Oui, bien sûr,*' he growls. 'But not until you have heard the first cuckoo sing.'

My first thought is that this must be some sort of a joke; a send-up of old-fashioned rural ways. And then I remember that Serge may show constant good humour in the face of dusty adversity, but what he does not do is jokes.

Monsieur Jadot, my trusty *potager* consultant, does jokes. After I have wandered up the old cart-track to his house, my feet crunching through the frosted leaves underfoot, I ask him when the first cuckoo is expected.

'*Ah-ouf,*' he exclaims. Jadot elevates his arm as if about to demonstrate a trick with a Butterfly yo-yo. 'Look: the doctor has poisoned me.'

At first I cannot quite see what he means, until I notice that his hand has disappeared into his sleeve.

I chuckle, playing along, and ask him if he cut it off by mistake with his chainsaw.

He looks so hurt at this suggestion that I panic, remembering how one of Gilles's fingers is just such a sawn-off stump. I can feel my cheeks turning scarlet with remorse. I am doing my best to back-pedal. But my brain is getting no traction on the black ice of my unreliable French.

'Not that,' he says. '*Ça!*' He jabs at his raised arm with his other hand. 'That's as far as I can lift it. Do you think I'm becoming paralysed?' Monsieur Jadot has a somewhat exaggerated regard for my medical expertise, largely because I have told him that Alice is an intensive-care nurse.

Not wishing to disappoint, I give him my quack diagnosis.

'I think it's a frozen shoulder,' I say. 'You'll need to take it easy for a while.'

'*Putain!*' he exclaims, his eyes widening as if he had seen a cuckoo in November. 'But that's exactly what my doctor said.'

Jadot says the doctor has told him to rest his shoulder, and that it will not recover for six months. Particularly since Jadot still insists on swinging his sledgehammer every day.

'Is that before or after the first cuckoo sings?' I ask.

He purses his lips; squints at me; looks troubled, as if he has just remembered that he left his car keys hanging on the horns of one of his cows. Above our heads, a solitary chestnut – one of the very last – flutters down from the denuded trees. It will not be long before everything is dead and frozen. For winter cannot be far away.

Desolate news is blinking on the answerphone when I return to La Folie. Le Grand Mermoz has had a heart attack. I cannot quite believe it: the big man himself, a sportsman to the core, felled by a blow that I have always associated with bloated stress-mongers and lard-basted sofa-slugs.

It seems that Mermoz was out walking in the mountains with Jeanne, his wife, when he complained of a vice-like grip on his chest, and then just collapsed in the woods. Fortunately Jeanne, being a nurse, knew exactly what to do. He is now staring at the ceiling of the vast factory hospital in Limoges, contemplating a life without tennis or other vices.

When I drive through the rain to visit him, gaggles of moody gendarmes stand at every roundabout, as if in response to a national emergency. They must have heard that Le Grand Mermoz is down and almost out.

The big man, when I knock on the door of his private room and tiptoe in, looks surprised, too. He is lying on his side, with one arm under his head. The room is bare and shabby, except for an iron bed from which the white gloss is beginning to chip, and the black cube of a television, suspended high on the opposite wall. From outside the door there comes a constant din: not of *beep-beeper-beep* alarms, but the crash-bang-slam of boxes and trolleys being shifted in a hurry.

For a moment, his eyes struggle to focus on the stranger who has entered his room. 'It's the Englishman,' he murmurs at last. 'Don't tell me I've woken up in London.'

'You look well,' I reply.

I had not expected him to look so sick: his eyes, always sparkling with good humour, seem clouded with doubt; his skin is creased and grey as a worn-out five-euro note.

'You've come to challenge me to a match, haven't you?' he growls, hauling himself up with the help of a triangular handle suspended like a cat's toy above the bed. I notice for the first time that he is wired to a black box about the size of a car battery. 'You think this is your chance finally to beat me.'

'Yes, and we'd better play soon, because you'll be fully fit by next week,' I reply. Bloke-banter is international. Even across the language-barrier of my faltering French, I know that Mermoz's joking is to hide the fact that he is touched that I have come. And we both know that mine is to hide the fact that I am worried about him.

'Oh, I'm not sure about that,' he says, suddenly serious. 'I don't feel so good.'

I eye Mermoz's black box, wondering if I should tell him that this may be because they've given him an elephant pace-maker by mistake. 'That's just to record the rhythm of my heart,' he says, guessing my thoughts, 'before they operate.'

Mermoz and I chat for a while, and he asks about how everything is going with *la ravissante* Alice. I'm surprised that he knows what she looks like, but of course: *le bouche à oreille*, news travels fast on the Jolibois bush-telegraph. So I tell him about our struggle to know what to do for the best; about the conflict between our wanting to be together somehow, and her needing to be closer to her family in England.

'You are thinking of returning to *Angleterre*?' he says, pulling hard on the triangular handle as though he needed it to help raise his eyebrows.

'I might have to. She matters more than anything now.'

'You *Anglais* are so passionate; it's always surprising to me. I thought you just drank tea and played cricket in the fog.'

'We do quite a lot of that, too.'

'But look: this is important.' Mermoz places his hand on his chest, as if to reassure himself that his heart is still beating. 'You have to go and get her; persuade her to come. If she goes to England, and settles into some new job, it will be too late. You will lose each other in the fog.'

He searches my eyes; wants to be sure that I have understood. And then he adds, with touching earnestness, that I must keep an eye on her, too, because beautiful nurses are always being chased by doctors. 'I should know,' he says. 'I'm married to one myself.'

We sit in silence for a while, watching the net curtains in the window being blown by the wind. Mermoz has never spoken to me so personally before. We tend to josh about nonsense, when he is not lecturing me about his hard-left principles. A flint-faced nurse in a white uniform puts her head round the door, peers fiercely at us both, and then shuts it again.

'Sometimes, of course, the doctors don't chase them quite so fast,' murmurs Mermoz, with a twinkle, pursing his lips.

At last, I rise to leave, and he takes me by the hand. 'This is the time you need to be together,' he says, his tired eyes shining, 'when the first sparks are still flying, and the fire has only just been lit. And we will be kind to her, you'll see, if she comes.'

'I know you will,' I reply, relieved to hear Mermoz talking about a future that is still likely to include him. 'But right now, I have to go and start training for our match.' Shaking his cold hand, and instructing him to get well soon, I slip quietly out of the room.

And then I drive home through the rain with his words ringing in my mind. I think about Alice and Spitfires, struggling to lighten my mood, which feels almost as grey as the sky. And things only get worse when I return to La Folie.

The atmosphere in the chicken house has never quite recovered from Titus's death, back in August. I suppose I should have guessed that it would be only a matter of time before the fox returned. But I wasn't expecting Monsieur Renard to come in broad daylight.

Tonight, as I trudge through the puddles to put the chickens to bed, it soon becomes clear that all is not well. There are too many empty spaces on the perches; more aircraft call-signs to rub off the blackboard. Four of our planes are still unaccounted for, skipper.

It doesn't take long to identify three of the missing pilots: Hotspur, the new squadron leader; Melissa, my bossy white *poule de Bresse*; and Margot, an affectionate foot-fetishist who likes nothing better than tugging on a leather bootlace or pecking at the hairs on one's toes. All are out there, somewhere, in the darkness.

Strange, that the fox should have a knack for taking my most characterful chickens. It is the spirited adventurers – the ones who travel furthest from the safety of La Folie – who are being picked off, while the quiet nonentities from the bottom perch live on.

And then, as I continue to gaze at the birds who are left on the depleted perches, the truth begins to dawn.

Martha has vanished, too. Martha, my special friend, who has spent more time on the window-sill beside my desk than all the other chickens put together, and who will sometimes sit on my lap on the terrace, watching the stillness of the trees across the valley. Martha, who could turf one of her sisters out of a nesting box as pitilessly as an angry super-model faced with a queue for the ladies' loo.

This lump in my throat is silly, I know. Martha is just

another chicken, after all. But these chickens – Martha, Margot and Melissa – had been with me since the beginning of my time at La Folie. They were my familiars; a part of my living landscape. They kept me sane and cheerful in the depths of brutal winters and at the height of burning summers. The sight of a bevy of ex-battery chickens blossoming in the freedom of the countryside is a tonic for the most jaded soul. And now the only survivor from my original six girls is Meg, who has been under the weather for months. Like the little crippled boy in the story of the Pied Piper, I suppose she simply could not keep up with the others, and so has survived to tell the tale.

At first I cannot find a single one of Martha's beautiful feathers – each as gold and black and graceful as a gondola gliding through a silent canal – to keep in remembrance or, at the very least, to be sure of her fate. And then, one day, Meg leads me to a small patch of nettles behind the *potager*, and here I find a tell-tale scattering of black and gold.

I select the best feathers I can find, and make a circle of them in the earth beneath the Lone Pine, in the place where all my other favourites have been buried: Emil, Nemo, Silent Mary and the rest.

'Thank you, Martha,' I whisper, blinking at all that is left of my favourite chicken. How often I held her on my lap, stroking her gondola plumage, taking comfort from the silent connection we seemed to share. Whenever I would drive back to La Folie, in sunshine or in rain, it was Martha who would come – *puck puck puck puck* – scampering out to greet me; to peck at my laces; to submit, clucking her doubts, to my caress. She it was, more than anyone, who settled me into my solitary life at La Folie. And now here she is: a fistful of feathers, stuffed into the earth.

Exhausted by the turmoil of the past few weeks – when I have come close to losing so much that is so precious to me – I watch my tears soak into the earth amid all that is left of

Martha; a circle of feathers; rain upon Stonehenge. At my feet, her sister Meg pecks at the wet earth, too busy gobbling up worms to say goodbye.

# 16

## DECEMBER

The early morning frosts are once again so hard that the sheep are white when I trudge out to break the ice on their water-trough and scatter the granules that make up for the lack of grass. April – when Digby can fly to Europe at last, liberating Alice from Baltimore – is still so far off, like the end of a rainbow that keeps getting further away, no matter how swiftly you advance upon it.

I console myself with the thought that it is only a few days until Alice returns to La Folie for another of her flying visits. Meanwhile I spend much of my time online, searching for cheap apartments to rent in Baltimore or Anapolis, or on the scenic waters of Chesapeake Bay.

'What do you think about America in February, Cat?' I ask her, as she sits in her Sphinx-like pose, watching me for any hint of a twitch towards the food cupboard.

I pore over the European regulations for importing live animals, too, because there are so many hoops through which Digby must jump. The rabies jab is only the start of it. Then there are the export forms to be signed by a government vet. The microchip that must be readable by UK scanners, at a time when US microchip manufacturers are bent on Betamaxing each other by adopting their own, incompatible standards. The travel crate that must conform to IATA minima. The tick and tapeworm treatment. The canine air-ticket. And so on.

I read the official jargon again and again, trying to make sense of it all. And then I come across something which sends a tingle of electricity up my spine. How did I not spot this before?

When it comes to importing dogs from the USA, Britain insists upon a delay of six months after a successful rabies blood test. But France, in her wisdom, demands a delay of only *three* months. And Digby had his blood test at the beginning of October. So he and Alice could theoretically fly across the Atlantic to La Folie next month.

*Vive la France!*

Ralph the artist always told me I should find myself a dog, to save me from my terminal isolation. And in a funny way, it turns out that he was right.

From Alice's silence at the other end of the line, I can tell that she doesn't consider my suggestion of using La Folie as a canine halfway-house between Baltimore and Blighty entirely the worst idea in the world. And I am sure that it is pure coincidence that Cat chooses just this moment to go clattering out through the cat-flap with unusual urgency.

'Even if you think you could put up with me,' Alice reminds me, at last, 'you're not going to think that once you meet my dog.'

'Oh, nonsense,' I reply, cheerfully. Because of course I haven't met Digby yet.

I am speeding through Jolibois, on my way to meet Alice at Limoges airport for her final visit before D-Day, when a car on the opposite side of the road starts flashing its lights at me. Perhaps it is *les flics*, policing stray juggernauts. But as I pull away, the driver winds down his window and shakes his fist at me.

'Look, I'm still here!' he yells.

I recognize – a split second too late – Le Grand Mermoz, beaming at me and the world with such astonished delight that you would think he had just come back from the dead.

And finally, after a wait that has lasted for ever, Alice is back at La Folie, like sunshine after rain. In fact, it rains sideways for most of her stay. This is probably a good thing, for I would hate to give her the misguided impression that France basks in wall-to-wall sunshine, even in the howling run-up to winter.

No, I would rather she saw La Folie for what it is, than for what she might dream it to be. This is what I tell myself when the electricity trips off in a storm, the chimney begins to rattle on the roof, and the old river once again begins to flow through the kitchen from behind the oven and fridge, trickling down the steps, and dribbling off out through the front door. December may be hard, but January – when she and Digby are now due to arrive – will be worse.

In a rare dry spell, we wander down the sunken path that winds through the trees into Jolibois, holding hands like a pair of children.

And there, after we have passed beneath the railway viaduct, is the river. Usually this slides through the park at the bottom end of town as slowly as syrup sliding off a spoon, but today it is gurgling along like a swimmer in the fast lane, splashing and kicking and daring anyone to get in its way.

'It's beautiful here,' she says, as we stand on the nine-hundred-year-old Gothic bridge upon which I have stood and dreamed so many times before, yet never with so much sky in my heart. 'I can't believe Digby and I are maybe going to come and live here.'

'When does it stop being "maybe", and start becoming "definitely"?' I ask, slipping my arm round her waist.

'All right, definitely,' she says, hiding her face in my collar. 'If you're sure you're sure.'

'I'm sure.' And the truth is that I am amazed at how completely and utterly sure I am. I am in uncharted territory, as I reach out to grab with both hands this future that was buried in my past.

'Meeting you is like the first time I met La Folie,' I tell her. 'And I just *knew*. The place was everything I had ever wanted; it ticked every box. And then it added a whole list of extra ticked boxes that I hadn't even considered before. Here was this amazing house that nobody else wanted. And it was perfect.'

'Are you saying I'm ramshackle and unwanted?' she asks, narrowing her eyes.

'I'm saying you have amazing views and considerable potential,' I reply, giving her a squeeze that makes her yelp.

'Hm.' Through the cotton of my shirt and the felt of my jacket, I can feel Alice's mind whirring like the cogs of a clock that is about to strike.

And then the church clock, on the steep crag high above our heads, does strike with a series of bongs and clangs and rattles. Midday.

'Time for lunch?' I ask, gently.

'Don't you think,' replies Alice, not moving, 'that perhaps you were just worried that the music was about to stop? That I was the first person who came along?'

I assume she is joking; make some glib response. But Alice is serious. So I tell her about the slow, circuitous route that led me from a school in Sussex, where a homesick little girl fetched sticks to help me build camps in the woods, to today; to this moment on a twelfth-century stone bridge in a nondescript town in the middle of darkest France.

'Either people seemed right, and I didn't feel crazy about them, or else I felt crazy about them, and knew that it wasn't quite right.'

'Snap,' says Alice, ruefully. 'As Toby is so fond of reminding me, I've kissed a few frogs in my time.'

I tell her about how, just before we met, I had finally reached a point where I didn't *need* anyone any more to make my life complete. 'So I drew a line in the sand. I said to myself that I was happy by myself. I stopped looking; trusted the universe to provide. And about five seconds later, Toby emailed me out of the blue to say that you were learning to fly.'

We watch as a pair of ducks – a male in a green silk helmet, trimmed with white, and a female in Burberry browns and blacks – glide out from under the bridge beneath our feet.

'I just wasn't expecting all this to happen quite so fast,' I add.

'Nor was I,' laughs Alice as, arm in arm, we begin to walk up the steep path via the ramparts into town.

'But you started it,' I continue. 'I mean, you were the one who played footsy-footsy under the table.'

'I was feeling ignored,' she says, indignantly, 'while you and Toby were banging on about internet dating as if I wasn't there.'

'Well, I'm ever so glad that you did, because I would never have dared if you hadn't.'

'Then so am I,' she says, smiling to herself. 'Glad and amazed.'

We walk on in silence for a while, our breaths becoming shorter as the path grows ever steeper. 'But I was the same,' she adds. 'I would happily have waited my whole life for the right person to come along, rather than settle for someone just because I felt rushed by my body into choosing.'

She tells me about a patient she once nursed, a lady who had remained single all her life. 'And then, at the age of eighty, she found love in an old people's home.' We stand aside as an old man, bent almost double beneath a bundle of sticks, comes down the path towards us, thanking us with a toothless grin as he passes. 'She finally married this man who was everything she had ever wanted. And that would have been me. I would have waited all my life, if I had to.'

Onwards and upwards we walk, past the ramparts of the medieval town, and up towards the church. Jolibois has never looked more beautiful to me than it looks on this grey, dank day. Around us, everyone seems to be smiling. And there is a freshness in the air which makes me feel zingingly alive.

'May I ask you something?' I turn towards Alice, and she looks suddenly nervous.

'Is there something wrong?' she says.

'It's just that you strike me as being such an amazing catch,' I reply, smiling. 'I mean, here you are: you're gorgeous, switched-on and delightful. You don't labour under the delusion that the world should somehow devote itself to satisfying your wants. You have girlfriends who go back a long way. You know how to be happy. You work hard. You eat properly, but are not a candidate for the whale-scanner. You are neither vegetarian nor teetotal. You're kind. You do not have a twisted or non-existent relationship with your parents. From my point of view, you're pretty much perfect. So I suppose I just can't help wondering why you haven't already been snapped up. Is there anything I should know?'

'I don't really know what to say to that,' she says, at last, 'except that I have had thirty-two hours of dual-instruction on a Cessna 172, and my instructor still doesn't think I'm quite ready to fly solo. I don't think he ever will, to be honest. But as I've already told you: when it came to love, I was happy to wait.' And then she confesses that she has wondered the same thing about me, too. 'Does it mean you have some dark secret?'

'*Touché*,' I laugh. 'Fortunately, I think I've already told you all my dark secrets. You know I used to collect stamps, was a keen bellringer and that the first record I ever bought was *The World of the Organ*.'

'That's true. That's pretty dark.'

'But the truth is that I think I just wasn't ready, until now, to have the kind of relationship of which I've always dreamed. And now I've met you, and all the pieces of my life have suddenly fallen into place.'

As we walk up the rue du Coq, we stop to look in the windows of the shops. In one, there stands a stuffed fox in a glass box, baring its jaws.

'It's so awful, what they do to these poor animals,' says Alice.

'You should have seen what Monsieur Fox did to Martha.'

'Even so. I can't bear stuffed animals.'

'I couldn't agree more,' I reply, as we walk on. 'Although I did persuade my mum to buy one for me once.'

'Which was?'

'When we were in Colombia, I found this stuffed baby alligator in a shop. It was carrying a briefcase and holding an umbrella, and baring all its teeth in a perfect smile. The shopkeeper said it was a magic alligator; that it could help you find things you had lost. But I just thought it was the coolest thing I had ever seen. So I made my mum buy it for me.'

'That's so weird,' says Alice, putting her hand over her mouth. Her eyes are round and dark as Liquorice Allsorts, as if she has just seen a ghost. 'For years, we had one exactly the same, in our bathroom in Islington. No one knew where he had come from. But he used to stand there, with his little yellow briefcase and his yellow umbrella, smiling down at me like a guardian angel, always keeping an eye on me.'

The few locals who are out shopping in the rue du Coq today must be puzzled at what is wrong with the funny Englishman, the one who is always losing at tennis and sometimes plays the organ for Mass, as he stands doubled up in the middle of the road, laughing fit to burst. Alice has to pull me out of the way of a car that is coming down the street, which turns out to be driven by Le Grand Mermoz, with Jeanne in the passenger seat beside him.

'Crazy guy,' roars Mermoz, winding down his window. And then he catches sight of Alice and grins at me, punching the air on my behalf.

The steel railings that run down each side of the rue du Coq are already draped with shiny fake parcels and ragged offcuts of Christmas tree. I lean on one of the railings, and the metal feels cold in my hot hands: reassuring simplicity, in the midst of a universe that is beginning to make me feel like a character in someone else's novel. The Magic Alligator is found, having found Alice Melbury for me. It never occurred to me that Survival-Kit Toby might have kept the shiny creature for all these years, or that it might have been grinning pruriently down at my future paramour as she luxuriated in her bath.

But this is real life, I remind myself. And it really is happening to me.

Next day, before we set off for Limoges airport at the start of Alice's long journey back to Baltimore, we walk into Jolibois once more, and eat lunch in the Café du Commerce, the only benighted place that is desperate enough to open on this dank grey Monday. It is raining outside, and still it feels cosier on the street than it is when one steps inside the frozen wastes of the Commerce. Yet nothing – not even a starter of pig's snout – can dim the glow of the moments that I spend with Alice, which feel like fleeting trailers for a film that I have been waiting all my life to see.

And in this unprepossessing place, as we sip our coffees, wishing that they would last for ever, and Johnny Hallyday sings something overblown on the juke-box in the corner, we have a conversation that I never in my life expected to have.

I ask Alice how she feels about the idea of having a child

one day. And before long, we are talking about how very wonderful it would be if we could have a child together.

Beside our table, a stunned-looking robin begins to tap its beak on the etched glass window of the café, as if to warn us both that something is amiss; that this goes utterly against the grain of everything I have ever felt about children before.

'But what if we can't have children?' asks Alice, suddenly serious, when we have already reached the stage of discussing colours for the walls of the nursery. 'How would you feel about that?'

'I don't know,' I tell her truthfully. The world has too many children in it. It does not need me to add to the excess. Nor does my own little life, which feels quite busy and complete and rich enough as it is, thank you very much.

And yet quite suddenly, with Alice Melbury and her blasted dog shortly to transform my daily existence, I can think of nothing more important in the world.

'Look. I bought you a present,' I say, as Alice and I say our goodbyes at Limoges airport, just feet from the spot where we met a few months ago, on her first visit with Survival-Kit Toby. How different the world feels to me now. I hand her my gift, wrapped in silver wrapping-paper which – I notice only now – has a snowflake pattern.

'You didn't need to do that.'

'I know, but I wanted to.'

Alice begins to unwrap her present. I watch her face frown, then smile, then frown again.

'*Stick and Rudder*,' she reads, peering at the shiny blue-and-yellow cover. '*An Explanation of the Art of Flying*, by Wolfgang Langewiesche.'

I am bouncing up and down, barely able to contain my excitement.

'So what do you think?' I blurt. 'Are you pleased?'

'Published in 1944, I see,' she says, raising her eyebrows, managing not to let her ecstasy get the better of her.

'And never bettered. It's the ideal introduction to flying tailwheel aircraft.'

'Excellent.' She considers this for a moment. 'You know I don't fly tailwheel?'

'I know, but you soon will, when we start flying the Luscombe together. Jethro can teach you. Tailwheels are the future.' I cough. 'Even though they don't make them any more. Obviously.'

Alice glances out of the terminal window, at the shiny new 737 that is taxiing towards us.

'So why has that one got a nosewheel?' she asks.

'Well, it may be a little safer,' I reply. 'But it's also a lot less fun.'

Alice laughs. 'Like my old life,' she says, looking down at the book in her hands. 'Before I knew I was coming to France with you.'


Once upon a time, I was frightened of being alone. I dreaded the idea of being by myself for one evening, let alone for three years on a remote hillside in a foreign country. With time, I have grown to appreciate how lucky I am; how rare it is, in a crowded world where a hundred thousand people are crammed into the space once occupied by a handful, to be able to sit alone, night after night, *sans* distractions, and have the time to do no more than sit and think. And sometimes, just to sit.

So whilst I cannot wait for Alice and Digby to arrive from Baltimore in a few weeks' time, I am aware, too, that their coming will spell the end of something: the end of this long, deep silence that Cat and I have shared with the sheep and the chickens and the grasshoppers. And as I contemplate the move up from a double scull to a coxless four, I am doing my best not simply to pine for Alice, but to appreciate these last few weeks of being alone, just Cat and me, still bobbing along in our little pea-green boat on the wide ocean.

And then there is Digby. On the cusp of the arrival of my new house-guest from the United States, I am well aware how vital it is, at the start of such a relationship, to begin on the right foot; to demonstrate who is in charge from day one. I must assert myself; be recognizably the boss from the off.

Unfortunately, Digby is almost certainly having the very same thoughts. The Special Relationship between Britain and America has always been a complex one. And from everything Alice has told me about Digby – 'he is extremely strong and likes to get his own way' – I have much to teach the Baltimore Bullet about civilized British values of tact and self-restraint. The fact that I have never even trained a puppy before, let alone a fully grown squirrel-chasing psycho with ingrained antisocial habits and a sock fetish, is a minor detail.

I have ordered several books with promising titles such as *Outwitting Dogs*, *The Dog Whisperer*, *Winning Ugly* and *Think to Win*. True, the last two are about tennis, but the same principles must apply: seek out your opponent's weak spot, run him ragged, and don't be alarmed if he retrieves simply everything you throw at him. I have also ordered a fat tartan bean-bag from Belgium, and a large box of liver-flavoured dog treats for use as bribes.

Gilles spies my dog books when he drops round for *un apéro*.

'So you're going to get a dog?' he asks, raising his eye-brows.

'Actually, I've already found one. *Un labrador, qui vient de Baltimore, avec Alice.*'

Gilles strokes his beard. Watching Gilles stroke his grizzled goatee has made me understand why men bother with beards, beside the obvious reason of wanting a place to store surplus food. It is to inform your funny English neighbour that you think he is about to do something unusually stupid, only you can't quite bring yourself to tell him so.

'You don't think it's a good idea?' I ask.

The beard-stroking intensifies, as if Gilles were a boy scout trying to ignite his tinder, with storm-clouds approaching.

'A labrador will terrorize the chickens, and chase your sheep,' he says, wagging his finger at me. 'You'll keep it chained up outside the house?'

'No, he'll be indoors with us,' I chirp. Gilles rolls his eyes. French dogs, if they are larger than handbags, live outside. 'But of course,' I add, trying to sound stern, 'I'll be training him very strictly, and he won't be allowed upstairs.'

'Ah,' says Gilles, gazing down at the table, his eyes twinkling.

Later, Alice phones.

'I'm worried that if you can't stand Digby, you'll want to get rid of both of us,' she says.

'Haven't we been through this before?' I chuckle.

'But you haven't *met* him. You have no idea how pushy Digby can be. And what about the cat and the chickens? He can't resist chasing things.'

'I shall train him to leave the chickens alone,' I say firmly. 'The cat will fend for herself.' There is a long silence at the other end of the line.

'Do you know anything about dog training, then?' asks Alice, with what sounds suspiciously like a giggle.

'Well . . . I've bought some books. And we had a dachshund when I was growing up.'

'Would that be the one that ate the neighbours' guinea-pigs?'

'What's Digby doing now?' I ask, changing the subject.

'He's lying on my bed with his head on my chest, breathing his poison breath in my face. I am feeding him olives, one at a time.'

I order two more books from Amazon: *So Your Dog's Not Lassie* and *How to Right a Dog Gone Wrong*. They don't seem to have any books about re-training Roman emperors.

'I'm so sorry,' I murmur, as Cat slinks in through the cat-flap, tragically unaware of the horrors to come.

Each step forward I take at La Folie is generally followed by at least seventeen steps back. I have begun to learn the lesson: I must never count my chickens, even when I am convinced that they are safely tucked up on their perches in the chicken house. Yet, even by the usual standards of out-rageous fortune, I am utterly unprepared for the blow that falls, without warning, from the sky today, just as I am spreading marmalade on my toast for breakfast.

The phone rings, and I can see from the caller display that it is Alice. She must be in the middle of another night-shift.

'There's something I have to tell you,' she begins, nervously, as if she were a child about to admit smashing a window with a cricket ball. 'I thought I could wait until I came to France, to tell you in the flesh, in case you decided that you didn't want me to come and be with you at all. And now I realize that I have to do this now, before it's too late.'

I sit down at my desk, leaning my elbows on the time-smoothed oak.

'Do what?' I ask, in little more than a whisper. Behind her, in Baltimore, I can hear the bleeping of the alarms. 'And do you have to get that alarm, or are you all right to speak?'

The alarm is for someone else's patient; they have already responded to it. But something has happened, she says; something that she cannot change. 'And the upshot is that I won't be coming to live with you at La Folie after all.'

Beneath my feet, the stone floor of the winter sitting-room is transformed into molten lava, sublimates and vanishes. I teeter above a black abyss spangled with stars.

Unaware of my floor problems, Alice emits a muffled sob, and continues in a trembling voice: 'I think we should stop seeing each other. I think you should find someone else. Probably.'

'No way,' I reply, my mind racing. What can have brought on this sudden change of heart? I cling by my fingertips to the jagged rocks that overhang the abyss. 'There isn't anyone else in the universe but you.'

'You're so sweet,' she sniffs, blowing her nose. 'But I miss my family, I always have, ever since Windlesham. You know I was always the most pathetically homesick little girl in the school. I don't speak French. And there's no way I could do ICU nursing in France. I had to learn a whole new vocab, just to start all over again in America. I'm too old to do that again. And I don't know the first thing about sheep.' In the background, I can hear another alarm begin its insistent *beep-beeper-beep*. She takes a deep breath. 'I can't do this to you. It's not fair. You deserve better.'

My mind whirls. So many reasons. She has stacked up so many of them that I cannot help wondering which is the real one, on which all the others are balanced. Is some secret about to leap out of the past to threaten our future together? *Beep-beeper-beep*.

'Gotta go,' she blurts. 'Call you again later.'

I am left staring at the dead receiver, like someone in a film. This certainly doesn't feel like my life, the life that I was peacefully and happily living until one minute ago. I stare down at my toast: a brown shape on a plate that I barely recognize. Cat, too: a stranger. She must be a mind-reader, for she chooses this moment to leap up on to my lap, lightly brushing my lips with her tail. But I am in no mind for caresses. Instead I shove her roughly back down on to the floor, and she stalks away, the antenna of her tail faintly shuddering with disgust.

The sound of a car outside the front door announces the

arrival of the postman, and I go to collect the letters from him.

'*Bonjour,*' he chirrups with his usual sing-song good cheer.

'*Bonjour, monsieur,*' I sigh, struck by the incongruity of the smile with which he is sorting through the post in the cardboard box beside him. Handing me a blue airmail envelope, he opens his mouth to speak. But when his eyes meet mine, his face falls and he simply touches the peak of his cap and drives away.

The letter is from Alice. I open it quickly, somehow expecting to read an explanation for the cataclysm so recently unleashed in my life. But on the contrary, it is a love-letter, telling me how she cannot wait to come to La Folie, and for us to be together at last.

I shiver. It is so cold in the kitchen that I can see my breath in the air, and there are no logs sawn for the fire. I do not want to leave the comfort of being near the telephone but I know that it may be hours before Alice phones back. So I trudge out to the barn, whip the chainsaw into life, and set about carving a new stack of logs for the stove. The heavy work helps. I concentrate on the weight of the chainsaw vibrating in my hands; on the smell of the sawdust in my nostrils. Nothing else matters, I tell myself. Then I stand one or two of the logs on end, and split them into kindling with the axe.

Behind the barn, alerted by the noise, the Rastafarians begin to bellow, bleating for their breakfast. I head round to their feed-trough; shake granules from a sack, and watch as they snuffle for the food with their soft muzzles. Gaston, the watchful chief, lifts his head to peer at me from time to time. I think how much less painful life might be if I were a sheep.

Two hours later, the phone rings again. Wrong number.

A minute later, it rings once more. I am about to tell *madame* that *je suis désolé* but, no, this is not the number for

Les Restos du Cœur, when I realize that it is, after all, the voice I am desperate to hear. Very simply and quietly, Alice tells me what she knows.

We will not be having a child together, after all.

She had a hunch, she says, that something was wrong. And now, after an exhaustive series of tests from a professor regarded as one of the leading fertility experts in America, the truth has emerged: she will never become pregnant, now or in the future.

'But there's always IVF, isn't there?' I ask, feeling myself enmeshed in a clumsy bundle of conflicting emotions. Do we really have to split up over this? An iron-grey ball of sadness has lodged itself, since breakfast, in my chest; is turning to silver as we talk.

'Not in my case, apparently. He just started banging on about how they were doing amazing things with DNA these days, and not to give up hope.'

'He wanted to clone a child?'

'I don't know. I'm afraid I was so upset that I wasn't really listening. I never wanted children until I met you. And now here we are, and it turns out that we can't. That *I* can't. I'm so, so sorry. I guess this changes everything. If you want to end things now, I promise I'll understand.'

For a moment, I cannot speak. Not because of my disappointment that I shall never be a father after all, but because I feel so moved by the absurdly beautiful sacrifice that Alice is prepared to make for me. As if I could ever be happy without her. A great wave of relief, ringed with sadness, crashes over me. I am not about to lose this woman it took me so long to find, after all.

'This changes nothing,' I reply, wishing I could wrap her in my arms, 'except that I love you even more than I did before you rang, if that is possible. And we'll also have a lot more time to go flying together. If we are not to be granted the happiness of children, then so be it. But I would still far rather remain childless with Alice Melbury, than be a reluctant father with anyone else.'

Three thousand miles away, amid the alarms, blood transfusions and cardiac arrests of an intensive-care unit, I hear a brave nurse sigh, wipe away her tears and quietly go back to her work.

Reading dog-training manuals is all very well, and Cat has bravely humoured my attempts to attach a lead to her collar and drag her round the house for walkies. But what I really need, if I am to become the Dog Whisperer of Jolibois before D-Day, is a bona fide dog to practise on. So when Gilles asks me to keep an eye on his sheep over the weekend, and offers me his flea-bitten border collie, Rose, to take with me when I go to *faire le tour*, I almost slobber over his shoes with excitement.

'I didn't think you liked dogs, Michael,' he says, doubtfully.

'Nor did I.'

I have always known that Rose is not your average sheepdog. I can tell this from the mounting exasperation in Gilles's voice when he is roaring '*Derrière! Derrière! À côté! À côté!*' at her, while the pair of them attempt to cajole a flock of sheep to go through a narrow gateway. Rose mostly ignores him. I suppose that, like Josette, she has heard it all before.

On Saturday I drive into Gilles's farmyard for work. And Rose comes bounding out of the barn to greet me.

'*Sit*,' I announce, strident as Barbara Woodhouse, as she jumps up at my chest. On command, Rose plants her paws on my shoulders and slobbers all over my face with a tongue the length of the Millau Viaduct.

Pointing at the ground, I try again. In French, this time: '*Assis!*' At this, she leaps into the front seat of the Espace and beams at me.

'*Très bien,*' I sigh, patting her head.

And so Rose and I travel from field to field: she steaming

down the paths, I galumphing in her wake, my heart in my mouth every time she show-jumps a barbed-wire fence, praying she will not rip herself open like a Jiffy bag. It's good having a dog, I decide. I am almost looking forward to doing this with Digby.

But when we reach the last field on my list, across the valley in St Sulpice, I encounter a problem. *Un gros problème.* A gate has come unlatched, and at least half of Gilles's eighty-odd ewes have escaped from their denuded field into the lush grass of the neighbouring orchard. I stand and stare, as utterly out of my depth as if they were half a swarm of bees playing truant from their hive. So now I have to attempt to round up forty hungry sheep; I, who have almost never managed to round up my own little flock of wily Ouessants, even on a good day and with a pocketful of bribes.

Rose watches as – whooping and puffing and waving my arms – I run round behind the escapees, and somehow coax them back into their field. All except one. One unusually independent *brebis* remains at large in the orchard, like the last ball-bearing in the Christmas puzzle. And I can see at once that if I attempt to pursue her through the open gateway, her sisters will be off again.

Ewe and I stare at each other. Desperate times call for desperate measures. I have no option but to test-fire my secret weapon.

'*Rose*,' I call. '*Viens-là.*'

Like a shot, Rose leaps up and comes to my side.

'*Derrière! Derrière!*' I call, just as I have heard Gilles shout, pointing at the lone ewe. I am half-joking really, like a child holding up a gun and saying 'bang'. But I feel my skin tingle with excitement, as Rose now races round behind the stray sheep, nose to the ground, and begins to steer her towards me. My jaw drops, as if I had just seen a UFO, or Rex Harrison were striding towards me in silk pyjamas.

By Jove, Pickering, I think she's got it. I stand aside as, with Rose in hot pursuit, the ewe comes careering through the open gateway and hurtles to join her sisters.

'For you, ze war is over,' I announce, shutting the gate with a triumphant clang.

Resisting a victory dance, I fall upon Rose's neck, showering her with hugs and kisses of praise and gratitude. Rose, unused to such public displays of affection, backs away for a good scratch of her resident population.

Later that night, I phone Alice.

'No need to worry about Digby and the chickens,' I tell her, breezily. 'I've got the whole dog-training lark sorted.'

'Oh, really? That's brilliant. What's the secret?'

'It's easy,' I reply, thinking back over my dazzling success with Rose. 'You just give them the instructions in French.'


Four days before Alice and Digby's arrival at Paris Charles de Gaulle, the telephone rings. Not another crisis, I think to myself.

'Mr Wright?' says a woman's voice I recognize. '*Warbird* magazine here.'

'Oh, right.'

'You know why we're ringing, don't you?'

'Er . . . no.' I gulp. Stay calm. Above all, stay calm.

But yes, I think I do know. And the sparks are already shooting up and down my spine.

'You've won the Spitfire flight,' she says, with laughter in her voice. 'From the moment we read your letter, we were hoping you would. And now you have.'

I want to phone Alice, but there is someone else I have to telephone first.

Jethro is silent as he digests my news. He already knew how many entries I had put in for the competition.

'Mr Wright,' he says at last, with emotion. 'I am deeply thrilled for you, and I am absolutely bloody green with envy.

Every pilot in Britain will be. But you deserve it, you bastard, you deserve it. Just make sure you bag a couple of Me-109s for me, will you?'

'I'll see what I can do, Jez,' I laugh. 'Until soon, my friend.'

'You bet. Fly safe.'

Next I phone Alice at home.

'I won, I won it,' I tell her, all in a tumble. Confused, she begins to ask if I was playing tennis today with Yves-Pascal the notaire.

'No, the *competition*. I'm going to fly a Spitfire at last.'

I can hear her almost bouncing up and down with excitement on the other end of the line. And no wonder. For she has news that trumps mine by far.

'You'll never believe this,' she says, 'but I flew solo today myself, for the very first time. It was my very last flying lesson in America; my very last chance. My instructor just climbed out of the plane, without a word. And I didn't crash or anything.'

'Amazing,' I laugh. 'I'm so proud of you.'

'If you'd seen my landings, you would have been.'

Finally, I telephone my mother, to tell her about my Spitfire flight. And she simply bursts into tears.

In the toasty kitchen of the Moulin Vaugelade, Josette is stirring a pot on the wood-burning stove. I am going to miss this place so much. So I cannot imagine how Gilles must be feeling, after thirty years here.

'Are you really driving to Paris?' asks Josette, her wooden spoon suspended in mid-air.

'*Oui. Pourquoi?*'

'I've never been there myself,' she sighs, glancing at Gilles. 'And I suppose now I never will.'

I blink. Josette is fifty and a bit. She has lived all her life no more than three hours' drive from the beating heart of French culture, widely regarded as one of the four greatest cities in the world. Yet she has never seen Notre Dame or the Eiffel Tower. She has not gazed down the Champs Elysées, wandered beside the Seine, climbed the steps to Montmartre, nor queued to discover that the Mona Lisa is quite a lot smaller than she thought it would be.

'Oh, you don't want to go there,' growls Gilles, with a nervous laugh. '*C'est fou*. Dirty and expensive and full of politicians.' Country people, worldwide, share the same instinctive fear of the city.

'Well, that's where I'm going anyway,' I announce, 'to fetch a girl and a dog.'

Josette glances wistfully out of the window, but I manage to stop just short of asking if she would like to come along for the ride. For this trip is no time for taking a country woman to the city, when I shall be doing exactly the reverse.

# 17

## JANUARY

An icy afternoon, grey as pigeons. After months of waiting, about a billion phone calls, and a fierce tussle with the complex bureaucracy of shipping an American dog to France, my entire being is now focused upon just one final challenge: turning up on time to meet Alice and Digby at Charles de Gaulle airport tomorrow morning.

'You *will* be there, won't you?' Alice asked me, with unusual tension, last time we spoke. 'Digby is likely to be pretty wired after the flight.'

'Of course I'll be there,' I replied. And it never occurred to me, not for a second, that I might not.

Fortunately, the odds are stacked in my favour. I have allowed almost eighteen hours for a journey that should take only three. And I have booked a hotel beside the airport, so as to be on the spot to meet the flight from Washington DC, which is due in at 6.30 am.

Two hours after leaving La Folie, I am barrelling up the autoroute towards Paris in the Espace. Wonderful car, the Espace: the old girl may be beyond the age of consent and smell of dead dog, but she only cost me nine hundred euros three years ago, and has never let me down.

Night is falling, and heavy rain with it, but the world looks especially beautiful tonight. Even the headlights of the approaching cars have a dazzling loveliness about them.

No sooner have I registered this thought, than the Espace begins to judder. It judders as if I had just dropped a fork into a waste-disposal unit, or like that time when I filled up my dad's diesel car with four-star, and it tried to shake itself to pieces on Clapham High Street. Red warning lamps glow through the dust on the dashboard, including one particularly discouraging one that says STOP. Call me a pessimist, but this is not a good sign. Not tonight, of all nights.

I limp into the next *péage* and switch off the engine. It is too dark to see much under the bonnet. This is a blessing, since it stops me having to try to fix anything. All I can do is top up the oil with a few glugs of multigrade, and splash half a bottle of Evian into the radiator. Or is that the brake fluid reservoir? No, it's definitely the radiator. Unless it's the power-steering fluid filler? No, I'm sure it's the radiator.

The thought crosses my mind that I may be forced simply to abandon the Espace here, hitch a lift into Paris, and do my best to rent a car at dawn to pick up Alice and Digby from the airport. Either that, or pay for a dog-friendly taxi all the way back to La Folie.

I give the dashboard of the Espace an encouraging pat, turn the key and almost yelp with surprise as the engine fires first time. The warning lights have disappeared for a tea-break, and the car sounds calmer as we head off on our way. Either this is a miracle, or else I am a competent mechanic after all. On balance, I think it is probably a miracle.

The airport hotel I have booked looks swankier than it did online, and the uniformed flunky who emerges to frown at the Espace doesn't offer to help me with my luggage as he grimaces at the creased bodywork. He appears to be hoping that I have come to the wrong place.

After a fitful night of hotel sleep, I awake at 6.15 am. The flight is due to arrive at 6.30 am, but since Alice will then have to wait for Digby and his paperwork to be pawed and pored over by *les douaniers* with their scanners, we have agreed that it will be more like 7.30 am before they appear, assuming that Digby has not already been deported or destroyed. Plenty of time for a shower and breakfast, then.

At 6.25 am, I am brushing my teeth when the phone in my hotel room rings. This will be my wake-up call from the front desk.

'*Bonjour, c'est Michael*,' I mumble, through a foam of Aquafresh, into the receiver. But the phone doesn't stop ringing. I stumble over to the desk, and answer my mobile instead.

'Where *are* you?' asks a voice I feel unusually dismayed to hear. 'We're already through customs.'

'Oh gawd. So you're—'

'In the Arrivals hall. Can you see us?' Alice speaks with the weariness of a woman who has just flown across the Atlantic with a hyperactive dog, only to find that the man on whom she has been pinning her hopes is not there to meet her.

'Not exactly.' My scalp prickles. 'You're so *early*.'

'Where are you? Are you in the terminal yet?'

'I . . . I'm on my way.'

Now I do a thing that I have only ever seen in those films where a man manages to scoop up all his belongings and fly out of a hotel room less than four seconds after receiving a tip-off that the KGB are downstairs. It is easy to move fast, I discover, when you are about to be exiled to Siberia. Or Coventry, at least.

Unlike in the films, I manage to get lost on the way to the airport. Considering that my hotel is only five minutes from Charles de Gaulle, with a big red arrow pointing towards the airport, this is impressive, even by my standards.

Seconds tick like hours, until at last I reach the illuminated yellow sign for the terminal, and I am confronted with a scene so primitive that it makes me wonder whether I am in the right continent, let alone the right airport.

At Heathrow or Gatwick, you get a warning from a man with a sub-machine gun if you dally longer than two minutes on the double-yellows out front. Here at Charles de Gaulle in Paris, a scrum of beaten-up cars and taxis is parked willy-nilly beneath the sodium lights, like bodies on a battlefield or ants on a *pain au chocolat*. I simply abandon the Espace a few feet from the grubby main doors, and dash into the squalid terminal.

Inside, there is no sign of Alice in the mêlée. No sound of a crazed labrador howling in an American accent. No mention of their flight on the Arrivals board, either, possibly because – as the harassed lady on the information desk tells me when I jump the queue – I have come to the Departures terminal. Groaning my despair, I gallop back to the Espace and hurtle off to the next body-strewn battlefield.

Just inside the revolving doors, standing poised and alert, gazing at the world as peacefully as a toy beagle nodding on the parcel-shelf of an Astra, stands the most beautiful creature you ever saw in your life. And there, attached to him by a scarlet leash, is the rear view of what I am hoping is my future.

'I am so sorry,' I gasp.

'You're here,' laughs Alice, turning to wrap herself around me.

'And so are you. And you're *early*,' I protest. 'What the—'

A large furry head forces itself between us, like a dwarf Victorian chaperone with a facial hair problem.

'Hello, Digby,' I cough, already beginning to feel the adrenaline pulsing in my shins and forearms, as I face up to the fear that he may be about to savage me. 'Good to meet you, too.' I bend down to receive an earful of saliva flicked off the end of a slobbery velvet tongue.

'They just waved us straight through,' says Alice. 'Didn't look at his papers. Didn't scan his microchip. Nothing. I just came into the baggage hall, heard him barking, and there he was, in his crate.'

'You mean, after *all that*?'

'Total waste of time.'

Digby gazes up at me, beaming with pride. I am disturbed to find that his facial expression vaguely reminds me of George W. Bush just before he invaded Iraq.

'I'm so sorry I wasn't here,' I murmur.

'You're here now.'

'So, are you ready to go?'

'Yes,' says Alice firmly. 'Let's go home.'

As we head out of the terminal building into the sodium gloom of an early morning on the outskirts of Paris, I haul Alice's luggage while Digby – straining on his leash in front of us like a sled-dog at the head of a team of huskies – hauls me.

His palpable excitement at having a whole continent's-worth of new smells to sniff makes me wonder at the dour expressions of his fellow tourists as they wander out of the terminal. Strange, that people should always look so glum on the cusp of new experiences. Mind you, I'll bet I look pretty uncertain myself, as I gaze at the hundred pounds of Baltimore labrador I have just adopted.

'What's lucky for both of us,' Alice told me on the phone a few weeks ago, 'is that neither of us comes with any baggage.'

'No children, bankruptcy or obvious psychosis,' I agreed. Because I had not met Digby yet.

Anxious to set off on the right foot with Digby, and following the advice in my dog-training manual, I have brought with me my large box of liver-treat bribes and transferred a small stash of them into my trouser pocket. As we reach the Espace, I offer one to Digby, as a reward for not biting me, barking at me or peeing on my leg at our first meeting.

Unfortunately, Digby must have read a different dog-training manual from me. Instead of taking the treat from my hand, he buries his snout in my pocket, like a wet ferret disappearing down a rabbit-hole.

I am already struggling not to hyperventilate when the ferret begins to chomp in the most alarming fashion.

'Help,' I yelp. 'I mean, "Digby, *no*." ' Grabbing his collar, I attempt to manhandle the slavering jaws away from my particulars.

Alice clearly thinks this is hilarious.

'Thank you for your support,' I mutter, doing my best to squeeze the drool from the masticated fabric of my inside-out pocket.

'I told you he could be rather pushy,' she giggles.

'Don't worry, I think Digby and I both know who's the boss,' I say, as I open the boot of the Espace for my new master.

After a moment's hesitation, Digby leaps inside and lies on his haunches, his tail flapping like a fish in the bottom of a boat while I load up the suitcases behind him.

'What's he got?' asks Alice sharply.

'Perhaps he can smell the sheep?'

'No, he's definitely got something.' The tone of her voice rises as she walks around the side of the car. 'Oh, Digby.' And then, 'Oh, Michael.'

Alice holds up a soggy piece of cardboard. 'I'm so sorry about your . . .' – she peers at the cardboard – '. . . liver treats.'

In one swift move, Digby has scoffed my tactical advantage over him. He has only gone and eaten every last one of the wretched things. I am the gladiator who has lost his sword; the exam-cheat who has mislaid his cribsheet. I throw him a glance which I hope Alice doesn't see, and tell myself that I love dogs. Even this one.

From the moment we set off, Digby wedges himself between Alice and me like the Berlin Wall, his wet snout smearing the inside of the windscreen with vapour trails of slime.

'He likes to drive,' explains Alice.

'Fine. He can take over at Orléans,' I reply, jamming my elbow into a wall of solid muscle to change gear.

At last we cross the little bridge over the river at the bottom of the drive to La Folie, and Digby starts shrieking and panting like a pressure-cooker that's about to explode.

'You'd think he'd been here before,' I yell, above the din.

'Labradors are water dogs,' explains Alice.

'You can say that again,' I reply, feeling something damp soaking through the fabric of my shirt.

As we rumble up the drive, the towering trees on either side of the steep track seem to wave their bare branches in welcome, and the rain has abated, if only for a day. Two members of the Egg Squad flutter out of the bushes, scampering ahead of us like pygmy outriders. The pitch of Digby's shrieking ratchets up another notch in response.

'Let's hope that a hundred and twenty liver treats have taken the edge off his appetite,' I murmur.

Suddenly there is a flash of something white and grey to our left. Digby emits a gasp and stands paralysed between us, like a cowboy who has been shot in a movie.

'Is he all right?' I ask, in a panic.

'Oh, no,' murmurs Alice slowly. 'I think he's seen the cat.'

Next morning, I leave Alice to sleep. A welcome glimmer of milky sunshine has melted the morning frost, and the fields all around the house are glistening with dew. Now I do not know the first thing about dogs. But I do know that watching a four-year-old labrador from suburban Baltimore attempting to make sense of the French countryside is one of the loveliest things I have seen in months.

From the moment he first jumped out of the Espace, the canine Rambo has been galloping around as if he were entirely at home and yet all at sea on some strange new planet; sending up clods of dirt behind him as he tracks mysterious new smells, snorting with surprise when the smells lead his wet snout into clumps of withered stinging nettles, and generally comporting himself with that you-don't-scare-me swagger which Americans adopt when they feel afraid or abroad or both.

Digby's antics make me realize that my own first impressions of La Folie were almost entirely visual; mental snapshots with a silent soundtrack. The cat, by contrast, cared more about how the place sounded than how it looked. I watched as she conducted a cautious aural reconnaissance, her body still as a statue, her ears twitching and twisting like hi-tech scanners atop an armoured personnel carrier as she took in the whirring of the crickets, the drone of the bourdons having one-for-the-road in the wisteria, and the scuttlings of unseen snacks in the undergrowth. All I had noticed was that you couldn't hear the traffic.

Yet Digby is not interested in looking or listening. His first impressions are entirely olfactory. Like a Japanese tourist, he crouches behind the high-definition video camera that is his snout, and follows it everywhere; into corners and crevices and bushes and barrels and basically anywhere he can shove it. I make a mental note to bear this in mind next time he is standing behind me.

In some ways, I think he must be in heaven. But he also makes frequent and heartbreaking runs to the Espace, wagging his tail as if to say thank you for the swell smells. And that now, if we don't mind, he is ready to go home.

Little does Digby know that his past really is another country; that his present is now his future, too.

On this first night, he lies down at the foot of the stairs with a resigned groan, and goes to sleep with his eyes wide open.

'So much for the expensive Belgian bed I bought him,' I whisper, as I head into the bathroom to brush my teeth. 'I thought he'd want to sleep beside the wood-burning stove.'

'It's early days,' says Alice, beginning to tiptoe upstairs to bed. 'He's sleeping there for my security.'

'That's so sweet.'

And it *is* sweet to see a big dog protecting his mistress from the foot of the stairs. At least until the moment comes when I want to climb the stairs myself, to go to bed.

I could swear I hear a low rumble as I approach Digby, though he does not raise his head. Perhaps it is his tummy. Alice should have warned him to steer clear of the in-flight meal.

I stop, and the rumble stops. I take another step forward, and it starts again.

'That's some tummy you've got there, Digby,' I chirp, to steady my nerves. Now he raises his head, bares his teeth by lifting the spiky black curtains of his jowls, and growls in a way that I would not describe as loving.

No problem. Wandering over to the fridge, I open a packet of two *steaks hachés*, toss one of them into the beast's slavering jaws, and head purposefully for the stairs. But the *steak haché* is mincemeat before I reach the bottom step. And Digby is growling again, the fur on his back standing stiff as a hairbrush.

I pick up the telephone, and press the internal call button.

'Any chance you could come down and call off Cerberus?' I ask, doing my best to hide the tremor in my voice.

*

Next morning, Digby follows me outside when I go to feed the Rastafarians. As far as I can tell, the further away from Alice I am, the happier he becomes.

His first meeting with the sheep is not a success. Seeing the dark, primeval forms of my tiny Ouessants, he rears up in a panic and barks wildly at them, at me, at the sky, everything. The fur between his shoulder-blades bristles like a mohican.

'Settle down, Digby,' I tell him.

On command, Digby hurls himself at the sheep.

Unfortunately, the sheep are separated from us by a wire fence which Digby sees a split second too late. I shut my eyes.

Though he is not visibly injured by the encounter, I feel for this all-too-willing dog. I, too, have experienced that juddering, percussive shock of walking slap-bang into a toughened plate-glass door that you didn't know was there. I know how horrid it feels. And I manage to resist the urge to high-five with Cat at Digby's come-uppance.

'I think perhaps we'll leave meeting the chickens until tomorrow,' I tell him, bending to comfort him. He is all snorty and jumpy and waggy as he gazes back at me with his soft, confused eyes.

In the kitchen, things go from bad to worse. Cat's pupils are dilated to the size of Maltesers as she stands atop the kitchen table like Horatius on the bridge, facing the Etruscan hordes. Her electrified fur makes it look as if she is wearing a monster-suit, even before she turns side-on to Digby and gives him the full broad-side, like when she sees her own reflection in the mirror, hissing like a leaky hose as she stiffens her tail and arches her body into an inflated 'h'.

Digby, bless him, gamely shuffles forward for a sniff. Amiable American that he is, he wants to make friends. And, in a blur of white, he receives two swift swipes of a clawed paw across the chops for his pains.

A pinprick of bright blood gleams on the damp snout. The

velvety ears crumple and Digby, visibly shocked, begins to run in circles round the kitchen table, panting and snorting like a cart-horse.

Cat sits, Egyptian-style, licking her paw as casually as if she were a lady assassin blowing smoke from the barrel of a pearl-handled revolver. Their pecking order is established. I am saying nothing. And Digby's first impression of Cat will not, I think, be one that he easily forgets.

# 18

## FEBRUARY

My life has changed, and it is taking me a while to adjust. So I cannot imagine what being at La Folie is like for Alice, as she swaps the hushed intensity of a Baltimore intensive-care unit for the intense hush of a wild hillside in darkest France.

'Do you realize, Michael,' my friend Jérôme tells me one day, 'that in the last six months, your French has not improved one little bit?'

'*Mais . . . mais . . .*' I can feel my mouth opening and shutting, as I struggle to come up with a response. Jérôme isn't being unkind; he's simply telling the truth.

Alice, bless her, is determined to do better. Hence the fact that she has been visiting the fragile Nicole for daily French lessons, and spending long hours at the kitchen table, staring at a list of French irregular verbs like a sheep gazing at a cattle-grid. I think it may take a while before she tiptoes across it. 'Most of us remember a little rusty French from O-level,' declares Lucinda, her older sister, on the phone from Australia. 'But Alice doesn't even seem to have that. We're not sure what she can have been doing at school.'

In an attempt to help her settle in, I have bought her a pair of brown wellies that she swears she will not wear, and an old brown Renault 19 that we call the Princessmobile, because it so obviously was not built for a princess.

'That's so brilliant,' she said, when she first saw it. '*Thank* you. Now, where shall I drive to?' And we both laughed, because she had a point.

I do worry that there are no lives for her to save, here at La Folie; no use for the years of nursing experience she has worked so hard to gain.

'It's not nursing I miss,' she tells me one day, after Shouty Pauline the cleaning lady has just been on one of her weekly cleaning raids. 'It's working with a brilliant team at the ICU; the camaraderie we had. Yes, I clean up a lot of disgusting stuff, and a lot of my job involves wiping people's bottoms. But at least I know – I knew – I was good at my job. Whereas here: there's nothing like people yelling at you in a foreign language you don't understand, to make you feel small,' she sighs.

'I'm sorry about Pauline.'

'It's not just her,' she says, putting her face in her hands. 'It's *everyone*.'

This is not the moment to ask her about the little foil packets of pills I have been finding, stuffed into drawers and cupboards; even the glove-box of the car. I don't like to examine them too closely, but something tells me they are not vitamins.

'I'm very adaptable,' Alice assured me, before she arrived. 'And I have enough insight to know that I'll be fine.'

The odd wobble is natural, I remind myself, when you are starting a whole new life. I had enough of them myself when I first arrived at La Folie. And, on the whole, Alice appears to be settling in rather well. It is the vacuum cleaner and the washing machine I am worried about. I have never had much use for either machine, personally, but now both seem to be running at full war-boost power, as Alice does her best to undo the effects of one man and a cat living by themselves for three years in a remote house heated only by dusty fire-wood.

I can hear her now, padding around upstairs, dragging the Miele hoover behind her, rather as Digby shadows her every move downstairs. And for the first time in my life, I find myself feeling moved by the sound of a vacuum cleaner. For this is a sound of childhood: the sound of someone taking care of me.

My worst gaffe to date comes when I ask Alice if she would mind going to fetch some kindling from the barn.

'We only need a few sticks,' I tell her, glancing up from where I am lying beneath the hot-water tank, trying to work out why it has become a cold-water tank. 'Do you mind?'

At this, a strange look comes into her eyes, halfway between fear and outrage, like when I threw away her Paula's Choice moisturizer by mistake. 'Yes, I do mind.'

'But I've got my hands full here. If you want the fire lit . . .'

'I'm not collecting sticks for your camp any more,' she says, firmly. 'That's your job now.'

'What do you mean, *now*?'

'I mean that, even if I do bring in your blasted sticks, you'll probably shut me out again, just like you and Toby did before.'

And I am left with my mouth opening and shutting, like a fish on a slab.

Then there is the time when I offer Alice one of the top jobs at La Folie: taking charge of the Egg Squad.

'You *are* joking?' she asks, quietly.

'No, no, I'm serious,' I reply, amazed at my own generosity. 'You really can, if you want.'

'Please don't make me do the chickens.'

'I didn't mean it like that. I thought you'd be pleased.'

She considers this for a second.

'That's very sweet,' she giggles, putting her arms around me until, a split second later, a whiskery, fawn-coloured muzzle with attached labrador forces itself between us. 'And if it's all right with you,' she adds, 'I'll just stick to blitzing the house.'

The truth is that I like the simplicity of this indoors-outdoors division of labour. I like having a clearly delineated role. It makes me want to beat my chest and grunt with caveman pleasure.

One evening, I am staggering in from the barn with an armful of logs piled so high that I can't see over the top of them – the load a man will attempt to carry is always directly proportional to the attractiveness of the woman he is trying to impress – and my forearms are burning as I stumble in through the back door.

'Michael!' shouts Alice, in an urgent voice, from the bathroom. I can hear the water running. 'Michael, are you there?'

Something must be wrong. Has another viper come to call? I hear Digby go galloping into the bathroom, claws-a-clatter, like all of the Keystone Cops turning up at once. Bending my knees, I attempt to dislodge a few logs into the wood-basket. But I appear to be stuck.

'Michael!' Alarmed now, I simply shut my eyes and drop the logs; I yell as a jagged lump of oak catches me full on the shin, just in that very spot where I always whack myself with my own tennis racquet whenever a first serve goes awry. A cloud of sawdust and wood-mites and sublimated pain rises into the air.

As fast as I can, I hobble to the bathroom to rescue the stricken Alice.

'Oh, there you are,' she says, gazing dreamily up at me from the bath. 'Can you pass me my conditioner from the cupboard, please?'

*

A week later, and a thick fog has wrapped La Folie in its dank blanket. Alice, Digby and I are marooned in the polar white-out.

France? We could be anywhere. Indeed, were I a Frenchman waking from a coma, I would swear I was in England.

Jolibois and La Folie seem to feel a little less French, the longer I am here, and not simply because Jolibois now has an English tea-room, an English barber called 'Men Only' and a cavernous café called Le Pub which serves Guinness in cans.

Alice and I have been busily overpainting the garish blues and greens of all the doors and windows at La Folie – as daubed by Zumbach and his wife – with a bland-but-grand off-white. My retinas feel more comfortable as a result. But I cannot help feeling that the house has lost something, too: a Frenchness that I could never have come up with myself.

I know that La Folie also feels less French simply because I have stopped noticing things: the heavy shutters framing the windows; the oversized buttons of the light-switches; the campness of the curved mouldings on the doors. I am no longer aware of the crazy slope of the upstairs corridor, which used to make me feel like a trawlerman leaning into a gale. Some nights, we even manage to sleep through the rapacious scuttlings of Georges the *fouine* and his murderous comrades in the roof.

This is one of the many good things about Alice's arrival from Baltimore. Not the fact that I am sleeping better, now that Cat, if not Georges, has been banned from crunching her mice upstairs, but the fact that everything has been made new and strange again, now that I am seeing the world through someone else's eyes.

'Everybody brings their own shopping bags to the till,' observes Alice, after a trip to Carrefour. 'And there's a whole aisle of UHT milk, no proper cream, and only one tiny fridge with a few cartons of fresh milk. What's that all about?'

'Well . . .' I begin, confidently, even though I haven't the foggiest.

'And there's laundry hanging on all the washing lines. In America, people run their tumble-driers for a single pair of socks. But at least they have customer service.'

'Ah, so you've discovered Bricomarché?'

I wonder where Digby imagines himself to be.

'Where's home, Digby?' Alice will ask him, when we are walking back up the old cart-track from Jolibois, and reach the crossroads. She says this is one of the words he knows. But from the fretting circles in which he spins as she repeats the question, I think it will be a while before he connects it with La Folie. From Digby's point of view, his old garden in Baltimore could, I suppose, be just over the next hill. And judging from the excited jogging-on-the-spot he does whenever he is waiting to be let out – like a wind-up toy buzzing against a skirting-board – he appears convinced that his own private Narnia will be on the other side of the back door next time someone opens it. Car doors and aircraft doors work like that, when you are a dog. Each time they open, you find yourself with a new set of smells to sniff. Why should house doors not be the same?

Today, when I open the back door for Digby, we both stand and gaze out at the wet, white landscape whose dankness does not beckon us. After a few moments, he licks my hand as if to say 'Don't worry, mate, I've just had a better idea' and trots over to stand at the front door instead. At first I chuckle at his stupidity. And then, touched by his stubborn optimism, I open it for him.

I have to squint and cover my eyes as a dazzling shaft of sunlight breaks through the trees. The sky has brightened almost to blue on this side of the house, and I can feel the palpable warmth of the sun on my face.

Digby beams up at me, wagging the entire rear half of his body. 'You see? You *see*?' he seems to say.

So much for my wanting to see the world through fresh eyes. Winter is coming to an end. And our Baltimore Boy is settling in fast.

Not content with human home-making, Alice has been lobbying hard for a proper sheep house for the Rastafarians, and insisting that Cat needs a proper bed, too, now that she has been banished from ours.

Her concern for the animals reminds me of the start of my time at La Folie, and makes me realize how blasé I have become. Back then, I would lie awake at night, worrying if the sheep and chickens were warm enough. These days, I take the ruggedness of the Rastafarians for granted, after the winters they have weathered with only a wall, a few fir trees and a roof-on-sticks for shelter. Ouessants are wild creatures, after all. This is lucky, since it has now taken me more than three years not to build a sheep house for them.

Eighteen months ago, at the height of my Rugged phase, I bought various books about shed construction. I consulted Gilles about agricultural roofing techniques. I even asked two moustaches in hard hats to scoop out a patch of earth for me with their mighty engine-of-war, after they rumbled across the fields to erect a *poteau* for the electricity supply. And that's as far as I got.

Action is now called for, and it is good Monsieur Jadot who comes to my aid. The wily old gardener points out that with a bit of clever fencing, the sheep could use the old stone outhouse that is spliced on to the chicken house; the one that is currently filled with several dusty oak barrels, two wooden ploughs, an ancient weighing machine and the regulation kitchen sink.

I slap myself on the forehead. Why build a new house, when an old one will serve? My middle-English brain must have become so adapted to seeing outbuildings only as potential *gîtes* or home offices, that it is difficult to see them in the role for which they were originally intended.

And so I set to work, clearing out relics from the time when La Folie was somebody else's home. Inside, the earthen floor is embedded with broken glass and rusted iron. I find empty eggshells, too, from where a more recent resident – Georges the *fouine*, perhaps – has been taking his breakfast. And dusty spiders' webs, thick as curtains: more past inhabitants, briskly swept aside.

The sheep are teenagers on a first date as they follow the feed-bucket tremulously into their scrubby new field. A few steps forward; a galloped retreat. They stop only to take another excited mouthful of lush weeds. I suppose I imagined they'd gallop straight into the sheep house and start measuring up for curtains. Instead they stop, spooked, unwilling to venture into the darkness beyond. But at least toothless old Gaston now knows that there is a haven for him, out of the wind and the rain, should he need it.

Meanwhile, Cat is thrilled with the new bed that Alice has provided for her, on an armchair in front of the wood-burning stove. She is lying there now, upside down with one paw extended, in her inverted Superman pose. Digby lies curled up on his bed in the corner, balefully staring at her with one unsleeping eye. I am happy about this, because at least when he is staring at Cat, he cannot stare at me. From the way he still growls when I come anywhere near Alice, he is beginning to make me feel like her stalker.

As for me, Alice has moved me to a new work-space, too, in the unheated *maison des amis*, where she says there are fewer distractions than at my old desk in the winter sitting-room. I cannot help thinking that this idea is most likely to have come from her furry canine pal. Perhaps, come springtime, it will be a cheery place to work. For now, I am wrapped up in my sheepskin flying-jacket and RAF winter trousers, huddled beside a paraffin heater which I am hoping will take the chill off the air in which I can see my own breath. *Ça caille*, as the French say when they shiver. But at least when the sheep sidle past my window, their chestnut fleeces white with frost, I can look them in the eye at last.

As in Britain, so in France: snow has fallen, snow on snow. There I was, thinking how uncanny it was to see new grass sprouting in the sheep-field, and then suddenly, in the space of two hours, everything has changed. If La Folie were a fruitcake, it would by now have been thoroughly iced.

The Rastafarians are out there now, just in front of my window, digging snow-holes with their front hooves to reach the wet grass beneath; Eskimos going fishing. I hurry out to give them a small heap of hay, which they ignore, and also some of Gilles's barley straw, which two or three of them begin to munch without relish.

Gaston is beginning to decline again this winter. When the other six sheep lie down in the snow to ruminate on their morning feed, he simply stands and looks miserable, his back legs tucked in close to his front ones, as if he were having to balance on a dinner plate. Which, to date, is a fate that none of my sheep has suffered.

Gaston and I stare at each other as he peers in through the window of my new office. Twice in the past, I have been forced to give the old boy antibiotics for the pneumonia to which he appears susceptible in winter. But this is a wretched business, because so little flesh is left on the scrawny fellow. So every injection is a trial, or at least it was until a full-time nurse moved into La Folie.

'What can I do for you, Gaston?' I ask him now, out loud.

Gaston stares back, his head rocking gently as he struggles for breath. A globule of snot drips permanently from one nostril, like an icicle. In fact, I think it *is* an icicle.

In the kitchen, Alice is baking a cake when I stagger in

through the door, bearing another armful of logs for the stove. On the mantelpiece, the glint of something metallic catches my eye: another two strips of pills. It's now or never, I tell myself, as I approach Alice with the evidence.

'Darling, I hate to pry, but . . .'

'Oh, gosh, you found those,' she says, embarrassed. 'I'm sorry, I'm trying to stop, really I am. But it's hard, after all those years in nursing.'

'I haven't looked at what they are,' I assure her. 'I'm really not spying on you.'

Alice bursts out laughing. She may be high on the stuff right now.

'These are hard drugs,' she says, taking the packets from me. 'Super-high-strength caffeine. Everyone takes them in nursing: caffeine strips, Pro-Plus tablets, you name it. And that's on top of all the tea and coffee and Diet Coke, too. I thought that here at La Folie I'd be able to stop, but it's harder than I thought, what with driving on the wrong side and trying to learn French.'

I sink into a chair, relieved and amazed at my own silliness. Digby leaps up from his bed and – just to rub it in – launches his front paws on to my chest. Then he starts wildly slobbering all over my face and neck with gloopy strokes of his velvet tongue, his whole body wagging with pleasure at the task.

'All I ask is that you don't ever, ever let this horrible hound get his paws on that stuff,' I gasp, from somewhere beneath my tormentor.

# 19

## MARCH

Returning to La Folie after a trip down to Jolibois to play the organ for Mass, I am surprised to find a large cardboard box outside the front door. Now the postman sometimes leaves us a parcel or two – books from Amazon, perhaps, or Luscombe spare parts from America – but the boxes *he* leaves never have several large holes drilled in the sides. Sometimes they rustle when you shake them. This one is rustling. And I haven't even touched it yet.

Moving closer, I gingerly place my eye up to one of the holes, and recoil like a Bofors gun. For there, through the Round Window, is a scaly claw, roughly the colour of curdled milk.

I stand and gaze around me. I feel like Piglet on the edge of the Heffalump trap, wishing Pooh were here with a Bright Idea.

Out of nowhere, Digby arrives with a bright idea. He begins clawing at the holes in the box with his paw, shrieking and barking at the strange smell from within.

Shooing him away, I carry my gift inside. At least, I *hope* it's a gift, and not the beginning of one of those stories about babies left on doorsteps that you see on the news. I take another look through one of the holes. Someone is staring back at me. Someone with a very beady eye, whose panicky pupil dilates and contracts so fast in the middle of its yellow iris that it makes me think of a glistening heart beating.

'Any idea who this is from?' I ask Alice. She is standing at the stove, stirring a pot of something that smells deliciously like *coq au vin*. 'It was on the doorstep.'

She shakes her head. 'Digby did start barking a while ago, so perhaps there was a car. But I didn't see anything, because I've been struggling with Delia.'

'You *are* good,' I put the box down on the kitchen table, and kiss her hair. 'Thank you for cooking.'

'You may not still be saying that when you taste it,' she says.

I'm about to remonstrate when the telephone makes me jump.

'Have you found them?' asks a voice I recognize.

'*Monsieur Jadot, bonsoir*,' I sigh.

'It is a gift,' says my sometime gardener, triumphantly.

'*Ah, merci*.' I hope he can hear the lack of conviction in my voice.

Cautiously, cradling the receiver in my chin, I peek once again into the top of the box; see white wings, mottled feathers, a comb like broken sealing wax and another one of those yellow eyes.

'You were needing a cockerel,' he says.

'Yes, but I don't need *three* of them,' I wail. I have lived long enough in the French countryside, and had enough difficulty in giving away my own young male chickens, to know that this is no time for fawning gratitude. 'Where do you expect me to put them?'

'Put them all in the pot.' Jadot roars with laughter.

'Look,' I protest, 'I gave away three of my own cockerels, a year or two ago, because I couldn't bear to kill them myself, so what makes you think—'

'Ah, yes, but these three brothers are *très mignons*,' he lies. 'They'll do well together.'

I have to admit – though not to Monsieur Jadot – that I have read that there is a virtue in keeping precisely three cockerels, this being the only number that will not attempt to claw each other to pieces. On the Duchy of Cornwall estates of the Prince of Wales, they *always* have three cockerels, as a matter of course.

On the other hand, these cockerels of Jadot's are ugly little blighters compared with the Holbeinesque magnificence of poor Hotspur and Titus, RIP. Their plainness does not tug at my heartstrings. Yet their fear does. If I give them back to Jadot, I doubt he'll even trouble to pluck and eat them. He'll just put a boot on their necks, and throw them out with the slops.

Stop, stop, stop. I am not entirely stupid. A gift of three males, of any species, is no gift at all. I have to say no. I look beseechingly at Alice, in search of moral support: help me to say no. Puzzled, she peers into the box of chickens, grimaces and recoils. This is exactly the support I wanted, but I fear it won't be enough.

'While we're talking about animals,' I ask old Jadot, changing the subject, 'would you be willing to feed mine – the cat, sheep and chickens – again, next time we go away?'

'*Bien sûr*,' he says. 'How many chickens do you have these days?'

'I have four hens,' I reply, watching a small, frightened eye blink at me through one of the holes in the cardboard box. I take the deep breath of a man about to do something he knows to be deeply foolish. 'And three young cockerels.'

It is only a couple of months since Alice and Digby arrived at La Folie. Yet as Einstein neglected to mention, time passes at a different speed when two of you live alone in the French countryside. Already I feel a conviction about our relationship, and a committedness to Alice, that I have never felt about anyone before.

The subject of children rears its head often, and we share our sadness at the thoughts of the parents we will never be.

I even find myself thinking about marriage, too, despite the fact that, in my former London life, I had begun to convince myself that marriage was an outmoded anachronism, cherished by those with more religion than sense; a charmingly primitive idea that free-thinking people could never come up with today, if it were not already woven into the fabric of their conventional expectations.

It never occurred to me that these arguments might be the product of my own brittle egoism; that, in the absence of anyone who could mend the cracks in my heart left by Clara Delaville, Ellen Gonn or Zara Malkin, I might have tricked myself into believing that such a commitment was not worth making anyway. It took more than two years of earth and sheep and chickens and solitude at La Folie before I began to unravel this deception, and to mend my heart myself. A minute after it was mended, and I was blinking in dazzled wonder at the arrival of Alice Melbury in my life. And now I find myself fearlessly contemplating the idea of binding the rest of that life to hers.

Admittedly, Alice has not actually given any indication that she wants to marry *me*. So my attention is suddenly piqued when – during a heavyweight discussion of fundamentals, such as whatever happened to Spangles, and is it true that you could blow up a pigeon with a packet of Space Dust – she tells me something I never knew: that the embossed letter inside the plastic lid of a tube of Smarties tells you the initial of the person you are going to marry.

At first I simply assume that this is one of those mystic pieces of arcane wisdom – such as which clothes go together, how to write neatly, and how to get your own way on everything, every time, without anyone noticing – to which only girls are privy. But of course it is not long before I simply, absolutely, have to get my hands on a tube of Smarties.

Not just any old tube of Smarties, either: I need one with an M on the lid. Not as a proposal, exactly. No, the Smarties will be more of a wind-tester, in the spirit of the amateur golfer who carefully tosses a few blades of grass into the air, prior to slicing his ball miles into the deep rough.

Unfortunately, as I soon discover, Smarties do not come in tubes any more. Instead, they come in hexagonal boxes with no plastic lid and certainly no matrimonial forecasting device. But somehow this just makes my quest all the more urgent and – after a long search, while Alice is away in London, catching up with her girlfriends – I finally manage to procure a couple of old-style tubes and lids from two dif-ferent sellers on eBay. And, from my brother Nick, enough Smarties to construct a pair of my secret weapons.

On the day of Alice's return from Stansted, I drive to Limoges airport to pick her up. My hands are tremulous with excitement, as I reach into the glove-box of the Espace, and hold out the two tubes of Smarties.

'English chocolate!' she exclaims, indulging me.

'Go on, which one do you want?' I ask. Her hand hesitates, wavering over first one tube, then the other, like the volunteer for a magic trick, who doesn't guess that the cards are already marked. At last she chooses the left-hand tube, snaps off the lid, and examines it carefully.

'Oh,' she says, holding it up. 'It's an E.'

'What?' I ask, aghast.

'Look.' We both frown at the lid in her hand.

And then I turn it through ninety degrees, so that it is the right way up.

'*Now* try,' I tell her.

'Ah, M,' she says, with such studied carelessness that my experiment is inconclusive. Thank goodness I bought two tubes, I think to myself, as I hand her the second one.

'Open this one,' I suggest. 'Let's see what it is.'

'Another M!' she exclaims. 'How did you do that?'

'My secret,' I reply, smiling at the success of my experiment.

They're here. Cat is asleep but Digby raises his head, ears twitching at the unfamiliar sound. After all this time, I had begun to believe they would never come. But now they have arrived, at last.

'Alice, quickly,' I shout into the kitchen. 'You have to come *right now*.'

'What? What is it?' she asks, alarmed. She wipes her hands on a dish-cloth and runs to join me outside the front door.

'Look,' I announce, pointing at the sky. And we both stare, transfixed, as the cranes float their majestic skywriting across the cloud-base in a V-formation as wide as the sky. Their wings are leather-bound bibles, beating in the wind. Their plangent calls, a thousand bugles blown by seraphim still practising their notes. I know this is the first time Alice has seen them. I could watch them for ever myself.

And then a second wing of birds sweeps into view, joining the first, making a giant W in the sky.

'W for the end of winter,' I murmur. 'Doesn't it make you wish we could fly?'

'To me it looks more like an M,' she murmurs, slipping her hand into mine.

I watch and listen, too transfixed to respond.

'Thank you for calling me,' she adds, in a whisper, blinking up at the sky. And I cannot be sure if it is me she is thanking, or the cranes.

Two days after the cranes, as I gaze out at the perfect blue morning, I feel like a small boy standing on the high diving-board at the swimming pool. For I am about to ask someone I have known since I was a child to marry me. And she, poor love, has no idea.

'Let's go flying today,' I announce over breakfast, reaching into my pocket to touch the polished rosewood box that I have already secretly opened sixteen times since getting up.

'Is the plane fixed, then?' gasps Alice, with a childlike excitement that touches my heart.

'It's flying perfectly. Although it will fly all the better with you sitting beside me.'

Alice does a little dance around the table, and races off to find her headset. 'Don't you dare go without me,' she yells, over her shoulder.

At the aerodrome an hour later, Alice and I work through the pre-flight check-list together. I do my best to look methodical as – with adrenaline drumming in my fingertips – I chock the Luscombe's main wheels. I lean down to check the eight brake clips held in place by eight tiny studs, each the size of the small brilliant-cut diamond that is burning a hole in my pocket. Let us hope none of them fails today.

'Are you all right?' asks Alice, her voice crackling over the intercom as we sit side by side in the Luscombe's leather-lined cockpit.

'Yes, why?'

'You seem nervous,' she says.

'Well, it's always touch and go whether the wings will fall off, isn't it?'

'And that could ruin your whole goddamn day.'

'Right,' I laugh, recognizing the line from the Cessna groundschool CD-ROM. 'I must say, I do like having a co-pilot.'

'Actually, I'm the first officer.'

And then we are off, up, up, over the fields of France.

'Wow,' exclaims Alice, reaching over to put her hand on my arm as we climb towards the sun.

Very soon, however, I realize that the weather isn't doing what it was supposed to do today. No, what looked like a perfectly clear sky, when we were standing down there looking up, suddenly seems as opaque as onion soup now that we're up here, peering down. I pictured myself asking Alice to marry me in the limitless expanse of a polished crystal sky. Instead, we appear to be trapped inside a small pearl lightbulb. Yes, we are fairly and squarely in the murk: with this clag, I thee wed.

'I think I'll just climb a little higher,' I tell her. 'See if we can get above this inversion.' Round and round we fly, carving a helix in the haze. I tell myself that the situation can only get better, just before it gets a whole lot worse.

'I need to pee,' announces Alice, her voice crackling in my headset.

'Are you serious?'

'I'm really sorry. Do you mind if we start heading back?'

The only sound that will come out of my mouth is a shrill giggle.

'Why is that funny?' she asks.

'It's just . . . I brought you up here because there's something I want to ask you.' We are not looking at each other. She is watching the altimeter, while I am staring into the glaring murk all around us, searching for military jets and the right words. 'Actually, I've got something for you. It's in the glove-box in front of you.'

'Is this it?' she asks, pulling out a waxed airsickness bag.

'No,' I gulp. I twiddle the squelch control on the intercom, attempting to reduce the hiss. 'There's a wooden box.'

Finally the polished rosewood box is in her hands. And with a deep breath, I take a running jump off the end of the diving-board.

'I wanted to ask you . . .' Alice is opening the box.

I pull the Luscombe round in a steep turn. As I do so, we finally edge clear of the clag, and pure, unfiltered sunlight comes streaming into the cockpit. 'I wanted to ask you if you would be willing to be my wife.'

There is a howl like feedback in my headset, and for a nasty moment I think the radio has exploded.

'OhhhhmyyyyyGoddddd!' she shrieks. And then again (this time in bold capitals, heavily underlined): '<u>OHHHHHMYYYYYGODDDDD!!!</u>'

I am not sure; this thing could still go either way. But I think this is a good sign.

'Oh my God,' she repeats, quietly. And then, 'Is this really for me?'

'Yes, of course. I'm asking you to marry me.'

'Oh my God. But it's beautiful.'

'Is that a yes, then?'

'I don't believe it,' she says, shaking her head.

'Darling, you have to say yes or no.'

'Yes, yes, sorry, of course it's yes,' she laughs. 'But I'm just so shocked. Are you *sure*?'

'Of course I'm sure,' I reply, pulling out the carb heat knob and surreptitiously checking the revs. 'You'd better see if the ring fits.'

'It's perfect – look,' she says, sliding it on to her finger; making the brilliant diamond glitter in the dazzling sunlight. 'And I love it.'

'Thank goodness. Now . . .' – jittery with elation, I peer back down through the clag – '. . . we'd better see if we can still find the airfield and land this thing.'

This is easier said than done. For the emotion I might be feeling at this point is not an aspect of the flight I had considered during my pre-take-off checks. What a shame it would be, I think to myself, if all that was left of us at the end of this flight were a small, rather special diamond found in the charred wreckage of a vintage aircraft. And then I think: *tant pis*. For this may be a whole new beginning, but already it feels like the happiest of endings, too.

# 20

## APRIL

Being engaged to Alice Melbury, and to refer to her in Jolibois as *ma fiancée*, feels even better than I expected.

I always heard the word *engaged* as a kind of cage-like limitation; that state of unavailability that tends to befall telephone lines and lavatories the moment you want to use them. Whereas the reality is not limitation but liberty. I am free at last from the worry of whether I shall ever meet the right person, because I already have. Now there is just the small matter of asking Alice's father's permission for her hand in marriage, organizing a small wedding, and then setting about the interesting business of living happily ever after.

Surprisingly, perhaps, the animals of La Folie have shown little excitement at the fact that Alice and I are now engaged, let alone the fact that I shall be off to Duxford in a week's time to fly a Spitfire at last. And Gilles is far more exercised with the death of a veal calf that he bought only two weeks ago, as a hedge against his retirement.

'That's five hundred euros down, just like that,' he growls, as I gaze at the lifeless body in its stall, its legs frozen in mid-gallop.

Monsieur Jadot is not filled with rapture at my news either, perhaps because he is too busy lamenting his own failure to find a willing *copine* who can cook proper French food.

'But what about Madame?' I ask, thinking of the pale woman who clung to the back of his tractor. 'She seemed so nice.'

'Too possessive,' he harrumphs. 'I couldn't stand it, in the end.'

'*C'est vrai?* But I rather like the fact that *ma fiancée* feels possessive over me.'

'Yes, but I bet she doesn't follow you around everywhere in her car, does she?'

'No, I have to admit that she doesn't,' I concede, scratching my chin.

In the *boulangerie*, meanwhile, the conversation remains firmly stuck to the weather, the Russian moon, and the fact that Young Boulesteix drank a skinful at the *Foire des Chapons*, and has managed to break his wrist.

I am obliged to accept that the transformation in my own life has, remarkably, not transformed everyone else's life, too. I like it this way. I like the fact that life in the countryside quietly ticks out the hours, regardless of what is happening in Paris or London or La Folie. And what I especially like about living with sheep and chickens and cats is the way that, even when I think the universe has changed utterly overnight, they just keep plodding and pecking and purring along in their own easy rhythms, *comme d'habitude*; fill up the trough and make it snappy please, *chef*.

So here I am, zingy with elation and amazement at the fact that I have met someone I want to marry who actually wants to marry me. And the Rastafarians, heedless, continue to graze as if nothing had happened. Five elasticated black lambs have been born in the past month. I watch them playfully head-butting each other in the field behind the house, where the rich new grass has somehow gone from sea-grass matting to shag-pile overnight. I know they are preparing for that day in the future when they will have to fight their own battles to win a mate.

The Egg Squad have shown even less interest in my life-changing news, although Big Melanie did have a bit of a go at pecking the diamond out of Alice's engagement ring when we had lunch on the terrace yesterday. Otherwise they are far too busy sorting out their own polygamous pecking order to worry about our much simpler arrangements.

Three cockerels, I now see, is far too many for four hens. And I feel worst of all for Meg, the last survivor of my original Egg Squad, weakened by grief. A frail old dear with something of the air of a bronchitic librarian about her, Meg deserves better than to be constantly propositioned by these three priapic pests.

'There's an obvious solution to this,' I warn Alice, thinking about all the empty space in our cavernous chest-freezer.

'Yes,' she says, brightly. 'We need more hens.'

Our families in general profess themselves delighted by the news, and Survival-Kit Toby, in particular, says he's thrilled. But only Digby, bless him, is beside himself with excitement about our engagement, shrieking and wagging and attempting to leap 360s in the air like a hot-dogging skateboarder, as if I'd mentioned a W–A–L–K or a banana. I like to think that this reflects a certain psychological development; that he is beginning to see me less as his love-rival and more like his boss. Although perhaps I did cheat just a little, by jingling his lead when I told him the news.

Nature herself gives no outward sign of being awed by our decision. Whenever the wind blows, I think about the wobbly chimney at La Folie, threatening to smash down through our bedroom with every gust. But the cuckoo remains unmoved. Every morning, I listen to the dawn chorus, as it mingles with the shrill clarion of Cat and the whiffling of Digby downstairs, both clamouring for their breakfast. And still there's no trace amid the whistle-twittering of that descending minor-third that is my signal to phone Serge the stonemason, who will not come to call until I have heard the first cuckoo sing. But at least I find myself paying attention to the noises of nature more closely than ever, and hearing sounds that I never heard before.

According to Jadot, the ancient sages of Jolibois have decreed that summer this year will be a wet one. Because of the ants, obviously. They say the little fellows are building their hummocky *fourmilières* in the open, beside the roads and ditches, rather than deep in the woods. And this means that water is on the way. Jadot has conveniently forgotten that his same sages also declared that last winter would be a fearsomely cold and harsh one, because the bramble tendrils were longer and more droopy than usual. Well, if brambles can lie (which they did), then ants probably can, too.

Even if they are wrong, I cherish the fact that there are still walnut-faced *paysans* in the countryside who keep such a close eye upon nature, and who still have enough confidence in their inherited folk-wisdom to extract meaning from what they see.

'Never go and get your hair cut during a new moon,' Gilles used to tell me. 'It'll grow back too quickly.' He and Josette are coming to lunch next week, so I'm hoping that he will not notice that I have had a sly trim without consulting the lunar calendar.

This afternoon, the rain is lashing down, and a fierce wind has begun to howl around La Folie.

'What are you writing about this week?' asks my fiancée, back from her French class in town. Even now, as I watch her delicately chopping an onion, her glossy hair gleaming beneath the kitchen lights, I find it hard to believe that this gorgeous woman will one day be my wife.

'About the chimney,' I reply, 'and how Serge won't come and fix it until we've heard the cuckoo sing.'

'But the cuckoo's been singing for weeks.'

I gulp, rooted to the spot. 'W . . . wh . . . why didn't you say?'

Alice hesitates. 'In fact, I think it might have been a woodpecker,' she says, with a hopeful smile. 'Doesn't that count?'

We both laugh, and I think how blessed I am to share my life with such a sweetly supportive soul; a fellow ex-townie who is doing her level best to get to grips with the inchoate mysteries of the French language and countryside. Then I laugh again, as I picture Serge's response to her woodpecker argument. Together, we gaze out of the rain-spattered window at the bushes swaying in the gale. Spring weather, indeed. I just hope things are better at Duxford next week, before they wheel out the Spitfire for my flight. And I can only hope and pray that our chimney does not fall before good Monsieur Coucou deigns to call.

The day of my Spitfire flight has finally come, and I can hardly keep still as I sit on the grass beside the control-tower at Duxford aerodrome, waiting to fly in the graceful war machine that is looping and rolling and roaring across the sky above my head. ML407 is a rare two-seat Spitfire variant that still carries a bullet-hole it picked up on D-Day.

And then the beautiful aircraft lands, and I can see the lady pilot shaking her head in the front cockpit as the fitters clamber on to the wings to help her out of her straps.

'Radio's fried,' I hear someone say. 'All flying cancelled until further notice.'

I sit in shock, staring at the dream machine. No one is quite clear when or if there will be another chance for me to fly. Is it over so soon, the flight of my life?

I have grown my potato. I have found the woman of my dreams. And with my head hanging in disbelief – like

Digby's when nightfall comes and he has still not had his walk – I fold up my Spitfire dream once more, tuck it into my back pocket, and fly back to La Folie on the fastest way to Abroad.

For days, Gilles has been insisting that Alice and I must go with him and Josette to eat crêpes at his friend Gérard's house. It doesn't seem to matter that *mardi gras* has been and gone. The crêpe season is a long one, *chez* Gérard.

'Actually, it's not exactly a house, where he lives,' coughs Gilles, as we set out to drive through the rain.

'What is it, then?'

'It's a bit special. You'll see.'

Half an hour later, we are standing in a muddy farmyard. Before us, I can see the silhouette of a large house, with a small outbuilding attached.

'*Et voilà*,' says Gilles.

The door of the outbuilding swings open, and a man with a torch ushers us inside. I reach out for Alice's hand. Even by the rough standards of La Folie, this place feels as primitive as an Iron Age camp.

Gérard is a genial, hulking presence, with white hair and a few teeth, which remind me of a handful of broken golf-tees stuck in a withered apple. He appears to be wearing about ten shirts and a pair of once-fluffy slippers that look as if they may have passed through a cow. But if the man is Gothic, his home is something else.

The hot blast of the fire is what hits me first. And then, in the flickering gloom, I see that we are in a small stone room whose walls and ceiling are jammed with jumble. The beams are hung with iron tools, mousetraps, oil cans, manila envelopes, bits of string, shearing implements, rusted chains, and a wooden tennis racquet that must have looked old-fashioned in the 1930s. In the background, an accordion record crackles on an old turntable.

'This is my night club,' whispers Gérard, beaming.

Living in darkest France has often felt to me like living fifty years in the past. But this place, this time-capsule, makes La Folie seem gleamingly modern. It is perfect. I grin at Alice; am relieved to see that she is smiling, too.

Gérard points to a rubicund woman who has emerged from the shadows. 'And that's my wife. She lives next door.' He is so delighted with this thought that he begins to slap his thigh, roaring with laughter, until she gently touches him on the arm, and he switches into crêpe-making mode, his face engraved with concentration as he ladles batter from a huge tureen into a frying pan balanced over the flames.

Gérard splashes cider into glasses. 'I came from Normandy in 1952, with all my cows on the train,' he says, beginning to pull objects off the walls and ceilings, explaining their significance. 'I didn't learn a thing at school – not a thing, did I, Gilles? – and it didn't matter. Whereas today, you have to pass all sorts of exams, and you leave not knowing a thing about the land.'

Beside me, Alice says something I do not understand. And then I realize why. Slowly and haltingly, she is speaking French. 'It is the same with the nurse *en Angleterre*,' she says, fumbling and stumbling and making perfect sense. Her pale skin flickers in the reflected glow of the fire. Gérard leans forward; Josette nods; Gilles sits on the edge of his chair. I sit transfixed, my eyes wide with wonder. I have never heard her do this before. 'I learned with the other nurses,' she says, 'to do the bed, take the temperature, mop the floor. Now they learn with the books. They are too proud to mop the floor.'

'*Oui, c'est ça*,' says Gérard, slapping his thigh again and nodding into the fire. Gilles stares at Alice, as if seeing her in a new light. I want to stand and applaud.

'*Bravo*,' whispers Josette, patting Alice's arm. '*C'est formidable*.'

The crêpes keep on coming, carefully sugared and folded by Gérard's wife. After three apiece, Alice and I hold up our hands: we're done. But Gérard isn't. 'You have to finish all that,' he growls, indicating the vast tureen of batter, still almost three-quarters full. 'You're not allowed to stop eating.'

I chuckle, thinking this is funny. Beside me, Alice is very still. Gilles glares at me. So it's not a joke, then.

After four crêpes, I can feel myself sweating pure butter.

After five, I am wondering whether it's dark enough to risk loosening my belt. Gilles's face is shiny and glowing, and he shows no sign of flagging. Nor does Gérard, with his deadly ladle. I have to go on. For Gilles's sake, and for *Angleterre*.

Six, and I swear I shall eat nothing but lettuce ever again.

'And you say you do this twice a week?' I ask Gérard, beginning to understand why France is beginning to move up the international obesity tables.

Seven, and I feel as if I have swallowed an anvil.

When Gérard slaps the eighth crêpe on to my plate, he eyes me carefully, like a trainer considering whether the boxer in his corner is fit to continue the bout. Gilles looks very still and meditative, almost like Buddha.

At last the tureen is drained, and Gérard lays down the dreaded ladle.

'I've done my job,' he says, proudly.

'You can say that again,' I sigh, leaning against the wall for support.

And we all bask in a lardy daze around the fire.

'Do you prefer to live in the past, then, Gérard?' I ask him. He grins and points at all the calendars on the walls. I thought they must date back to the 1950s, but each is – I now see – open at this month of this year.

'You can still live in the present, even when you live in the past,' he laughs. And all I can think, as we stagger out into the night, and back to the twenty-first century, is that I personally can't wait for that day in the future, when a woman from my past becomes a part of my eternal present. And I will never again have to eat another crêpe.

A few days later, and I receive an apologetic phone-call from *Warbird* magazine. They explain that Spitfire ML407 may never fly again.

*What*?

The company which sponsors the plane's insurance has been vaporized by the credit crunch. Without their help, the Spitfire's vast premiums will be impossible to sustain.

I slump into an armchair and gaze out of the window for a very long time.

Meg, the last remaining chicken of the six in my original Egg Squad, has never regained the strength that she lost when her sisters were taken by the fox. A tiny Rhode Island Red, she was weak even before that, and the prognosis is not good. She now spends most of her life in the kitchen, squatting motionless on the quarry tiles, waiting for me to bring her scraps of bread or muesli, occasionally dipping her beak into the small bowl of medicated water I provide for her. She may not have long to live, but I am determined that the rest of her life should at least be as comfortable as possible.

Alice and Digby are not convinced. But Meg is so unobtrusive that even the cat puts up with her, shooting only the occasional sidelong glance to indicate her resentment at the presence in the kitchen of a half-dead bird not personally imported by her.

Pauline, our shouty cleaning lady, comes while we are out, and leaves a note after she has finished cleaning. '*S.V.P. Pas de poules dans la maison!*' To be fair, she does have a point. Sick Meg's ablutions are alarmingly distinctive. I resolve to keep her outside in future.

A few days later, and though Meg has been sticking close to the house, she, too, vanishes. Not another one. The patient is nowhere to be found when I put the other chickens to bed. By the morning, there is still no sign of her. I have to accept that she will not be coming back.

And then I am making a sullen cup of tea for myself and Alice, when I am struck by the sight of something on the window-sill. It is a ragged-looking chicken, slouching like a tramp at a soup kitchen.

'Isn't that . . . ?' I begin, barely daring to finish the question I have started. I am only a step away from imagining goblins sitting on toadstools and Elvis buying brioche at the *boulangerie*. It is easy to mistake one chicken for another, in certain lights. But I step outside for a closer look.

It *is* Meg. The prodigal has returned. And I feel like hopping with happiness.

'Please don't bring her inside,' begs Alice.

'You don't care,' I retort.

'You don't have to clean the floor.'

And there is nothing I can say to this.

Poor Meg is not in great shape. Her neck is matted with something dark, and one eye is closed and watery. Nevertheless, she's alive.

For a moment, I think back to Shouty Pauline's note: No chickens in the house.

And then I pick up my favourite chicken, and carry her indoors.

# 21

## MAY

From the way that Gilles is leaning against the front of his white van, unwilling to approach the front door, I can see that he brings uncomfortable tidings.

'*Salut, Gilles,*' I chirp, as cheerfully as possible, before submitting my hand to his iron death-grip.

'*Salut, Michael,*' he says, not really looking at me.

'*Alors, quoi de neuf?*' I feel a little leap of triumph at the base of my spine, because usually Gilles beats me to the toughest question in the world to answer – what's new? – and for once I have got in there first.

He shifts from foot to foot, examining the ground as if scouting for mushrooms.

'*Ah-ouf*, nothing really,' he says. 'But we've found a house.'

'*Ah, c'est formidable!*' I exclaim. In the distance, a cuckoo begins to call. 'Where is it?'

'That's just it,' he replies, quietly. 'It's quite a long way from Jolibois. It's not what we wanted, but it's all we could find.'

'Because everything is so expensive?'

He nods, as I beckon him inside. The cuckoo can wait.

'Because of *les Anglais*, I suppose?'

'*Ah-ouf*, I don't know about that,' he growls.

'You have to haggle, Gilles, that's the thing,' I tell him, playing back to him his favourite advice to me. But he doesn't laugh.

'How . . . far?' I can feel my heart sinking, as if I'd just heard of the death of an old friend, or the cancellation of a flight in the most beautiful aircraft in the world. I'm not just feeling sorry for myself, either. I am sorry for Gilles and Josette, too. They have lived in Jolibois for thirty years. I know they didn't want to have to leave.

'It's in a hamlet just on the other side of Lézard-le-Duc,' he says. 'Maybe twenty minutes away.'

I bite my lip. I had not imagined that he would move so far from Jolibois.

In London, a twenty-minute drive is no distance at all. I have spent that long just waiting for a bus to come, and used to think nothing of travelling for an hour to meet a friend for a drink on the other side of town.

Here in darkest France, twenty minutes is the distance between different worlds. Life is local. When I drive twenty minutes outside Jolibois, I feel like a child entering the evil forest; an explorer venturing into the unknown. I happen to know Lézard-le-Duc, and it is another country to Jolibois. The roads are surfaced in a paler tar; the *cantonniers* who clear the ditches wear different uniforms; the grimly rendered houses lining the main street are of an entirely different kilter to the higgledy-piggledy relics that make up the centre of our town.

I know I will be losing a friend. And I cannot imagine how I will manage without him. Worst of all, I now have even less time than I feared to chip away at the mountain of my debt to Gilles. Thank goodness it is the sheep-shearing next month, when I am back on wool-gathering duty. One last, paltry service I can render to the peasant mentor who has done so much for me since I arrived at La Folie.

'Is there anything I can do for *you*, Gilles?' I ask, as Gilles rises to leave, though not before he has promised to deliver three stout corner-posts for my new fence behind the *potager*. But no, he will not accept any money for the *poteaux*. And no, I cannot help lift them on to the tractor, because Josette's back is almost better, so she will do all the heavy lifting. She is only fifty-one, after all. And no, no tasks suitable for a tractorless townie spring to Gilles's mind.

'Unless . . .' he says.

'*Oui?*'

'Our new house has quite a big garden, which is going to need mowing. But it's too small for a tractor.' I can already feel the tingle of excited anticipation in my spine, as he continues: 'Would it be too much trouble for you to put your ride-on mower in the Espace, and come and cut the grass for me, once or twice, over the summer?'

'Ah, Gilles, *merci, merci bien*,' I blurt, dizzy with gratitude. For with all due respect to those high-minded souls who once taught me Latin and Greek, honed my intellectual curiosity and encouraged my literary aspirations, I can think of no finer commission, just now, than being offered the chance to mow the lawn for a French farmer whose many kindnesses I shall never be able to repay.

Night after night, as Alice and I sit on the terrace with our sundowners, listening to that blasted cuckoo, we discuss our favourite subject: where to get married, and how to stop La Folie from becoming a subterranean kingdom, as the hill behind the house steadily bears down upon us, like a wet sponge squeezed against a sugar-lump. Serge and the chimney will have to wait. It is expensive to change the landscape of one's life. And never mind the old church-versus-registry-office quandary; we haven't even chosen a country yet.

Besides the fact that it is where we live, the obvious advantage of marrying in France is that – thanks to the existence of blue-and-yellow aircraft – it is now easier and cheaper for our British friends to reach than is most of England. Yet from reading between the lines of her protestations about how wonderful France is, I sense that Alice would far rather marry in Britain, and not just because of her ongoing tussles with the lingo. She says it would somehow seem more proper than marrying here in France. And I think I know what she means. Would a French marriage *count*?

I know it would be legal and all that. I have already seen the list of paperwork we would need for the *Mairie*, a bureaucratic bonanza that makes me think of Digby's immigration paper-chase, or Jarndyce vs. Jarndyce crossed with *The Crystal Maze*. Yet I, too, have my own niggling sense of doubt. The idea of a French marriage, rather than a British one, is a bit like contemplating a cup of Lipton's Yellow Label instead of PG Tips; *pâté en croûte* instead of pork pie; or a pan of home-cooked *haricots blancs* instead of a sky-blue tin of baked beans with white-on-black lettering. And I know that when Alice uses the word home, she is either referring to her mother's house in Westbury, or to Britain in general. She is certainly not talking about La Folie.

On the other hand, getting married in England would mean choosing a particular location. And we soon discover that there is no one place to which either of us feels we unquestionably belong. The best I can do is a street in Eastleigh named after my grandfather, George Wright, who won a brace of gold medals for England at the Empire Games in the 1930s. But there is nowhere to get married in George Wright Close. And Eastleigh has never been my home.

I know that for Alice it is the same, after four years of working in Baltimore, and with parents who live at either end of southern England. She is already beginning to discover that the more time she spends in France, the further away England begins to seem. Going there is like returning to a school where you used to be a pupil and finding that it is no longer yours.

How I envy those lucky souls with primordial ties to some Betjemanesque village with a pub, a post office and a church. Instead, Alice and I both come from the kind of mobile middle-class backgrounds that entail stints of living abroad, several years at far-flung boarding schools, and parents who have gradually moved west across England, from London via suburbia to the countryside. Home is wherever we happen to live at the time.

'Where do you come from?' ask the locals in Jolibois, and I always say *Londres* because it is mostly true, and because it is less embarrassing than trying to explain Weybridge.

In France, the place where you were born matters. It is the place where the chapter headings of your life – birth, marriage, children and death – are stored, much like the old parish records in England before we all took to living on the M25. Yet Alice and I have, as yet, no chapter headings in France. So there would be a kind of freedom in marrying here, as if we were signing our names on a blank page.

The first I know of the start of the *grands travaux* at La Folie, in which much of the hillside from behind the house will be shifted to the front of it, is a low rumble in the distance, like an approaching storm. Cat begins to growl, her fur standing on end in a full-body mohican. Digby goes bananas, too, as if he had just caught the ghost of Banquo sniffing at his Dog Chow. Moments later, the kitchen goes dark. Has the sky fallen on our heads? No, it's just a bulldozer the size of the Arc de Triomphe going past the window.

*Nom de Dieu.* That thing looks big enough to move a

mountain range, let alone shift a few cubic metres of earth from behind a small farmhouse in darkest France. And the driver, when he clambers down to shake my hand, shares more than a passing resemblance to his vehicle. His belt must be as long as I am tall.

'Is there another way up to this place?' he asks.

'Not really,' I reply. 'Why?'

'Philippe's coming up in the Big One, and I'm not sure he'll be able to get it up here.'

'You mean Philippe's digger is even bigger than this?'

'They're both twenty-four tonnes,' he shrugs. 'But the Big One's quite a lot wider.'

'Ah, *très bien.*'

I was expecting *le patron* who gave me the quote to be here, to supervise. Instead, I can merely stand and gape, as a complete stranger starts demolishing the hillside behind La Folie. I do not even have time to get nervous about what he might hit, largely because he has already hit something much, much worse than I could have possibly imagined.

Water gushes from a hole in the earth, in a foaming torrent that makes me think of Kate Winslet screaming in a torn silk dress, or the spangly murk churned up behind a cross-Channel ferry out of Dover.

'*Mon Dieu*, is it the water main?' I shout, above the din.

Bulldozer Man shakes his head.

'It's much too big for that, *monsieur*,' he says, ruefully.

'Shall I call the water people?' I ask. Great lumps of hillside are being carried away by the flood.

'Good idea,' he nods.

Minutes later, a red-and-white-striped van turns up, and an angry-looking moustache erupts from it.

'*Ça va, monsieur?*' I ask.

'Not particularly, no,' he storms. '*You* just spoiled my day.'

'Ah.'

Together, we gaze at the gashed pipe. You could canoe on those rapids.

'Nobody in any of the villages above Jolibois will have any water now, thanks to you,' seethes the moustache. 'The switchboard will be jammed. Calls will be passed on to Toulouse. There'll be no hushing this up. And someone must pay.'

Feeling an urgent need for a cup of very strong tea, I phone Yves-Pascal the notaire to ask whether I am likely to go to prison for life. Ariane answers.

'Ah, Michael, how are the great works coming?' she says, her voice dancing with delight. 'I am *so* pleased you are opening up the place at last; getting rid of all those trees and darkness.'

'Have you got any water?' I ask.

'*Oui, bien sûr,*' she replies, surprised. 'Do you want some?'

'Would you like to check?'

'That's funny,' she says, a few moments later. 'It seems to have stopped.' The water people must have turned off the big tap marked 'Limousin'.

Alone of all the creatures at La Folie, the Rastafarians appear to be enjoying *les grands travaux*. With the fences down, they are charging and splashing around the luxuriant slopes of La Folie like children staying in a grand hotel for the first time, pressing all the buttons in the lift, going round and round in the revolving doors. The Egg Squad have vanished in the direction of the Lone Pine, there to rue the loss of their favourite dust-bath. From the window-sill, Cat gazes out, wide-eyed with rage and regret, as her mouse tenements and lizard slums are bulldozed, one by one. Digby has been on edge all day, too. Every so often, shrieking like a smoke-alarm, he races out to snap at the caterpillar tracks of the digger as if he thought he could take it on. 'C'mon, if you think you're hard enough,' he barks, in his Baltimore twang. Unmoved, the mechanical brontosaurus surges onward.

La Folie is changing fast. Though I like the fact that we now have daylight in the bathroom, because it is no longer underground, this is not a source of rapture. No, one moment we are gazing out over an ancient natural landscape that probably has not changed since the Battle of Crécy, and the next moment, a dusty plateau the size of Croydon has replaced the gentle slope that once led up to La Folie. Never mind infinity pools; we have created an infinity car park by mistake.

What makes things worse is that these are French *ouvriers*, not British ones. So they arrive at 7.30 am, don't have a single tea-break and refuse all other offers of refreshment. As a result, there is no let-up in the bombardment; no pause to reflect on the devastation we have sanctioned.

I wonder if anyone ever had this problem with Capability Brown. Back in the eighteenth century, it must have taken his navvies such a long time to get anywhere that there would have been plenty of time to stop them going too far. On the other hand, if you *did* start having second thoughts and murmuring that, now you come to think of it, that ha-ha is a little too far to the left, Mr Brown, and yonder grotto a tad too deep, all those pooped navvies would have been quite justified in telling you where you could stick your Grecian temple.

'Everything the diggers have done is reversible,' I mumble to Alice, in an attempt to reassure myself. But the words ring hollow in my ears. And so, channelling my inner dissident, I plant myself in front of Philippe's clanking, grinding digger and hope that it stops before he squishes me into a sheet of lasagne. Fortunately, it stops. I shout up to him that I didn't realize there would be *quite* so much earth, and could he by any chance move, say, two hundred cubic metres of it to the far corner of the bottom field? Philippe shrugs and lights another cigarette.

He aside, only one fellow seems entirely unfazed by the

carnage we have wrought. While the other sheep revel in pastures new, toothless old Gaston comes hobbling after me, head low, making a kind of rasping drone that is as close as he gets to a *baa* these days. Never mind cavorting about the countryside. When a fellow is so old that he cannot feed himself, all he wants is his cup of Horlicks of an evening, regular as clockwork. So Gaston – once so wild and proud a ram – meekly follows me into the sheep house and waits while I fetch him his handful of granules from the sack. As he munches, we gaze at each other: he, relieved to eat at last; I, relieved that he has lasted at all.

Tonight, Gilles and Josette are coming for dinner, and we have defrosted a pound of our best Porkinson Bangers in their honour, partly as a special treat and partly because the fridge is a bit of a blank page, too. Sausages are one of the few foods that Britain does better than France, whose so-called chipolata is a sour, greasy extrusion that even Cat has been known to reject. So we request British *saucisses* in every parental supply-drop, and guard them with our lives.

Stepping out of his white van, Gilles gazes about him, strokes his beard, and says nothing.

'So what do you think, Gilles?' I ask, nervously. Has he not noticed the flat, blasted landscape that the diggers have left?

'Don't worry,' he says, at last, reading my mind. 'This will grow.' He stretches out his arm; sweeps it over the landscape.

'You can see a long way from here,' adds Josette. 'I never knew.'

I usher them inside, and Gilles immediately asks if he can wash his hands. He says they haven't had any water since Tuesday. Alice and I exchange glances; say nothing.

And then we sit at the table, and it feels just like old times, as Josette sips her Pineau, and Gilles his Salers.

'So,' asks Gilles, as Alice begins to serve up, 'when are you two planning to get married?'

'September,' I reply.

'*En France*,' adds Alice, taking me by surprise. I know she still finds these evenings with our French friends a struggle.

At first, from the way Gilles wrinkles up his nose, I fear he may be appalled at our presumption. And then, from the way he is jabbing his fork as if to spear a goblin, I realize that we have made a tragic mistake with the sausages.

'Are they meant to be like this?' he asks, frowning at his plate.

'*Mange!*' hisses Josette, as if she were telling a child to shut up and eat. I blink. This is the first time I have heard Gilles's shy and silent wife tell her rock-like husband to do anything, ever.

'*C'est pas terrible*,' he harrumphs, looking seasick.

'*Mange,*' she repeats, in a softer tone.

I, for my part, feel mortified; as mortified as only a man who has just blown a pound of perfectly decent pork sausages on his unfeeling neighbour can feel. Yet I cannot blame Gilles, who, bless him, always tells it the way he sees it. Retirement may prove hard for my friend. But I am happy to see that his wife is beginning to dare to crawl out from under her rock.

# 22

## JUNE

Alice says she would like everyone at our wedding to be able to stay in the same place. So now we are searching for a simple chateau or a big, crumbling hotel, not too far from Jolibois. Unfortunately, it soon emerges that the Limousin, being one of the poorest regions in France, is scarcely the chateau capital of the universe. The few chateaux that do exist mostly resemble Bates Motel. And the hotels tend to be boxy, grey and functional, clustered like northern day-trippers in the bumbling heart of Limoges.

Hence today's recce to the somewhat swisher region of Bergerac, where – as part of a long weekend away – we have booked to stay the night at our last hope: a chateau which could sleep most of Jolibois, has its own restaurant and which, to my dismay and Alice's delight, accepts dogs.

'Why don't we make this a romantic break?' I ask her, as I pick up the phone to make the booking.

'But it wouldn't be romantic without him,' she replies, twigging at once that although Jadot has agreed to feed the chickens, I am thinking of leaving Digby behind to guard the house. 'Would it?'

Poor Digby can hardly believe it when I tell him that he is

coming too. He has been wearing his RSPCA face ever since he saw our bags being packed, and now you would think I had electrified the floor, from the way he explodes into the air and starts flinging himself around in a series of tight spins. It is very hard, with a labrador from Baltimore, to know how to break things to him gently.

At the chateau's reception desk, the lady manager does not visibly share Digby's rapture. Too late, it dawns on me that 'dogs accepted' is aimed at old ladies clutching chihuahuas, not gasping labradors dragging their owners behind them, like huskies hauling a sled. Even before *Madame* lets out the shriek – Digby was castrated as a puppy, but still has an embarrassing penchant for Frenchwomen's bottoms – I can see from the surfeit of porcelain at tail-height that this is really not Digby's kind of place.

'Do you think we should just cut our losses and leave?' I whisper to Alice.

'We're here now,' she replies firmly, squeezing my hand. 'It will be fine.'

I nod, as *Madame* makes a reluctant gesture in the direction of the staircase, as if sharing a secret she would far rather keep under wraps. I gulp. Narrow, wooden and carpeted with something antique and Persian, the idea of taking Digby up there feels a bit like driving a tank into a doll's house. Too late: our blond bombshell is already on his way up.

On the first half-landing, I manage to steady a willow-pattern vase before it falls. But there is nothing I can do about the two stately ladies tottering down, who end up clinging, white-knuckled, to the banisters, as the canine express thunders past.

'*Excusez-moi, mesdames,*' I blurt, clinging to the end of Digby's lead like a bungee-jumper on the way back up.

Once in the sanctuary of our room – which has a four-poster bed and more antique furniture than I had hoped –

Alice and I stare at each other as if we have just survived a mortar attack, knowing quite well that the full bombardment has yet to begin.

'We've got to take him outside,' says Alice. 'Try and tire him out before dinner.'

'But that means the stairs again.'

'Even so.'

I do my best to smile at *Madame* as I sprint past her desk for the second time: a waterskier clinging on for dear life.

'We'll be back,' I gasp, as cheerfully as I can.

I think it is fair to say that dinner is not a success. Alice and I have already decided that the chateau will not do for the wedding, so I feel wretched when the *maître d'* brings us a bottle of the local Pécharmant red wine with his compliments, suggesting that it might be suitable for our reception.

But that is not the problem. No, the problem is the howling of the hound of the Baskervilles, languishing in his far-flung turret upstairs. I see one aghast diner drop his fork with a clink at the sound.

'Don't react,' I whisper to Alice. 'Pretend he's not ours.'

But then my heart sinks. The two ladies Digby flattened on the stairs have entered the restaurant. The baying of Cerberus intensifies. Now the ladies are muttering and staring at us. And when the *maître d'* comes to take their order, one of them points a bony finger of denunciation.

'Sneak,' whispers Alice, wrinkling her nose.

'Time to go,' I murmur.

Next day, on the drive home, Alice is unusually silent.

'I'm just a little disappointed,' she says. 'It feels like a wasted trip.'

'Mm,' I reply. 'But at least now we know the kind of place we *don't* want.' And from the way Digby bounces out of the car at the bottom of the drive to La Folie – still giddy with delight at the memory of his first night on a four-poster – perhaps the trip wasn't entirely wasted, after all.

'Where's *home*, Digby?' I ask him, as he stands yelping with excitement in front of the car. And this is all the invitation he needs: he is off like a shot, hurtling up the drive ahead of us.

Before we unpack, I trudge out to the chicken house to see how everyone is doing. The landscape seems greener than we left it on Friday night and, to judge from the squelchiness underfoot, either it has been raining non-stop, or else I am in for a very nasty surprise from the *fosse septique*. The cat comes and rubs herself against my legs, before retreating to watch me from the stone steps. It is as if she knows something I don't, and wants me to discover it for myself.

I am surprised to find the chicken-house door still bolted. So old Jadot has not yet been up here today. I hope he came yesterday.

Meg is lying on the floor just inside the door, surrounded by her sisters. Jadot's three young cockerels-in-waiting scarper as I enter. She remains motionless. Meg, the last of my original Egg Squad and the gentlest chicken I have ever known, is always happy to be picked up; to sit on my lap when I work; to bait the cat by scouring the kitchen floor for crumbs. But not today.

No. I can see at once that there will be no more reconnaissance missions for Meg; no more scampering to greet me when I rattle up the hill to La Folie in the Espace.

With a sigh, I kneel beside her. The chestnut feathers still look glossy, but the legs are stiffly folded up beneath the stricken body like the partially retracted undercarriage of a Yak-52. Meg's neck is Meerschaum-twisted; her lidded eye as pale as the whitened yolk of a flipped fried egg.

Jadot warned me, weeks ago, that when a chicken is sick like Meg was sick, she would never recover. Yet I begged – and beg – to differ. Meg was becoming stronger with each day that passed, after a course of antibiotics injected by Alice into her scrawny breast. True, she had not laid an egg since the Middle Ages. Yet her rheumy right eye had cleared up; her rear end was no longer quite so matted with beige chalk; she seemed a perkier bird all round.

What she needed was fresh air and sunlight, not being shut up for a whole weekend in the damp darkness with her sisters. Chickens are not sentimental. It is quite possible that they pecked their weaker sibling to death.

Perhaps it is childish of me still to feel dismay at the death of a chicken. It is nothing, I tell myself, compared with the human deaths that Alice has had to face, again and again, as part of her daily working life. But there is a world of difference between a nameless layer being snaffled by a fox, and coming home to find an old friend laid out cold at your feet. Calm and always unruffled, despite her illness, Meg was my last remaining connection to the start of my life at La Folie. And now she is gone, and I am surprised at the gap she has left.

When Alice asks me where I am going, I say nothing. I cannot expect her to understand. I pick up the stiff brown body, place it in a blue bin-liner, and carry it through the rain to the Lone Pine, where one or two of Martha's feathers are still stuck in the earth; birthday candles on a cake.

Here, where Meg's sister Silent Mary is buried alongside Emil and Nemo, I begin to dig. But even with all this rain, the summer-baked ground is still too hard for my spade. So I fetch an iron bar to break up the earth, feeling a strange relief in this heavy labour beneath the rain.

I always meant to clean up the mucky clumps from Meg's rear end. Now, too late, I do it for her, pulling lumps of dry clay from her downy feathers. Then I place her scrawny body gently in the hole in the earth and gaze at what is left of Meg, wishing she were still here. I am glad that it is dry enough for her; I could not bear to lay her in a flooded grave. I shovel the dirt back into the hole, slowly at first, and then faster, because bits of Meg are still sticking out here and there, and it makes me feel funny inside.

From the window of my office at the end of the house, as I gaze down at the freshly dug earth beneath the Lone Pine, I am surprised to see Alice appear, walking towards the place I buried Meg. I have not seen Alice Melbury at this distance, like a character in someone else's life, since that day when I watched her through the chainlink fencing at Limoges airport: a slim goddess wandering across the sun-baked apron, hunched and irresistible, and coming to see *me*. I remember it was her first solo visit to France, and she carried a bag weighed down with pilot-training manuals that she didn't touch while she was here. Now she is carrying something, too, as her feet tread softly on the wet grass. It might almost be a bundle of sticks, to help her brother build a camp in the woods. But as I look more closely, and watch her kneel in the dirt beside Meg, I can see that it is a tiny bunch of wild flowers.

An unusually hot spring means that shearing-time has arrived early in the Limousin, and with it my annual opportunity to help Gilles. So it is quite a blow when Big Leif, the Dutch skyscraper who lives in the old signalman's cottage beside the Moulin Vaugelade – a domestic arrangement that makes me think of a grasshopper tucked into a matchbox – tells me that Gilles has asked him to *ramasser la laine* this year.

Sorry, Leif, but hasn't gathering the wool always been *my* job, these past summers?

Nothing is for certain these days. And, sure enough, as the sheep-shearing approaches, I receive a momentous call from Gilles, confirming the news. 'I won't need you to gather the wool this year, Michael,' he coughs. I cannot believe it. Were our sausages really as bad as all that? Or am I still in disgrace for the destruction of Monsieur Boudin's hedge by the

Jolibois Eighteen? Dismayed, I am about to protest when Gilles adds: 'I'm giving you *une promotion*.'

'*C'est vrai?*' I hold my breath as he speaks. Yes, it *is* true: I am to turn the sheep and set them on their rumps, presenting them thus to the shearer for their short-back-and-sides.

Oh, my word: the glory of it. I feel my head swell dangerously at the thought of the manly work that lies ahead of me. I can hardly wait to tell Alice, when she comes back from her French lesson. She will be so impressed. No more scrabbling around on my knees, pulling rank handfuls of khaki poo from the fleeces before I fling them into the sack; no more having to clamber into the woolsack myself, treading the wool down into the corners as if I were Fotherington-Thomas pushing shortcrust into a flan tin. *Non, monsieur*: I'm up there with the big boys, now, and we are cooking with gas.

Life in the countryside is changing, in France as in Britain. In my first summer at La Folie, Gilles's shearing barn seemed to be full of men helping the shearers do their stuff. A holiday ambience prevailed, especially after a robust lunch of *gigot d'agneau* prepared in silence by Josette, with hefty libations of Beaujolais Villages on the side.

Taking part felt like being written into a Thomas Hardy novel, or playing a film role intended for Gérard Depardieu. Each year since then, however, the numbers and the mirth have dwindled. The farmers are tightening their belts, notch by notch, year on year.

'I remember when I used to get fifteen francs a kilo for my wool,' laments Gilles, standing amid the shadows of his shearing barn, with seventy sweaty sheep bleating and barging behind him, like a crowd at a rock concert. 'And that was in the days when a franc was worth something. This year, they have offered me fifty cents a kilo, which won't even pay the shearer.' He casts a rueful glance down at Young Boulesteix, who sits crosslegged in the straw, his muscular shoulders bulging out from a vest that looks as if it has shrunk in the wash.

Boulesteix smiles, not looking up. A sheep-farmer himself, still at the start of the race whose finish-line Gilles has almost reached, he continues adjusting the combs of his Lister shearing-machine in silence, screwing up his eyes against the smoke from the Marlboro Light that is smouldering in the corner of his mouth. I am hoping that he has forgotten my slapstick routine, when he sat and watched me chase Gaston around his field, all those moons ago. But from the way he grins and nods when our eyes meet, I fear that the memory must still be giving him a tickle of pleasure.

Just four of us are here, this grey morning, at the start of two days of shearing: Young Boulesteix; Old Hubert, sturdy as a hay-cart, leaning on his crook; Gilles, looking more morose than I have seen him since Josette's accident; and me, the funny Englishman, in an embarrassingly white T-shirt which will be spinach-green by the end of the day. Big Leif has been laid low by a swollen disc in his spine, so will not be joining us, after all.

And so we begin. Shearers like to work in pairs, each cheered by the knowledge that someone else's legs and back are aching at least as much as their own. But the work is drying up, so today Young Boulesteix will be shearing alone. Hubert drags each sheep towards me with his crook. All I have to do is flip the animal over and sit it on its haunches, before hauling it into the barber's chair.

For the first thirty sheep or so, this feels as easy as flipping crêpes.

By the time we have done all seventy sheep in the first batch, my left wrist is already beginning to throb. I feel as if I have been using it to beat ostrich eggs into stiff peaks for several hours.

By the hundred-mark, I am thinking about asking for an off-games chit from matron.

Yet retiring hurt would be a slur on *Angleterre*. Boulesteix is the one who's doing all the work, after all, and it is only eight weeks since he broke his wrist, as testified by the sodden grey hankie still bound tightly around the joint. I'll bet his is hurting a lot more than mine. And besides: I have to justify my promotion.

Behind me, a ewe who must be the queen of the flock has been watching the proceedings as calmly as a grandma at a cricket match.

'Shall I catch that one next?' I murmur to Hubert.

'*Ah, oui, elle est tranquille*,' he grunts, glancing at Gilles with the flicker of a smile.

Turning, I grab the hefty sheep around the neck, pass quickly behind her, and flip her on to her rump. That's the theory, anyway. But before I can lift her hind legs from under her, she starts wildly galloping them, like a motorcyclist doing a wheelie on the spot, in a cloud of smoke and burning rubber.

I am still doing my best to hold on to the flailing mass of flesh and fleece when Grandma achieves traction. A split second later, and the old girl's off, scarpering into the heart of the flock. And I am still hanging on. Sheep are strong when they are frightened – and men are weak when they are laughing. I cannot explain quite *why* I am laughing. There is nothing funny about public humiliation, after all. But with uncharacteristic self-awareness, standing outside myself as if I were watching a character on a stage, perhaps I can see how utterly ridiculous I must look.

I am an ant clinging to a powder-puff as we hurtle into the braying melee. And then Grandma tosses her head, striking me two sharp uppercuts – bright light! bright light! – with her granite skull, and I think she may have broken my jaw.

Now I find myself hanging underneath the sheep, like Odysseus attempting to sneak past Polyphemus. Unfortunately, there are so many braying beasts pressing all around us that this is more like trying to hide beneath a Morris Minor going round Hyde Park Corner in the rush hour.

Still clinging to Grandma, I stagger to my feet. As I do so, I hear a roaring noise: concussion, perhaps? No, it is Hubert, the human hay-cart, leaning on the oak pillar at the centre of the barn, and laughing so much that dust is falling from the roof. I am laughing through the stars, too, though I dare not look at Gilles.

'*Je m'excuse*, Michael,' says Hubert, kindly, as he helps me to set up the sheep in front of Boulesteix. 'But one always laughs at the *malheurs* of others.'

'*Ah, oui*,' I reply, lost for words. Pétrus, my Marmite mate who grew up in Maida Vale, once told me that the difference between French and English humour is that the French like to laugh at other people, whereas we English are happiest laughing at ourselves. I do not know if this is true. But I do know that – whilst I feel sheepish at the thought that Gilles has promoted me way beyond my level of incompetence – I feel strangely reassured, too, by the timeless ability of beasts to make fools of men.

There are British storms. There are French storms. And then there are the kind of witches-on-the-heath, flash-bang-walloping cataclysms favoured by second-rate horror movies, in which our hero staggers towards a wind-machine that is spewing out Force Nine on the Beaufort scale, navvies just off camera hurl buckets of water over him, the sound-man shakes a sheet of zinc the size of my barn doors, and the streetlamps in neighbouring towns are made to flicker by a drunken electrician holding a frayed electrical flex in each charred hand.

That is what last night's storm was like in Jolibois, after the first day of Gilles's sheep-shearing. Graves opened. Grown men wept. Only Alice remained calm, lying on the cold stone floor of the winter sitting-room beside Digby, stroking his head and whispering stories about the Baltimore Orioles, his favourite baseball team, to keep him calm.

At 3 am, there is a crash like the sound of Hubert the hay-cart falling through a greenhouse. The chimney must have come down. I stumble outside in my waterproofs to investigate, and stand motionless at the sight that confronts me. It is worse than I feared. The chimney is still standing. But the old box tree has been hit. The gnarled, ivy-covered trunk is splintered like a snapped twig. The upper part, carried on the wind, has smashed down through the windscreen of the old Renault 19 I bought for Alice to drive, and is now sticking out of the car like a giant plant in a novelty pot. I stare at the decapitated trunk of my old friend, silhouetted against the flashing sky, while the rain streams down my face.

The earth and rubble I had laboriously spread on the steepest section of the drive last week, in an attempt to fill in the lunar craters, have all been washed away. So I shall have to start again.

But the shearing must go on. And so, with that dull grogginess of head and limb that follows a sleepless night, I head off once again to Gilles's barn in the Espace, its tyres throwing up sheets of standing water on every bend.

When I arrive, things are not looking good. I was hoping we might have a few reinforcements this morning; substitutes racing on to the pitch with fresh legs, to inject a little energy and pace. Yet the same three weary handshakes greet me as I climb over the gate into the sheep-filled barn: Gilles himself, still stroking his beard; Hubert the hay-cart, with his face like the Pyrenees; and Young Boulesteix, my neighbour, puffing furiously on another Marlboro Light. This is his first season as a full-time shearer and, from the way he stomps around the barn like Douglas Bader, I can see that his legs are already shot.

I can also see that he does not want to start. None of us does. With only one stiff shearer, today is going to be a long, long day. But at last Boulesteix takes a final drag on his cigarette, jerks the cord on his Lister, making it buzz into life, and nods for his first victim. Hubert hooks the beast with his crook, I heave it on to its haunches, and Gilles – overseeing this last gasp of his life's career – prepares to gather up the greasy fleeces once again.

The air hangs heavy in the shearing-barn, the buzz of the Lister mingling with the baying of the sheep and the cursing of Boulesteix as he sweats and grapples with beast after beast.

'*Putain!*' he roars, as yet another fractious ewe struggles from his grasp. 'Will there be a single one that doesn't fight?'

'It must be the storm,' says Gilles, gently. 'They're stressed.' I nod, and look away.

Boulesteix keeps asking what the weather is doing outside: have the storm-clouds returned? No one in his right mind will shear in a thunderstorm; it is too risky.

'I'll just do one more,' he says. But with a deep and distant rumble, the thunder begins, and Gilles warns him to switch off his machine.

'*Excusez-moi,*' says Hubert, with an apologetic shrug.

'*Quoi?*' asks Gilles.

'I think it's the pills I'm taking,' murmurs Hubert, with a beatific grin. And then with a sound like the Soup Dragon clearing her throat, or mashed potato being shot from a Bofors gun, he lets rip another one.

'*Nom de Dieu!*' exclaims Gilles, a great beam of mirth spreading from cheek to cheek. 'What on earth did you eat last night?' He has a point, too. There are certain clod-snorting, bellows-rending thunderblasts that just make you fear for a chap's safety.

'Look, has the storm come or not?' demands Boulesteix, glancing at each of them in turn.

'*Non*,' says Hubert, indignantly.

'*Si!*' insists Gilles, jabbing him in the ribs.

'Yours are worse,' mutters Hubert, under his breath. The two old friends beam at each other.

'What's so funny?' asks Boulesteix, glaring at the three of us.

I'm sorry: it may be very childish of me, but there is just something deeply hilarious – and strangely life-affirming – about watching a pair of old French shepherds joshing about each other's farts in the middle of a thunderstorm.

Outside, the thunder and lightning begin in earnest, and we stand and watch the rain pelt down. But everyone is cheerier now. The heavy mood is broken. We shall find a way through this long day, after all.

The storm abates, and the rain stops. Boulesteix is just reaching up to restart the Lister when a last, mighty thunderclap rends the silence.

'Sorry,' says Hubert, with a polite cough. 'That's definitely the last one.'

Getting married in France is, I am fast discovering, not for the faint-hearted. It helps that Alice and I do actually live in Jolibois because, for the local *Mairie* to agree to a marriage, we have to prove that at least one of us has been resident in the commune for a minimum of forty days. And the first document to be signed – the so-called *Attestation sur l'Honneur* – promises six months in prison for anyone who pretends to be living in St Tropez when really they're living in Basingstoke, despite the fact that this is obviously a very easy mistake to make.

I suppose that, like Obélix falling into the magic potion as a baby, the French become immune to superfluous bureaucracy in childhood, just as they grow used to those exercise books with far too many lines in them.

The mandatory visit to the doctor for a medical certificate, followed by blood tests for syphilis and other diseases popular in the Napoleonic era, are merely the start of it. By some patriarchal anachronism, only women are legally obliged to undergo these various blood tests, although Dr Vaux, our lady *médecin*, is having none of this.

'It is an outdated law,' she snorts. 'And besides: you, *monsieur*, will want to show some solidarity with your fiancée, won't you?' she says, briskly filling in the form before I can formulate a reply to what was, I sense, not really a question at all. It is quite obvious that Dr Vaux has no idea just how badly the combination of needles and white coats gives me the willies.

Alice and I must also each provide an original birth certificate translated into French by an officially designated translator. Just to stop boringly organized people doing too much in advance, these must be dated no more than three months before the marriage. Never mind that one of the characteristics of a birth certificate is that it does not tend to change very markedly from day to day or year to year.

Then there must be a copy of our passports. And a copy of the passports of each of the four people who will be witnesses at the civil wedding, along with their addresses, occupations, inside-leg measurements, and so on.

After this, there are the two pairs of certificates – a *certificat de célibat* and a *certificat de coutume* for each of us – which Madame Lemuel, the fearsomely efficient lady who runs the *Mairie*, tells us we should be able to get from our local authority in Britain.

To my surprise, the woman I phone at Southwark Council seems to think she can help with the certificates and says that I am welcome to come in for an interview. Except that they don't have any appointments available for the next few months.

Good news comes a few days later, however, when it emerges that the website of the British Embassy in Paris provides the *certificat de célibat* as a free download. Rule Britannia! This admirable document states, beneath an emphatic royal crest, that there is no such thing as a certificate of celibacy under British law.

And so it goes on. I do not mind having to hurdle all these gates. If we wish to marry in France, we must expect to do things the French way, after all. And there is something reassuring about the thick folder of forms and certificates we are beginning to amass; a grim satisfaction, as we emerge from the labyrinth, in looking back upon what we have endured. I suppose this is why Alice keeps all her old essays from nursing, even though she will never read them again. And I see a kind of cold beauty in the rigour of it all, when each completed form, each box ticked, takes us another step closer to being wed.

All we have to do now is find a church, someone willing to marry us, and then somewhere lovely to have a bunfight afterwards.

Alice – who enjoys being the centre of attention almost as much as she enjoys the crunching of Cat munching mouse-skulls and lizards beneath the breakfast table – is adamant that the wedding should be family only. But, thanks to the breeding habits of her clan, this means that we are already up to fifty guests before we have even started. As for me, I do not mind how many people come, just so long as I do not have to play the organ.

A glossy pile of scary wedding magazines mysteriously appears on the kitchen table and, together, Alice and I talk about the best weddings we have known. As far as I can see, what they all had in common was very simple: the bride and groom were palpably in love, well matched and really wanted to marry each other. Compared with this, it really doesn't seem to matter very much how the napkins are folded.

But there is a place that touched me, not so long ago. An

old stone barn where, even as I sat amid a scene of joshing conviviality, embarrassed at having no manly pocket-knife with which to slice my *saucisson*, I gazed up at the great beams of dusty oak supporting the roof and thought what an ideal place it would make for someone's wedding. I just never quite imagined it might be mine.

So I take Alice to meet my friend Maurice, up at the big chateau where the hare-hunt was held all those months ago. He leads us past the old stone fountain and out across the grass, where the huntsmen belched their brassy triplets from their coiled horns of black and gold. And then we tiptoe into the stillness of the ancient barn, and stand in silence, all at sea in the soaring space.

'The cracks in the walls, we can fix,' says Maurice, in English, expressing his embarrassment with a dip of his head.

'Oh, please don't,' says Alice, speaking for us both. 'The cracks are the best bit.'

Next, leaving Alice to concentrate upon finding a florist and The Dress, I drive down to Jolibois to visit Raphaël the priest, to ask if he is allowed to marry us. And, if not, whether he might let us use one of his Catholic churches for an Anglican wedding.

I like to think I have a bit of an understanding with Raphaël. Both of us are reformed townies, after all. He now keeps cows and grows raspberries; I do the same thing with weeds and very small sheep. I also like the way that he knows that I know that he knows I was brought up an unwashed Anglican, yet still happily allows me to accompany the Catholic Mass in the churches of his parish, only occasionally ticking me off for falling short.

Unfortunately, this is one of those occasions. We have only just sat down in the shadows of his *presbytère*, overlooking the roofs of the disused tanning factories by the river, when Raphaël starts wagging his finger at me.

'The Mass must not be made to wait,' he declares.

I know immediately what he is talking about. During last Saturday's Mass, I got myself trapped in the middle of a Karg-Elert chorale prelude at the end of the *Offertoire*, and took for ever to improvise my way towards a clumsy coda. Faced with this situation in England, your average patient vicar would wait. But Raphaël cut me off with his microphone before I could reach the final chord. 'It is the organist who follows the liturgy,' he continues, 'not the other way round.'

'*Ah, oui, bien sûr, mais . . .*'

'No exceptions,' he says.

Raphaël is, I have to say, fairly hard-core. What he really longs for, he says, is a choir of true believers, because he is convinced they would make a more beautiful sound than a choir full of infidels. Nevertheless, I have promised Alice that I will ask him about marrying us. As I do so, I feel as if I am in a Lancaster bomber, roaring across a lake at tree-top height, lining up on the watch-towers of a dam. Steady, skipper, steady . . .

'I was just wondering if you might be willing to marry Alice and me, even though neither of us is Catholic,' I tell him, wringing my hands. 'Being the deputy organist, and everything.' Bombs gone, skipper.

Raphaël's eyes widen, and a bottomless silence yawns between us for what feels a whole lot longer than a Karg-Elert chorale prelude. I squirm in my chair, sensing the bomb bouncing across the still waters of the lake.

'I shall put it to the bishop,' he says at last.

'You don't mind my having asked?' I scan the dam for traces of the blast, but my bomb must have failed to detonate.

'*Pas du tout*,' laughs Raphaël. '*C'est une question très intéressante.*'

Relieved, I limp back to base, to fly another day. Raphaël

may not have said *oui*, but he did not shoot me down in flames, either.

In my old, single life, the summers at La Folie would drift by as slowly as Cleopatra's barge, burnished and glowing in the sun. Yet now that a wedding is in the offing, everything is in a hurry: the weeks are unwilling conscripts on a forced march, struggling to get their feet in line. And even the *potager* has succumbed to the encroaching stress.

Gone are the days when I thought that growing vegetables was a tranquil business; gone, my illusions of the *potager* as a place of refuge, where a chap could plant his shallots and weed his aubergines in peace. No, today I have donned my tin hat, and my mattock is at the ready. For an invader is in our midst, sneaking past me while my back was turned and my nose was buried in bureaucracy at the *Mairie*.

And who is my enemy? Only the dreaded *doryphore*, that's who, otherwise known as the ten-striped spearman, *Leptinotarsa decemlineata*, or – more commonly – the Colorado beetle.

I know this doesn't sound like much, compared with facing a Napoleonic blood test for syphilis, coming *this* close to flying a Spitfire, and trying to find 140 chairs and some-one to do simple flowers for a French wedding, when chairs are scarce and the florists of Jolibois are all in the grip of neo-Modernism, shrinking in horror from such banned words as *rustique*, *simple* and *naturel*. But just now, in the midst of the biggest life-change I have known since I was born, I can think of little else. Squirmy brown beetle larvae fill my dreams. My every waking nightmare is of massed baked beans with legs.

Nor am I alone. At the tennis club, I hear Jean-Michel and Le Grand Mermoz worriedly whispering about the arrival of *les doryphores* as if they were the secret police or an unwashed punk band from Lille. Marie, too, in the *boulangerie*. I heard people having these same conversations last June, and I suppose I was complacent. It was my first season as a potato-grower, and only a few *doryphores*, cruising the neighbourhood, had discovered my virgin *potager*.

I really couldn't see what all the fuss was about. Fully grown, the cream-and-black beetle is a handsome little fellow, whose striped glossiness makes one think of a well-sucked mint humbug, or an ice-hockey referee who has spilt tea down his front. His scarab-shaped carapace is about the size of one of Alice's delicate fingertips. The underside is a glossy mahogany, with six legs partially tucked up inside, like poor Meg when she died, or the undercarriage of a Dakota.

*Les doryphores* – more crawly than creepy – did no obvious damage to my last year's crop. I simply picked off the intruders with my fingers, and then sprayed all the plants with an organic potion to discourage repeat offenders. It never dawned on me that these chaps might tell their friends, nor that the friends would tell *their* friends, just as the old farmer who waves at the pair of friendly hippies driving a caravan into his field has no conception of the drug-fuelled rave they are about to ignite.

Now, however, the cataclysm is upon me. Each day, another phalanx of beetles crawls up out of the earth to lay their eggs. For the first time, I understand what the French must feel when they see another wave of *Anglais* emerging from the Ryanair flight at Limoges. Every female Colorado beetle can lay eight hundred eggs at a time, three times a year. By my calculations, that means that I could have 128 million insects munching away before we are married.

Each morning, Digby and I stride out to my 120 potato plants and, while he helps by barking like a crow-scarer just outside the gate, I begin the grim work of picking the adult beetles off the leaves, crushing them between two stones. I cannot bring myself to do this with my bare hands, as Gilles and Monsieur Jadot do. Then I check carefully under each leaf, looking for the tell-tale clusters of bright yellow eggs, which – holding my breath – I squish with my fingertips. Sometimes I am too late, and every stem and leaf of the plant is already dotted with red-brown blobs, each of which – out, vile jelly – must be individually squashed.

I can see why Britain jealously protects its status as a *doryphore*-free zone. The entire European population of Colorado beetles grew out of a handful of stowaways which arrived in Bordeaux from America in 1919, over-paid, over-sexed and over here. Their impact makes me feel relieved that our own American import, the Baltimore Bullet, was neutered as a puppy. One Digby is, I feel, quite enough for France.

There are many good things about getting married. Friends from my past life, whom I think about often yet have not seen for years, will at last be parachuting into my present life to help us celebrate. A beautiful woman with a dimpled smile sends me to London, with instructions to buy myself a beautiful waistcoat from the Burlington Arcade. And, best of all, I shall finally get to participate in a wedding without playing the organ.

To be fair, one of the loveliest things about playing the organ is being invited to play at friends' weddings. This month alone, I have been losing sleep over an English one, near Carcassonne, and a French one, near Orléans. This is a blessing, for it stops me losing sleep over our own nuptials, now only weeks away. It is not the getting married that worries me. It is whether we shall have to eat standing up, after I cunningly forgot to order any chairs before they were all booked up for village feasts and the kind of *soirée dansante* where everyone knows the paso doble except me.

My parents have heroically agreed to drive down and look

after Digby and the rest of the food-chain at La Folie while we are away. They look stunned at the change wrought by the earthworks, as they stiffly climb out of their car.

'I know you said it was pretty extreme,' says my father, gazing at the wide-open space that has replaced the rough alley, bounded with Christmas trees, that used to lie in front of the house. 'But I assumed you were exaggerating.'

'I think it's lovely,' adds my mum quickly, cutting him off before he can say more. 'I see you've kept what's left of the box tree. And there's so much more light. And room to turn the car round, and everything. Just look at the view.'

They have arrived laden with gifts and sausages and a huge pile of press releases addressed to the old Michael Wright – the shallow, critical one, who used to write about music and dance and theatre, before he started squashing beetles from dawn till dusk.

My mother has also brought the usual food parcel of PG Tips and Marmite, along with a couple of tins of Branston baked beans which she thought I might like to try, as a change from Heinz. Under normal circumstances, I might. But when Alice pours the gleaming, slithering mass of beans into a pan a few days later, I am disturbed to find myself checking to see if they have legs.

I always love it when my parents visit La Folie, but it feels particularly special now that Alice is here. They have met once before, and I watch her charming them again with her easy chatter and her readiness to laugh. Tongue-tied shyness is what they always dread in others; afraid, perhaps, to catch themselves reflected there. Animated poise is what they adore, and the tinkling laughter of a beautiful young woman so comfortable in her own skin that she helps theirs to feel less scratchy for a while.

It feels good to see my parents let their guards down and relax; to glimpse the smiles they exchange when Alice brings a perfect chicken-and-leek pie to the kitchen table, or when she describes the Landmark Trust houses in which she holidayed as a child, and it turns out that they, too, have stayed in Tixall Gatehouse and would love to try Fort Clonque. Sometimes parents like playing Snap as much as children do.

I do not need to ask what Mum and Dad think of Digby. I can see it in the way they glance at each other for re-assurance whenever he bounds into the house from outside, his jowls green with tell-tale smears of sheep poo, and jumps up to slick their flinching faces with one of his sloppy-tongued greetings. The door of my dad's Volvo bears the mark of the beast: two sets of four vertical scratches etched into the paintwork, from where Digby came to say hello when they first arrived. They lend us this car now for our long drive down to Carcassonne, because it has air-conditioning, and does not smell of dead dog.

The Carcassonne wedding is special to me, because the bride, Alix, happens to be the grown-up version of one of the two little girls whom – twenty-odd years ago – I tutored in Maths and Latin at an old wooden table beside a swimming pool not far from Toulouse.

Sometimes I even wonder if I would ever have searched for La Folie, had I not spent that idyllic fortnight in the French countryside with my friend Jon, teaching *hic haec hoc* to Alix and Sarah on a shaded terrace in the mornings, discovering the pleasures of fresh sardines and local cheeses at lunchtimes, and cycling, wobbly with wine, along sun-bleached roads through avenues of poplars in the afternoons.

I am reminded of that youthful delight today, as Alice and I drive down to Carcassonne, the earth becoming redder, the cows paler and the light more brilliant the further south we go. But I begin to feel jittery with nerves when we step out of the oven outdoors and I lug my electronic keyboard into the cool of Camon's beautiful twelfth-century abbey for the rehearsal. Everything here feels much grander than I was expecting. The air in the silent church is thick with stress. And this will be me and Alice in a few weeks' time.

Suddenly, from behind me, I hear a woman's voice whispering my name. 'Mike?'

Turning, I come face to face with a tanned and imposingly beautiful creature in a jaunty green dress and heavy-framed specs, grinning nervously at me as if she had just pranged my car.

'Sarah?' I gamble. Is this really the stern, thirteen-year-old stripling who forced me to brush up on my trigonometry?

'And you must be Alice,' she says, clapping her hands and hugging her like an old friend. 'Alix and I are *so* pleased for you both.' I blink as Sarah hugs me, too. Her smile is green and red and yellow and purple and white, as a thin shaft of multicoloured sunshine slices through the stained-glass window above our heads, and the abbey seems less forbidding than it did a second ago.

'I can't *believe* you're getting married,' she tells me, in a stage whisper, as she drags us both by the hand to sit with her in a pew in one of the transepts. 'I thought you swore you never would.'

'That was before I found Alice again,' I laugh.

'You mean you knew each other before?'

'It's a long story,' I reply, giving Alice's hand a squeeze.

The more I absorb of the hushed, ornate ambience of the ancient abbey, the more I have a nasty feeling that the full-gospel-welly arrangement of 'Amazing Grace' I have practised for the service could be a horrible mistake. I must remember to ask the bride what she thinks. And whilst I knew I'd have to accompany a couple of soloists, I had no idea that one of them would be a professional tenor with a distinguished international career. I feel a bit like an old donkey in a straw hat on Blackpool beach, informed that Frankie Dettori will be my jockey in the next race. From behind my music stand, I glance at Alice, who is sitting with

Sarah at the back of the church, and give her a little wave. She waves and smiles back at me, like a sunbather on a beach, not guessing that the man waving at her from the water is in fact drowning.

'Would you like to try that again?' murmurs Ted, pressing his palms together as if in prayer, after I have just made the opening bars of his beloved Donizetti sound more like Donny Osmond. 'I'm so sorry,' I stammer. 'I'll do better tomorrow.'

'Yes, that would be good,' says Ted, raising his eyes to the ceiling.

And then he begins to sing. And as the first notes of '*Una furtiva lagrima*' float up into the lofty recesses of the crumbling abbey, and the sun shimmers through the stained glass, and the ladies doing the flowers stiffen into awestruck statues, and I can sense Alice sitting very wide-eyed and still at the back of the church, I am torn between feeling transfixed by the weird beauty of this moment – two Englishmen making Italian music in a French church, in preparation for the wedding of a child I once knew – and utterly unworthy of it, too, my fingers fumbling over the keys while Ted's voice somehow makes the thickened air of the darkened abbey seem to sway with rapture.

Though Ted's wedding-day performance is perfect, it is the memory of our rehearsal that I shall treasure. 'Amazing Grace' is another matter. As we reach the end of the first verse, with the congregation droning away, I make a fateful decision. Carried away by the excitement of the occasion, I hit the 'Gospel Organ' pre-set on my keyboard, whack the volume up to max, hold my breath, and stab the next few blues-style chords as if we were in Memphis.

The congregation's response to this is immediate and overwhelming: there is an appalled silence, as if I had just wheeled a barrel-organ into the British Library. No one sings a note. Out of the corner of my eye, I see Sarah and Alix's old and distinguished father, a former clerk to the House of Lords, turn and stare at me, eyebrows raised, head tilted forward in disbelief. As I cringe, my mind racing with adrenaline, it dawns on me that I never did ask Alix what she thought about souping-up the hymn.

Then, suddenly, from behind me, comes a trumpet-like sound; a burnished war-cry that sends tingles down my spine. Don't look now, but it's Ted. And his voice is on fire. As his blazing tenor fills the air, I sense the grinning souls in front of me beginning to latch on, like Lilliputians clinging to Gulliver, until they are all bellowing out the words with a lusty riotousness that takes me by surprise. Here, in this holy French place, I cannot help feeling a wholly English pride at the glorious din my countrymen are making. And no one more so than the former clerk to the House of Lords, who is singing his heart out.

Afterwards, I glance across at Alix, nervous at having lowered the tone of her special day. And I feel at once deeply impressed and inexplicably sad. Impressed, because the little girl I once taught, now a poised and beautiful woman, has the presence and kindness, in the midst of her own wedding, to give the poor old organist a thumbs-up and a smile. And sad, because it is a smile I remember from a world I still miss, as we sat at an old wooden table in France, on a summer's day just like today.

A day after this English wedding comes a French one. So Alice and I are back on the autoroute, this time heading north towards Orléans for the marriage of Roman and Sophie, the young couple I met at Arlette's house over dinner eighteen months ago. I promised to play the organ for them, after Roman promised to introduce me to some of the single women of Poitiers. Thank goodness Alice saved us both – and the good women of Poitiers – from his having to carry out his side of the bargain.

Ninety minutes before the wedding, having left Alice at the *chambres d'hôtes* where we will be spending the night, I sprint into the church. I should be just in time for a rehearsal with the young *animateur* who is to lead the singing. Yet as my eyes adjust to the darkness, I see that it is deserted. Have I come to the right place? True, there are a couple of lavish arrangements of white flowers on pedestals, but this doesn't mean a thing, since churches all over France boast such displays, as unwithering in their decorousness as smart French ladies of a certain age. I squeeze a petal. Ah, not silk or plastic: so this must be the place for the wedding, after all.

I wait. And then I wait some more. Suddenly the doors of the church fly open.

'*Je suis désolé*,' pants a young man in a silk suit, galloping up the aisle towards me.

'*Ah, ce n'est pas grave*,' I lie, guessing from his haunted appearance that this must be the *animateur*, whose job is to sing lustily and make sure that everyone comes in on time. The omens, thus far, are not promising.

We have about twenty different pieces of music to rehearse, and – I glance at my watch – at least five minutes in which to practise them. So Guillaume and I do the only decent thing under the circumstances: we panic. He sprints around the church, hunting for the microphone, while I – fingers trembling with adrenaline – attempt to familiarize myself with the single manual of the tiny English pipe-organ that sits up near the altar.

It would help if I could switch the blasted thing on. Never mind that it was built in 1789 and boasts ivory stop-knobs yellowed with time and the clammy hands of myriad other nervous organists on myriad other wedding days; never mind that each stop-knob bears the beautiful copperplate script of a John Russell who built the thing more than two hundred years ago: it still needs juice. There is no longer a handle for a half-drunk bellows-boy to pump for his thruppence. We need electricity, and I cannot for the life of me see how to plug the thing in.

As if by magic, Peter Viola appears, with his wife June beside him. My old friend has a habit, like the shopkeeper in *Mr Benn*, of turning up just in the nick of time.

'You look smart,' I blurt, hastily shaking hands. I have never seen Peter in a suit before.

'And you look worried,' he replies, with a wink. 'Can I help?'

So I tell him how I cannot find the power switch for the organ. Peter looks across at his wife, and gives her a nudge. June walks forward, shuts her eyes and then points at a small wooden panel that I have failed to spot on the side of the organ case. 'There it is,' she shrugs. Peter opens the panel and flicks the switch.

'Thank you,' I gasp, my mouth open, as the organ-bellows begin to hiss into action.

'That's my girl,' he says, with a proud smile at June.

Thankfully, my musical duties are simplified by the fact that Sophie – like many French brides – has decided to come in and go out to the accompaniment of pop music on CD. So it is a bit of a blow when, just as everyone stands for her arrival, a handsome young man – even more panicked than Guillaume – comes dashing up to me.

'The CD player hasn't arrived,' he blurts. 'Can you play Enya?'

My mouth opens in a silent scream. Helpless to help, I shake my head.

'Well, can you play . . . *n'importe quoi?*'

I nod, my mind racing. I just hope that *n'importe quoi* is what I think it is, and not a well-known ballad by Johnny Hallyday.

Seconds later, we are all saved, as yet another young man comes sprinting down the aisle, with a large black box held high above his head like a tray of burnt cakes. And, in defiance of every known law of nature, it is almost a relief to hear Enya's floaty swirl echoing through the church.

The next two hours – French weddings last longer than some marriages – pass in a blur of feverish concentration for me and Guillaume, and in floods of tears for Sophie's family. I just hope this is not because of my organ-playing.

And then it is over, and at nightfall Alice and I are sitting for dinner in a candle-lit marquee big enough for the Russian State Circus, on the front lawn of a moated chateau which is the groom's family seat.

Arlette, Roman's mother, appears, her face crinkled into the happy-sad smile of a mother who is letting go of her son to a woman whom she loves. I stand, we kiss, and I introduce her to Alice.

'I'm so sorry you didn't manage to find *une Française*,' she tells me, holding both of our hands as she gazes into my eyes. 'But I think Alice is much better for you.'

Later, leaving Alice deep in conversation with Peter Viola, I excuse myself and carry my glass of wine outside, standing for a moment to gaze at the chateau's lit-up façade reflected in the moat beneath. And then I wander away, towards the huge trees on the edge of the forest, and turn to see the marquee's translucent canvas glowing deep orange, as if it were a beautiful hot-air balloon about to take off into the night.

It is cool out here, and I feel more at home with these big trees than with the hubbub inside the marquee. I am better off on the outside, I think to myself, as I listen to the hum of conversation filtering from within. I know I shall always be on the outside, in some sense, if Alice and I continue to live here in France. And yet, and yet, there is something beguilingly universal about that hum from within, which could as easily be English, or Colombian, or Malay.

Here I am at a glorious French wedding, surrounded by many people whom I count as friends, and accompanied by a wonderful woman who will soon be my wife. And – in a moment of recognition that must, in the end, be common to every exile – it dawns on me that I am almost beginning to feel that I belong.

Back at La Folie, my parents are preparing to leave. Usually this gives me the familiar back-to-school feeling; a heaviness in my heart. But not today. Today, my parents, too, seem unusually upbeat. This may be because they can finally say goodbye to Digby, despite his best attempts to leap into the back of the Volvo to accompany them. But I prefer to think it is because something has changed between us; a weight has been lifted; a hidden switch has been flicked.

I kiss my mum and hug my dad, who is taking some of the storm-sheared wood from the box tree with him. He says he cannot bear the thought of it being burnt or thrown away.

They can leave La Folie more lightly, now that Alice is here, than when I was here by myself. And I, in turn, do not feel that lump in my throat that is my usual response to the sound of my dad turning the key in the Volvo's ignition. Yes, I do feel a sadness. But it is the sadness of a child who has grown too big for his hobby-horse; too tall to play in the Wendy house any more. This weight in my chest is not at the fact of their going. It is because I am aware, for the first time in my life, that I can begin to let them go.

'Are you all right?' asks Alice, studying my face carefully, as I turn after shutting the front door.

'Yes, fine. Why?'

She reaches out and takes my hand, holding it between hers. 'It's always hard saying goodbye to parents.'

'Yes, and it's worse, the further apart you live.'

'Tell me about it,' she sighs. And then, brightening, adds, 'Do you think your mum likes me?'

'She says she thinks you're tough as old boots,' I reply,

laughing, putting my arms around her. 'And, believe me, coming from her, that's a compliment.'

Sensing our embrace, our friendly neighbourhood policeman comes trotting up from his bed and attempts to wedge his whiskery snout between us. And then, perhaps thinking better of it, he snorts and wanders away.

When Digby first arrived at La Folie, I worried how he would bear up under the strain of living in a foreign country. Both my mother and Alice's mother, on the other hand, worried about the cat, and sent us copious advice on how to avoid her being marginalized, psychologically tortured or murdered in her bed by the Beast of Baltimore. Yet, as I am still discovering, the very fact of living abroad creates bonds between the unlikeliest creatures.

With time, Cat and Dog are beginning to come to an uneasy truce. She has stopped cuffing Digby every time he saunters past one of her vantage points, and – in return – he has stopped attempting to sniff her bottom whenever her back is turned. It would be wrong to say that Cat and Digby are *friends*, exactly, but some of the looks she casts him could, in some lights, be deemed coquettish. And I have occasionally spied them touching noses, when they think no one is looking.

Today the house is feeling unusually empty, after my parents' departure. So it is a pleasure when Big Leif and Anna, the towering Dutch couple who live down by the level-crossing, drop in out of the blazing sunshine for a glass of wine. I feel like a Lilliputian as they bow their heads to fit through the front door and Leif grins down at me from somewhere beyond the troposphere. I remember from *Blue Peter* that pole-vaulting across canals is popular in Holland. Leif could do it without the pole.

'You've got a dog,' he announces, as Digby leaps up and imprints his muddy paws all over the front of Leif's perfectly pressed chinos.

'Enthusiastic dog,' yelps Anna, reaching behind her to extract Digby's nose.

'Sorry about him,' I reply. 'He's American.'

'Oh,' they both nod, uncertain how to respond.

'How's your back, Leif?'

'Much better, thanks, although I still have to lie down in the car.' He rubs his lumbar region with both hands. 'I was sorry to miss the shearing.'

'We missed you, too,' I reply.

I like Leif and Anna. We appear to share the same cheerful stoicism that comes of having grown up beneath the iron-grey skies of Northern Europe; the same desire for a simple rural life that comes of having been frazzle-dazzled by London and Amsterdam respectively. Yet we are different enough, too. *Les Anglais* in Jolibois remind me, uncomfortably, of one of those fitting-rooms that has a mirror on every wall.

Digby appears to like Leif and Anna, too. And when they stride off home like a pair of Giacomettis, he begins to follow them down the drive.

'Do you think you ought to call your dog?' asks Leif.

'No, you're welcome to him,' I joke. 'He's obviously hoping for a better life.' Digby never ventures beyond the gates of La Folie, so he will not follow them far.

Several hours after they have left, Alice comes to find me in the barn.

'Something's wrong with Cat,' she says. 'She just keeps yowling at me, then dashing out of her cat-flap, before coming back to yowl at me some more.'

'Where's Digby?'

'I thought he was out here with you.'

I shake my head. 'He's probably up behind the house, barking at the sheep.'

But Digby is not behind the house, nor in any of his usual haunts. He is not in the side field, where he sometimes goes to smell the smells. He is not rooting for rotten vegetables in the compost heap, nor searching the chicken house for eggs. He has vanished.

Suddenly the cat skids into the barn and starts clawing at my trouser-legs, growling with angst.

'What is it, Cat?' I ask, following her out of the barn.

In the dusk, we stand and listen. All I can hear is the white noise of the river at the bottom of the hill, like the hiss of an intercom; the reedy screeches of the buzzards; the faint barking of a dog on a distant farm.

Next moment, I am running down the drive towards the river, my clod-hopping, cracked-leather boots hammering on the track. After four hundred metres, I stop to tie up my flying bootlaces and listen.

The barking is closer now. And there is another sound, too: the mewling of a cat.

Turning my head, I glimpse Cat scampering after me, her eyes glittering. I have never seen her so far from the house before.

'All right, Lassie,' I pant. 'You can come, too.'

Digby must have followed Leif and Anna. In the distance, I can hear a train coming. At the road, I turn left to race along the river-bank beside the railway line, following the yelping anguish. He must be here somewhere; trapped, perhaps. Now the bells of the level-crossing are ringing, and still no sign of Digby.

A shriek of metal grinding upon metal, and the train thunders past. And there is Digby: standing knee-deep in the freezing waters of the river; shivering, panicking, barking his head off.

'Come on, Digby,' I call. 'Let's go home.'

But Digby cannot hear me. Wild-eyed and grey with cold, he is far too busy yelling at the sky.

Again, I shout, 'Digby, it's me!'

Now he turns his head, still barking, lost in his private terror, looking right through me.

There is only one thing for it. I must use the spell. I must speak the dread words only to be uttered in the most desperate circumstances, when nothing but the most primeval magic will work upon the canine soul.

'Digby,' I cry. 'Digby, do you want a *biscuit*?'

Suddenly the liquorice-black jowls hang lank. The sky is silent at last. For a split second he stares at me, a question on his lips. And then he is careering straight for me, like a locked-on missile.

As we race, side by side, up the drive, we are met by a welcoming committee of one: Cat, waiting anxiously at the top of the avenue of trees, her fur electrified at the sight of the approaching projectile.

As he passes, I see her cuff Digby with a clawed paw. 'Don't you *dare* do that again', this seems to say. Either that, or else it is intended to stop me thinking that Cat has gone soft over a dog.

Next day, when I come downstairs, someone has left a dead mouse in Digby's bed.

# 23

## JULY

Suddenly everything is happening at once. I know this is my own fault. I have approximately 279 pressing things to do, yet still spend far too much of my time just gazing out over the valley, thinking about how spiffing life is, how spiffing Alice is, and how even more spiffing it all will be when she and I are finally married. Not because this will change the way we think about each other, but because it will be a celebration of the fact that we do not have to worry about the wedding any more.

In the meantime, I feel like some end-of-the-pier plate-spinner, fatally distracted by his glamorous assistant, turning round to find every single one of his plates on the point of wobbling off their poles.

How people with proper jobs find time to fit everything in, I cannot imagine. People with children, ditto. Even without a wedding to plan, I could have a busy life just doing all the incidentals that fall through the gaps: squishing *doryphores*; mucking out the chickens; cleaning my plane; discussing the sheep with Gilles; doing the washing-up at least once a week.

Admittedly, my inherited tendency to down tools for a

drink at six o'clock sharp does tend to shorten the day more than is strictly necessary, especially now that I can spin out the pause even longer with Alice as my co-conspirator. But I would not say I was *lazy*, exactly. I just think that – like most men – I am easily distracted.

There is always something more important to do, just when one is about to settle down to the thing one has been meaning to do for days, especially if that thing involves putting up shelves or any variation on a theme of tidying up. And the more pressing the deadline, the more tempting becomes the activity chosen to displace it. It is always when I have something that simply will not wait that I remember that there are nettles behind the house which urgently need to be cut down.

With the wedding to organize, and about a hundred guests flying out from Blighty, it does not help that the Jolibois open tennis tournament has come round again. So my services as international cannon-fodder are required, just when the Jolibois Festival, of which I have risen to the giddy heights of *secrétaire adjoint*, is about to start.

In the midst of everything else, Alice is about to fly off to California for two weeks to complete her flying training, and I am beginning to feel quite whimbly – her word – at the thought. I feel for her, having to be there, on the other side of the world, when I know she would rather be here. And it will be strange to be alone again myself.

At the start of my adventure at La Folie, many people told me how brave I was, to come and live in France all by myself. And sometimes – as I have chased down a ewe in a blizzard, or attempted to flirt in a foreign language – I have almost caught myself believing them.

But as anyone who has ever ventured abroad alone will know, the truth is that the solo traveller has a supreme advantage over those who travel in groups. Life feels lighter when nobody is depending on you – and uncharacteristically simple when there is no one else upon whom to rely.

It is always easier to approach a stranger and strike up a conversation when you are one, not two. From the outside, a couple is a closed, self-sufficient unit: two particles fused with an ionic bond. Whereas a single person walking into a bar is an atom fizzing with spare electrons in its outer shell, waiting to connect. So people talk to you. Few jokes begin with the words 'A couple walks into a bar . . .'

Being alone has forced me, time and again, to make an effort: to be the one who turns up at the club and asks, 'May I join in?' or walks into the church and asks 'May I play?' with one hopeful finger pointed at the organ-loft.

Brave? No, I do not think so. Not when the alternative was simply continuing in the old ways, getting and spending, watching myself waste my life. It is Alice who has been brave, for she is giving up far more than me, with none of the benefits of the solo traveller. Sometimes I do still wonder if Zumbach was right: that La Folie is no place for a woman.

Today, with Alice en route to California, I am flying solo myself once more, in the kitchen at La Folie. Almost, but not quite. For I still have Digby butting me with his wet snout, lobbying for a you-know-what. I cannot imagine why people will spend thirty quid an hour on a personal trainer, let alone invest in a rowing-machine, when a dog will happily do the same job for free.

Despite Digby's insistence, I can already detect a tantalizing whiff – the merest sniff – of my former life, when I lived in these old walls *tout seul*, trudging out to check on the sheep, and returning, time after time, to Cat and an empty house.

At first, I feel a guilty pleasure in rediscovering this feeling I had almost forgotten; that romantic sense of not knowing what comes next. There is a beauty in uncertainty, and in the world of possibilities that lies behind each new face and façade.

This excitement lasts for approximately five minutes. And then I find myself wishing that Alice were here. Her plane to Los Angeles will not even have landed yet. How quickly a person can get under your skin when you live in a submarine together, marooned at the end of the world. Living together is easy, when you are lucky enough to be with someone generous and open and happy in themselves. It is living alone that takes practice. And I appear to have lost the knack.

A few hours later, the phone rings, and I hear a female voice that I recognize but cannot place.

'Is that Michael?'

'Yes. Who is this?'

'Are you free to go flying the day after tomorrow?' says the voice.

'Well, I . . .'

'In the Spitfire,' says the voice.

'Just try and stop me,' I reply, feeling a whoosh of electricity shooting up my spine. What the hell I am going to do with Digby, with Alice still away, does not immediately spring to mind. But nothing, now, is going to come between me and my Spitfire dream. Even if I have to row the Baltimore Bullet across the Channel and carry him on my shoulders to Duxford, I'll be there.

Two days later, I am at Duxford once again, standing beside the gleaming form of Spitfire ML407, now insured by a new sponsor, as she points her nose purposefully at the sky. A real Spitfire, too. Not one of my Airfix models, painstakingly painted in Humbrol enamel by my dad, and then riddled with bullet-holes, using a hot needle, by me. Not one of the Spitfire silhouettes in the dog-eared aircraft-recognition book that my friend Davenport brought to school.

My whole body is smiling as Carolyn, ML407's owner and pilot, goes through the pre-flight briefing. *I am about to fly a Spitfire.* Past and future have become two cones, their opposed tips meeting in a single moment. My entire life is about to be funnelled through this one, brief encounter. What bothers me is whether I am humanly capable of absorbing it. The flight is supposed to last for only twenty minutes. And those twenty minutes have to last me for the rest of my life.

Suddenly I feel a hand on my shoulder, and feel the fingers digging in. Wrenching myself free, I spin on my heels and come face to face with Jethro in a khaki flying-suit, grinning from ear to ear as if he had just won a win-a-flight-in-a-Spitfire competition. Jethro, with whom I used to fly down for lunch at Compton Abbas, our planes in loose formation at a couple of thousand feet; or scudding low over the frothing waves off the isle of Sheppey; Jethro, with whom I would swan out across the Channel – my heart in my mouth – for *moules frites* in Le Touquet and home before dusk.

'Sorry to interrupt, ladies and gentlemen,' he says, twirling an imaginary moustache. 'I just wanted to shake this joker by the hand and wish him a pleasant flight, the lucky bugger.'

'It's brilliant to see you, Jez,' I tell him, giving him a hug. 'I'll see you later.'

'I'll be watching you,' he says. 'Look: I've brought my video camera and all.'

'You're great. Sorry, Carolyn. Where were we?'

And then she invites me to climb up on to the Spitfire's wing. I take a deep breath, haul myself up, and I am there, standing beside Douglas Bader and Johnny Johnson and the rest, as they prepare to take off on another sortie. My skin tingles as I lean into the Spitfire's cockpit. For now I am gazing through a prism into the 1940s. Every edge and dial and detail stands out in sharp relief before my eyes, as I feed hungrily on the cold beauty of this miracle machine. My breathing is calm. My mind is clear. I am present as I have never been before. Quietly and methodically, Carolyn points out the airspeed indicator, throttle settings, undercarriage lever, flaps, trim and magneto switches. Though every hard, gleaming surface is made of metal or bakelite or perspex, my impression is one of enveloping reassurance, not brutal functionality. It is hard to believe that this was a killing machine.

Carolyn asks if I have any questions. I have just one. And when she replies that, yes, if I feel comfortable, she will of course let me take the controls, my heart leaps, filled up with sunlit sky.

'Now, anything in your pockets?' she asks, patting the zips of her own flying-suit as she carefully scans mine.

'Just this,' I say.

'What on earth is it?' she demands, gazing without rapture at the grey lump in my hand, smooth as a pebble on a beach.

'It's my very first potato from last summer; from my life,' I explain, suddenly embarrassed. 'I can't quite explain why I brought it.'

Carolyn watches carefully as I lob the potato to Jethro, who, without lowering his video camera, somehow manages to catch it in his left hand. 'Look, you haven't got any other stray objects in your pockets that might come loose in the plane, have you?' she demands.

'Only this photo,' I reply, pointing at the upside-down snap in one of the transparent map-pockets on the knees of my flying suit.

'Your wife?' she asks, glancing down at it.

'My fiancée. She's a pilot herself.'

'You're lucky,' replies Carolyn, smiling for the first time. 'My husband was, too.'

A fitter helps me into my parachute; hands me a flying-helmet and goggles. And as I climb over the riveted metal sill of the cockpit, and down into its welcoming depths, all my doubts and fears about being present enough to experience this moment for the epiphany that it is are swept aside. I feel relief, more than anything. I am *here*. And it is as if a woman I had unrequitedly adored for thirty years had suddenly changed her mind and whispered 'yes'.

In the silence, I scan the instruments, their heavy needles as grand as the hands of a cathedral clock.

'Ready to go?' comes Carolyn's voice in my headset.

'Ready to go,' I repeat. And how. I have been ready for this moment for more than thirty years.

The fuselage begins to rock as the heavy propeller is turned by the starter-motor, and I laugh out loud as the Merlin engine explodes into life: fifteen hundred horses shaking me in my straps, wrapping me in a warm cloud of vaporized aviation oil. It really feels as if we are not just sitting *behind* the engine, but slap bang inside the guts of a belting, snorting monster. Now the needles in front of me are dancing into life as the monster slowly rouses herself from her sleep.

And then the monster lets out a roar as Carolyn nudges the throttle, unchaining her, and we surge forward over the grass before she closes it again to test the brakes.

A voice crackles in my headset. 'Duxford traffic, caution the Spitfire lining up two-zero.' *Caution the Spitfire*. And, bloody hell, that's *us*. Already I feel like punching the air, and we haven't even taken off.

Full power. The noise is quite devastating. The monster has gone wild, and the jelly in my eyes is starting to vibrate. The whole world is shaking, and I am grinning as if I had only just learned how to smile. This is it.

I am sitting in a Spitfire that is slowly accelerating on to the grass runway of a Battle of Britain fighter station. I am a child. I am an adult. For this instant, I feel like a god.

Out of my left eye, I glimpse Jethro waving furiously with one arm, video camera clutched to his face in the other. Now we are thundering like a racehorse on the gallops, the control-column in front of me eases forward and I sense the Spitfire's tail rising beneath me as if I were in the Luscombe, except that now we have about a hundred times more power and I am riding the Mallard on rails, not a cart dragged behind a donkey, bump, bump, bump. And then the altimeter needle is spinning as we climb fast and steeply, effortlessly accelerating into an iron-grey sky.

We bank hard left, the world spins right, and I yell with delight as we continue the climb, unable to resist sharing the visceral thrill I feel at the invincible power that surges us sky-wards, making my stomach flip with raw delight. I am flying over the English countryside in a Spitfire, and it is even more dazzling than I dreamed.

Closing my fingers cautiously around the cold steel of the control-column, with its spade-grip and knurled brass gun-button, I allow myself to sense Carolyn's control-inputs from the front cockpit. Like this, I can feel the Spitfire being flown, as if I were resting my fingers on the fluttering keys of a pianola, feeling a ghost pianist ripple out Rachmaninov. I feel as if I am touching the flying of all my pilot heroes, too, as we slice through the air at three thousand feet in the most beautiful aircraft ever built.

On my left and right, I stare down at the deep-blue and red roundels dominating the camouflage paint on the wings, my gaze drawn ineluctably to the perfect ellipses at their tips; archetypal loveliness carving up the fields beneath. This is what *they* saw, I remind myself, as if I were not already excited enough.

There is no buffeting; no hint of that constant jostling that I feel in the Luscombe, as the flimsy yellow bird is pushed and pulled and barged by the very air in which it flies. We are not simply riding on the air; we are drilling our own Spitfire-shaped tunnel through it, like a corer through an evanescent apple.

'Cambridge on your left,' snaps Carolyn over the

intercom, as if we were on a sightseeing trip, rather than the ride of my life. I glance down for a second; recognize the Gothic filigree of King's College chapel glowing in the sun, where Alice's dad sang in the choir half a century ago, even as my parents were sipping tea in their rooms at Girton and at Trinity Hall. But now is not the time for all that: now, I just want to feel the sky, not scan the earth. I want to soak up every last electron of the experience of flying this wheeling-banking-rolling-looping ineffable dream machine.

For a moment, I pull my headset away from my ears and laugh to hear the raging Merlin monster in all its brutal glory as Carolyn dives, watching the airspeed build before she pulls up and, pushing the stick hard right, makes the horizon perform a perfect roll around the nonchalant Spitfire. I always thought my Luscombe sounded deafeningly loud inside its tiny, tinny cockpit. But it is the distant whine of a gnat compared with the hornet explosiveness of the Spitfire, with its dizzying din. The mighty engine sounds as if twenty-four men with pneumatic drills are all working down the same manhole, which just happens to be hurtling across the sky at three hundred mph.

And then comes the question I have been waiting all my life to hear.

'Do you want to have a go at flying her?' asks Carolyn.

'Yes, please,' I croak, the excited child inside me trying to sound like a grown-up.

'Right, she's trimmed in the cruise. You have control.'

'I have control,' I acknowledge. 'Oh my God.'

'What's the matter?'

'Nothing,' I say. 'I'm just so happy.'

I hear Carolyn chuckle over the roar of the engine, and then I am flying a Spitfire over the fields of Cambridgeshire. *I am flying a Spitfire.* And it feels so sleek; so natural; so exactly how I always thought flying should feel, until I first sat at the stodgy controls of a beaten-up Cessna and wondered what all the fuss was about. This is, quite simply, the finest, most beautiful thing I have done in my whole life.

Glancing at the photograph, I whisper Alice's name, and she is with me, too.

And now it is time to return to base. Yet instead of a sense of panic that the fairground ride is ending far too soon, I feel ready as Carolyn pulls the Spitfire up into the sky for one last, ecstatic victory roll and rejoins the circuit at Duxford. For my heart is full of sky, and I know that every second that has passed between me and the Spitfire will stay with me for ever.

As we taxi to a halt, I feel utterly at peace with the world. One of the plot-strands of my life is complete. And it is odd, but as I tell Jethro when he comes running to greet me, and I step, sweaty and reluctant, from the best seat in the world, I have the sneaking suspicion that this will not be the last time that I fly a Spitfire.

Later, we have a beer together in The Three Willows, and Jethro fills me in on his new life as a flying-instructor, and his progress with his skywriting. He says he has almost given up trying to draw a heart in the sky, because everyone says it is impossible with just one aeroplane. But things are going great with Sasha, and he has a new sponsor for his flying displays over the summer.

I can never keep up with my old friend's life, and tonight is no exception.

'Sasha and I are planning to move in together in a few weeks' time. I tell you, mate: she may not be a pilot, but I really think she's the one.'

So we toast each other's good fortune, and he asks me what my new flying goal will be, now that I have laid the Spitfire ghost to rest.

And I tell him that I know it is not going to be easy, and I know it will take a while. But now, after today, I want to fly a Spitfire of my own.

'Well, here's to flying,' he says, clinking my glass. 'And women. And the future.'

Next day, with my head still in the clouds, I meet up with Alice at Stansted, and we fly back to Limoges together on Ryanair. She is basking in glory, too, for she has passed the skills test for her pilot's licence with flying colours. She is now officially qualified as a private pilot, licensed to commit aviation.

'Who would have thought that I would marry a woman with a pilot's licence?' I say out loud, gazing up at the lurid blue and yellow of the aircraft's interior as the 737 taxis to the hold at Stansted. 'You've no idea how impressed Jethro is. He'd be so jealous, if he weren't already in love himself.'

'But he hasn't even met me yet,' she laughs.

'He doesn't need to. I've told him all about you.'

'That's all I need,' she groans. 'What did you tell him?'

'Only the good stuff. In fact, there's only good stuff, isn't there?' I take hold of Alice's hand, smile at the diamond glittering in her engagement ring, and give her hand a squeeze. 'When are you going to let me know if there's anything that isn't utterly exquisite about you? You know – appalling habits, bodies under the patio, a secret love-child, that sort of thing.'

'I'm sure there are *lots* of things,' she says, holding her smile. She glances out of the window as the aircraft's engines begin to roar, and we are pressed back in our seats as it accelerates down the runway, rumbling thunder. 'But I don't keep a list in my head, if that's what you mean. And even if I did, I wouldn't tell you. Not until after we're married, anyway.'

'But by then it will be too late.'

'Precisely,' she giggles.

The rumbling stops, and we are flying.

*

Back in Jolibois, we have been invited to the house of Claude, the electrician with the strong forehand, to watch England play France at rugby. All my best friends from the tennis club are here – Le Grand Mermoz, Maxim, Blaise, the Proustian Madeleine and the rest – and there are whoops of laughter at the sight of my brand-new England supporter's shirt, with its scarlet swirl, red rose and all.

'You do realize that that vile thing won't be worth much by tomorrow, don't you?' chortles Mermoz.

'*Peut-être*,' I reply. 'But if *les Anglais* should happen to win . . .'

'. . . Then we'll rip it off you and cut it up before you leave,' says Claude, slapping me on the back and roaring with laughter. Fortunately the national anthems now strike up, and we all turn to watch Claude's vast flat-screen television.

'Why aren't you two singing?' demands Jeanne, seated on my left. So Alice and I grimly do our best to sing along to 'God Save the Queen', before *les Français* respond with a rousing Marseillaise. And then the game starts, and an appalled silence falls over everyone as – almost immediately – England score a try. I leap to my feet, fist clenched, until Alice tugs at the back of my shirt, and I quietly sit back down.

'*C'est pas vrai*,' murmurs Le Grand Mermoz.

'*C'est pas possible*,' adds Blaise, his head in his hands.

'Right, that's it,' says Claude. 'No food for Alice and Michael until France score.'

I know from my experiences on the tennis courts of Jolibois that the French hate losing with a passion. Yet tonight, the atmosphere in the room remains genial and playful. Even so, as the match progresses, I can feel myself trembling with nerves. It is a strange feeling, sitting in a room full of French people in France, watching England play rugby ferociously well. Of course I desperately want England to win – yet I am somehow dreading that they will. Dry-mouthed, I do my best to pour myself some water, embarrassed at the clinking of jug on glass that shows how much my hands are shaking.

By the time England kick a penalty to take them five points clear, everyone except Alice and me has decided that the French team are useless, and that it's all over: a lost cause.

'But look, there are still five minutes to go,' I protest. 'Anything could happen.'

'No, it's no use,' says Mermoz, glumly. 'We don't deserve to win, playing like this.'

Come the final whistle, and I feel a weird mix of emotions: thrilled that we won, sorry – and ever so slightly guilty – that they had to lose.

'Aren't you going to celebrate, Michael?' asks Claude.

I shake my head, attempting to explain that it is a lot more fun to beat Australia than to beat the French. But I am not sure that they quite believe me.

'We can't possibly come to your wedding after this,' says Mermoz, his head in his hands. 'All your English friends will be laughing at us.'

Much of July has been a wash-out, yet the next day dawns bright and clear, so Alice and I decide to fly south-west in the Luscombe to celebrate her pilot's licence.

'You handle the approach and circuit, and I'll do the landing,' I tell her, as we cruise over the caves at Lascaux, 'because your approaches are always far better than mine.'

'But I don't know how to fly a tailwheel aircraft,' she protests.

'In the air, this thing is just the same as a Cessna. It's only when you're on the ground that it handles differently to a tricycle undercarriage.'

'If you say so.'

'You obviously haven't read that book I bought for you: *Stick and Rudder* by Langewiesche.'

'Yes, I did,' she protests. 'But my mind was on other things at the time.'

At Libourne aerodrome, amid the vineyards of St Émilion, there is a restaurant right beside the apron with a perfect view of the planes as they take off and land.

'I'm so sorry at what the cooks have done, *monsieur*,' says *Madame*, bringing my *onglet aux échalotes*. I gaze at my steak, wondering if they have frazzled it into old shoe-leather, and burst out laughing. For there, in plastic numerals planted in the *gratin de courgettes*, is the score from last night's match: 14–9.

'People say that the French are bad losers,' I say to Alice, over the intercom, as we fly back to St Juste. 'But it's simply not true.'

Next I dial up the frequency for St Juste, announcing that we are inbound. There is no air-traffic control at St Juste, so it is a surprise to hear a voice crackle in response.

'*Michael?*' says a voice I recognize as that of Antoine, the white-haired ace mechanic. 'I regret to inform you that English pilots are no longer welcome at St Juste.'

Laughing, I turn to Alice. 'See what I mean?'

# 24

## AUGUST

A little watery sunshine has arrived in a belated parody of summer, just to remind us what we have been missing.

'*Ça va . . . avec le beau temps?*' asks each person who arrives at La Folie. They all say it: Gilles; Monsieur Laveille the burly joiner who always wears shorts, even in winter; Didier the postman, who is still trying to get Digby to acknowledge him each time he bounces up the drive in his little yellow Clio.

'*Bonjour, chien,*' chirps Didier, day after day. '*Ça va, avec le beau temps?*'

And, day after day, Digby – having barked at the arrival of the car as furiously as if it were a siege-engine arriving outside the walls of Poitiers – ignores him. Alice and I think our dog may have Asperger's. But I cannot tell the postman that, so I blame it on the fact that French wasn't on the curriculum at his Baltimore puppy-camp, and just stand there beside Digby, embarrassed, wishing he would at least try to bite the poor man or something: anything rather than this daily brutality of sending him to canine Coventry.

'*Aagh-ta-ta-ta-taagh!*' roars Gilles when he drives up in his white van, and Digby tries to climb in through the window on the driver's side. I think it is fair to say that Digby loves Gilles more than Gilles loves Digby.

I know how Digby feels, too, for I do not know what I shall do without my heroic neighbour and peasant mentor when he leaves. It was he who, right at the start of my time in France, sagely encouraged me to buy sheep that are very easy to lift and very hard to kill by mistake. And rarely does Gilles's white van rumble up the drive to La Folie without my gleaning some vital piece of folk-wisdom, such as how to plough with cows, or why I must never plant during a Russian moon.

'I've just treated my sheep for the last time, and I have a few doses left,' he says today, after bumping up the drive, yet again, in the familiar white van. 'Wondered if you'd like what's left of *le produit* for yours? I won't be needing it any more.'

For a long time, I was adamant that my Ouessants did not need any treatments or drugs. They are wild, rustic animals, after all, and products from the vet only come in vast, brutally expensive flagons, intended for commercial flocks. But there is no doubt that Gaston and his gang have fared better in those winters when I have injected them with a little of Gilles's moonshine.

'You can do them yourself this year, can't you?' he says, with a twinkle. At first I take this as a reference to the fact that I now have a trained intensive-care nurse on the premises. Alice may not share my enthusiasm for trudging out in wellies and pyjamas to feed the chickens, but she is a different woman as soon as she has a syringe in her hands. I feel sure this is why I have not had a cold since she arrived at La Folie. The germs are frightened of her.

And then I realize what is behind his words – that looming retirement; that wretched move to a house in a distant village – and I fear that Gilles is attempting a subtle hand-over of power, like a parent inveigling a child into tying his own shoelaces for the first time. He needs to see me stand on my own two feet, so that he can shuffle off into the shadows without worrying too much about his English apprentice. He wants me to let go.

'*Oui, c'est vrai*,' I concede, reluctantly. '*Je peux les faire.*'

Often Gilles and I stand outside to chat, gazing out across the valley. But today I can see from the way he is stroking his beard that he has something else he wants to ask me, so I invite him inside.

'Actually, I wondered if I could ask you for *un service*,' he says, slumping into a chair at the kitchen table. And suddenly his face darkens, as if a cloud had passed in front of the moon, and he looks very old and very tired. 'A farmer from Aubusson promised two months ago that he'd buy my sheep – all five hundred and fifty of them – and now he's not answering my calls. Time is running out, and the prices have dropped again, what with first the foot-and-mouth, and then the blue tongue disease.'

I nod, glumly acknowledging my personal responsibility, as the token *Anglais*, for the state of the French meat market. Is Gilles expecting me to buy his sheep?

'I was wondering,' he says. 'I don't really understand the internet, but perhaps you could advertise them for me on there?'

I explain that I'm not sure how many French farmers spend their evenings Googling for fresh flocks. There may be nobody to read such an advertisement.

'Perhaps some of the younger ones . . .' he entreats. I gaze at my old friend, trying not to think of poor old Gaston standing out there in his field, weakening with each winter that passes, no longer the ram he once was.

So I promise Gilles that I will indeed look for a website where we can advertise his sheep, and then I pour him his customary snifter of bright yellow Salers – a distillation of gentian flowers, which looks like alien horse-piddle and tastes like Bitrex – before splashing Pastis into a glass for myself and clouding it with water from the tap.

'*À la tienne*,' we cough, as we clink glasses for what must be the hundredth time. I can see from Gilles's weary face that he cannot imagine what he will do, if he cannot sell his sheep. And, selfishly, I cannot imagine what I am going to do, in a couple of months' time, when my mentor retires. I shall not be losing my friend, for we intend to stay in touch. But I shall be losing my neighbour, which – as anyone who has ever lived next door to a wise and generous man will know – is a far more daunting prospect.

Day after day, I trudge out to open up the chicken house in the morning, and shut the Egg Squad up at night. I check on the Rastafarians; scoop toothless Gaston's granules into the feed-trough as silently as I can, so as not to alert the competition. I pick beans in the *potager*; brushcut the nettles; cut the grass.

Compared with the mounting strain of organizing a wedding at the end of the world, I like my little routines; like the fact that the animals and vegetables show no sign of sharing the rising stress levels inside the house. I have never had a gift for multi-tasking, and can already feel my brain beginning to fry as the day of our wedding approaches.

Fortunately my organ-playing for Mass in the villages around Jolibois appears to have weighed in my favour with Raphaël the priest, and so – a day after the civil ceremony at the *Mairie* – we are to be married in the tiny Catholic church of St Sornin-les-Combes, in a service officiated by a cheery Anglican priest from Poitou-Charente, before decamping to Maurice's epic barn at the top of the hill for dinner and Anglo-French revelry.

The only problem is that the church is so small that it will already be a squeeze, without any extras. Yet Le Grand Mermoz has warned me that some people may decide to come to our wedding service who haven't actually been invited to it; the devoted old ladies known as *les grenouilles de bénitier*, for example, who come to every service in the book.

Gilles says that we really should have a *vin d'honneur* for all comers, on top of anything else we plan: cocktails and canapés after the service for everyone we can think of, including anyone whose moustache might be twitched if we don't invite them, and any waifs and strays who happen to turn up.

He assures us that *les Français* are quite used to slipping away, if they have not been invited to the dinner afterwards. For Alice and me, however, this is way too much of a cringe. I simply cannot imagine having to announce that dinner is served – oh, but some of you aren't invited, so would you mind just drinking up and going home? When in Rome, and all that – but, just this once, we are going to do as *les Anglais* do.

For better or worse, then, richer or poorer, we have decided that everyone invited to the wedding had better be invited to all of it. Le Grand Mermoz and the rest of my tennis chums; Yves-Pascal the notaire and his wife Ariane; Jérôme and Jacqueline from Les Sablonnières; Arlette and Bernard with Roman and Sophie, the newly-weds; Renée and Céline from dance class; Big Leif and Anna; and so on.

The only significant gap on the guest list will be Digby. Alice says he would make the most wonderful bridesmaid. I say my rival for her affections cannot be trusted in an open field, let alone a church.

With wedding pressures building inside my head, and only just over a month still to go, it feels a relief to escape to St Juste, and the calming effects of a large gathering of vintage aeroplanes. At the little aeroclub, with its three Robins and its thirty or so flying members, the gendarmes estimate that fourteen thousand people have come to watch the annual *fête aérienne*. Planes arrived throughout yesterday afternoon, and now the early-morning sun glints through the mist on a sight to gladden the heart.

Two ranks of gleaming machines are lined up on the dewy grass, their engines silent, their noses pointing expectantly into the wind like a pack of old hounds, still keen to scent the breeze. They make me think, too, of a parade of veterans standing proudly with their medals and berets, at attention beside an empty tomb.

Here are two stately Morane-Saulnier 317s that somehow survived the war; here, a clutch of Nords and Broussards, all of which seem to share that deeply French characteristic of looking as if they have just had a jolly good lunch. Beside them stands a thumping great pair of Harvards that give me a jolt of happy recognition, alongside a trio of Piper Cubs, a Stearman, a Stinson and a Pitts. In vain I scan the silhouettes for a Spitfire, but at least there's a Tiger Moth – or a *T.J. Mott*, as the French pronounce it – flown by a very tall and elegant Dutchman with the air of a rich philanthropist. I bet myself that he runs a huge Edam factory, but it turns out that he is a retired 747 captain who used to fly Starfighters with the Dutch air force, and has even displayed at Duxford.

My humble Luscombe is part of the static line-up, too, although I haven't been asked to display it in flight. So rather than rubbing shoulders with the moustaches in the pilots' tent, I am working as a marshal. I am the chap who waves the lollipops to show the visiting aircraft where to park. Except that there are four of us on marshalling duty – four beacons of incompetence in our hi-vis jackets – and we only have one set of lollipops between us. This feels a bit like being a sheriff without a gun; a fairy without a wand. We are making do.

Fortunately, the only thing that needs marshalling, first thing this morning, is a pair of young roe deer, their hind legs looking far too big for them, who have wandered on to the deserted runway. Plane-spotters come in all shapes and sizes.

The day begins to pass very slowly. I am struck by how tiring it is to stand in one place for several hours, doing nothing all, when one is not used to it. And the problem with wearing a fluorescent waistcoat is that it makes it very difficult to slope off for a five-minute break without being rumbled. Nevertheless, when some of my friends from the tennis club appear – Maxim the boxer, Claude the electrician, and their families – I feel impelled to go over to welcome them.

'Which is your plane, Michael?' asks Matisse, Claude's ten-year-old son. Matisse doesn't attempt to hide his disappointment when I tell him it's not one of the pair of hulking great Harvards with their open-mouthed Pratt & Whitney radial engines; not one of the two twin-tailed Broussards that could each carry ten men; not the Pitts, nor the Stampe, nor the Stinson.

'No,' I reply, 'it's that little yellow one on the end of the line.' There is a pause as, squinting, his eyes focus on my Luscombe. Then he looks down at the ground; kicks an imaginary stone.

'I thought it might be,' he sighs.

'Well, it does look fairly new,' says Claude, trying to make good his son's visible disappointment. 'When was it built?'

'1946,' I reply. The electrician's mouth flies open like a cat-flap flung wide by a spooked kitten.

'*Quand même!*' he whispers, under his breath. And I can see him making a mental note that Matisse will not be coming flying with me any time soon.

And still we marshals must stand, and stand. From the ache behind my knees, I sense that I have not missed my vocation as a policeman on the beat; a sentry on parade. Yet Rémy the glovemaker – a pale figure in a leather cowboy hat, whose defiant blinking gives him the air of a mole disturbed in mid-dig – is exultant.

'I stand all day long at my workbench,' says Rémy, 'so this is easy. It's sitting down that's hard for me. During long lunches, I have to pretend I need to *aller faire pipi*, just to stretch my legs.'

For lunch today, we volunteers have been promised *un sandwich* at the back of the hangar. My English brain immediately pictures a tray of neat Mother's Pride triangles, white as cotton wool, shot through with yellow-grey seams of egg or tuna or – in a particularly gruesome childhood flashback – bloater paste. Here in France, *un sandwich* appears to mean a sack filled with crusty baguettes, which two ladies with purple hair are noisily hacking apart, their glinting knives making the sound of goblins skating on oystershells. The bread we fill ourselves, from great trays of ham, pâté, Camembert and cornichons, while a man in fireman's uniform gurgles Gamay into plastic cups from a twenty-litre vat of red wine. Life is good; a chair would make it better; Alice being here would make it perfect. I have left her at La Folie, organizing dresses for her bridesmaids.

One of the other marshals turns out to be a farmer, Jean-Pierre, who was once a mechanic in the French air force. So in between pushing aeroplanes, we talk about sheep and cows and jet engines. You can learn a lot if you listen to farmers.

'All the children today, they have become disconnected from the earth,' sighs Jean-Pierre, as we watch the Pitts flicking and twisting through its aerobatic display like a fish on a line. I met its pilot over lunch, a handsome German aerobatic ace called Kai, who is precisely what Alice says is missing in aviation: a dashing young flying-instructor who doesn't swagger, and doesn't look as if he would be much happier holding a clipboard in a shopping centre. Kai told me he knows Jethro, too.

'Ah, yes – Jethro Gilroy,' he smiled. 'Excellent pilot. Everyone knows who Jethro is. And I guess he likes it that way.'

The Pitts rolls across the sky, and Jean-Pierre continues to shake his head about how children have become *déconnectés de la terre*.

'Adults, too,' I reply. I know this, because I was one of them, and not so very long ago. 'It's why I came to the French countryside in the first place: to learn, and to reconnect with nature.'

'You're lucky,' he says, 'because you realized it was important for you. Most people don't even notice what they have lost; do not recognize what is missing in their lives.'

Perhaps not, though I happen to suspect that many do. I have seen their grey faces on the London Underground; have watched them losing themselves in books and music and computer games, eager for escape. I have sensed the wistfulness and frustration these people feel at the urban lives in which they feel trapped. I recognize their palpable desire to escape into a sweeter, simpler life, at one with nature rather than with their mobile phone; with trees, not concrete; not with the internet, but with the sea and the sky and the stars.

'So why don't they?' asks Jean-Pierre, as a Gipsy Major engine roars into life behind us.

And I do not really know the answer to this, any more than I can guess – as the Tiger Moth climbs gracefully into the crystal sky, and heads south, silhouetted like an angel by the setting sun – why everyone in the world does not wish to learn to fly.

Alice greets me on the doorstep of La Folie, looking worried.

'What's the matter?' I ask.

'You have to phone this number,' she says. 'Someone called Benj; says he works for Virgin Atlantic.'

The phone only rings once, before a woman answers.

'Hello, Karen speaking,' says a voice I recognize. Surely it can't be *that* Karen, the one who threatened to shoot Jethro? And then a man's voice comes on the line, too, on another extension.

'It's all right, Kaz, I've got it,' he says. 'Is that Michael? How's the Luscombe?'

The formalities dealt with, he tells me about Jethro.

There has been a crash, on the way back from a display. I do not hear all the details. At first it sounds as if Jethro is paralysed and in a wheelchair. But then Benj puts me straight. My old friend has broken his wrist, but should make a full recovery. It is his passenger, a young woman called Sasha, who is the one who is seriously injured. I put down the receiver, and shut my eyes. Jethro in a wheelchair would have been unthinkable. But this, this, for Jethro, will be infinitely worse.

Here in the French countryside, I imagined I would find an unchanging world, insulated by trees and grass and sheep from the fretful transience of the city. Yet living close to nature has made me more conscious than I ever was in my London life of how sharply life mutates and metamorphoses; how suddenly it ends and begins. Meeting Alice, and deciding to spend our lives together, feels like simply another thread in the same web in which the animals and trees and plants, too, are enmeshed. Jethro and Sasha, also. The web changes so fast.

One moment the landscape is zinging with colour, and young lambs are jerkily frisking away like a speeded-up film in the field behind the house. The next minute, the trees are a tangle of old wire coat-hangers, and Gaston is close to death again.

Over the next few days, I slowly piece together the story of Jethro's crash from pilot friends and news reports. And then

Jethro himself phones, and he tells me where he is, and it sounds like a very dark place indeed.

'All I can think, all of the time, is that I wish it was me in Stoke Mandeville, lying there staring at a hospital wall, wondering if my body will ever be mine again,' he says.

I listen.

'She's the love of my life, Michael. And what I've done to her, it's almost worse than if I'd killed her. Can you imagine?'

I shake my head; cough to let him know that I am still there on the other end of the line. Sasha has already had two operations on her spine, and there are many more to come.

'Pretty much everything below the waist is shot,' he says. He is currently driving six hours a day to visit her; hopes to rent a flat beside the hospital, so that he can be there full time. 'And walking is just a distant dream. But we're in this together; she's adamant that she doesn't want us to split. I tell you, Michael, the love that's in that girl.' And his voice begins to crack.

'So what are you going to do?' I ask, after a long pause.

'I've told her I want her to sue me,' he says. 'It's the only way to make the insurance pay out enough. This way, all I will lose is everything. Whereas she has already lost far more than that.'

We both sit in silence for a while. It never occurred to me, until now, that my dashing friend might, beneath the bravado, be a very much more complex human being than I ever guessed.

'How is Sasha doing in herself?' I ask.

'That's the worst thing about it,' he says, hoarsely. 'Sash is completely amazing. I go in there, and she smiles at me. *She asks me how I am*. And she tries to look after me.' He pauses, blowing his nose. 'And here am I. I'm the one who did this to her. And I'm a complete wreck.'

'Give yourself some time, Jez. I wish you'd be a little gentle on yourself.'

'Don't worry,' he says, clearing his throat. 'I'll still be there for your wedding. I'm going to fly over in the RV4.'

'You're joking. That's ridiculous, Jez. You've got a broken arm. Sasha needs you there.'

'We've already discussed it. She wants me to come.'

'Don't give it another thought. *Please*.'

'Thanks for being there for me, mate.'

'Always, Jez.

'Fly safe.'

'Bye.'

'Bye.'

Gilles's sheep are, at last, all sold. And he and Josette drive up to La Folie to say goodbye.

'It's all finished,' he says, with such a brave smile that my heart goes out to him. Josette, hands thrust deep into the pockets of her quilted jacket, stares at the ground.

The Moulin Vaugelade, the house that they called home for thirty years, stands empty now. I drive down there a few hours later, in the rain-swept darkness, to take a look.

The farmyard is silent. The windows are shuttered, except on the upper floor, where the shutters still hang – as they have always hung – broken from their hinges, like the doors of an advent calendar opened by an over-excited child.

Why am I here? I suppose I needed to see for myself, to convince myself that Gilles really has left. But as I shine my torch over the broken pots and buckets in the yard, and the light picks out the wan glitter of a strand of last year's tinsel above the front door, it is impossible to believe that he is gone.

Here is where he greeted me, on that very first day, when he invited me for my first-ever drink in a proper French

JE T'AIME À LA FOLIE

house. This is where we drank champagne in a ramshackle tent with Leif and Anna and old Hubert the shepherd, to toast his son's wedding. On that half oil-drum, Gilles and Young Boulesteix grilled great hissing hunks of lamb. This is the spot where he demonstrated to me how to kill a chicken, and just over there is where Cool Hand Luke, his brain heated with sheep-shearing and wine, jumped into the river, fully clothed. Just inside the barn, I can still see the indentation in the straw where Rose, the sheepdog who listened to me, would sleep. I drive away with a heavy heart, and an inkling of how hard it must have been for them to leave all this behind.

In the morning at La Folie, the grumble of a familiar diesel engine sends Digby into his usual frenzy.

'Did you change your mind?' I ask, blinking with surprise.

'I wondered if you'd like a couple of chickens,' shrugs Gilles, after managing to beat off Baltimore Boy. 'I know you've lost a few recently.'

And so we receive our first wedding present. Two French hens are no replacement for two old friends who have gone to live too far away. But I appreciate the unconscious symbolism of the gesture, even so. A little bit of the old peasant life of the Moulin Vaugelade will live on here, at La Folie.


Next morning, Didier the postman brings a letter, post-marked Toulouse. Though the twisty French handwriting is unfamiliar, I recognize the name written in capitals beneath the unfussy signature at the bottom of the page: ZUMBACH. Yet this letter, written in English, is not from Ludo. It is from his wife, the poised and birdlike woman whom I met only once, when she handed me the keys to my future at the office of the notaire. I know she never could stand the isolation of La Folie.

*Dear Guardian of La Folie*
*The very first time I saw La Folie, I immediately knew she would be my house. Weary to not find one buyer, the owner didn't want any more to sell it.*

*I succeeded to convince himself, and so to sell more hilly ground. First, he just wanted to sell the part in front of the house. But I wanted the well and the beautiful false acacia at the top of the hill.*

*I succeeded to have them. It was my house. She had waited me.*

*I always knew that the houses choose themselves their guardian, not the opposite. Sometimes they find it, sometimes they don't.*

*The first time I saw her, it was cold wet weather and it was foggy.*

*To reach her, there was not asphalt road but much mud and very strange atmosphere.*

*I immediately loved her. L'Ogre did not agree with me. He did not want to buy her. (He is not a land man.)*

*I was in harmony with the landscape every season. I planted over and over again many trees. In summer, I took care of each tree and I watered them with watering cans and buckets.*

*I had an old oak (downstairs, on the left) and against it, I recharged my battery. Also, I loved silver birch song in front of the house . . .*

*And then, I left La Folie. (L'Ogre was too nasty.)*

*I came back one year after to sign at the notaire.*

*What change!!!*

*It was a neglected house, almost despair.*

*A part of my oak was dead and my bees have left their hive. (People say they do not stay when a couple is divided.)*

*I felt very nerve-racking waves. It was difficult for me, but La Folie held something against me because I deserted her.*

*Today, your book has put my mind at rest and quiet.*
*I know my trees are in good hands (too my fishes).*
*Please, take care of all my (sorry, now it is yours) oaks,*
*Christmas trees (planted after every Christmas), my cypress,*
*my chestnut trees, my hazel trees, medicinal plants, my*
*hornbeam (at the top of the hill). Thank you very much,*
*new guardian.*

*The Birdlike Woman*

I sit in silence for a while. I read the letter again, more slowly this time. Then I carefully fold it up and gaze out of the window of my office.

I stare at the old oak at the bottom of the hill; attempt to picture a slim, poised woman leaning against its trunk, drawing strength from its strength as she blinks back her tears. I imagine her tending her bees in a white gauze helmet and a pair of old gardening gloves; watch her picking medicinal flowers as she wanders up to sit with the snakes by the ruined well; listen with her to the music of the wind playing in the leaves of the silver birch, as the sun falls warm on her face.

And I want to say sorry, as I glance across at the space where her Christmas trees once were, hoping that she will understand. I want to say thank you, too. Because for the first time since I fell in love with La Folie, the doubt that her husband planted has slipped away at last.

# 25

SEPTEMBER

Early morning on the day of our *mariage civil* at the *Mairie*, and I have never felt so tense in my life. I know that the male brain was not created for multitasking. Yet mine – overwhelmed with things left undone, as our church wedding tomorrow hurtles towards me like a charging ram – is now officially beginning to melt. The muscles in my back are taut as violin strings in winter. My nerves are beginning to shriek. It is not that I am nervous about getting married. Far from it; I cannot wait. It is just that I don't have *time* to get married, when I am far too busy organizing a wedding.

This is silly, of course. I have only been entrusted with the incidental errands (order of service, organ, trumpeters, band, amplification, church, wine, champagne, tables and chairs, seating plan and lighting), whereas Alice is dealing with all the really monumental tasks (worrying about the dress; worrying about the dress some more). Actually that is unfair. Alice is also busy with more important things, such as worrying about her hair.

In rural France this century, it appears to be *de rigueur* for all women in their thirties and forties to have their hair cut short and dyed the colour of rogan josh. Attempt to diverge from this accepted look, pioneered by Duracell, and you are on your own. This may explain why Alice is almost in tears when she returns from a trial wedding-styling session with a recommended *coiffeur*. With her flounced, tousled, and heavily lacquered bouffant hair-do, my future wife looks like nothing so much as a 1980s Hot Gossip dancer disguised as a gypsy fortune-teller.

'Don't you *dare* laugh,' she says, her lip trembling as she attempts to brush the horror from her hair.

'I'm not, I'm not,' I reply, truthfully. 'It's much too scary for that.'

While Alice organizes the flowers, table-settings, transport and last-minute accommodation niggles of a hundred guests from Britain, California and Australia, I have spent most of the past two days in the Espace, ferrying clinking wine-crates from the cash-and-carry in Limoges. Monsieur Brûlé the *traiteur* assures me that twenty-four bottles of rosé will be enough for 140 people. And I assure Monsieur Brûlé, with an apologetic smile, that he obviously doesn't know *les Anglais*.

Today may be the day of the civil wedding, but it is also the day when 140 chairs, fourteen tables, a sound-system and a lighting rig are to be delivered to Maurice's barn at the top of the hill. Thank goodness my brothers have now arrived from London, to help me set everything up. Thank goodness, too, for Madame Lemuel at the *Mairie*, who makes me think of Ariadne with a ball of wool, leading Alice and me through the labyrinth of French bureaucracy.

At first Madame Lemuel struck me as having a certain *hauteur* about her – until I realized that her head is invariably tilted back, not in disdain, but in response to the tendency of her glasses to slip down her nose. There is never a moment to push them up, after all. No, you can tell from the way Madame Lemuel riffles athletically through the folders in her filing cabinet that she gets an almost sensual pleasure from doing things fast. Whatever other disasters may befall our wedding, at least we know that our paper-work is in order.

The thing that is making my last-minute labours all the more tricky, however, is the fact that I am having to do most of them in secret.

'What matters are the people coming,' Alice reminded me last night, 'not the angle of the lighting or the spelling of the hymns. We see our families, and our friends, so little. We need to be with them.' Things become so beautifully simple, the way Alice explains them. And so, whilst the sense of anticipation and excitement that is beginning to zing through the quiet streets of Jolibois steadily rises, I enlist my dad to help me carry tables and my brothers to set the chairs and lights, while my mother cheerfully greets our friends arriving from Limoges airport in their shiny rental cars.

After a final lunch *en famille* at the Café Limousin, I race back to La Folie to change into a jacket and tie. Madame Lemuel is a stickler for punctuality: our civil wedding will not wait.

Alice has gone on ahead, so here I am, blinking into the sunlight as I drive down to town alone, on this road whose twists and turns I know so well. I wave at old Monsieur Giblin, who waves back from the doorway of his cottage by the level-crossing. There is no hurry now, I tell myself, for this is the last drive I shall ever make as a single man. I could almost be driving to Lepeltier's *boulangerie* for bread, or to the shop owned by the Nicest Man in the Universe for fire-lighters. I might be going to have my hair cut by Sylvie; to the tennis club for ritual humiliation; or to the church to play the organ for Mass. I might be doing any of these things. But instead, today, in a few minutes' time, I am going to be married. For ever.

We do not know for sure which of Jolibois' various *maires adjoints* will be doing the honours. So I am thrilled and relieved to see the beaming face of Agnès – the first lady of Jolibois tennis club, and the waltzing-partner upon whose toes I once trod – waiting to greet us in a rather splendid tricolore sash at the top of the steps, as if she had just been crowned Miss France. Or Madame Jolibois, at the very least.

As our families file into the *Mairie* and sit in rows on the shiny blue leather seats of the *conseil municipal*, I am surprised to spot the long-haired journalist who always covers the Jolibois tennis tournament for *Le Populaire*. My first thought is that this must be because I finally made it through the first round this year, until I remember that Madame Lemuel says we are the first *Anglais* ever to get married at the *Mairie*.

'Now, if I may, before we begin,' says Agnès, in French, standing beneath the smiling gaze of a gold-framed President of the Republic, 'I should just like to say a few words about Michael.'

I was not expecting this. And I am touched to see that her hands are shaking as she reads from a crumpled piece of paper, held at arm's length. Touched, too, by how she manages to make my catalogue of defeats on behalf of the Jolibois men's over-35s second tennis team sound like a dazzling contribution to Jolibois life, and indeed to the sporting glories of France as a whole. Dazed by her kindness, I do not catch everything she says.

Alice squeezes my hand. She had no idea, until now, that she was marrying an international athlete. And I just feel so proud and happy to be here, getting married in the little French town that has become my home, to a girl I have known since I was child.

The actual marrying part of the *mariage civil* is over very quickly: we both say '*oui*' to the little paragraph Agnès reads out, and that's that. We shake hands with Agnès, kiss each other, and Madame Lemuel presents us with a small and rather lovely piece of Limoges porcelain, as a gift. I begin to flounder for words of gratitude, but she stops me.

'*C'est normal*,' she laughs. 'We give the same to everyone who marries here.'

And then survival-kit Toby is taking pictures of us all outside the *Mairie*, and my father turns round to Alice to present her with a small cardboard box.

'Wedding present,' he says. Inside are two of the most gleamingly beautiful wooden egg-cups I have ever seen.

'You made them yourself?' she gasps.

His face flickers with the hint of a smile. 'I thought you might recognize the wood,' he says.

Alice gazes down at the box-wood egg-cups, lost in her thoughts, as we drive back to La Folie.

'Do you feel married?' I ask.

'I *think* so,' she says. 'But I'm glad we're getting married again tomorrow.'

'Me too,' I reply, cheering myself with the thought that a French civil wedding may last only five minutes, but we now have the whole of the rest of our lives to recover from the paperwork that preceded it.

Next day, the rain is falling like water from a colander. If one more person in town says to me '*Mariage pluvieux, mariage heureux*', I swear I shall smite them with a rolled-up copy of *Le Populaire*.

Sorry. I am just a little highly strung just now. As soon as I have worked out a perfect seating plan for 140 French and English guests, printed out the covers for the order of service, photocopied the music for the trumpeters, delivered my electronic keyboard to the church, rehearsed a few songs with the band and written my speech, I shall feel a whole lot more relaxed. Unfortunately, I am not likely to have all this done before Tuesday. And the wedding – or wetting, as the weather seems to promise – is in seven hours' time.

Nor does it help that Alice has vanished, wisely opting to spend her last few hours as an almost-single woman with her friends and family, rather than with her haunted-looking civil husband, a burnt-out husk of a man whose conversation – limited at the best of times – is now reduced to an inane, maundering babble about seating plans and trumpet parts and where the hell is that very expensive waistcoat I bought in the Burlington Arcade?

In my heart I know that Alice is right about spending time with our families and friends. I have so much to learn from her. Yet something keeps me poring over the order of service, trying to make the French and English versions of the *Notre Père* precisely line up on the page.

The weather would not matter, except that I am worried about Jethro. A month after his crash, the news reaches me that Jethro is flying himself to France in an aerobatic two-seater and this filthy weather. I know he is planning to land at St Juste; feel relieved that Antoine will be there to help him refuel. I just hope the pair of them will be okay.

I hope Alice's uncle Peter will be all right, too. For he has agreed to play my electronic keyboard for our humble little wedding, despite being one of Britain's greatest living organists.

'Not *the* Peter Hurford?' I asked Alice, when she told me with whom she was holidaying in Blakeney, all those months ago.

'Yes, why?'

Her uncle turns out to have been one of the performers on *The World of the Organ*, the first LP I ever bought. His celebrated performances of Bach, recorded on the finest pipe-organs in the world, breathe exceptional poetry and humanity into music that can easily be made to sound ponderous and four-square. And now he has come to St Sornin-les-Combes, for one of the last gigs in his glittering international career.

Unfortunately, I find it hard to describe the look of sublimated pain that flickers across the great man's face – halfway between a smile and a grimace, as if he had stubbed his toe at a funeral – when I show him the instrument that he will be playing today. Picture a soldier about to be sent over the top, armed only with a spud gun and a small supply of King Edwards, and you have the general idea.

'*I say*,' he declares, as people do when – lost for words – they feel obliged to make do with the verb alone. We both gaze at my electronic keyboard, a polyphonic synthe-sizer purchased just off the Charing Cross Road about fifteen years ago. 'Is that *it*?'

I nod, staring at my feet.

'It's a Korg T2,' I tell him, in case this helps.

'Is it,' he replies, without a question mark.

I feel as if I am asking Beethoven to play a toy piano. And I also happen to know that Beethoven can make a toy piano sound like nothing on earth.

'Isn't there a pedalboard?' asks Britain's greatest living organist. He peers, glum as Eeyore, into the keyboard's black-and-steel flight-case.

From the carrier bag in my left hand, I pull out a small black foot-switch with a wire attached. 'Well, there's this,' I reply.

The silence that follows is deep enough for me to hear the band beginning to rehearse 'Daydream Believer' in the barn, half a mile away.

'We'll manage,' says Peter's wife, Pat, grabbing the little pedal from me with a brave smile. 'Somehow. Now, what about these trumpeters? Are they professionals?'

'So I'm told,' I reply. 'I haven't met them, but the local *école de musique* is supplying them. Brass teachers, I imagine.'

'Hm,' growls Peter, clearing his throat.

And then he takes me by surprise. From a carrier bag of

his own, he presents me with a battered blue hardback that looks almost familiar.

'This is for you,' he says, his eyes twinkling behind his glasses. 'My old aircraft-recognition book.'

And as I flip through the silhouettes of Harvards and Heinkels and Messerschmitts on the yellowed pages, I can feel my fingers almost tremble with forgotten longing. I remember how much I coveted a copy of this very same book when it was in my friend Davenport's hands at school.

'I was mad-keen on planes myself, as a child,' says Peter, grinning with pleasure. 'I just thought you ought to have it.'

Around lunchtime, with only a few minutes left in which to anguish over how to seat 140 people for dinner in two languages, Jérôme, my old friend with nine horses, nine donkeys and nine bicycles for his nine grandchildren, suddenly drives up to the house. He is wearing a bow-tie and struggling beneath the weight of a glazed urn the size of the Arc de Triomphe.

'What the hell are you doing here, Jérôme?' I roar at him, quite unfairly. Of course he and Jacqueline are invited to the wedding. I just don't want to see him, right now, in the midst of my blind panic.

'*Je m'excuse*,' he stammers, visibly shocked at my Jekyll-and-Hyde metamorphosis. 'I just wanted to drop off your present, which was too heavy to post.'

'Oh, Jérôme, it's so kind of you,' I reply, shamefacedly wringing my hands as the seventy-year-old ex-soldier and banker hurries back to the safety of his car. 'Forgive me,' I beseech him. 'I . . . it's the seating plan.'

Jérôme waves; smiles; is gone.

By the time Jon, my best man, arrives to pick me up, I am in quite a state. He stands in the doorway of La Folie and bursts out laughing.

'Are you all right?' he asks. 'And shouldn't you be getting changed?'

'Just a few more tables to do,' I burble, tugging at my hair, in case this helps me to remember which of our French friends speak English and which of our English friends speak French.

'Eat this,' he instructs, placing a plate of bread and cheese in front of me. 'I'll polish your shoes. We leave in five minutes.'

Beside me, poor Digby keeps racing back and forth between my desk and the hook beside the stove, where his lead hangs. This he jingles meaningfully with his snout.

'Any chance of a walk?' beseech his big, dark eyes.

'Later,' I bark. And then I feel a pang of remorse as, ears crumpled, Digby retreats to curl himself up in a tight, defensive ball on his bed. 'I'm sorry, mate,' I whisper, kneeling beside him, and laying my hand softly on his velvet head. 'It's just that I have to get married today.'

Digby leaps to his feet, pretending not to hear. He knows that his best-ever chance of being a bridesmaid is fast slipping away. And then, with one last mournful glance, he clambers slowly back on to his bed, and curls up beside Cat.

The phone rings, and it is Josette.

'It's Gilles,' she says, sounding stricken.

Please do not tell me my heroic ex-neighbour has had a heart attack in his new garden; not today. '*Ça va?*' I ask, cautiously.

'*Oui, oui, ça va,*' she replies. 'But . . . but . . . does he need to wear a tie?'

Relieved, I now get into a frightful muddle as I attempt to say yes and no at the same time, because I cannot be sure whether Gilles is the sort of rugged *paysan* who will even possess a tie. In doing my best to explain that it doesn't much matter what he wears, as long as he's comfortable, I end up warning her that he really shouldn't come without his trousers.

Josette laughs. '*Donc à tout à l'heure,*' she chirrups, hanging up.

An hour later, I am sitting in the little church at St Sornin-les-Combes, and my fluttering heart-rate is finally beginning to subside. In front of me is a *tableau vivant* of my past and present lives, and I feel almost overwhelmed by the waves of love and delight I can feel washing over me. Amid the animated throng of Alice's friends and family, here are my parents: my mother excited, my father nervous. And here, my Sherborne chums and Edinburgh pals; long-standing friends from East Dulwich; new ones from Jolibois. I catch sight of Mrs Charles, our old headmistress from Windlesham, glamorous as ever in a wide-brimmed hat; Gilles in a tie; Alix and Sarah; Le Grand Mermoz; Phoebe Yates. I try not to dwell on those I wish were here, and aren't: Ralph and Olga, not yet ready to return to Jolibois; Peter Viola, who fell off his bicycle in Kent; Ellen Gonn, who almost came, but the Swiss ambassador's schedule clashed; Antoine, my ace mechanic, who says he still feels wobbly about weddings; and Jethro, most of all. And then the opening bars of one of the Schübler chorale preludes come rippling down from the gallery, and soon a tiny woman from the *gendarmerie* and a couple of local urchins are blasting out Purcell on their trumpets in the gallery, playing more than half of the right notes, and Alice is standing beside me at last.

Now everything begins to feel even better. Raphaël the priest makes a brief and touching introduction in French; Robin, the seraphic Anglican vicar, adds something in English, and I am soon lost in the strange magic of this moment, as my old and solitary life ends in a new beginning. Survival-Kit Toby stands in the high pulpit to read a poem called 'The Co-Pilot'. My old schoolfriend Giles reads 1 Corinthians, in French. And Alice holds my hand, as if we were strolling through an icy playground together, crunching a path through the frozen leaves.

By the end of the service, it is raining so hard that no one can leave the church. Fortunately I feel far too elated to care. But Maurice and Pétrus come up with a brilliant escape plan, and we are released.

Married at last, Alice and I stand together in Maurice's great barn in the grounds of the chateau at the top of the hill, basking in the strange thrill of it all.

'I can't believe I'm married to Alice Melbury,' I tell her.

'That's because you're not,' she replies, squeezing my arm.

'Aren't I?' I gulp.

'No, you're married to Alice Wright.'

The rain eases up, and before long we are even able to move outside. A sliver of sunlight silvers the iron clouds that hang over the distant hills.

'It doesn't look as if he'll make it,' I murmur to Alice. 'In this weather, not even Jethro . . .'

I had hoped so much that Jethro might be here today. But in this gloom, not even the birds are flying.

And that's when I spot something, just above the horizon. It couldn't be, could it? Two gleaming lights, blazing straight at us from a mile or so out, barrelling through a hole in the wall-to-wall murk like a steam train roaring from a tunnel. I point, want to say something, but the words won't come out. Hot-cold excitement shivers up my spine, and I can feel my skin beginning to tingle.

'Look! Look!' I finally blurt, jumping in the air and spilling champagne all down my arm. *Il est là! Il est là!*

Everyone looks up, mouths open, glasses suspended in mid-air as – with a searing roar – a sleek white aeroplane with a beacon blazing on each wing-tip and smoke billowing from its belly rockets through the raging sky above our heads. Upside down.

'Oh. My. God!' gasps Alice beside me, amid a widespread barrage of asterisk-laden expressions of awe, both English and French, from all around us.

'I *knew* he'd come,' I whisper, putting my arm around her, not taking my brimming eyes off the gleaming arrow that has now rolled wings level, and is beginning to pull up, up, up towards the vertical, drawing a chalk smoke-trail across the charcoal canvas of the clouds.

Everyone is clapping and laughing by the time Jethro rolls off the top of his first loop, and when he has climbed skywards to paint his second, a huge gasp of a cheer goes up. For we have seen what he is drawing in the sky.

'It's a heart, a great heart in the sky,' shouts a man behind me, tracing the shape with his outstretched finger.

'So beautiful!' exclaims someone else, in French, with a catch in her voice. '*Un grand cœur dans le ciel*.'

Everyone is pointing, smiling, cheering at the sky. Even Gilles, in his natty tie, looks awestruck, while Mrs Charles, our beautiful headmistress from another life, gently dabs at her eyes.

'Do you want to hear my news?' whispers Alice, as we watch Jethro dancing in the air above our heads. I nod, not taking my misty eyes off the gleaming flying machine.

And this is when she tells me that she is pregnant. We are going to have a child next year.

'But it's impossible,' I whisper. 'The experts said you couldn't . . .'

'Impossible is just a word,' she replies, sunlight dancing in her eyes. 'And besides, what do experts know?'

Alice Wright, *née* Melbury, pulls me towards her. And as the impact of her news dawns upon me, a spangled wave of stars explodes inside my heart, filling it with sky.

Behind me, I hear a cheer, as Alice and I kiss. With a final victory roll, Jethro ends his display. And we are about to head towards Maurice's barn, to run the gauntlet of my unfinished seating plan for dinner, when another aircraft appears low overhead, rocking its wings, its white-haired pilot raising his arm in salute. Antoine. Even through the blur of my tears, I recognize the red, white and blue machine at once. It is Antoine, who was waiting for a sign; who swore he would never fly again, until the time was right.

And as I gaze up into the sky, and draw Alice closer to me, I can hardly believe that all these pieces of my life are finally connected up.

# ACKNOWLEDGEMENTS

If *Je t'aime à La Folie* is forgettable, that is entirely my fault. If it has any lasting value, that is thanks to:

Five miracle women who taught me about love: Lell, Florence, Sara, Claire and Marisa.

The pilots whose skill and pleasure in the sky have inspired my own flying, especially Anand Arora, Helene Shaw, Richard Meredith, Justyn Gorman, Peter Valentine, Philippe Mayence, Stuart McKinnon, Stratton Richey, Anna Walker, Carolyn Grace and Julian Harris, who died doing what he loved.

My special friend and fellow Rude Mechanical, Jon Stock, who suggested, long ago, that I might like to write about my adventures at La Folie for a newspaper.

My patient editor, Simon Taylor, a man as generous as he is visionary, who first mooted the idea of this book sometime in the middle of the nineteenth century.

My dashing young agent, Mark Lucas, who sent me happily back to the drawing board when I thought the book was already done.

My brother Steven, who read the manuscript twice in about ten minutes, and immediately came up with several characteristically brilliant suggestions for making it better.

My artist friend, Nicholas Peall. What Nick has drawn, straight off the top of his head, goes way beyond my wildest hopes for the endpapers of this book.

My favourite botanist, Rosemary Duckett, who gave the manuscript an extra spit-and-polish; Brenda Updegraff, who copyedited the text with such exquisite care and flair, and Kate Samano, queen of proofs.

My French friends in Jolibois, who have made me feel so welcome, despite the limitations of my backhand.

With particular love and respect, I acknowledge Charles and Elizabeth-Ann Malden, one of the truly great head-teaching partnerships of the twentieth century, who gave me and several of the characters in this book the most wonderful possible start in life at Windlesham House School.

I bow to my loyal support group: Cat, for her forbearance, and Digby, for his enthusiasm. My sister and brothers – Jane, Steven and Nicholas – for sharing so much with me. And my parents, Anne and Peter, for my life. I love you all.

Finally, there is the one to whom I owe my purest debt of love, who inspired this book, and whose sacrifices have given me the time and space and willingness to write it. Thank you, my darling: I only hope, now that it is finished, that you will feel that it was all worthwhile.

# IN MEMORY OF

Titus

Martha

Meg